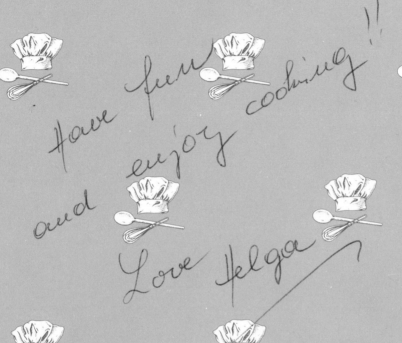

Have fun
and enjoy cooking!!
Love Helga

10 COOKBOOKS IN 1

THE
Pleasures
OF
Cooking

ISBN: 1-56173-900-6

Library of Congress Catalog Card Number: 92-61807

Cover photography by Sacco Productions, Ltd., Chicago,
Illinois.

Pictured on the front cover *(clockwise from top left)*: Santa Fe
Burrito Bake *(page 71)*, Streusel Raspberry Muffins *(page
346)*, Spicy Beef with Noodles *(page 262)*, Piña Colada Cake
(page 498), Chicken with Cucumbers and Dill *(page 55)* and
Jam-Filled Chocolate Sugar Cookies and Chocolate-Caramel
Sugar Cookies *(page 542)*.

Pictured on the back cover *(clockwise from top left)*: Turkey
and Rice Quiche (page 156), Glazed Apple Custard Pie *(page
402)*, Garlic Skewered Shrimp *(page 286)*, Deluxe Fajita
Nachos *(page 10)*, Rocky Road Brownies *(page 532)* and
Tropical Treat Muffins *(page 349)*.

8 7 6 5 4 3 2 1

Manufactured in U.S.A.

Microwave ovens vary in wattage and power output; cooking
times given with microwave directions in this publication
may need to be adjusted. Consult manufacturer's instructions
for suitable microwave-safe cooking dishes.

10 COOKBOOKS IN 1

THE Pleasures OF Cooking

Publications International, Ltd.

CONTENTS

INTRODUCTION

Welcome to the creative world of **The Pleasures of Cooking.** We've combined ten of our most popular cookbooks in one easy-to-use volume to give you hundreds of outstanding recipes, perfect for everyday meal-planning, party ideas or entertaining menus. You'll love the versatility and diversity of this cookbook.

Today's busy lifestyles leave little time for creativity in the kitchen, but this masterful collection promises to show you how to put the pleasure back into your cooking. Each and every one of the over 600 sensational recipes, many from your favorite brand name companies, has been kitchen-tested to assure delicious, successful results. Whether you need a simple supper to feed your family or an elegant dinner to impress your boss, the easy-to-follow directions guarantee a meal that will please everyone. Paging through the book you'll be amazed at the beautiful full-color photos and captivating variety.

Dozens of tantalizing chicken dishes that are quick to make can be found in "Hurry-Up Chicken Recipes." There is everything from snacks and sandwiches to dishes suitable for gala entertaining in this section. "Casseroles, Stews, Soups & More" will show you the ease of cooking one-dish meals, such as scrumptious stews, soups and quiches plus delicious casseroles, skillet dinners and stir-fries.

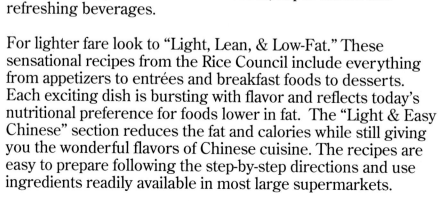

A fantastic chapter on grilled recipes and other dishes perfect for warm weather cooking will have you firing up the barbecue in no time. "Barbecue & More" is full of helpful tips for the novice or master of the grill, plus fantastic barbecue go-withs, like tasty sauces and marinades, super salads and refreshing beverages.

For lighter fare look to "Light, Lean, & Low-Fat." These sensational recipes from the Rice Council include everything from appetizers to entrées and breakfast foods to desserts. Each exciting dish is bursting with flavor and reflects today's nutritional preference for foods lower in fat. The "Light & Easy Chinese" section reduces the fat and calories while still giving you the wonderful flavors of Chinese cuisine. The recipes are easy to prepare following the step-by-step directions and use ingredients readily available in most large supermarkets.

Looking for a no-fail, lavish dessert guaranteed to impress friends and family? "Jell-O® Easy Entertaining" has both classic and creative new uses for Jell-O® Brand Gelatin and Pudding that are suitable for all occasions—small impromptu gatherings, children's parties or year-round holiday festivities. This glorious collection will bring back fond childhood memories and create delicious new traditions for today's generation of Jell-O® lovers.

Large or small, sweet or savory—muffins are a perfect treat any time of day and "The Muffin Cookbook" has dozens of magnificent muffins to fit any occasion. Serve them as an early morning breakfast, a sensational snack-time delight, a lunch or dinner accompaniment or even as a unique dessert! They are a breeze to make, so bake a bunch to brighten your day.

Picture-perfect pies of every type imaginable are included in "New Borden® All-American Pies." Dish up a piping-hot main-dish pie for a simple savory supper. Or, choose from a dazzling array of dessert pies, in every popular flavor from luscious apple to refreshing lemon, rich chocolate to crunchy pecan.

"Duncan Hines® Celebrates Baking" by showing you how to create luscious desserts using Duncan Hines® mixes. You won't believe how simple it is to make these magnificent cakes, cookies and pies. There's even a whimsical group of recipes designed for you and your children to make together. There's no better way to bring fresh-baked goodness into your kitchen.

What cookbook would be complete without a chapter on America's favorite flavor—chocolate!

"Baker's® Easiest-Ever Chocolate Recipes" offers a spectacular variety of chocolate recipes including decadent brownies, cookies and candies plus super-rich cakes, pies and desserts. It's so easy—most of these recipes can be prepared in just minutes with a single bowl!

Page after page, you'll be amazed at the variety of recipes and over 300 eye-catching photos. With hundreds of taste-tempting recipes to choose from you're sure to find meal and party planning a snap. It won't take long before this comprehensive recipe collection becomes an indispensable kitchen reference. So, join us in the exciting journey to discover **The Pleasures of Cooking**.

HURRY-UP
CHICKEN
RECIPES

Clockwise from bottom left: Mexican-Style Almond Chicken Salad (page 23), Double-Coated Chicken (page 47) and Chicken Macadamia (page 55)

Deluxe Fajita Nachos

2½ cups shredded cooked chicken
  1 package (1.27 ounces) LAWRY'S®
       Spices & Seasonings for Fajitas
  ⅓ cup water
  8 ounces tortilla chips
1¼ cups (5 ounces) grated
       Cheddar cheese
  1 cup (4 ounces) grated Monterey
       Jack cheese
  1 large tomato, chopped
  1 can (2¼ ounces) sliced ripe
       olives, drained
  ¼ cup sliced green onions
       Salsa

In medium skillet, combine chicken,
Spices & Seasonings for Fajitas and
water; blend well. Bring to a boil;
reduce heat and simmer 3 minutes.
In large shallow ovenproof platter,
arrange chips. Top with chicken and
cheeses. Place under broiler to melt
cheese. Top with tomato, olives,
green onions and desired amount
of salsa.

*Makes 4 appetizer or
2 main-dish servings*

Presentation: Garnish with guacamole
and sour cream.

Hint: For a spicier version, add sliced
jalapeños.

New Yorker Pita Sandwich

  ¾ pound boneless skinless
       chicken breasts, cut into
       ¼-inch strips
  ½ cup chopped onion
  ½ cup green bell pepper strips
  1 tablespoon vegetable oil
  1 can (16 ounces) HEINZ
       Vegetarian Beans in Tomato
       Sauce
  2 tablespoons HEINZ Horseradish
       Sauce
  ¼ teaspoon salt
       Dash black pepper
  4 pocket pita breads (5-inch
       diameter)
  8 slices tomato
       Leaf lettuce

In skillet, sauté chicken, onion and
green pepper in oil until vegetables
are tender-crisp and chicken is
tender. Stir in beans, horseradish
sauce, salt and pepper. Simmer
5 minutes to blend flavors. Cut pitas
in half and tuck 1 tomato slice and
lettuce into each half. Fill each with
about ⅓ cup bean mixture.

*Makes 4 servings
(about 3 cups mixture)*

Deluxe Fajita Nachos

Barbecued Chicken on a Bun

1 teaspoon seasoned salt
⅛ teaspoon coarsely ground black pepper
2 whole boneless chicken breasts, halved
4 buns, split and toasted
4 slices (1 ounce *each*) Swiss cheese
4 slices (1 ounce *each*) baked ham, warmed
Peach-Mint Salsa (recipe follows)
Lettuce leaves
Savory Grilled Peaches (recipe follows)

Combine seasoned salt and pepper. Loosen one edge of chicken skin and rub seasoning mixture underneath skin. Cook chicken skin-side down on covered grill over medium, indirect heat about 30 to 35 minutes or until chicken is tender and no longer pink. Remove and discard skin. Serve chicken on buns topped with cheese, ham and salsa. Garnish with lettuce. Serve with Savory Grilled Peaches.

Makes 4 hearty sandwiches

Conventional Oven Method: Prepare as above. Roast skin-side up in 350°F oven for about 30 minutes or until chicken is tender and no longer pink. Continue as directed.

Tip: Sandwiches are delicious served either hot or cold.

Peach-Mint Salsa

1 fresh California peach, chopped (about ⅔ cup)
⅓ cup chopped green onions
1 tomato, chopped
1½ tablespoons chopped fresh mint
¼ teaspoon chili powder

In small bowl, combine all ingredients. Refrigerate leftovers.

Makes about 1½ cups

Savory Grilled Peaches:

Cut 4 fresh California peaches in half. Cook on covered grill over medium, indirect heat 4 minutes. Turn and cook an additional 4 minutes or until heated through.

Makes 4 servings

Favorite recipe from **California Tree Fruit Agreement**

Chicken Luncheon Sandwich

1½ cups chopped cooked chicken
1 cup (4 ounces) shredded Wisconsin Cheddar cheese
½ cup finely chopped celery
¼ cup green bell pepper
1 green onion, chopped
1 tablespoon chopped pimiento
½ cup mayonnaise
½ cup plain yogurt
Salt and pepper to taste
Rolls or bread
Lettuce leaves

Combine chicken, cheese, celery, bell pepper, onion, pimiento, mayonnaise and yogurt. Season with salt and pepper. Stir until well blended. Refrigerate until ready to use. Serve on rolls with lettuce.

Makes about 4½ cups

Favorite recipe from **Wisconsin Milk Marketing Board** © 1993

Chicken Luncheon Sandwich

Chicken Kabobs in Pita Bread

¼ cup olive or vegetable oil
¼ cup lemon juice
½ teaspoon salt
½ teaspoon dried oregano leaves
¼ teaspoon garlic powder
⅛ teaspoon pepper
1 whole boneless skinless chicken breast, cut into 1-inch cubes
2 large pita breads
1 small onion, thinly sliced
1 tomato, thinly sliced
½ cup plain yogurt
  Parsley, if desired

1. Mix oil, lemon juice, salt, oregano, garlic powder and pepper in medium glass bowl. Add chicken; toss to coat completely. Cover and refrigerate at least 3 hours or overnight.

2. Remove chicken from marinade, reserving marinade. Thread chicken onto 4 small metal skewers. Place kabobs on greased broiler pan. Broil about 5 inches from heat until chicken is golden, 8 to 10 minutes, brushing often with marinade. Turn kabobs over and brush with marinade. Broil until chicken is tender and no longer pink, 5 to 7 minutes.

3. Cut each pita bread in half; gently pull each half open to form a pocket. Remove chicken from 1 kabob and place inside 1 pocket; repeat with remaining kabobs. Top with onion, tomato and yogurt. Garnish with parsley. Serve hot.

Makes 4 servings

Bandito Buffalo Wings

Preparation time: 15 minutes
Total time: 55 minutes

1 package ORTEGA® Taco Seasoning Mix
12 chicken wings, split with tips removed (about 2 pounds)
½ cup ORTEGA® Thick and Chunky Salsa, Green Chile Salsa or Picante Sauce

Place seasoning mix in heavy plastic food storage bag. Add a few chicken wings; shake until well coated. Repeat to coat all pieces. Place in lightly greased baking pan. Bake at 375°F for 35 to 40 minutes or until chicken is tender and juices run clear. Serve hot with salsa for dipping.

Makes 2 dozen appetizers

Microwave Directions: Prepare chicken as above. Place 8 pieces on 9-inch microwaveable pie plate with meaty portions toward edge of plate. Cook at MEDIUM-HIGH (70% power) for 8 to 10 minutes or until chicken is no longer pink near bone, turning dish after 4 minutes. (Chicken should reach an internal temperature of 180°F.) Repeat with remaining pieces. Serve as above.

Grecian Chicken Salad Sandwiches

2 cups chopped cooked chicken
1 cup seeded chopped cucumber
1 cup seeded chopped tomato
⅓ cup sliced green onions
¼ cup REALEMON® Lemon Juice from Concentrate
¼ cup vegetable oil
1 teaspoon sugar
½ teaspoon salt
¼ teaspoon dried basil leaves
1 clove garlic, finely chopped
2 cups shredded lettuce
4 pita bread rounds, halved

In medium bowl, combine chicken, cucumber, tomato and onions. In jar or cruet, combine ReaLemon® brand, oil, sugar, salt, basil and garlic; shake well. Pour over chicken mixture. Cover; marinate in refrigerator 2 hours. Just before serving, toss with lettuce. Serve in pita bread. Refrigerate leftovers.

Makes 4 sandwiches

Chicken Kabobs in Pita Bread

Curried Chicken Puffs

½ cup water
⅓ cup PARKAY® Margarine
⅔ cup flour
   Dash of salt
2 eggs
1 8-oz. pkg. PHILADELPHIA BRAND®
   Cream Cheese, softened
¼ cup milk
¼ teaspoon salt
   Dash of curry powder
   Dash of pepper
1½ cups chopped cooked chicken
⅓ cup slivered almonds, toasted
2 tablespoons green onion slices

• Bring water and margarine to boil. Add flour and dash salt; stir vigorously over low heat until mixture forms ball. Remove from heat; add eggs, one at a time, beating until smooth after each addition.

• Place level measuring tablespoonfuls of batter on ungreased cookie sheet.

• Bake at 400°F, 25 minutes. Cool.

• Combine cream cheese, milk, ¼ teaspoon salt, curry powder and pepper, mixing until well blended. Add chicken, almonds and onions; mix lightly.

• Cut tops from cream puffs; fill with chicken mixture. Replace tops. Place puffs on cookie sheet.

• Bake at 375°F, 5 minutes or until warm.
   Makes approximately 1½ dozen

Note: Unfilled cream puffs can be prepared several weeks in advance and frozen. Place puffs on a jelly roll pan and wrap securely in moisture-vaporproof wrap.

Muffin Divan

Prep time: 20 minutes
Cooking time: 15 minutes

2 cups chopped cooked chicken
1 cup mushroom slices
⅓ cup picante sauce
¼ cup MIRACLE WHIP® Salad
   Dressing
2 tablespoons green onion slices
3 English muffins, split, toasted
1 cup chopped cooked broccoli
½ lb. VELVEETA® Pasteurized
   Process Cheese Spread,
   sliced

Preheat oven to 350°F. Combine chicken, mushrooms, sauce, salad dressing and onions; mix lightly. Top muffin halves with chicken mixture and broccoli. Place on ungreased cookie sheet. Bake for 10 minutes. Top with process cheese spread; continue baking until process cheese spread begins to melt.
   Makes 6 sandwiches

Cajun Chicken Burgers

1 pound fresh ground chicken
1 small onion, finely chopped
¼ cup chopped green or red
   bell pepper
3 scallions, minced
1 clove garlic, minced
1 teaspoon Worcestershire sauce
½ teaspoon TABASCO® Brand
   Pepper Sauce
   Ground black pepper

In medium bowl, combine chicken, onion, bell pepper, scallions, garlic, Worcestershire sauce, Tabasco® sauce and black pepper. Form into five 3-inch patties. Broil or grill 6 minutes; turn over and broil an additional 4 to 6 minutes or until no longer pink. Serve immediately.
   Makes 5 servings

Hot Chicken and Pepper Pita

1½ tablespoons vegetable oil
2 whole boneless skinless chicken breasts, cut into cubes
½ teaspoon garlic salt
1 medium-size onion, sliced into thin rings
1 medium-size red bell pepper, cut into strips
1 medium-size yellow bell pepper, cut into strips
1 medium-size green bell pepper, cut into strips
2 teaspoons finely chopped pickled hot pepper rings, drained well (optional)
1 package (12 ounces) OCEAN SPRAY® Cran-Fruit™ Sauce, any flavor
2 tablespoons soy sauce
½ teaspoon ground ginger
⅓ cup cashews
2 cups shredded lettuce
4 large pita breads, halved

Heat oil in skillet at medium heat 2 to 3 minutes. Add chicken; cook and stir until lightly browned. Sprinkle with garlic salt. Add onion and peppers; cook and stir 3 minutes. Stir in Cran-Fruit™ Sauce, soy sauce and ginger. Reduce heat to medium; cook uncovered 5 to 8 minutes until vegetables are crisp tender. Remove from heat; toss lightly with cashews and lettuce. Spoon into pita breads.

Makes 8 sandwiches

Glazed Ginger Chicken

5 tablespoons KIKKOMAN® Soy Sauce
3 tablespoons plum jam
1 tablespoon sesame seed, toasted
1 tablespoon cornstarch
1 tablespoon minced fresh ginger
1 clove garlic, pressed
8 small chicken thighs (about 2 pounds)

Cut eight 8-inch squares of aluminum foil; set aside. Combine soy sauce, plum jam, sesame seed, cornstarch, ginger and garlic in small saucepan. Bring to boil over medium heat, stirring constantly. Remove from heat and cool slightly. Stir in thighs, a few at a time, to coat each piece well. Place 1 thigh, skin-side up, on each foil square. Divide and spoon remaining sauce evenly over thighs. Fold ends of foil to form a package; crease and fold down to secure well. Place foil bundles, seam-side up, in single layer, on steamer rack. Set rack in large pot or wok of boiling water. (Do not allow water level to reach bundles.) Cover and steam 30 minutes or until chicken is tender. Garnish as desired. Serve immediately.

Makes 8 appetizer servings

Mexican Appetizer Cheesecake

3 (8-ounce) packages cream cheese, softened
2 teaspoons WYLER'S® or STEERO® Chicken-Flavor Instant Bouillon
1½ teaspoons chili powder
½ teaspoon hot pepper sauce
2 eggs
½ cup *hot* water
1 cup finely chopped cooked chicken
1 (4-ounce) can chopped green chilies, well drained
Salsa, shredded cheese and sliced green onions
LA FAMOUS® Tortilla Chips

Preheat oven to 325°F. In large mixer bowl, beat cream cheese, bouillon, chili powder and hot pepper sauce until smooth. Add eggs and water; mix well. Stir in chicken and chilies. Pour into 9-inch springform pan. Bake 30 minutes or until set; cool 15 minutes. Carefully run knife around edge of pan; remove side of pan. Top with salsa, cheese and green onions. Serve warm or chilled with tortilla chips. Refrigerate leftovers.

Makes 10 to 12 appetizer servings

Garlicky Gilroy Chicken Wings

2 pounds chicken wings (about 15 wings)
3 heads fresh garlic,* separated into cloves and peeled
1 cup plus 1 tablespoon olive oil, divided
10 to 15 drops TABASCO® Brand Pepper Sauce
1 cup grated Parmesan cheese
1 cup Italian-style bread crumbs
1 teaspoon black pepper

Preheat oven to 375°F. Disjoint chicken wings, removing tips. (If desired, save tips to make chicken stock.) Rinse wings; pat dry. Place garlic, 1 cup oil and pepper sauce in food processor or blender container; cover and process until smooth. Pour garlic mixture into small bowl. Combine cheese, bread crumbs and black pepper in shallow dish. Dip wings into garlic mixture, then roll, one at a time, in crumb mixture until thoroughly coated. Brush shallow nonstick pan with remaining 1 tablespoon oil; arrange wings in a single layer. Drizzle remaining garlic mixture over wings; sprinkle with remaining crumb mixture. Bake 45 to 60 minutes or until brown and crisp. Garnish as desired.

Makes about 6 appetizer servings

*The whole garlic bulb is called a *head*.

Favorite recipe from **The Fresh Garlic Association**

Bits o' Teriyaki Chicken

½ cup KIKKOMAN® Teriyaki Sauce
1 teaspoon sugar
2 whole boneless skinless chicken breasts, cut into 1-inch pieces
1 tablespoon water
1 teaspoon cornstarch
1 tablespoon vegetable oil
2 tablespoons sesame seed, toasted

Combine teriyaki sauce and sugar in small bowl. Stir in chicken; marinate 30 minutes, stirring occasionally. Remove chicken; reserve 2 tablespoons marinade. Combine reserved marinade, water and cornstarch in small bowl; set aside. Heat oil in hot wok or skillet over medium-high heat. Add chicken and sesame seed; stir-fry 2 minutes. Stir in cornstarch mixture. Cook and stir until mixture boils and thickens and chicken is tender, about 1 minute. Turn into chafing dish or onto serving platter. Serve warm with wooden picks.

Makes 6 appetizer servings

Cheddary Chicken Salad Grills

Prep time: 15 minutes
Cooking time: 10 minutes

2 cups chopped cooked chicken
¼ lb. VELVEETA® Pasteurized Process Cheese Spread, cubed
¼ cup chopped celery
¼ cup KRAFT® Real Mayonnaise
12 whole-wheat bread slices
KRAFT® Strawberry Preserves
Soft PARKAY® Margarine

Combine chicken, process cheese spread, celery and mayonnaise; mix lightly. For each sandwich, spread one bread slice with preserves; cover with chicken mixture and second bread slice. Spread sandwich with margarine. Grill until lightly browned on both sides.

Makes 6 sandwiches

Garlicky Gilroy Chicken Wings

Fresh Fruity Chicken Salad

Yogurt Dressing (recipe follows)
2 cups cubed cooked chicken
1 cup cantaloupe melon balls
1 cup honeydew melon cubes
½ cup chopped celery
⅓ cup cashews
¼ cup green onion slices
Lettuce leaves

Prepare Yogurt Dressing; set aside. Combine chicken, melons, celery, cashews and green onions in large bowl. Add dressing; mix lightly. Cover. Chill 1 hour. Serve on bed of lettuce. *Makes 4 servings*

Yogurt Dressing

¼ cup plain yogurt
3 tablespoons mayonnaise
3 tablespoons fresh lime juice
¾ teaspoon ground coriander
½ teaspoon salt
Dash of pepper

Combine ingredients in small bowl; mix well. *Makes about ½ cup*

Chicken Noodle Soup

5 (14½-ounce) cans ready-to-serve chicken broth
2 cups water
1 small onion, cut into small wedges
1 cup sliced carrots
1 cup sliced celery (including leaves)
2 tablespoons WYLER'S® or STEERO® Chicken-Flavor Instant Bouillon
1 teaspoon parsley flakes
1 teaspoon basil leaves
¼ teaspoon pepper
½ (1-pound) package CREAMETTE® Egg Noodles, uncooked
2 cups chopped cooked chicken

In Dutch oven, combine broth, water, onion, carrots, celery, bouillon, parsley, basil and pepper. Bring to boil. Reduce heat; simmer 15 minutes. Prepare noodles according to package directions; drain. Add egg noodles and chicken to soup; heat through. Garnish as desired. Refrigerate leftovers. *Makes about 4 quarts*

Fresh Fruity Chicken Salad

Chicken Potato Salad Olé

2 large ripe tomatoes, seeded
   and chopped
¾ cup chopped green onions
¼ cup chopped fresh cilantro
1 to 2 tablespoons chopped,
   seeded, pickled jalapeño
   peppers
1½ teaspoons salt, divided
1 cup HELLMANN'S® or BEST
   FOODS® Real, Light or
   Cholesterol Free Reduced
   Calorie Mayonnaise
3 tablespoons lime juice
1 teaspoon chili powder
1 teaspoon ground cumin
2 pounds small red potatoes,
   cooked and sliced ¼ inch
   thick
2 cups shredded cooked chicken
1 large yellow or red bell pepper,
   diced
   Lettuce leaves
   Tortilla chips, lime slices, whole
   chili peppers and cilantro
   sprigs for garnish (optional)

In medium bowl combine tomatoes, green onions, chopped cilantro, jalapeño peppers and 1 teaspoon of the salt; set aside. In large bowl combine mayonnaise, lime juice, chili powder, cumin and remaining ½ teaspoon salt. Add potatoes, chicken, bell pepper and half of the tomato mixture; toss to coat well. Cover; chill. To serve, spoon salad onto lettuce-lined platter. Spoon remaining tomato mixture over salad. If desired, garnish with tortilla chips, lime slices, whole chili peppers and cilantro sprigs.

Makes 6 servings

Mexican-Style Almond Chicken Salad

4 boneless skinless chicken breast
   halves, poached
1 cup BLUE DIAMOND® Blanched
   Slivered Almonds
⅓ cup plus 2 teaspoons vegetable
   oil, divided
6 tablespoons lime juice
3 cloves garlic, finely chopped
5 teaspoons ground cumin
⅛ teaspoon cayenne pepper
½ teaspoon salt
6 tablespoons mayonnaise
1 small red onion, chopped
2 oranges, peeled and chopped
4 flour tortillas
   Vegetable oil for frying
   Lettuce leaves, sliced avocado,
   peeled orange slices, red
   onion rings and BLUE
   DIAMOND® Blanched Slivered
   Almonds for garnish

Cut chicken into 1-inch cubes; reserve. Sauté almonds in 2 teaspoons oil until golden; reserve. Combine lime juice, garlic, cumin, cayenne and salt. Beat in mayonnaise and remaining ⅓ cup oil. Add chicken, onion and reserved almonds. Gently fold in oranges. Fry tortillas in 2 inches oil, one at a time, turning once, until crisp, puffed and golden; drain and reserve. (A ladle can be pressed in the center of the tortilla while frying to form shell.) To serve, line each tortilla with lettuce leaves and top with ¼ of chicken salad. Garnish each serving with avocado slices, orange slices, onion rings and almonds.

Makes 4 servings

Chicken Potato Salad Olé

Hearty Chicken and Rice Soup

10 cups chicken broth
1 medium onion, chopped
1 cup sliced celery
1 cup sliced carrots
¼ cup snipped parsley
½ teaspoon cracked black pepper
½ teaspoon dried thyme leaves
1 bay leaf
1½ cups chicken cubes (about ¾ pound)
2 cups cooked rice
2 tablespoons lime juice
Lime slices for garnish

Combine broth, onion, celery, carrots, parsley, pepper, thyme and bay leaf in Dutch oven. Bring to a boil; stir once or twice. Reduce heat; simmer, uncovered, 10 to 15 minutes. Add chicken; simmer, uncovered, 5 to 10 minutes or until chicken is tender. Remove and discard bay leaf. Stir in rice and lime juice just before serving. Garnish with lime slices. *Makes 8 servings*

Favorite recipe from **USA Rice Council**

Mandarin Chicken Salad

1 whole chicken breast, halved
2 cups water
4 tablespoons KIKKOMAN® Soy Sauce, divided
Boiling water
¾ pound fresh bean sprouts
1 carrot, peeled and shredded
½ cup slivered green onions with tops
2 tablespoons minced fresh cilantro or parsley
¼ cup distilled white vinegar
2 teaspoons sugar
½ cup blanched slivered almonds, toasted

Simmer chicken in mixture of 2 cups water and 1 tablespoon soy sauce in covered saucepan 15 minutes or until chicken is tender.

Meanwhile, pour boiling water over bean sprouts. Drain; cool under cold water and drain thoroughly. Remove chicken and cool. (Refrigerate stock for another use, if desired.) Skin and bone chicken; shred meat with fingers into large mixing bowl. Add bean sprouts, carrot, green onions and cilantro. Blend vinegar, sugar and remaining 3 tablespoons soy sauce, stirring until sugar dissolves. Pour over chicken and vegetables; toss to coat all ingredients. Cover and refrigerate 1 hour. Just before serving, add almonds and toss to combine. *Makes 4 servings*

Cucumber Chicken Salad

3 tablespoons CROSSE & BLACKWELL® Worcestershire Sauce
2 tablespoons cider vinegar
2 tablespoons vegetable oil
1 tablespoon sesame oil
1 teaspoon sugar
1 teaspoon Dijon-style mustard
1 teaspoon grated fresh ginger
2 cups chopped cooked chicken
1 cup cooked spinach pasta (½ cup uncooked)
1 cucumber, peeled, seeded and sliced
1 red bell pepper, diced
¼ cup dry roasted peanuts

In large bowl, combine Worcestershire sauce, vinegar, oils, sugar, mustard and ginger. Add chicken, pasta, cucumber and red pepper; toss lightly to mix well. Top with peanuts. *Makes 4 servings*

Hearty Chicken and Rice Soup

Paella Salad

Garlic Dressing (recipe follows)
2½ cups water
1 cup uncooked rice
1 teaspoon salt
¼ to ½ teaspoon powdered
    saffron
2 cups cubed cooked chicken
1 cup cooked deveined medium
    shrimp (about 4 ounces)
1 cup diced cooked artichoke
    hearts
½ cup cooked peas
2 tablespoons chopped salami
2 tablespoons thinly sliced green
    onions
2 tablespoons chopped drained
    pimiento
1 tablespoon minced fresh
    parsley
    Lettuce or fresh spinach leaves
1 large tomato, seeded and
    cubed

1. Prepare Garlic Dressing.

2. Place water in 1-quart saucepan; heat to boiling. Stir rice, salt and saffron into water. Reduce heat; cover and simmer 20 minutes. Remove from heat; let stand until water is absorbed, about 5 minutes. Refrigerate about 15 minutes.

3. Place rice, chicken, shrimp, artichoke hearts, peas, salami, onions, pimiento and parsley in large bowl; toss well. Pour dressing over salad; toss lightly to coat. Cover and refrigerate 1 hour.

4. Arrange lettuce on large serving platter or 4 serving plates; top with salad mixture. Garnish with cubed tomato. *Makes 4 to 6 servings*

Garlic Dressing

¾ cup olive or vegetable oil
¼ cup white wine vinegar
1 teaspoon salt
½ teaspoon pepper
1 clove garlic, pressed

1. Mix all ingredients in tightly covered jar. (Dressing can be refrigerated up to 2 weeks.)
Makes 1 cup

Chicken Ragout with Chilies, Tortillas and Goat Cheese

1 cup BLUE DIAMOND® Sliced
    Natural Almonds
6 tablespoons vegetable oil,
    divided
6 corn tortillas
4 boneless skinless chicken breast
    halves
1 cup chicken stock or broth
1 onion, chopped
1 red bell pepper, cut into strips
1 can (7 ounces) whole green
    chilies, cut crosswise into
    ¼-inch strips
1½ teaspoons ground cumin
1 cup heavy cream
½ pound goat cheese
1 tablespoon lime juice
½ to 1 teaspoon salt

Sauté almonds in 1 tablespoon of the oil until golden; reserve. Heat 4 tablespoons of the oil and soften tortillas, one at a time, for about 30 seconds. Drain. Cut tortillas into ½-inch strips; reserve. Poach chicken breasts, in covered saucepan, in barely simmering chicken stock, about 10 minutes or until just tender. Reserve chicken stock; slice chicken into strips. In large skillet, sauté onion and bell pepper in the remaining 1 tablespoon oil, until onion is translucent. Add chilies and cumin; sauté 1 minute longer. Stir in reserved stock and cream; simmer 2 to 3 minutes. Add chicken. Stir in goat cheese; *do not boil*. Add lime juice and salt. Fold in tortilla strips and almonds. *Makes 4 servings*

Tucson Chicken Salad

1 (8-ounce) container BORDEN® or
   MEADOW GOLD® Sour Cream
2 teaspoons WYLER'S® or STEERO®
   Chicken-Flavor Instant Bouillon
1 tablespoon REALIME® Lime Juice
   from Concentrate
½ teaspoon ground cumin
   Dash hot pepper sauce
½ pound smoked cooked chicken
   or turkey breast, thinly sliced
½ pound Cheddar cheese, thinly
   sliced
1 medium apple, cored and
   sliced
1 cup sliced celery
½ cup thin strips pared jicama
   Lettuce leaves
½ cup chopped walnuts, toasted

In medium bowl, combine sour
cream, bouillon, ReaLime® brand,
cumin and hot pepper sauce.
Cover; chill 1 hour. Arrange chicken,
cheese, apple, celery and jicama
on lettuce. Top with nuts. Serve with
dressing.* Refrigerate leftovers.

Makes 4 servings

*For thinner dressing, add milk to
desired consistency.

Chicken and Bacon Salad

1 pound boneless skinless
   chicken breasts, cubed
2 teaspoons CHEF PAUL
   PRUDHOMME'S POULTRY
   MAGIC®
2 teaspoons Worcestershire sauce
4 tablespoons olive oil or
   bacon fat
½ cup minced onion
½ cup minced celery
12 ounces bacon, fried crisp,
   drained and crumbled
2 cups chopped purple cabbage
2 cups chopped green cabbage
1 cup chopped iceberg lettuce
1½ cups Green Onion Salad
   Dressing (recipe follows)
4 large romaine or iceberg
   lettuce leaves
8 tomato wedges or cherry
   tomatoes for garnish

Sprinkle chicken breast with Poultry
Magic® and work in well with your
hands, then work in Worcestershire
sauce.

Heat olive oil in large, heavy skillet.
Cook chicken pieces in hot oil,
stirring quickly with wooden spoon.
Brown chicken on all sides, about
3 to 4 minutes. Add onion and
celery; cook 4 minutes. Place in
large bowl; cover and chill.

Add bacon, cabbages, chopped
lettuce and Green Onion Salad
Dressing to chicken. Cover and
chill. Stir before serving. Serve on
lettuce-lined salad plates garnished
with tomatoes.

Makes 4 servings

Green Onion Salad Dressing

1 egg plus 1 egg yolk*
1 cup plus 2 tablespoons
   vegetable oil
   Scant ½ cup chopped green
   onions
1½ tablespoons Creole mustard or
   brown mustard
1 tablespoon white vinegar
½ teaspoon CHEF PAUL
   PRUDHOMME'S VEGETABLE
   MAGIC®

In blender or food processor, blend
egg and egg yolk until frothy, about
2 minutes. With the motor running
add oil until dressing is thick and
creamy. Add remaining ingredients;
blend well. Refrigerate until ready
to use.   *Makes about 1½ cups*

*Use clean, uncracked eggs.

Zucchini Chicken Soup

Prep time: 10 minutes
Cook time: 10 minutes

½ cup chopped onion
½ cup chopped carrot
1 clove garlic, minced
1 tablespoon butter or margarine
1 cup diced cooked chicken
1 can (16 ounces) DEL MONTE®
   Zucchini with Italian-Style
   Tomato Sauce
1 can (14½ ounces) chicken broth

Saute onion, carrot and garlic
in butter, about 5 minutes. Add
remaining ingredients. Heat through
and serve.   *Makes 5 cups*

ONE-DISH MEALS

Dairyland Confetti Chicken

CASSEROLE:
- 1 cup diced carrots
- ¾ cup chopped onions
- ½ cup diced celery
- ¼ cup chicken broth
- 1 can (10½ ounces) cream of chicken soup
- 1 cup dairy sour cream
- 3 cups cubed cooked chicken
- ½ cup (4 ounces) sliced mushrooms
- 1 teaspoon Worcestershire sauce
- 1 teaspoon salt
- ⅛ teaspoon pepper

CONFETTI TOPPING:
- 1 cup sifted all-purpose flour
- 2 teaspoons baking powder
- ½ teaspoon salt
- 2 eggs, slightly beaten
- ½ cup milk
- 1 tablespoon chopped green bell pepper
- 1 tablespoon chopped pimiento
- 1¼ cups (5 ounces) shredded Wisconsin Cheddar cheese, divided

For casserole: In saucepan, combine carrots, onions, celery and chicken broth. Simmer 20 minutes. In 3-quart casserole, mix soup, sour cream, chicken cubes, mushrooms, Worcestershire sauce, salt and pepper. Add simmered vegetables and liquid; mix well.

For confetti topping: In mixing bowl, combine flour, baking powder and salt. Add eggs, milk, green pepper, pimiento and 1 cup of the cheese. Mix just until well blended. Drop tablespoons of topping onto casserole and bake in 350°F oven for 40 to 45 minutes or until golden brown. Sprinkle with remaining ¼ cup cheese and return to oven until melted. Garnish as desired.

Makes 6 to 8 servings

Favorite recipe from **Wisconsin Milk Marketing Board © 1993**

Quick 'n Easy Country Captain

- 3 tablespoons minced onion
- 1 clove garlic, minced
- 2 teaspoons curry powder
- 1 tablespoon butter or margarine
- 1½ cups chicken broth or bouillon
- 1½ cups UNCLE BEN'S® Rice In An Instant
- 1½ cups cubed cooked chicken
- 1 tomato, chopped
- ¼ cup raisins
- ⅓ cup salted peanuts (optional)

Cook onion, garlic and curry powder in butter in medium saucepan 2 to 3 minutes. Add broth; bring to a boil. Stir in rice, chicken, tomato and raisins. Cover and remove from heat. Let stand 5 minutes or until all liquid is absorbed. Sprinkle with peanuts, if desired. *Makes 4 servings*

Dairyland Confetti Chicken

Chicken Milano

Prep time: 5 minutes
Cook time: 20 minutes

2 cloves garlic, minced
4 boneless skinless chicken breast
 halves
½ teaspoon basil, crushed
⅛ teaspoon crushed red pepper
 flakes (optional)
 Salt and pepper to taste
1 tablespoon olive oil
1 can (14½ ounces) DEL MONTE®
 Italian Style Stewed
 Tomatoes*
1 can (16 ounces) DEL MONTE® Cut
 Green Italian Beans or Blue
 Lake Cut Green Beans,
 drained
¼ cup whipping cream

Rub garlic over chicken. Sprinkle
with basil and red pepper. Season to
taste with salt and pepper, if desired.
In skillet, brown chicken in oil. Stir
in tomatoes. Cover and simmer
5 minutes. Uncover and cook over
medium heat, 8 to 10 minutes or
until liquid is slightly thickened
and chicken is tender. Stir in green
beans and cream; heat through.
Do not boil.   **Makes 4 servings**

*You may substitute Del Monte®
Original Style Stewed Tomatoes.

Country Skillet Chicken

5 large cloves fresh California
 garlic
1 tablespoon lemon juice
4 large chicken pieces (about
 2 pounds)
2 tablespoons butter
1 tablespoon vegetable oil
1 cup sliced fresh mushrooms
¾ cup dry white wine
1 bay leaf
½ teaspoon salt
1 teaspoon Dijon-style mustard
½ cup chicken broth
1 tablespoon chopped parsley

Peel garlic. Finely mash, or put
through garlic press, 1 clove garlic.
Mix with lemon juice and rub over
chicken pieces. Let stand 10 minutes.
Melt butter with oil in large skillet
over medium-low heat. Add chicken
pieces and sauté 15 minutes, turning
once. Add mushrooms, wine, bay
leaf, salt and remaining 4 cloves
whole garlic. Cover and cook
10 minutes.

Blend mustard with chicken broth.
Pour over chicken and continue
cooking, covered, until chicken is
tender, 10 to 15 minutes. Remove
chicken and whole garlic cloves to
serving platter; keep warm. Discard
bay leaf. Bring pan liquid to boiling
and cook rapidly a few minutes to
reduce and thicken slightly. Pour
over chicken and sprinkle with
parsley. Serve a whole clove of
soft-cooked garlic with each
portion, to mash into the sauce
as chicken is eaten.

Makes 4 servings

Favorite recipe from **The Fresh Garlic
Association**

Chicken Milano

Orange Chicken Oriental

3 whole boneless skinless chicken
  breasts, cut into 2-inch strips
½ teaspoon salt
¼ teaspoon ground ginger
2 tablespoons vegetable oil
1 small garlic clove, minced
1 can (8¼ ounces) pineapple
  chunks, undrained
1 cup Florida orange juice,
  divided
1 teaspoon instant chicken
  bouillon granules
2 tablespoons wine vinegar
⅓ cup sliced celery
1 small green bell pepper, cut into
  ¼-inch strips
1 small onion, sliced
1 small tomato, cut in wedges
3 tablespoons flour
2 tablespoons soy sauce
1 tablespoon sugar
  Hot cooked rice

Sprinkle chicken with salt and
ginger. Heat oil in large skillet over
medium heat; add chicken and
garlic and cook 5 minutes. Add
liquid from pineapple, ¾ cup of the
orange juice, the bouillon and
vinegar. Cover; simmer 10 minutes
or until chicken is tender.

Add celery, green pepper and
onion. Cover; cook 5 minutes longer.
Add tomato wedges and pineapple
chunks. In small bowl, blend
together flour, soy sauce, sugar and
remaining ¼ cup orange juice. Add
to skillet and cook, stirring constantly,
until mixture thickens and comes to
a boil; cook 1 minute longer. Serve
over rice, if desired.

Makes 4 servings

Favorite Recipe from **Florida
Department of Citrus**

Chicken Pot Pie

Preparation time: 45 minutes

1 10¾-ounce can cream of
  chicken soup
1 cup milk, divided
½ cup chopped onion
1 3-ounce package cream
  cheese, softened and cut up
¼ cup chopped celery
¼ cup shredded carrot
¼ cup grated Wisconsin Parmesan
  cheese
3 cups cubed cooked chicken
1 10-ounce package frozen cut
  broccoli, cooked and
  drained
1 cup packaged complete
  buttermilk pancake mix
1 cup (4 ounces) shredded
  Wisconsin Sharp Cheddar
  cheese
1 egg, slightly beaten
1 tablespoon vegetable oil
¼ cup sliced almonds

In large saucepan combine soup,
½ cup of the milk, onion, cream
cheese, celery, carrot and Parmesan
cheese. Cook and stir until mixture
is hot and cream cheese is melted.
Stir in chicken and broccoli; heat
through. Pour into ungreased 2-quart
casserole.

For topping, in medium mixing
bowl combine pancake mix and
Cheddar cheese. In small mixing
bowl stir together egg, remaining
½ cup milk and oil. Add to pancake
mixture; stir until well combined.
Spoon topping over hot chicken
mixture. Sprinkle with nuts. Bake in
a 375°F oven for 20 to 25 minutes or
until topping is golden brown and
chicken mixture is bubbly around the
edges. *Makes 6 to 8 servings*

Favorite recipe from **Wisconsin Milk
Marketing Board** © 1993

Orange Chicken Oriental

Hearty Chicken Bake

3 cups hot mashed potatoes
1 cup (4 ounces) shredded
  Cheddar cheese
1 can (2.8 ounces) DURKEE® French
  Fried Onions
1½ cups (7 ounces) cubed cooked
  chicken
1 package (10 ounces) frozen
  mixed vegetables, thawed
  and drained
1 can (10¾ ounces) condensed
  cream of chicken soup
¼ cup milk
½ teaspoon DURKEE® Ground
  Mustard
¼ teaspoon DURKEE® Garlic
  Powder
¼ teaspoon DURKEE® Ground Black
  Pepper

Preheat oven to 375°F. In medium
bowl, combine mashed potatoes,
½ cup cheese and ½ can French
Fried Onions; mix thoroughly. Spoon
potato mixture into greased 1½-quart
casserole. Using back of spoon,
spread potatoes across bottom
and up sides of dish to form shell.
In large bowl, combine chicken,
mixed vegetables, soup, milk and
seasonings; pour into potato shell.
Bake, uncovered, at 375°F for
30 minutes or until heated through.
Top with remaining cheese and
onions; bake, uncovered, 3 minutes
or until onions are golden brown. Let
stand 5 minutes before serving.

Makes 4 to 6 servings

Chicken Almond Stir-Fry

5 teaspoons soy sauce
3 teaspoons cornstarch, divided
2 whole boneless skinless chicken
  breasts, cut into 2 x ¼-inch
  strips
1 cup boiling water
1 teaspoon instant chicken
  bouillon granules
½ teaspoon ground ginger
¼ cup CRISCO® Oil, divided
2 cups fresh broccoli flowerettes
  or 1 package (6 ounces)
  frozen Chinese pea pods,
  thawed
1 medium onion, cut into 1-inch
  pieces
1 clove garlic, minced
½ red or green bell pepper, cut
  into 1½ x ¼-inch strips
¼ to ½ teaspoon dried crushed
  red pepper
½ cup sliced almonds, chopped
  walnuts or peanuts
  Hot cooked rice

1. Combine soy sauce and 1
teaspoon of the cornstarch in
medium bowl. Add chicken; stir
to coat. Refrigerate 30 minutes.

2. Combine water and bouillon
granules in small bowl. Stir
until dissolved. Add remaining
2 teaspoons cornstarch and
ginger; stir.

3. Heat 2 tablespoons of the Crisco®
oil to 365°F in electric skillet or on
medium-high heat in large heavy
skillet. Add broccoli, onion, garlic
and bell pepper. Stir-fry until
crisp-tender. Remove from skillet with
slotted spoon to serving dish.

4. Heat remaining 2 tablespoons
Crisco® oil in same skillet to 365°F or
on medium-high heat. Add chicken
mixture and crushed red pepper.
Stir-fry until chicken is no longer pink.
Return vegetables to skillet. Add
bouillon mixture. Stir until thickened.
Stir in nuts. Serve with rice.

Makes 4 servings

Hearty Chicken Bake

One Skillet Spicy Chicken 'n Rice

¼ cup all-purpose flour
1 teaspoon LAWRY'S® Seasoned Salt
6 to 8 chicken pieces, skinned
2 tablespoons vegetable oil
2 cans (14½ ounces each) whole peeled tomatoes, undrained and cut up
1 package (1.25 ounces) LAWRY'S® Taco Spices & Seasonings
1 cup thinly sliced celery
1 cup long-grain rice
½ cup chopped onion
Chopped parsley

In plastic bag, combine flour and Seasoned Salt. Add chicken; shake to coat well. In large skillet, brown chicken in oil; continue cooking, uncovered, over low heat 15 minutes. Add remaining ingredients except parsley; blend well. Bring to a boil. Reduce heat; cover and simmer 20 minutes or until liquid is absorbed and chicken is cooked through. Garnish with parsley. ***Makes 4 to 6 servings***

Ginger Spicy Chicken

2 whole boneless skinless chicken breasts, halved
Salt
2 tablespoons vegetable oil
1 medium-size red bell pepper, cut into 2 × ¼-inch strips
1 medium-size green bell pepper, cut into 2 × ¼-inch strips
1 can (8 ounces) pineapple chunks in juice, undrained
½ cup PACE® Picante Sauce
2 tablespoons chopped cilantro or parsley
2 to 3 teaspoons grated fresh ginger *or* ¾ to 1 teaspoon ground ginger

Sprinkle chicken breasts with salt. Heat oil in large skillet over medium heat. Add chicken; cook about 5 minutes on each side or until light brown and tender. Remove chicken; keep warm. Add pepper strips, pineapple with juice, picante sauce, cilantro and ginger to skillet. Cook, stirring frequently, 5 to 7 minutes or until peppers are tender and sauce is thickened. Return chicken to skillet and heat through. ***Makes 4 servings***

Brown Rice Chicken Bake

3 cups cooked brown rice
1 package (10 ounces) frozen green peas
2 cups cubed cooked chicken breast
½ cup cholesterol free, reduced calorie mayonnaise
⅓ cup slivered almonds, toasted (optional)
2 teaspoons soy sauce
¼ teaspoon ground black pepper
¼ teaspoon garlic powder
¼ teaspoon dried tarragon leaves
Vegetable cooking spray

Combine rice, peas, chicken, mayonnaise, almonds, soy sauce and seasonings in bowl. Transfer to 3-quart baking dish coated with cooking spray. Cover and bake at 350°F for 15 to 20 minutes. ***Makes 6 servings***

Favorite recipe from **USA Rice Council**

One Skillet Spicy Chicken 'n Rice

Chicken & Pasta Sicilian

4 to 6 boneless chicken breast
halves, lightly seasoned and
coated with flour and paprika
Vegetable or olive oil
½ (1-pound) package CREAMETTE®
Spaghetti or Fettuccini,
cooked and drained
⅓ cup chopped walnuts, toasted
¼ cup margarine or butter, melted
1 (26-ounce) jar CLASSICO®
Di Sicilia (Ripe Olives &
Mushrooms) Pasta Sauce,
heated

In large skillet, cook chicken breasts
in oil until tender and golden on
both sides. Slice crosswise; set aside.
Toss together hot cooked pasta,
walnuts and margarine. To serve,
arrange chicken and pasta on
plate. Spoon hot pasta sauce over
chicken. Garnish with fresh basil, if
desired. Refrigerate leftovers.

Makes 4 to 6 servings

Lemon Honey Chicken

¼ cup CRISCO® Oil
6 tablespoons lemon juice
2 tablespoons honey
1 teaspoon grated lemon peel
Dash salt and pepper
6 chicken pieces

1. Combine Crisco® oil, lemon juice,
honey, lemon peel, salt and pepper
in glass baking dish. Stir well.

2. Place chicken pieces in baking
dish. Turn to coat. Marinate at room
temperature 20 minutes.

3. Preheat grill.* Remove chicken
from marinade, reserving marinade.

4. Grill chicken 15 to 20 minutes.
Brush with marinade. Grill on other
side 15 to 20 minutes or until meat
near bone is no longer pink.

Makes 4 to 6 servings

*Broiler may also be used.

Chicken & Pasta Sicilian

Baked Chicken Parmesan

Prep time: 15 minutes
Cooking time: 1 hour

1 broiler-fryer chicken, cut up, skinned (2½ to 3 pounds)
¾ cup MIRACLE WHIP® Salad Dressing
1 cup POST TOASTIES® Corn Flake Crumbs
½ cup (2 ounces) KRAFT® 100% Grated Parmesan Cheese
Dash of salt and pepper

• Heat oven to 350°F.

• Brush chicken with salad dressing; coat with combined crumbs and cheese. Sprinkle with salt and pepper.

• Place in 13x9-inch baking dish. Bake 1 hour or until tender.

Makes 3 to 4 servings

Variation: For Cajun Chicken, omit salt. Add 1 teaspoon *each* ground cumin and onion powder and ½ teaspoon *each* ground red pepper and garlic powder to salad dressing; mix well. Substitute 1½ cups crushed sesame crackers for corn flake crumbs and parmesan cheese. Continue as directed.

Note: For crispier chicken, place chicken pieces on rack of broiler pan to bake.

Mexican Chicken Kiev

2 whole boneless skinless chicken breasts (about 1 pound), halved and pounded
4 ounces Monterey Jack cheese, thinly sliced
1 can (4 ounces) chopped green chilies, drained
⅓ cup seasoned dry bread crumbs
1 teaspoon chili powder
½ cup bottled salsa

Preheat oven to 375°F.

Top each chicken breast half with equal amounts of cheese and chilies; roll up and secure with wooden toothpicks. Roll in bread crumbs combined with chili powder, coating well.

In lightly greased shallow baking pan, arrange chicken rolls and bake 20 minutes. Top with salsa and bake an additional 20 minutes or until chicken is tender and no longer pink. Serve, if desired, with additional salsa.

Makes about 4 servings

Microwave Directions: Prepare chicken breasts as above. In lightly greased 2-quart microwave-safe oblong baking dish, arrange chicken. Microwave covered with plastic wrap at HIGH (Full Power) 5 minutes. Rearrange chicken, then top with salsa. Microwave 3 minutes or until chicken is tender and no longer pink. Let stand covered 5 minutes.

Favorite recipe from **Thomas J. Lipton Co.**

Patio Chicken Salad

Prep time: 20 minutes

½ lb. VELVEETA® Pasteurized Process Cheese Spread, cubed
2 cups cubed cooked chicken
1 8-oz. can pineapple chunks, drained
1 cup celery slices
1 cup red or green grape halves
MIRACLE WHIP® Salad Dressing

In large bowl, combine process cheese spread, chicken, pineapple, celery, grapes and enough salad dressing to moisten; mix lightly. Serve on lettuce-covered plates.

Makes 6 servings

Variation: Add ⅓ cup sliced almonds, toasted.

Baked Chicken Parmesan

Chicken Picante

½ cup medium-hot chunky taco
  sauce
¼ cup Dijon-style mustard
2 tablespoons fresh lime juice
3 whole boneless skinless chicken
  breasts, halved
2 tablespoons butter or margarine
  Plain yogurt

Combine taco sauce, mustard
and lime juice in large bowl. Add
chicken, turning to coat. Cover;
marinate in refrigerator at least
30 minutes.

Melt butter in large skillet over
medium heat until foamy. Remove
chicken from marinade; reserve
marinade. Add chicken to skillet;
cook about 10 minutes or until brown
on both sides. Add marinade; cook
about 5 minutes or until chicken
is tender and marinade glazes
chicken. Remove chicken to serving
platter. Boil marinade over high heat
1 minute; pour over chicken. Garnish
with cilantro or lime slices, if desired.
Serve with yogurt.

Makes 6 servings

Favorite recipe from **National Broiler
Council**

Southern Barbecued Chicken

⅔ cup HEINZ Tomato Ketchup
1 tablespoon honey
2 teaspoons lemon juice
  Dash hot pepper sauce
1 (2- to 2½-pound) broiler-fryer
  chicken, cut up

In small bowl, combine ketchup,
honey, lemon juice and hot pepper
sauce. Broil or grill chicken 25 to
30 minutes, turning once. Brush
ketchup mixture on chicken; cook
additional 5 to 10 minutes or until
chicken is tender, turning and
brushing with ketchup mixture.

*Makes 4 to 5 servings
(about ¾ cup sauce)*

Jiffy Chicken 'n Rice

1½ cups cooked unsalted regular
  rice (½ cup uncooked)
1 jar (8 ounces) pasteurized
  processed cheese spread
¼ cup milk
2 cups (10 ounces) cubed cooked
  chicken
1 package (10 ounces) frozen
  peas, thawed and drained
1 can (2.8 ounces) DURKEE® French
  Fried Onions

Preheat oven to 375°F. To hot rice in
saucepan, add cheese spread,
milk, chicken, peas and ½ *can*
French Fried Onions; stir well. Spoon
into 1½-quart casserole. Bake,
uncovered, at 375°F for 25 minutes
or until heated through. Top with
remaining onions; bake, uncovered,
3 minutes or until onions are golden
brown.   *Makes 4 to 6 servings*

Microwave Directions: Prepare rice
mixture as above; spoon into
1½-quart microwave-safe casserole.
Cook, covered, on HIGH 8 to
10 minutes or until heated through.
Stir rice mixture halfway through
cooking time. Top with remaining
onions; cook, uncovered, 1 minute.
Let stand 5 minutes.

Ortega® Salsa Chicken

4 boneless chicken breast halves
  (about 1 pound)
1 tablespoon vegetable oil
1 (12-ounce) jar ORTEGA® Thick 'n
  Chunky Salsa

In large skillet over medium-high
heat, brown chicken in hot oil; drain
fat. Add salsa and heat to a boil.
Reduce heat to low; cover and
simmer 15 minutes or until chicken is
tender, turning once.

Makes 4 servings

Chicken Picante

Batter Fried Chicken

1 (2½- to 3½-pound) broiler-fryer
    chicken, cut up
1 cup water
1 stalk celery (including leaves),
    cut into 2-inch pieces
1 small onion, cut in half
1 clove garlic, cut in half
½ teaspoon salt
⅛ teaspoon pepper
    Fritter Batter (recipe follows)
    Vegetable oil for frying

1. Place chicken, water, celery, onion, garlic, salt and pepper in 5-quart Dutch oven. Heat to boiling. Reduce heat to low; cover and cook until chicken is almost tender, 20 to 25 minutes.

2. While chicken is cooking, prepare Fritter Batter. Remove chicken from Dutch oven, drain and pat dry with paper towels. Cool slightly.

3. Pour oil into deep fryer or 5-quart Dutch oven to 2½ to 3 inches deep. Heat to 350°F.

4. Dip chicken in Fritter Batter to coat. Add several chicken pieces to oil. (Do not crowd; pieces should not touch.) Fry, turning occasionally, until chicken is golden, 5 to 7 minutes.

5. Place fried chicken on cookie sheet lined with paper towels; keep warm in 200°F oven until ready to serve. *Makes 4 servings*

Fritter Batter

1 cup all-purpose flour
1 teaspoon baking powder
1 teaspoon salt
¼ teaspoon white pepper
2 eggs
¾ cup milk
1 tablespoon vegetable oil

Combine flour, baking powder, salt and pepper in medium bowl; add eggs, milk and oil. Beat with fork or small whisk until well mixed.
Makes about 1½ cups

Chicken Scandia

1 jar (12 ounces) HEINZ HomeStyle
    Chicken Gravy
¼ cup dairy sour cream
2 teaspoons lemon juice
1 teaspoon dried dill weed
4 boneless skinless chicken breast
    halves, grilled or sautéed
    Hot cooked noodles

In small saucepan, combine gravy, sour cream, lemon juice and dill; heat over low heat, stirring, until smooth and warm. *Do not boil.* For each serving, slice chicken diagonally across grain into 4 slices. Arrange on a bed of noodles; spoon gravy mixture over chicken. Garnish with lemon wedges, if desired.
Makes 4 servings

Batter Fried Chicken

Chicken Couscous

1½ cups couscous*
2½ cups chicken broth, divided
6 tablespoons butter or
    margarine, divided
1 cup chopped onion
2 tomatoes, peeled and cubed
2 carrots, pared and diagonally
    sliced
1 green bell pepper, cut in strips
½ small butternut squash, pared
    and cubed (2 cups)
1 teaspoon salt
2 cups cubed cooked chicken
1 zucchini, sliced
1 can (20 ounces) chick peas,
    drained
½ cup raisins
1 teaspoon lemon juice
½ teaspoon ground cinnamon
½ teaspoon TABASCO® Brand
    Pepper Sauce
¼ teaspoon ground turmeric
¼ teaspoon paprika
    Hot Sauce (recipe follows)

Place couscous in bowl. Add
1½ cups broth and soak 20 minutes
or until all broth is absorbed. Rub
couscous between fingers to remove
any lumps. Place in colander over
simmering water. Cover; let steam
1 hour. In large saucepan melt
3 tablespoons butter; sauté onion
until tender. Add tomatoes, carrots,
green pepper, butternut squash and
salt. Cover; cook over low heat
30 minutes. Add remaining 1 cup
chicken broth, chicken, zucchini,
chick peas, raisins, lemon juice,
cinnamon, Tabasco® sauce,
turmeric and paprika. Cook
10 minutes longer. Drain off 1 cup
broth to make Hot Sauce. Add
remaining 3 tablespoons butter to
couscous and mix well. Serve
couscous with chicken-vegetable
mixture and Hot Sauce.

Makes 6 servings

*If using quick-cooking couscous,
cook according to package
directions and omit steaming step.

Hot Sauce

1 cup broth drained from chicken-
    vegetable mixture
½ to ¾ teaspoon TABASCO® Brand
    Pepper Sauce
½ teaspoon paprika

Combine all ingredients in small bowl.

California Chicken Risotto

1 pound boneless skinless
    chicken breasts, cut into
    1½-inch pieces
¾ teaspoon salt (optional)
¼ teaspoon ground red pepper
1 tablespoon olive oil
1 large onion, coarsely chopped
    (2 cups)
1 clove garlic, minced
1⅓ cups UNCLE BEN'S® CONVERTED®
    Brand Rice
2 cans (14½ ounces each) ready
    to serve chicken broth
1 small yellow or green bell
    pepper, diced (1 cup)
1 package (3 ounces) cream
    cheese, softened and cut
    into cubes
1 large tomato, chopped
    (1½ cups)
¼ cup fresh basil leaves, thinly
    sliced*

Sprinkle chicken with salt, if desired,
and red pepper; set aside. Heat oil
in 10-inch skillet over medium heat.
Add onion and garlic; cook and stir
3 minutes. Add chicken; cook and
stir until no longer pink. Add rice;
cook and stir 1 minute. Add broth to
skillet; bring to a boil. Reduce heat;
cover tightly and simmer 20 minutes.
Stir in bell pepper. Remove from
heat. Let stand covered until all
liquid is absorbed, about 5 minutes.
Stir in cheese until melted and
creamy. Stir in tomato and basil.

*You may substitute 1 teaspoon
dried basil for fresh; cook with
chicken.

Chicken Tetrazzini

8 ounces uncooked long
    spaghetti, broken in half
3 tablespoons butter, divided
¼ cup all-purpose flour
1 teaspoon salt
½ teaspoon paprika
½ teaspoon celery salt
⅛ teaspoon pepper
2 cups milk
1 cup chicken broth
3 cups chopped cooked chicken
1 can (2 ounces) mushrooms,
    drained
¼ cup pimiento strips
¾ cup grated Wisconsin Parmesan
    cheese, divided

In large saucepan cook spaghetti according to package directions; drain. Add 1 tablespoon of the butter; stir until melted. Set aside. In a 3-quart saucepan melt remaining 2 tablespoons butter; stir in flour, salt, paprika, celery salt and pepper. Remove from heat; gradually stir in milk and chicken broth. Cook over medium heat, stirring constantly, until thickened. Add chicken, mushrooms, pimiento, spaghetti and ¼ cup Parmesan cheese; heat thoroughly. Place chicken mixture on ovenproof platter or shallow casserole; sprinkle remaining ½ cup Parmesan cheese over top. Broil about 3 inches from heat until lightly browned. *Makes 6 to 8 servings*

Favorite recipe from **Wisconsin Milk Marketing Board** © 1993

Double-Coated Chicken

7 cups KELLOGG'S® CORN FLAKES®
    Cereal, crushed to 1¾ cups
1 egg
1 cup skim milk
½ cup all-purpose flour
½ teaspoon salt
¼ teaspoon pepper
3 pounds broiler-fryer chicken
    pieces, washed and
    patted dry
3 tablespoons margarine, melted

1. Measure crushed Kellogg's® Corn Flakes® cereal into shallow dish or pan. Set aside.

2. In small mixing bowl, beat egg and milk slightly. Add flour, salt and pepper. Mix until smooth. Dip chicken in batter. Coat in crumbs. Place in single layer, skin-side up, in foil-lined shallow baking pan. Drizzle with margarine.

3. Bake in preheated 350°F oven about 1 hour or until chicken is tender. Do not cover pan or turn chicken while baking.
Makes 6 servings

Citrus Chicken Iberia

1 (2½- to 3½-pound) broiler-fryer
    chicken, cut into quarters
2 tablespoons all-purpose flour
½ teaspoon salt
⅛ teaspoon pepper
2 tablespoons butter or margarine
2 tablespoons olive oil
1 clove garlic, minced
1 can (6 ounces) Florida frozen
    concentrated orange juice,
    thawed, undiluted
½ cup chicken broth or water
1 teaspoon dried oregano leaves
1 green bell pepper, cut into strips
1 red onion, sliced
½ pound mushrooms, sliced
½ cup black olives, sliced

Wash chicken; pat dry. Combine flour, salt and pepper. Coat chicken with flour mixture. In large skillet, heat butter and oil; sauté garlic until lightly browned. Add chicken and brown on both sides.

Combine orange juice concentrate, chicken broth and oregano; pour over chicken. Cover. Cook for 15 minutes. Baste chicken with pan juices. Add green pepper and onion. Cover; cook 5 minutes longer. Add mushrooms and olives. Cover; cook 5 minutes or until chicken is tender. *Makes 4 servings*

Favorite recipe from **Florida Department of Citrus**

Caribbean Pineapple Chicken

Preparation Time: 10 minutes
Cook Time: 20 minutes

1 DOLE® Fresh Pineapple
1 tablespoon vegetable oil
2 boneless skinless chicken breast
    halves
1 clove garlic, pressed
2 teaspoons all-purpose flour
¼ cup water
2 to 3 tablespoons honey
1 to 2 tablespoons soy sauce
    Grated peel and juice from
    1 lime
¼ teaspoon coconut extract
    Pinch ground red pepper
1 tablespoon flaked coconut,
    optional
1 to 2 teaspoons minced cilantro
    or green onion, optional

• Twist crown from pineapple. Cut pineapple in half lengthwise. Refrigerate half for another use. Cut fruit from shell with knife. Cut fruit crosswise into 6 slices.

• In 8-inch nonstick skillet, sauté pineapple in oil over medium-high heat until slightly browned. Remove to plates.

• Rub chicken with garlic; sprinkle with flour. In same skillet, sauté chicken, covered, in pan juices over medium-high heat until browned; turn once.

• Mix water, honey, soy sauce, lime juice, coconut extract and red pepper in cup; pour into skillet. Cover; simmer 12 to 15 minutes or until chicken is tender. Remove chicken to serving plates.

• Arrange chicken on plates. Spoon sauce over top. Sprinkle with coconut, lime peel and cilantro.

Makes 2 servings

Delicious Chicken Pasta

2 whole skinless boneless chicken
    breasts (about 12 ounces)
3 teaspoons CHEF PAUL
    PRUDHOMME'S MEAT MAGIC®,
    divided
1 cup chopped onion
½ cup chopped celery
½ cup chopped bell pepper
2 cups defatted chicken stock,
    divided
2 tablespoons all-purpose flour
3 cups thinly sliced fresh
    mushrooms
1 teaspoon minced garlic
½ cup chopped green onions
6 ounces pasta (fettucini, angel
    hair or your favorite), cooked
    according to package
    directions

Cut chicken into thin strips; place in small bowl and combine thoroughly with 2 teaspoons of the Meat Magic®.

Place skillet over high heat and add onion, celery, bell pepper and remaining 1 teaspoon Meat Magic®. Cook over high heat, shaking pan and stirring occasionally (don't scrape), for 5 minutes. Add ½ cup chicken stock, scraping up the browned coating on the bottom of pan; cook another 4 minutes. Stir in the chicken mixture and cook 4 minutes. Add flour and stir well, cooking another 2 minutes. Add mushrooms and garlic, folding carefully so mushrooms don't break. Add ½ cup chicken stock and scrape bottom of pan. Cook 4 minutes and add another ½ cup stock, stirring and scraping. Continue cooking 5 minutes more; add green onions and remaining ½ cup stock. Stir and scrape well. Cook 5 more minutes or until chicken is tender; remove from heat. Serve with pasta. *Makes 6 servings*

Caribbean Pineapple Chicken

Creole Chicken Thighs

2 tablespoons butter or margarine
½ pound mushrooms, sliced
1 medium onion, chopped
½ cup chopped green bell
pepper
½ cup thinly sliced celery
2 cloves garlic, minced
1 can (16 ounces) tomatoes,
cut up
½ teaspoon salt
½ teaspoon sugar
½ teaspoon thyme leaves,
crumbled
½ teaspoon hot pepper sauce
2 bay leaves
8 broiler-fryer chicken thighs,
skinned
2 cups cooked rice

In fry pan, melt butter over medium-high heat. Add mushrooms, onion, pepper, celery and garlic. Cook, stirring constantly, about 3 minutes or until onion is translucent but not brown. Stir in tomatoes, salt, sugar, thyme, hot pepper sauce and bay leaves. Add chicken pieces, spooning sauce over chicken. Cook, covered, over medium heat about 35 minutes or until chicken is tender. Remove and discard bay leaves. Serve chicken and sauce over hot cooked rice. *Makes 4 servings*

Favorite recipe from **Delmarva Poultry Industry, Inc.**

Chicken Breasts Hawaiian

4 whole boneless skinless chicken
breasts, halved
¼ cup butter or margarine
2 teaspoons chili powder
¼ cup flaked coconut
1 egg, slightly beaten
¾ cup coarse dry bread crumbs
1 teaspoon salt
¼ cup plus 2 tablespoons CRISCO®
Shortening, divided
4 pineapple slices
2 cooked sweet potatoes,
quartered
2 firm bananas, peeled and cut in
half lengthwise
Toasted nuts and coconut,
if desired
Sweet and Sour Sauce (recipe
follows)

1. Rinse and pat chicken dry. Place chicken between 2 pieces of plastic wrap; flatten slightly.

2. Cream butter and chili powder. Blend in coconut. Divide into 8 portions.

3. Spoon 1 portion onto each chicken piece. Tuck in sides; roll and skewer. Chill at least 2 hours.

4. Preheat oven to 400°F.

5. Dip chicken rolls into egg, then roll in combined bread crumbs and salt to coat evenly.

6. Melt ¼ cup of the Crisco® in a large heavy skillet over medium-high heat. Add chicken rolls and brown evenly on all sides. Transfer to greased shallow baking dish and bake 20 to 25 minutes or until chicken is tender. Remove skewers.

7. Melt remaining 2 tablespoons Crisco® in a large heavy skillet over medium heat. Heat pineapple, sweet potatoes and bananas. Arrange with chicken rolls on a serving platter. Garnish with toasted nuts and coconut, if desired. Serve with Sweet and Sour Sauce.
Makes 8 servings

Sweet and Sour Sauce

2 tablespoons CRISCO®
Shortening
¼ cup finely chopped onion
½ cup catsup
½ cup apricot preserves
1 tablespoon brown sugar
1 tablespoon cider vinegar
½ teaspoon curry powder

1. Melt Crisco® in a small heavy saucepan over medium heat. Add onion; cook until tender. Stir in catsup, apricot preserves, brown sugar, vinegar and curry powder; blend well. Heat and keep warm.

Chicken Santa Fe

1¾ cups (14½-ounce can)
    CONTADINA® Stewed
    Tomatoes, cut-up
¾ cup chopped onion
¼ cup mild or hot green chili salsa
1 garlic clove, minced
¼ teaspoon salt
4 boneless skinless chicken breast
    halves (about 1 pound)
3 tablespoons all-purpose flour
2 tablespoons olive oil
2 cups hot cooked rice
¼ cup sour cream
1 small ripe avocado, peeled
    and pitted, cut into cubes
    Fresh cilantro or parsley

In medium bowl, combine tomatoes, onion, salsa, garlic and salt; set aside. Coat chicken with flour. In 10-inch skillet heat oil over medium heat. Sauté chicken for 3 to 4 minutes on each side, or until golden brown. Pour tomato mixture over chicken; cover and simmer for 15 to 20 minutes or until chicken is tender. Divide rice onto 4 individual plates. Top with chicken and sauce. Garnish with dollop of sour cream, avocado cubes and cilantro.

Makes 4 servings

Dijon Chicken & Pepper Rice Skillet

1⅔ cups water
2 tablespoons butter or margarine
1 package (5.1 ounces)
    COUNTRY INN® Brand Rice
    Dishes Creamy Chicken &
    Mushroom
2 teaspoons Dijon-style mustard
8 ounces deli-cooked chicken
    breast, cut into ½- to ¾-inch
    cubes
1 cup short thin mixed red and
    green bell pepper strips

Combine water and butter in 10-inch skillet. Stir in contents of rice and seasoning packets and mustard; bring to a boil. Cover tightly; reduce heat and simmer 8 minutes, stirring occasionally. Stir in chicken and pepper strips. Remove from heat; let stand covered 5 minutes or until desired consistency.

Makes 4 servings

Chicken Olé

2 tablespoons vegetable oil
1 large onion, chopped (1 cup)
2 cloves garlic, minced
1 can (10½ ounces) tomato purée
1 cup Florida orange juice
3 tablespoons chopped canned
    green chilies
1 teaspoon grated orange peel
1 teaspoon ground cinnamon
½ teaspoon dried thyme leaves,
    crushed
½ teaspoon salt
1 (2½- to 3½-pound) broiler-fryer
    chicken
    Salt and pepper
8 new potatoes
3 medium-size red bell peppers,
    seeded and sliced

Preheat oven to 350°F. In large skillet, heat oil; sauté onion and garlic until tender. Add tomato purée, orange juice, chilies, orange peel, cinnamon, thyme and salt. Cook 10 minutes, stirring occasionally.

Meanwhile, sprinkle chicken, inside and out, with salt and pepper. Place chicken in large baking dish. Pare a narrow strip around each potato. Arrange potatoes around chicken. Pour sauce over all.

Cover. Bake 45 minutes. Add red peppers; cover. Cook 45 minutes longer until chicken and potatoes are tender.   *Makes 4 servings*

Favorite recipe from **Florida Department of Citrus**

GALA ENTERTAINING

Chicken and Broccoli Crepes

½ cup half-and-half
½ cup all-purpose flour
½ teaspoon garlic salt
1¼ cups chicken broth
2 cups (8 ounces) shredded Wisconsin Cheddar cheese, divided
½ cup (2 ounces) shredded Wisconsin Monterey Jack cheese
1½ cups dairy sour cream, divided
2 tablespoons diced pimiento
1 tablespoon dried parsley flakes
1 teaspoon paprika
1 can (4 ounces) sliced mushrooms, drained
2 tablespoons butter
10 cooked Basic Crepes (recipe follows)
2 packages (10 ounces each) frozen broccoli spears, cooked and drained
2 cups cubed cooked chicken

Combine half-and-half, flour and garlic salt; beat until smooth. Blend in chicken broth. Stir in 1 cup of the Cheddar cheese, the Monterey Jack cheese, ½ cup of the sour cream, the pimiento, parsley and paprika. Cook sauce over low to medium heat until mixture thickens, stirring constantly. Sauté mushrooms in butter. On each crepe, place cooked broccoli, chicken and mushrooms. Spoon 1 to 2 tablespoons of sauce over each. Fold crepes. Place in large shallow baking dish. Cover and bake in a preheated 350°F oven 20 to 30 minutes or until throughtly heated. Pour remaining sauce over crepes. Top with remaining 1 cup sour cream and 1 cup Cheddar cheese. Bake, uncovered, 5 to 10 minutes longer or until cheese melts. Top with chopped parsley, if desired.

Makes 10 crepes

Basic Crepes

3 eggs
½ teaspoon salt
2 cups plus 2 tablespoons all-purpose flour
2 cups milk
¼ cup melted butter

Beat eggs and salt. Add flour alternately with milk, beating with electric mixer or whisk until smooth. Stir in melted butter.

Allow crepe batter to stand for 1 hour or more in refrigerator before cooking. The flour may expand and some of the bubbles will collapse. The batter should be the consistency of heavy cream. If the batter is too thick, add 1 to 2 tablespoons of milk and stir well.

Heat 7- to 8-inch nonstick skillet to medium-high heat. Spray lightly with vegetable cooking spray. With one hand pour 3 tablespoons batter and with the other hand lift the pan off heat. Quickly rotate pan until batter covers bottom; return pan to heat. Cook until light brown; turn and brown other side for a few seconds.

Makes about 30 crepes

Note: To store crepes, separate with pieces of waxed paper and wrap airtight. They may be stored frozen for up to 3 months.

Favorite recipe from **Wisconsin Milk Marketing Board** © **1993**

Chicken and Broccoli Crepes

Chicken with Cucumbers and Dill

2 whole boneless skinless
  broiler-fryer chicken breasts,
  halved
1 teaspoon salt, divided
3/4 teaspoon pepper, divided
4 tablespoons butter or
  margarine, divided
2 cucumbers, peeled, seeded
  and cut into 1/4-inch slices
1/2 teaspoon dill weed
1/4 cup lemon juice
  Lemon slices, for garnish

Sprinkle chicken breasts with
1/2 teaspoon of the salt and 1/2
teaspoon of the pepper. Melt 2
tablespoons of the butter in large
skillet over medium heat; add
chicken. Cook about 8 minutes or
until chicken is brown on both sides;
remove and keep warm. Melt
remaining 2 tablespoons butter in
same skillet. Add cucumbers; stir to
coat. Sprinkle remaining 1/2 teaspoon
salt and 1/4 teaspoon pepper over
cucumbers; cook 2 minutes. Stir in
dill weed. Push cucumbers to side
of skillet.

Return chicken and any collected
juices to skillet. Cook 2 minutes
or until chicken is tender. Place
chicken on serving platter; arrange
cucumbers around chicken. Cook
juices in skillet until light brown. Pour
lemon juice and pan juices over
chicken. Garnish with lemon slices.

Makes 4 servings

Favorite recipe from **Delmarva Poultry
Industry, Inc.**

Chicken Macadamia

6 whole boneless skinless chicken
  breasts
1 cup plus 1 tablespoon
  champagne
4 1/2 teaspoons butter
2 1/2 tablespoons flour
1 cup chicken stock or broth
1/4 cup heavy cream
1 1/2 teaspoons chopped fresh
  parsley
  Dash fresh ground pepper
2 1/2 cups Wisconsin Sharp Cheddar
  cheese, shredded
1/2 cup macadamia nuts, chopped
  and toasted

1. Pound chicken breasts to 1/4-inch
thickness. Place in large pan and
cover with 1 cup champagne.
Marinate for 2 hours.

2. Melt butter over low heat. Stir in
flour until smooth. Gradually add
chicken stock and cream to butter
mixture. Cook until smooth and
thickened, stirring constantly.
Add remaining 1 tablespoon
champagne, parsley and pepper.
Sauce should be medium thin.

3. Remove chicken from marinade.

4. Combine 2 cups cheese and
nuts. Sprinkle 1/3 to 1/2 cup on each
chicken breast. Roll up chicken,
tucking in sides; secure with skewers,
if necessary. Place seam-side down
on baking sheet.

5. Pour half of sauce over chicken
breasts; reserve remaining sauce.

6. Bake in 325°F oven for 45 minutes
or until chicken is tender.

7. Place chicken breasts on serving
plates. Top with remaining 1/2 cup
cheese. Heat remaining sauce;
spoon over cheese. Garnish with
additional toasted macadamia nuts
and chopped parsley, if desired.

Makes 6 servings

Favorite recipe from **Wisconsin Milk
Marketing Board © 1993**

Chicken with Cucumbers and Dill

Sierra Chicken Bundles

2 cups prepared Mexican or
    Spanish-style rice mix
¼ cup thinly sliced green onions
½ teaspoon LAWRY'S® Seasoned
    Pepper
4 whole boneless skinless chicken
    breasts
½ cup unseasoned dry bread
    crumbs
¼ cup grated Parmesan cheese
½ teaspoon chili powder
½ teaspoon LAWRY'S® Garlic Salt
¼ teaspoon ground cumin
¼ cup IMPERIAL® Margarine,
    melted

In medium bowl, combine prepared rice, green onions and Seasoned Pepper. Pound chicken breasts between 2 sheets of waxed paper to ¼-inch thickness. Place about ⅓ cup rice mixture in center of each chicken breast; roll and tuck ends under and secure with wooden skewers. In pie plate, combine remaining ingredients except margarine; blend well. Roll chicken bundles in margarine, then crumb mixture. Place seam-side down in 12×8×2-inch baking dish. Bake, uncovered, in 400°F oven 15 to 20 minutes or until chicken is tender and no longer pink. Remove skewers before serving. *Makes 4 servings*

Presentation: Serve with assorted steamed vegetables and corn bread.

Almond Chicken Paprika

1 cup BLUE DIAMOND® Whole
    Natural Almonds, toasted
2 whole boneless skinless chicken
    breasts, halved
    Salt and freshly ground white
    pepper
8 tablespoons butter, divided
2 teaspoons Dijon-style mustard
2½ tablespoons paprika, divided
    Flour
⅔ cup chopped onion
    Pinch cayenne pepper
1 cup chicken stock or broth
½ cup sour cream

Coarsely chop almonds; reserve. Lightly flatten chicken breasts. Season with salt and white pepper.

Melt 6 tablespoons of the butter. Whisk in mustard and 1 tablespoon of the paprika. Coat chicken in the flour, then in mustard mixture. Coat with almonds. Place on buttered baking sheet. Bake at 450°F for 10 to 15 minutes or until chicken is just firm. Meanwhile, melt remaining 2 tablespoons butter in saucepan. Add onion and sauté until translucent. Stir in remaining 1½ tablespoons paprika, 1 tablespoon flour, ½ teaspoon salt and cayenne. Cook 1 minute. Stir in chicken stock; simmer 5 minutes. Whisk in sour cream; heat through. *Do not boil.* Divide sauce among 4 serving plates and top each with a chicken breast.

Makes 4 servings

Chicken Americana with Wisconsin Blue Cheese

4 ounces Wisconsin Blue cheese
3 ounces cream cheese,
    softened
1 egg
2 tablespoons walnuts
3 tablespoons bread crumbs
1 tablespoon chopped parsley
¼ teaspoon pepper
6 whole boneless skinless chicken
    breasts, pounded
    Flour
    Butter

Cream cheeses until smooth; combine with egg, walnuts, bread crumbs, parsley and pepper; blend thoroughly. Place ⅓ cup cheese mixture on one side of each chicken breast. Roll to enclose filling; secure with toothpicks.

Flour the rolled chicken breasts lightly. Sauté the breasts in butter until golden brown. (This can be done ahead of time.) Place in baking pan. Bake in a 375°F oven for 20 minutes or until chicken is tender. Remove breasts and let stand 5 to 8 minutes. Slice and serve.

Makes 6 servings

Favorite recipe from **Wisconsin Milk Marketing Board © 1993**

Sierra Chicken Bundles

Stuffed Chicken with Apple Glaze

1 (3½- to 4-pound) broiler-fryer chicken
½ teaspoon salt
¼ teaspoon pepper
2 tablespoons vegetable oil
1 package (6 ounces) chicken-flavored stuffing mix, plus ingredients to prepare mix
1 cup chopped apple
¼ cup chopped walnuts
¼ cup raisins
¼ cup thinly sliced celery
½ teaspoon grated lemon peel
½ cup apple jelly
1 tablespoon lemon juice
½ teaspoon ground cinnamon

Preheat oven to 350°F. Sprinkle inside of chicken with salt and pepper; rub outside with oil. Prepare stuffing mix according to package directions in large bowl. Add apple, walnuts, raisins, celery and lemon peel; mix thoroughly. Stuff body cavity loosely with stuffing.* Place chicken in baking pan; cover loosely with aluminum foil and roast 1 hour.

Meanwhile, combine jelly, lemon juice and cinnamon in small saucepan. Simmer over low heat 3 minutes or until blended. Remove foil from chicken; brush with jelly mixture. Roast, uncovered, brushing frequently with jelly glaze, 30 minutes longer or until meat thermometer inserted into thickest part of thigh registers 185°F. Let chicken stand 15 minutes before carving. Garnish as desired.   *Makes 4 servings*

*Bake any leftover stuffing in covered casserole alongside chicken until heated through.

Favorite recipe from **Delmarva Poultry Industry, Inc.**

Chicken Provencal with Mushroom Wild Rice

3 whole boneless skinless chicken breasts, halved
1 tablespoon olive oil
½ teaspoon salt
¼ teaspoon freshly ground black pepper
2 cloves garlic, minced
1 can (14 to 16 ounces) Italian plum tomatoes, drained and chopped
¼ cup dry red wine
1 tablespoon drained capers
1 teaspoon thyme leaves, crushed
2 cups quartered mushrooms
2 tablespoons butter or margarine
2 cups water
1 package (6¼ ounces) UNCLE BEN'S® Original Fast Cooking Long Grain & Wild Rice
½ cup sliced green onions with tops

Pound chicken to ½-inch thickness. Cook chicken in oil in 12-inch skillet over medium-high heat until lightly browned, about 1 minute per side. Sprinkle with salt and pepper. Add garlic to skillet; cook 1 minute. Add tomatoes, wine, capers and thyme; stir. Cover and simmer over low heat until chicken is cooked through, about 3 minutes. While chicken simmers, cook mushrooms in butter in medium saucepan over medium-high heat until lightly browned. Add water and contents of rice and seasoning packets to saucepan; bring to a vigorous boil. Reduce heat; cover tightly and simmer until all water is absorbed, about 5 minutes. Remove chicken to serving platter; cook tomato mixture over high heat to desired consistency. Spoon over chicken. Stir green onions into rice; serve with chicken.   *Makes 6 servings*

Stuffed Chicken with Apple Glaze

Gourmet Chicken Bake

1 teaspoon seasoned salt
¼ teaspoon curry powder
¼ teaspoon dried savory, crushed
¼ teaspoon white pepper
3 whole broiler-fryer chicken breasts, halved
1 cup buttermilk or soured milk*
2 packages (6 ounces each) seasoned long grain and wild rice
5½ cups chicken broth, divided
1 pound fresh asparagus, trimmed
2 tablespoons toasted slivered almonds
2 tablespoons chopped pimiento

Combine seasoned salt, curry powder, savory and pepper in small cup. Sprinkle over chicken. Place chicken in large bowl; pour buttermilk over chicken. Refrigerate, covered, overnight. Arrange chicken in single layer in 13×9-inch baking pan. Pour buttermilk marinade over chicken. Bake at 350°F 1 hour or until chicken is tender.

Cook rice according to package directions, using 5 cups of the chicken broth for the water. Meanwhile, cut asparagus 3 inches from tip, then cut remaining stalks into 1-inch pieces. Place asparagus in remaining ½ cup broth in small saucepan. Cover and cook over medium heat 15 minutes. Set aside, but do not drain.

Remove chicken from baking pan. Remove 3-inch asparagus spears from pan; set aside. Stir rice, 1-inch asparagus pieces and broth from asparagus into baking pan. Arrange chicken over rice and place asparagus spears around chicken. Sprinkle with almonds and pimiento. Bake about 15 minutes or until heated through.

Makes 6 servings

*To sour milk, use 1 tablespoon lemon juice or vinegar plus milk to equal 1 cup. Stir; let stand 5 minutes before using.

Favorite recipe from **National Broiler Council**

Breast of Chicken Cordon Bleu

2 whole chicken breasts (about 1 pound each)
Salt and white pepper
½ cup milk
1 egg, slightly beaten
2 slices (1½ ounces each) ham
2 thick slices (2½ ounces each) Medium Wisconsin Aged Swiss cheese
½ cup all-purpose flour
2 cups finely ground dried bread crumbs
½ cup (1 stick) butter

Preheat oven to 350°F. While chicken is ice cold, remove all bones from each whole breast. Do not sever skin at any point. (You may wish to have your butcher do this for you.) Sprinkle both sides of chicken lightly with salt and pepper.

Combine milk and egg to make egg wash. Brush both sides of breasts completely with egg wash. Place each whole breast, skin-side down, on waxed paper. Place one slice of the ham and cheese on half of each breast. Brush ham and cheese liberally with egg wash and fold halves together, wrapping skin around all white meat.

Place flour, remaining egg wash and bread crumbs in 3 separate shallow dishes. Dip rolled chicken in flour, egg wash and crumbs. Be sure crumbs throughly coat chicken. Wrap the coated breasts in foil and refrigerate for 6 hours or overnight.

Remove from refrigerator and brown in butter. Remove from pan; reserve butter. Place chicken in baking pan. Pour reserved butter over chicken. Bake for 35 to 40 minutes or until tender. When ready to serve, cut each chicken breast in half.

Makes 4 servings

Favorite recipe from **Wisconsin Milk Marketing Board** © 1993

Gourmet Chicken Bake

Herb Marinated Chicken Kabobs

4 boneless skinless chicken breast halves (about 1 pound)
2 small zucchini, cut into ½-inch slices
1 large red bell pepper, cut into 1-inch squares
½ cup HEINZ Gourmet Wine Vinegar
½ cup tomato juice
2 tablespoons vegetable oil
1 tablespoon chopped onion
1 tablespoon brown sugar
2 cloves garlic, minced
½ teaspoon dried oregano leaves
½ teaspoon pepper

Lightly flatten chicken breasts; cut each breast lengthwise into 3 strips. In large bowl, combine chicken, zucchini and red pepper. For marinade, in jar, combine remaining ingredients; cover and shake vigorously. Pour marinade over chicken and vegetables. Cover; marinate in refrigerator about 1 hour. Drain chicken and vegetables, reserving marinade. Alternately thread chicken and vegetables onto skewers; brush with marinade. Broil, 3 to 5 inches from heat source, 8 to 10 minutes or until chicken is cooked, turning and brushing occasionally with marinade.   *Makes 4 servings*

Chicken Parisian

¼ cup unsifted flour
¼ teaspoon paprika
¼ teaspoon pepper
6 boneless skinless chicken breast halves (about 1½ pounds)
3 tablespoons margarine or butter
8 ounces fresh mushrooms, sliced (about 2 cups)
½ cup water
¼ cup dry white wine
2 teaspoons WYLER'S® or STEERO® Chicken-Flavor Instant Bouillon *or* 2 Chicken-Flavor Bouillon Cubes
2 teaspoons chopped parsley
¼ teaspoon dried thyme leaves

In plastic bag, combine flour, paprika and pepper. Add chicken, a few pieces at a time; shake to coat. In skillet, brown chicken in margarine; remove from pan. In same skillet, add remaining ingredients; simmer 3 minutes. Add chicken; simmer, covered, 20 minutes or until tender. Refrigerate leftovers.
Makes 6 servings

Coq au Vin

3 to 4 slices bacon, cut into ½-inch pieces
1 (2½- to 3-pound) broiler-fryer chicken, cut up
1 envelope LIPTON® Recipe Secrets Beefy Mushroom Recipe Soup Mix
½ teaspoon salt
¼ teaspoon dried thyme, crushed
1 clove garlic, minced
1½ cups dry red wine
½ cup water
2 cups frozen small whole onions
2 tablespoons chopped parsley

Cook bacon in large skillet over medium-high heat until crisp. Remove from skillet with slotted spoon; drain on paper towels. Brown chicken in drippings; remove and drain on paper towels.

Stir soup mix, salt, thyme and garlic into drippings in skillet. Then stir in wine and water. Add chicken, bacon, onions and parsley. Bring to a boil over high heat. Reduce heat to low. Cover and simmer 45 minutes or until chicken is tender, basting occasionally.
Makes about 6 servings

Dijon Chicken Elegant

4 whole boneless chicken
    breasts, halved
⅓ cup GREY POUPON® Dijon or
    Country Dijon Mustard
1 teaspoon dried dill weed
    or 1 tablespoon chopped
    fresh dill
4 ounces Swiss cheese slices
2 frozen puff pastry sheets,
    thawed
1 egg white
1 tablespoon cold water

Pound chicken breasts to ½-inch thickness. Blend mustard and dill; spread on chicken breasts. Top each breast with cheese slice; roll up.

Roll each pastry sheet into a 12-inch square; cut each square into 4 (6-inch) squares. Beat egg white and water; brush edges of each square with egg mixture. Place 1 chicken roll diagonally on each square. Join 4 points of pastry over chicken; press to seal seams. Place on ungreased baking sheets. Brush with remaining egg mixture. Bake at 375°F for 30 minutes or until chicken is done. Serve immediately.

Makes 8 servings

Chicken and Vegetable Roll-Ups

1 large carrot, pared and cut into
    thin strips
1 medium red bell pepper,
    seeded and cut into thin strips
1 medium summer squash, cut
    into thin strips
1 medium zucchini, cut into thin
    strips
6 boneless skinless chicken breast
    halves, pounded
2 tablespoons vegetable oil
1 cup plus 2 tablespoons water
1 cup sliced fresh mushrooms
2 teaspoons WYLER'S® or STEERO®
    Chicken-Flavor Instant Bouillon
    or 2 Chicken-Flavor Bouillon
    Cubes
1 tablespoon cornstarch
2 tablespoons dry sherry, optional
½ teaspoon dried tarragon leaves
    Hot cooked rice

Place equal amounts of vegetables on each chicken breast half; roll chicken around vegetables and secure with wooden picks. In large skillet, brown roll-ups in oil. Add *1 cup* water, mushrooms and bouillon; bring to a boil. Reduce heat; cover and simmer 15 minutes. Remove roll-ups from skillet. Combine remaining *2 tablespoons* water and cornstarch. Stir cornstarch mixture, sherry and tarragon into skillet; cook and stir until thickened. Spoon sauce over roll-ups and rice. Refrigerate leftovers.

Makes 6 servings

Champagne Chicken Valencia

½ cup flour
½ teaspoon salt, divided
½ teaspoon pepper, divided
3 whole boneless skinless chicken
    breasts, halved
¼ cup butter
¼ cup vegetable oil
1½ cups dry champagne or white
    wine
1 cup Florida orange juice
1 cup heavy cream
4 Florida Valencia oranges,
    peeled and sectioned*

Preheat oven to 350°F. In small bowl, mix flour with ¼ teaspoon salt and ¼ teaspoon pepper; coat chicken breasts completely with flour mixture.

In large skillet, heat butter and oil; cook chicken until golden brown. Remove from skillet and arrange on greased baking sheet. Bake in 350°F oven 20 minutes or until chicken is tender.

Meanwhile, discard excess fat from skillet. Add champagne, orange juice and remaining ¼ teaspoon salt and ¼ teaspoon pepper; bring to boiling. Add cream and cook over high heat until sauce measures about 2 cups. Place chicken breasts on heated serving platter; top with sauce. Garnish with orange sections.

Makes 6 servings

*When Valencia oranges are not in season, use any in-season orange.

Favorite recipe from **Florida Department of Citrus**

CASSEROLES,
STEWS, SOUPS & MORE

Clockwise from bottom left: Tortellini with Three Cheese Tuna Sauce (page 117), Quick Tamale Casserole (page 66), Santa Fe Stew Olé (page 74) and Paella (page 100)

GREAT BEEF

Quick Tamale Casserole

1 1/2 pounds ground beef
3/4 cup sliced green onions
1 can (4 ounces) chopped green chiles, drained and divided
1 can (10 3/4 ounces) tomato soup
3/4 cup mild salsa
1 can (16 ounces) whole kernel corn, drained
1 can (2 1/4 ounces) chopped pitted ripe olives (optional)
1 tablespoon Worcestershire sauce
1 teaspoon chili powder
1/4 teaspoon garlic powder
4 slices (3/4 ounce each) American cheese, halved
4 corn muffins, cut into 1/2-inch cubes
Mexican Sour Cream Topping (optional)

In medium skillet, brown ground beef with green onions. Reserve 2 tablespoons chiles for Mexican Sour Cream Topping, if desired. Stir in remaining chiles, tomato soup, salsa, corn, olives, Worcestershire sauce, chili powder and garlic powder until well blended; heat through. Place in 2-quart casserole. Top with cheese, then evenly spread muffin cubes over cheese. Bake at 350°F for 5 to 10 minutes or until cheese is melted. Serve with Mexican Sour Cream Topping, if desired.

Makes 6 servings

Mexican Sour Cream Topping

1 cup sour cream
2 tablespoons chopped green chiles, reserved from above
2 teaspoons chopped jalapeño peppers (optional)
2 teaspoons lime juice

Combine ingredients in small bowl.

Quick Tamale Casserole

Mandarin Beef

- **1 pound beef flank steak**
- **3 tablespoons lite soy sauce, divided**
- **6 teaspoons vegetable oil, divided**
- **1 tablespoon cornstarch**
- **3 teaspoons brown sugar, divided**
- **1/4 pound green beans, cut diagonally into 2-inch pieces**
- **1 package (10 ounces) frozen asparagus,* defrosted and cut diagonally into 2-inch pieces**
- **1/4 pound mushrooms, sliced**
- **2 tablespoons dry sherry**
- **6 green onions, cut into 2-inch slivers**
- **1/2 teaspoon Oriental dark roasted sesame oil***

Cut beef flank steak lengthwise in half. Cut steak across the grain into 1/8-inch-thick strips. Combine 1 tablespoon of the soy sauce, 1 teaspoon oil, the cornstarch and 1 teaspoon of the sugar; pour over beef strips and marinate 30 minutes. Heat nonstick frying pan over medium heat; add remaining 5 teaspoons oil. Stir-fry green beans 3 to 4 minutes in oil; add asparagus and mushrooms and cook 2 minutes. Remove vegetables; keep warm. Combine sherry, remaining 2 tablespoons soy sauce and 2 teaspoons sugar; reserve. Stir-fry beef (1/3 at a time) 2 to 3 minutes; reserve. Return beef, vegetables and sherry mixture to frying pan and heat through. Stir in green onions. Add sesame oil and stir. Serve immediately. *Makes 4 servings*

Preparation time: 15 minutes
Marinating time: 30 minutes
Cooking time: 15 minutes
Favorite recipe from **National Live Stock and Meat Board**

*Twelve ounces fresh asparagus may be substituted. Cut into 2-inch diagonal pieces; blanch 2 minutes before stir-frying.
**Dark sesame oil may be found in the imported (oriental) section of the supermarket or in specialty stores.

Mandarin Beef

Zesty Beef Stroganoff

1 (1- to 1¼-pound) sirloin
   steak, cut into ⅛-inch
   strips
¼ cup margarine or butter
8 ounces fresh mushrooms,
   sliced (about 2 cups)
½ cup sliced onion
1 clove garlic, finely
   chopped
2 tablespoons flour
1 cup water
3 tablespoons REALEMON®
   Lemon Juice from
   Concentrate
3 tablespoons dry red wine
2 teaspoons WYLER'S® or
   STEERO® Beef-Flavor
   Instant Bouillon
¼ teaspoon pepper
1 (8-ounce) container
   BORDEN® or MEADOW
   GOLD® Sour Cream, at
   room temperature
   CREAMETTE® Egg Noodles,
   cooked as package
   directs
   Chopped parsley

In large skillet, over medium-high
heat, brown sirloin in margarine;
remove from pan. In same skillet,
cook and stir mushrooms, onion
and garlic until tender; stir in
flour. Add water, ReaLemon®
brand, wine, bouillon and pepper;
cook and stir until slightly
thickened. Stir in sour cream then
meat; heat through. *Do not boil.*
Serve on noodles; garnish with
parsley. Refrigerate leftovers.
Makes 4 servings

Zesty Beef Stroganoff

Southwest Pot Roast

¼ cup all-purpose flour
2 teaspoons garlic salt
½ teaspoon ground red
   pepper
4 to 5 pounds boneless beef
   rump roast
1 tablespoon vegetable oil
1 (13¾-ounce) can
   COLLEGE INN® Beef
   Broth
2 tablespoons WRIGHT'S®
   Natural Hickory
   Seasoning
2 cups green or red bell
   pepper slices
2 cups onion wedges
3 ears corn-on-the-cob, cut
   into 1-inch chunks

In shallow bowl, combine flour,
garlic salt and ground red pepper.
Coat beef with flour mixture. In
8-quart saucepan, brown beef in
oil. Add beef broth and hickory
seasoning. Bring to a boil; reduce
heat. Cover tightly and simmer 2
hours. Add peppers, onions and
corn. Cover; simmer 45 minutes
longer or until vegetables and beef
are fork-tender. To serve, thinly
slice beef and serve with vegetables
and sauce. *Makes 6 servings*

Bistro Burgundy Stew

1 pound sirloin beef, cut
　　into 1¹/₂-inch pieces
3 tablespoons all-purpose
　　flour
6 slices bacon, cut into
　　1-inch pieces (about
　　¹/₄ pound)
2 cloves garlic, pressed
3 carrots, peeled and cut
　　into 1-inch pieces (about
　　1¹/₂ cups)
³/₄ cup Burgundy or other dry
　　red wine
¹/₂ cup GREY POUPON®
　　Dijon Mustard or
　　GREY POUPON® Country
　　Dijon Mustard
12 small mushrooms
1¹/₂ cups scallions, cut into
　　1¹/₂-inch pieces

Coat beef with flour; set aside.
In large skillet, over medium heat,
cook bacon just until done; pour
off excess fat. Add beef and garlic;
cook until browned. Stir in
carrots, wine and mustard; cover.
Simmer 30 minutes or until carrots
are tender, stirring occasionally.
Stir in mushrooms and scallions;
cook 10 minutes more, stirring
occasionally. Garnish as desired.

Makes 6 servings

Santa Fe Burrito Bake

1¹/₂ pounds ground beef
1 cup water
1 can (4 ounces) chopped
　　green chilies, undrained
1 package (1.25 ounces) taco
　　seasoning mix, dry
2 cups Wheat CHEX® brand
　　cereal, crushed to ³/₄ cup
1 loaf frozen bread dough,
　　thawed
1 cup (4 ounces) shredded
　　Cheddar cheese
1 teaspoon margarine or
　　butter, melted
　　Chili powder
　　Salsa, sour cream and
　　shredded lettuce

Preheat oven to 350°F. In large
skillet over medium heat cook
meat 5 minutes or until no longer
pink; drain. Stir in water, chilies
and seasoning mix. Add cereal,
stirring until well combined; set
aside. Roll bread dough into a
15x10-inch rectangle. Spread 2
cups reserved meat mixture in a
4-inch-wide strip lengthwise down
center of dough. Top with cheese.
Cover with remaining meat
mixture. Bring sides of dough up
over filling. Seal top and sides
well. Place seam side down on
ungreased baking sheet. Brush
with margarine. Sprinkle with chili
powder. Bake 30 to 35 minutes or
until golden brown. Slice and
serve with salsa, sour cream and
lettuce.　　*Makes 6 servings*

To decorate top: Cut 1-inch wide
strip from a short side of dough;
reserve. Decorate loaf with
reserved dough before brushing
with margarine.

Santa Fe Burrito Bake

Tex-Mex Two Bean Chili

Roman Meal®
Company Meat Loaf

1 pound lean ground beef
1/2 cup ROMAN MEAL® Wheat,
Rye, Bran, Flax or Oats,
Wheat, Rye, Bran, Flax
Cereal
1/2 cup milk or tomato juice
1/4 cup finely chopped onion
1/4 cup finely chopped celery
1 egg, slightly beaten
2 teaspoons Worcestershire
Sauce
1/2 to 1 teaspoon salt or garlic
salt
1/8 teaspoon pepper

Preheat oven to 350°F. In large
bowl combine all ingredients; mix
well. Shape into ring in 8-inch
cake pan. If desired, spread with
mixture of 2 tablespoons brown
sugar, 2 tablespoons catsup and
1 teaspoon prepared mustard.
Bake 40 to 50 minutes, or until
browned; let stand 10 minutes.
Makes 6 servings

Tex-Mex
Two Bean Chili

2 tablespoons olive oil
1 cup chopped onions
1 cup chopped green pepper
2 large cloves garlic, pressed
1 pound lean stew meat, cut
into 1/2-inch cubes
1/2 pound bulk hot Italian
sausage*
1 3/4 cups (15-ounce can)
CONTADINA® Tomato
Puree
1 3/4 cups (14 1/2-ounce can) beef
broth
1 1/4 cups water
2/3 cup (6-ounce can)
CONTADINA® Tomato
Paste
1/2 cup (4-ounce can) diced
green chiles
3 tablespoons chili powder
1 1/2 teaspoons ground cumin
1 teaspoon salt
1 teaspoon sugar
1 teaspoon dried oregano
leaves, crushed
1/8 teaspoon cayenne pepper
(optional)
1 1/2 cups (15-ounce can) pinto
beans, rinsed and
drained
1 1/2 cups (15-ounce can) kidney
beans, rinsed and
drained

*Note: If link sausage is used,
remove casings before sautéing.

In 6-quart saucepan, heat oil; sauté onion, green pepper and garlic 3 to 4 minutes, or until tender. Add stew meat and sausage, stirring to crumble sausage; cook 5 to 6 minutes. Blend in tomato puree, broth, water, tomato paste, green chiles, chili powder, cumin, salt, sugar, oregano and cayenne pepper. Bring to a boil. Reduce heat; simmer uncovered 1½ hours, stirring occasionally. Mix in beans. Cover and simmer additional 30 minutes. *Makes 6 servings*

Patchwork Casserole

2 pounds ground beef
2 cups chopped green bell pepper
1 cup chopped onion
2 pounds frozen Southern-style hash-brown potatoes, thawed
2 cans (8 ounces each) tomato sauce
1 cup water
1 can (6 ounces) tomato paste
1 teaspoon salt
½ teaspoon dried basil, crumbled
¼ teaspoon ground black pepper
1 pound pasteurized process American cheese, thinly sliced

Cook and stir beef in Dutch oven over medium heat until crumbled and brown, about 10 minutes; drain off fat.

Add green pepper and onion; sauté until tender, about 4 minutes. Stir in all remaining ingredients except cheese.

Spoon ½ of the meat mixture into 13×9×2-inch baking pan or 3-quart baking dish; top with ½ of the cheese. Spoon remaining meat mixture evenly on top of cheese.

Cover pan with aluminum foil. Bake in preheated 350°F oven 45 minutes.

Cut remaining cheese into decorative shapes; place on top of casserole. Let stand, loosely covered, until cheese melts, about 5 minutes. *Makes 8 to 10 servings*

Patchwork Casserole

Santa Fe Stew Olé

1 tablespoon vegetable oil
1½ pounds beef stew meat, cut into small bite-size pieces
1 can (28 ounces) stewed tomatoes, undrained
2 medium carrots, sliced into ¼-inch pieces
1 medium onion, coarsely chopped
1 package (1.25 ounces) LAWRY'S® Taco Spices & Seasonings
2 tablespoons diced green chiles
½ teaspoon LAWRY'S® Seasoned Salt
¼ cup water
2 tablespoons all-purpose flour
1 can (15 ounces) pinto beans, drained

In Dutch oven, heat oil; brown stew meat. Add tomatoes, carrots, onion, Taco Spices & Seasonings, green chiles and Seasoned Salt; blend well. Bring to a boil; reduce heat. Cover and simmer 40 minutes. In small bowl, combine water and flour; blend well. Add to stew mixture. Stir in pinto beans and simmer an additional 15 minutes. *Makes 4 servings*

Presentation: Serve hearty portions of stew with cornbread or warm tortillas.

Cottage Meat Loaf

1 pound ground beef
1 cup cottage cheese
⅓ cup fresh bread crumbs
1 egg, beaten
1 medium onion, finely chopped
¼ cup chopped green pepper
2 teaspoons paprika
½ teaspoon salt
¼ teaspoon pepper
⅛ teaspoon nutmeg
¼ cup chili sauce (optional)

Combine all ingredients except chili sauce in large bowl; mix well. Place in loaf pan or shape into round in pie plate. Pour chili sauce over top, if desired. Bake in preheated 350°F oven about 45 minutes or until no longer pink in center. *Makes 4 to 6 servings*

Favorite recipe from **Wisconsin Milk Marketing Board** © 1993

Santa Fe Stew Olé

Mexican Beef Stir-Fry

1 pound beef flank steak
2 tablespoons vegetable oil
1 teaspoon ground cumin
1 teaspoon garlic salt
1 teaspoon dried oregano
   leaves
1 red bell pepper, cut into
   thin strips
1 medium onion, chopped
1 to 2 jalapeño peppers,
   seeded and cut into
   slivers*

Cut beef flank steak diagonally across the grain into ⅛-inch-thick slices. Combine oil, cumin, garlic salt and oregano. Heat 1 tablespoon of the oil mixture in large nonstick frying pan until hot. Add red pepper, onion and jalapeño pepper; stir-fry over medium-high heat 2 to 3 minutes or until tender-crisp. Remove from pan; reserve. Stir-fry beef strips (½ at a time) in remaining oil mixture 1 to 2 minutes. Return vegetables to frying pan and heat through.

Makes 4 servings

Serving Suggestions: Mexican Beef Stir-Fry may be served on a lettuce raft, in taco shells or on tostada shells. Top with guacamole, if desired.

Preparation time: 15 minutes
Cooking time: 10 minutes

Favorite recipe from **National Live Stock and Meat Board**

*Wear rubber gloves when working with jalapeño peppers and wash hands with warm soapy water. Avoid touching face or eyes.

18-Minute Meatball Soup

1 pound ground beef (80% lean)
1 can (16 ounces) stewed tomatoes, broken up
1 can (13¾ ounces) beef broth
½ cup salsa or picante sauce
¾ teaspoon ground coriander
¾ teaspoon ground cumin
½ teaspoon salt
2 medium zucchini, thinly sliced
2½ tablespoons chopped cilantro

Combine tomatoes, beef broth and salsa in 2½-quart microwave-safe casserole. Cover and microwave at HIGH (100% power) 6 minutes. Meanwhile combine ground beef, coriander, cumin and salt; mix lightly but thoroughly. Pinch off 1-inch pieces of beef mixture to make approximately 32 free-form meatballs; place around the sides of 8-inch microwave-safe baking dish. Remove tomato mixture from microwave; add zucchini, cover and reserve. Cover meatballs with waxed paper and cook at HIGH 2½ minutes, rotating dish ¼ turn after 1½ minutes. Remove meatballs with slotted spoon and place in tomato mixture. Cook tomato mixture with meatballs, covered, at HIGH 4½ minutes. Garnish with cilantro.

Makes 4 servings

Preparation time: 5 minutes
Cooking time: 13 minutes

Favorite recipe from **National Live Stock and Meat Board**

Mexican Beef Stir-Fry

good

Santa Fe Casserole Bake

1 pound lean ground beef
1 package (1.25 ounces)
   LAWRY'S® Taco Spices &
   Seasonings
2 cups chicken broth
¼ cup all-purpose flour
1 cup dairy sour cream

sauce

1 can (7 ounces) diced green
   chiles
1 package (11 ounces) corn
   or tortilla chips
2 cups (8 ounces) grated
   Monterey Jack or
   Cheddar cheese
½ cup sliced green onions
   with tops

Santa Fe Casserole Bake

In medium skillet, brown meat and stir until crumbly; drain fat. Add Taco Spices & Seasonings; blend well. In small bowl, combine broth and flour. Add to meat mixture, bring to a boil to slightly thicken liquid. Stir in sour cream and chiles; blend well. In 13 × 9 × 2-inch lightly greased glass baking dish, place ½ of chips. Top with ½ of beef mixture, ½ of sauce, ½ of cheese and ½ of green onions. Layer again with remaining ingredients ending with green onions. Bake, uncovered, in 375°F oven for 20 minutes. Let stand 5 minutes before serving.

Microwave Directions: In 1-quart glass bowl, crumble beef. Microwave on HIGH 5 to 6 minutes, stirring once; drain fat. Add Taco Spices & Seasonings; blend well and set aside. In 1-quart glass measuring cup, combine broth and flour. Microwave on HIGH 5 minutes or until bubbling and thick, stirring once. Add to meat mixture; stir well. Stir in sour cream and chiles. In a 13 × 9 × 2-inch lightly greased microwave-safe baking dish, layer as stated above. Cover with waxed paper. Microwave on 50% power 15 to 18 minutes, rotating after 7 minutes. Let stand 5 minutes before serving.

Makes 6 servings

Presentation: Serve with gazpacho salad and Mexican-style rice.

Hint: Top with guacamole for additional flavor.

Very good!

Stir-Fried Beef and Vegetables

1 (³/₄- to 1-pound) flank
    steak, cut diagonally into
    ¹/₈-inch diagonal slices
1 large sweet onion, sliced
8 ounces fresh mushrooms,
    sliced (about 2 cups)
1 green bell pepper, seeded
    and cut into strips
1 clove garlic, finely
    chopped
2 teaspoons WYLER'S® or
    STEERO® Beef-Flavor
    Instant Bouillon *or*
    2 Beef-Flavor Bouillon
    Cubes
¹/₃ cup boiling water
¹/₄ cup soy sauce
2 tablespoons cider vinegar
2¹/₂ teaspoons cornstarch
1 teaspoon sugar
¹/₄ cup vegetable oil
1 (8-ounce) can sliced water
    chestnuts, drained

Prepare meat and vegetables.
Dissolve bouillon in water.
Combine soy sauce, vinegar,
cornstarch and sugar; stir into
bouillon mixture. In large heavy
skillet or wok, heat *2 tablespoons*
oil over high heat. Add garlic and
meat; stir-fry 2 minutes (meat will
be slightly pink in center). Remove
meat and juices. Wipe pan; heat
1 tablespoon oil. Add onion,
mushrooms, green pepper and
water chestnuts; stir-fry 2 minutes
over high heat. Add remaining
1 tablespoon oil around edge of
pan; add meat and juices, then
bouillon mixture. Stir; cover and
cook 2 minutes. Refrigerate
leftovers.   *Makes 4 servings*

Stir-Fried Beef and Vegetables

Beef Barley Vegetable Soup

1 pound beef shanks,
    cracked
7 cups water
1 (14¹/₄-ounce) can stewed
    tomatoes
³/₄ cup chopped onion
2 tablespoons WYLER'S® or
    STEERO® Beef-Flavor
    Instant Bouillon *or*
    6 Beef-Flavor Bouillon
    Cubes
¹/₂ teaspoon basil leaves
1 bay leaf
¹/₂ cup uncooked regular
    barley
3 medium carrots, peeled
    and chopped
1¹/₂ cups chopped celery

In large kettle or Dutch oven,
combine shanks, water, tomatoes,
onion, bouillon, basil and bay leaf.
Bring to a boil. Reduce heat; cover
and simmer 1 hour. Remove
shanks from stock; cut meat into
¹/₂-inch pieces. Skim off fat. Add
meat and barley; bring to a boil.
Reduce heat; cover and simmer 30
minutes. Add carrots and celery;
cook 30 minutes longer. Remove
bay leaf. Refrigerate leftovers.
    Makes about 10 servings

Cheeseburger Pie

1 (9-inch) unbaked pastry
    shell, pricked
8 slices BORDEN® Process
    American Cheese Food
1 pound lean ground beef
½ cup tomato sauce
⅓ cup chopped green bell
    pepper
⅓ cup chopped onion
1 teaspoon WYLER'S® or
    STEERO® Beef-Flavor
    Instant Bouillon *or*
    1 Beef-Flavor Bouillon
    Cube
3 eggs, well beaten
2 tablespoons flour

Preheat oven to 450°F. Bake
pastry shell 8 minutes; remove
from oven. *Reduce oven
temperature to 350°F.* Cut *6 slices*
cheese food into pieces. In large
skillet, brown meat; pour off fat.
Add tomato sauce, green pepper,
onion and bouillon; cook and stir
until bouillon dissolves. Remove
from heat; stir in eggs, flour and
cheese food pieces. Turn into
prepared pastry shell. Bake 20 to
25 minutes or until hot. Arrange
remaining *2 slices* cheese food on
top. Bake 3 to 5 minutes longer or
until cheese food begins to melt.
Refrigerate leftovers.

Makes one 9-inch pie

Beef Pot Roast in Beer

3- to 4-pound beef rump
    roast
2 tablespoons flour
1 teaspoon salt
    Dash pepper
2 tablespoons CRISCO®
    Shortening
1 can (12 ounces) beer
2 bay leaves
6 small whole onions, peeled
4 medium carrots, peeled
    and cut into 1-inch
    pieces
½ cup cold water
¼ cup flour
2 tablespoons catsup

Coat roast with 2 tablespoons
flour. Season with salt and pepper.
In Dutch oven or large skillet,
brown roast on all sides in hot
Crisco®. Add ½ cup of the beer
and the bay leaves. Cover tightly;
simmer 1½ hours. Remove bay
leaves. Add onions and carrots.
Cover and cook 1 hour more or
until meat and vegetables are
tender; remove to heated platter.
Skim fat from pan juices. Add
enough of the remaining beer to
make 1½ cups liquid. Combine
cold water and ¼ cup flour; stir
into juices with catsup. Cook and
stir until thickened and bubbly.
Cook and stir 2 to 3 minutes more.
Serve with meat and vegetables.

Makes 6 to 8 servings

Cheeseburger Pie

FABULOUS PORK

Sausage Skillet Dinner

12 ounces fully cooked
    smoked pork link
    sausage, cut diagonally
    into 1-inch pieces
2 tablespoons water
1 medium onion
2 small red cooking apples
2 tablespoons butter, divided
12 ounces natural frozen
    potato wedges
¼ cup cider vinegar
3 tablespoons sugar
½ teaspoon caraway seed
2 tablespoons chopped
    parsley

Place sausage and water in large nonstick frying pan; cover tightly and cook over medium heat 8 minutes, stirring occasionally. Meanwhile, cut onion into 12 wedges; core and cut each apple into 8 wedges. Remove sausage to warm platter. Pour off drippings. Cook and stir onion and apples in 1 tablespoon of the butter in same frying pan 4 minutes or until apples are just tender. Remove to sausage platter. Heat remaining 1 tablespoon butter; add potatoes and cook, covered, over medium-high heat 5 minutes or until potatoes are tender and golden brown, stirring occasionally. Combine vinegar, sugar and caraway seed. Reduce heat, return sausage, apple mixture and vinegar mixture to frying pan and cook 1 minute, or until heated through, stirring gently. Sprinkle with parsley. *Makes 4 servings*

Preparation time: 5 minutes
Cooking time: 18 minutes

Favorite recipe from **National Live Stock and Meat Board**

Sausage Skillet Dinner

Saucy Pork and Peppers

Saucy Pork and Peppers

2 fresh limes
¼ cup 62%-less-sodium soy
    sauce
1 teaspoon oregano leaves
½ teaspoon thyme leaves
    Dash cayenne pepper
4 cloves garlic, crushed
2 to 3 fresh parsley sprigs
1 bay leaf
1 pound pork tenderloin,
    trimmed and cut into
    1-inch cubes
1 tablespoon olive oil
1 teaspoon brown sugar
2 medium onions, each cut
    into 8 pieces
2 medium tomatoes, each cut
    into 8 pieces and seeded
1 large red bell pepper, cut
    into 8 pieces
1 large green bell pepper,
    cut into 8 pieces.

Squeeze juice from limes,
reserving peel. In small bowl,
combine lime juice, lime peel, soy
sauce, oregano, thyme, cayenne
pepper, garlic, parsley and bay
leaf; blend well. Place pork cubes
in plastic bag or non-metal bowl.
Pour lime mixture over pork,
turning to coat. Seal bag or cover
dish; marinate at least 2 hours or
overnight in refrigerator, turning
pork several times.

Remove lime peel, parsley sprigs
and bay leaf from marinade;
discard. Remove pork from
marinade, reserving marinade.
Drain pork well. Heat oil in large
skillet over high heat. Add brown
sugar; stir until sugar is dissolved.
Add pork cubes; cook and stir
about 5 minutes or until pork is
browned. Reduce heat to low. Add
onions, tomatoes, peppers and
reserved marinade; simmer 10 to
15 minutes or until pork is
tender.   *Makes 4 servings*

Favorite recipe from **National Pork
Producers Council**

Pork Sausage and Onion Soup

1 pound fresh pork sausage
2 large yellow onions
2 tablespoons butter or margarine
2 cloves garlic, minced
1 teaspoon brown sugar
2 cans (13 3/4 ounces each) single-strength beef broth
1/2 cup dry white wine
1/2 cup water
1 teaspoon Dijon-style mustard
Freshly ground black pepper
1 tablespoon chopped parsley

Pinch off 1-inch pieces of sausage to make approximately 32 free-form patties; cook sausage patties (1/2 at a time) in Dutch oven until browned on both sides. Remove patties; keep warm. Pour off drippings. Cut onions in half lengthwise; cut into thin slices. Add butter and onions to same Dutch oven; cook and stir over medium-high heat 5 minutes. Add garlic and sugar; continue to cook and stir 5 minutes. Add sausage patties, beef broth, wine, water and mustard; bring to a boil. Season with pepper to taste. Garnish with parsley.

Makes 4 servings

Preparation time: 15 minutes
Cooking time: 30 minutes

Favorite recipe from **National Live Stock and Meat Board**

Cajun Red Bean and Sausage Casserole

1 pound dried kidney beans
1/2 pound salt pork or ham, diced
3 cups chopped onions
1 cup chopped green onions
1 cup chopped fresh parsley
1 pound smoked sausage, cut into 1/4-inch slices
1 can (8 ounces) tomato sauce
1 tablespoon Worcestershire sauce
1 tablespoon LAWRY'S® Seasoned Salt
1 teaspoon LAWRY'S® Seasoned Pepper
1/2 teaspoon LAWRY'S® Garlic Powder with Parsley
1/2 teaspoon hot pepper sauce

Rinse beans. Place beans in large, heavy Dutch oven. Add water to level 2 inches above beans; let soak overnight. Add salt pork, bring to a boil; reduce heat, cover and simmer 30 minutes. Stir in remaining ingredients. Cover and simmer 45 minutes to 1 hour or until beans are tender.

Makes 8 to 10 servings

Presentation: Serve over hot cooked rice with a green salad and crusty bread.

Hint: Heat is more evenly distributed in a cast iron Dutch oven.

Classy Cassoulet

6 slices bacon
¼ cup seasoned dry bread
    crumbs
1 pound hot or sweet Italian
    sausage, cut into 1-inch-
    thick slices
1 medium onion, cut into 6
    wedges
3 cloves garlic, finely
    chopped
1 can (16 ounces) sliced
    carrots, drained
1 can (16 ounces) zucchini,
    drained
1 can (8 ounces) stewed
    tomatoes
½ cup chopped celery
1 teaspoon beef-flavored
    instant bouillon granules
1½ teaspoons dried parsley
    flakes
1 bay leaf
2 cans (15 ounces each)
    butter beans, 1 can
    drained, 1 can undrained

Sauté bacon in large skillet, turning until crisp and browned, about 8 minutes. Remove with slotted spoon to paper towels to drain. Set aside skillet with bacon drippings. Combine 2 tablespoons of the bacon drippings with bread crumbs in small bowl. Set aside.

Sauté sausage, onion and garlic in skillet with bacon drippings until sausage is no longer pink, 12 to 15 minutes. Drain off fat, leaving sausage mixture in skillet. Stir carrots, zucchini, tomatoes, celery, boullion, parsley, bay leaf and 1 can drained butter beans into skillet with sausage. Add can of undrained butter beans. Bring to a boil; lower heat and simmer, uncovered, for 10 minutes or until mixture is heated through and celery is tender. Remove bay leaf.

Place sausage mixture in one 2-quart or 6 individual broiler-proof casseroles. Crumble bacon over top; sprinkle with bread crumb mixture. Broil 5 inches from heat 1 minute or until crumbs are golden; be careful not to burn crumbs. Serve hot with garnish of sliced, canned cranberry sauce.

Makes 6 servings

Favorite recipe from **Canned Food Information Council**

Classy Cassoulet

Peachy Pork Picante

Peachy Pork Picante

1 pound boneless pork loin,
    cut into 1-inch cubes
1 tablespoon taco
    seasoning mix
2 tablespoons minced
    parsley
2 teaspoons vegetable oil
8 ounces bottled salsa,
    chunky style
¼ cup peach preserves

Combine taco seasoning and
parsley; coat pork cubes with
seasoning mixture. Heat oil in
heavy skillet over medium-high
heat. Add pork, cook and stir to
brown, about 3 to 5 minutes. Add
salsa and preserves to pan, reduce
heat, cook and simmer until
tender, about 15 minutes.
Makes 4 servings

Preparation time: 25 minutes

Favorite recipe from **National Pork
Producers Council**

Paprika Pork Stew

1 pound boneless pork
    shoulder, cut into 1-inch
    cubes
2 tablespoons all-purpose
    flour
2 tablespoons sweet paprika
1 teaspoon salt
2 tablespoons shortening
½ cup water
1 medium onion, cut in half
    lengthwise and sliced
4 small red new potatoes,
    quartered
2 tablespoons water
½ cup sour cream

Combine flour, paprika and salt;
mix well. Coat pork with flour
mixture. Reserve excess flour
mixture. Brown pork in shortening
in a large skillet or Dutch oven.
Pour off drippings. Add ½ cup
water and onion, cover tightly and
cook over low heat for 30
minutes. Add potatoes and
continue cooking, covered, 20 to
30 minutes or until pork and
potatoes are tender. Combine
reserved flour with 2 tablespoons
water; stir into pork mixture and
cook until thickened, stirring
occasionally. Remove from heat
and stir in sour cream.
Makes 4 servings

Preparation time: 15 minutes
Cooking time: 60 minutes

Favorite recipe from **National Pork
Producers Council**

Family Baked Bean Dinner

1 can (20 oz.) DOLE®
    Pineapple Chunks in
    Juice
½ DOLE® Green Bell Pepper,
    julienne-cut
½ cup chopped onion
1 lb. Polish sausage or
    frankfurters, cut in
    1-inch chunks
⅓ cup brown sugar, packed
1 teaspoon dry mustard
2 cans (16 oz. each) baked
    beans

Drain pineapple, save juice for
beverage. Place green pepper and
onion in 13×9-inch microwave-
safe dish. Cover, microwave on
HIGH (100% power) 3 minutes.
Add sausage, arranging around
edges of dish. Cover; continue
microwaving on HIGH 6 minutes.
In bowl, combine brown sugar
and mustard; stir in beans and
pineapple. Add to sausage mixture.
Stir to combine. Microwave,
uncovered, on HIGH 8 to 10
minutes, stirring after 4 minutes.
                  Makes 6 servings

Prep time: 15 minutes
Cook time: 20 minutes

Cajun Skillet Hash

1 onion, chopped
2 cloves garlic, crushed
2 tablespoons butter or
    margarine
1 large potato (about
    7 ounces), cooked,
    peeled and chopped
1 can (14½ ounces)
    DEL MONTE® Cajun (or
    Original) Style Stewed
    Tomatoes*
½ teaspoon thyme, crushed
2 cups cooked diced ham
1 green pepper, chopped
    Salt and pepper

In large skillet, cook onion and
garlic in butter until tender-crisp.
Add potato; cook 2 minutes. Stir
in tomatoes and thyme; simmer
over medium heat 2 to 3 minutes.
Add ham and green pepper. Season
with salt and pepper to taste.
Simmer, stirring frequently, 3 to 5
minutes. Season with hot pepper
sauce. Serve with eggs, if
desired.   *Makes 6 servings*

*If using Original Style Stewed
Tomatoes, add a pinch each of
cinnamon, ground cloves and
cayenne.

Prep time: 8 minutes
Cook time: 14 minutes

Southwestern Stir-Fry

1 pound pork tenderloin, cut in quarters lengthwise and then sliced 1/4 inch thick
2 tablespoons dry sherry
2 teaspoons cornstarch
1 teaspoon ground cumin
1 clove garlic, minced
1/2 teaspoon seasoned salt
1 tablespoon vegetable oil
1 green pepper, seeded and cut into strips
1 medium onion, thinly sliced
12 cherry tomatoes, halved
Green chile salsa

Combine sherry, cornstarch, cumin, garlic and seasoned salt in medium bowl; add pork slices and stir to coat. Heat oil over medium-high heat in heavy skillet. Add pork mixture and stir-fry about 3 to 4 minutes. Add remaining ingredients except salsa, cover and simmer 3 to 4 minutes. Serve hot with green chile salsa.

Makes 4 servings

Favorite recipe from **National Pork Producers Council**

Swissed Ham and Noodles Casserole

2 tablespoons butter
1/2 cup chopped onion
1/2 cup chopped green pepper
1 can (10 1/2 ounces) condensed cream of mushroom soup
1 cup dairy sour cream
1 package (8 ounces) medium noodles, cooked and drained
2 cups (8 ounces) shredded Wisconsin Swiss cheese
2 cups cubed cooked ham (about 3/4 pound)

In 1-quart saucepan melt butter; sauté onion and green pepper. Remove from heat; stir in soup and sour cream. In buttered 2-quart casserole layer 1/3 of the noodles, 1/3 of the Swiss cheese, 1/3 of the ham and 1/2 soup mixture. Repeat layers, ending with final 1/3 layer of noodles, cheese and ham. Bake in preheated 350°F oven 30 to 45 minutes or until heated through.

Makes 6 to 8 servings

Favorite recipe from **Wisconsin Milk Marketing Board** © 1993

Southwestern Stir-Fry

Sausage Stuffed Zucchini

Sausage Stuffed Zucchini

    3 medium zucchini (about
        2 pounds)
   12 ounces bulk Italian
        sausage, cooked and
        drained
1¹/₂ cups Wheat CHEX® brand
        cereal, crushed to ¹/₂ cup
  ¹/₄ cup water
    1 package (1.5 ounces) dry
        spaghetti sauce mix
  ¹/₄ cup chopped onion
    1 tablespoon olive oil
    1 clove garlic, minced
  ¹/₄ cup chopped green pepper
    2 cups chopped tomatoes
    1 can (8 ounces) tomato
        sauce

Preheat oven to 350°F. Cut zucchini in half lengthwise. Scoop pulp out, leaving ¹/₈-inch shell; set aside shells. Chop pulp; set aside. In medium bowl combine sausage, cereal, water and 2 tablespoons of the spaghetti sauce mix. Stuff reserved shells with sausage mixture. Place in ungreased 13×9×2-inch baking pan. Bake, covered, 25 to 30 minutes or until hot. In medium saucepan over low heat combine onion, oil and garlic. Cook 2 minutes or until onion is tender. Add green pepper and reserved zucchini pulp. Cook over medium heat 5 minutes or until zucchini is tender, stirring often. Add tomatoes, tomato sauce and remaining spaghetti sauce mix. Cook over low heat 10 minutes or until hot, stirring often. Spoon over stuffed shells. Return to oven 10 minutes or until hot.

Makes 6 servings

Microwave Directions: Prepare zucchini and pulp as above. In medium bowl combine sausage, cereal, water and 2 tablespoons of the spaghetti sauce mix. Stuff reserved shells with sausage mixture. Place in ungreased microwave-safe 13×9×2-inch pan. Microwave on HIGH, covered, 3¹/₂ to 4 minutes or until zucchini shells are crisp-tender; set aside. In 3-quart microwave-safe bowl combine onion, oil and garlic. Microwave on HIGH 1 minute or until onion is tender. Add green pepper and reserved zucchini pulp. Microwave on HIGH 2 minutes or until zucchini is tender. Add tomatoes, tomato sauce and remaining spaghetti sauce mix. Microwave on HIGH 3 minutes or until hot, stirring halfway through. Spoon over stuffed shells. Microwave on HIGH 1 minute or until hot.

Chop Suey

¼ cup flour
2 teaspoons salt
½ pound cubed veal
½ pound cubed pork
⅓ cup CRISCO® Shortening
1 cup chopped onion
1 cup celery, cut into 1-inch pieces
1 cup beef stock or broth
½ cup soy sauce
2 tablespoons molasses
1 can (16 ounces) bean sprouts, drained
Hot cooked rice

Combine flour and salt in large plastic food storage bag; add meat cubes and toss lightly to coat. Brown in hot Crisco® in Dutch oven; add onion and continue browning. Stir in celery, beef stock, soy sauce and molasses. Cover and cook over low heat for 25 minutes. Add bean sprouts; cook 15 minutes more. Thicken with additional flour, if necessary. Serve over hot cooked rice.

Makes 4 to 6 servings

Pork Loin Roulade

4 boneless center pork loin slices, about 1 pound
½ red bell pepper, cut into strips
½ green bell pepper, cut into strips
1 teaspoon vegetable oil
⅔ cup orange juice
⅔ cup bottled barbecue sauce
1 tablespoon prepared Dijon-style mustard

Place pork slices between 2 pieces of plastic wrap. Pound with mallet to about ¼-inch thickness.

Place several red and green pepper strips crosswise on each pork portion; roll up jelly-roll style. Secure rolls with wooden toothpicks.

In nonstick skillet, brown pork rolls in vegetable oil. Drain fat from pan. Combine orange juice, barbecue sauce and mustard; add to skillet. Bring mixture to boiling; reduce heat. Cover and simmer 10 to 12 minutes or until pork is tender. Remove toothpicks to serve. *Makes 4 servings*

Preparation time: 20 minutes
Cooking time: 12 minutes

Favorite recipe from **National Pork Producers Council**

Pork Loin Roulade

Sesame Pork with Broccoli

1 can (14½ ounces) chicken broth
2 tablespoons cornstarch
1 tablespoon soy sauce
4 green onions and tops, finely diced
1 pound pork tenderloin, trimmed
1 tablespoon vegetable oil
1 clove garlic, minced
1½ pounds fresh broccoli, cut into bite-size pieces (about 7 cups)
2 tablespoons sliced pimiento, drained
2 tablespoons sesame seed, lightly toasted

In small bowl, combine chicken broth, cornstarch and soy sauce; blend well. Stir in green onions; set aside. Cut pork tenderloin lengthwise into quarters; cut each quarter into bite-sized pieces. Heat oil in wok or heavy skillet over medium-high heat. Add pork and garlic; stir-fry 3 to 4 minutes or until pork is tender. Remove pork; keep warm. Add broccoli and broth mixture to wok. Cover and simmer over low heat 8 minutes. Add cooked pork and pimiento; cook just until mixture is hot, stirring frequently. Sprinkle with sesame seed. Serve immediately.

Makes 6 servings

Favorite recipe from **National Pork Producers Council**

Pork Cutlets with Garden Vegetables

1½ pounds pork cutlets
2 teaspoons vegetable oil
2½ cups peeled, chopped fresh tomatoes
1 can (8 ounces) tomato sauce
½ cup chopped onion
¼ cup chopped fresh chiles *or* 4-ounce can diced green chiles
1 clove garlic, minced
2 tablespoons fresh lime juice
½ teaspoon salt
¼ teaspoon ground cumin
1 cup julienne-cut carrots
1 cup julienne-cut zucchini
¼ cup raisins
¼ cup slivered almonds

Heat oil in nonstick frypan. Brown pork cutlets over medium-high heat. Stir in tomatoes, tomato sauce, onion, chiles, garlic, lime juice, salt and cumin. Cover; simmer 20 minutes. Stir in carrots, zucchini and raisins. Cover; simmer 10 minutes longer or until vegetables are tender. Stir in almonds. *Makes 6 servings*

Preparation time: 15 minutes
Cooking time: 30 minutes

Favorite recipe from **National Pork Producers Council**

Sesame Pork with Broccoli

Pineapple Ham Stir-Fry

1 can (20 oz.) DOLE®
    Pineapple Chunks in
    Juice
1 clove garlic, pressed
1 tablespoon finely chopped
    ginger
1 tablespoon vegetable oil
½ yellow onion, sliced
½ DOLE® Green or Red Bell
    Pepper, julienne-cut
⅓ cup chicken broth
1 tablespoon cornstarch
1 tablespoon soy sauce
1 tablespoon sherry
½ lb. cooked ham,
    julienne-cut
½ lb. sugar peas
½ lb. bean sprouts
    Hot cooked rice

Drain pineapple; save juice for beverage. In large skillet or wok, sauté garlic and ginger in oil. Add onion and green pepper, sauté 2 minutes. Combine broth, cornstarch, soy sauce and sherry; stir into skillet. Add ham, sugar peas, bean sprouts and pineapple to skillet. Cook and stir until vegetables are tender-crisp, 3 to 4 minutes. Serve with rice. *Makes 4 servings*

Prep time: 15 minutes
Cook time: 15 minutes

Sage and Rosemary Pork Stew

2 pounds boneless pork
    shoulder roast, cut into
    ¾-inch cubes
1 tablespoon vegetable oil
2 cans (14½ ounces each)
    chicken broth
1 cup water
½ cup sliced green onions
1 tablespoon minced fresh
    rosemary *or* 1 teaspoon
    dried rosemary
1 teaspoon minced fresh
    sage *or* ⅛ teaspoon
    dried sage
¼ teaspoon salt
⅛ teaspoon pepper
2 cups cubed, unpeeled new
    potatoes
½ pound fresh green beans,
    cut up
⅓ cup all-purpose flour
⅔ cup half-and-half

Heat oil in Dutch oven. Brown pork cubes over medium-high heat. Stir in broth, water, onions and seasonings. Bring to a boil; reduce heat. Simmer uncovered for 20 minutes. Stir in potatoes and beans; simmer 15 to 20 minutes or until tender. Combine flour and half-and-half; mix until smooth. Gradually stir into stew. Cook and stir until thickened.
Makes 6 servings

Preparation time: 15 minutes
Cooking time: 45 minutes

Favorite recipe from **National Pork Producers Council**

Pork Valenciana

Pork Valenciana

1½ pounds boneless pork loin,
    cut into ¾-inch cubes
2 tablespoons olive oil,
    divided
2 yellow onions, peeled and
    chopped
1 green pepper, seeded and
    chopped
2 cloves garlic, minced
1 8-ounce can whole
    tomatoes, undrained
½ teaspoon salt
1 bay leaf
¼ teaspoon pepper
4 cups water
2 cups uncooked rice
2 chicken bouillon cubes
½ cup sherry (optional)
⅛ teaspoon saffron threads
1 cup peas
1 small jar pimientos,
    drained
12 green olives

Brown pork in 1 tablespoon of the oil over medium-high heat in large skillet; remove. Add onions, green pepper, garlic and remaining 1 tablespoon oil. Continue cooking until slightly brown, about 5 minutes. Return pork to pan and stir in tomatoes, salt, bay leaf and pepper. Add water, rice, bouillon and sherry. Dissolve saffron in small amount of water and add to pan. Bring to boil, cover and simmer over low heat 15 minutes. Remove bay leaf. Garnish with peas, pimientos and olives.

Makes 8 servings

Preparation time: 15 minutes
Cooking time: 20 minutes

Favorite recipe from **National Pork Producers Council**

Tuscany Sausage and Rice Skillet

Tuscany Sausage and Rice Skillet

¾ pound Italian sausage, cut
    into 1-inch slices, casings
    removed
1 medium onion, cut into
    thin wedges
1 clove garlic, minced
1½ cups thin red and green
    bell pepper strips
1⅓ cups chicken broth
¼ teaspoon salt
1½ cups UNCLE BEN'S® Rice In
    An Instant
2 tablespoons grated
    Parmesan cheese

Cook sausage with onion and
garlic in 10-inch skillet until
sausage is cooked through. Pour
off all but 1 tablespoon drippings.
Add pepper strips, broth and salt.
Bring to a boil. Stir in rice; cover
and remove from heat. Let stand 5
minutes or until all liquid is
absorbed. Sprinkle with cheese.

Makes 4 servings

Pork Ball Stir-Fry

Boiling water
1 package (8 ounces) transparent Chinese noodles
1 pound ground pork
1 cup cracker crumbs
1 can (8 ounces) water chestnuts, drained and chopped
6 tablespoons soy sauce, divided
1 egg, beaten
1½ tablespoons grated ginger root, divided
1 clove garlic, minced
¼ cup almond or vegetable oil
1 cup diagonally sliced celery
¼ cup cider vinegar
2 tablespoons sugar
1 teaspoon grated orange peel
½ teaspoon red pepper flakes
1 cup sliced green onions
1 cup toasted whole almonds
2 tomatoes, cut into wedges
½ cup cilantro leaves

Pour boiling water over noodles; let stand 2 to 3 minutes; drain and set aside. Combine pork, cracker crumbs, water chestnuts, 2 tablespoons of the soy sauce, the egg, 1 tablespoon of the ginger root and garlic; mix well. Shape into 24 meatballs. Brown meatballs in hot oil, cooking 4 to 5 minutes. Add celery and sauté. Combine remaining 4 tablespoons soy sauce, ½ tablespoon ginger, vinegar, sugar, orange peel and red pepper flakes. Pour into wok or skillet and add noodles; heat through. Toss with green onions, almonds, tomatoes and cilantro.

Makes 6 servings

Favorite recipe from **Almond Board of California**

Pork Strips Florentine

1 pound boneless pork strips
1 package (6 ounces) seasoned long grain and wild rice mix, uncooked
1⅔ cups hot water
1 can (2.8 ounces) DURKEE® French Fried Onions
¼ teaspoon DURKEE® Garlic Powder
1 package (10 ounces) frozen chopped spinach, thawed and well drained
2 tablespoons diced pimiento (optional)
½ cup (2 ounces) shredded Swiss cheese

Preheat oven to 375°F. In 8×12-inch baking dish, combine pork strips, rice, contents of rice seasoning packet, hot water, *½ can* Durkee® French Fried Onions and garlic powder. Bake, covered, for 30 minutes. Stir spinach and pimiento into meat mixture. Bake, covered, 10 minutes or until pork and rice are done. Top with cheese and remaining onions; bake, uncovered, 3 minutes or until onions are golden brown.

Makes 4 servings

SPLENDID SEAFOOD

Paella

1 tablespoon olive oil
½ pound chicken breast
    cubes
1 cup uncooked rice*
1 medium onion, chopped
1 clove garlic, minced
1½ cups chicken broth
1 can (8 ounces) stewed
    tomatoes, chopped,
    reserving liquid
½ teaspoon paprika
⅛ to ¼ teaspoon ground red
    pepper
⅛ teaspoon ground saffron
½ pound medium shrimp,
    peeled and deveined
1 small red pepper, cut into
    strips
1 small green pepper, cut
    into strips
½ cup frozen green peas

*If using medium grain rice, use
1¼ cups of broth; if using
parboiled rice, use 1¾ cups of
broth.

Heat oil in Dutch oven over medium-high heat until hot. Add chicken and stir until browned. Add rice, onion, and garlic. Cook, stirring, until onion is tender and rice is lightly browned. Add broth, tomatoes, tomato liquid, paprika, ground red pepper, and saffron. Bring to a boil; stir. Reduce heat; cover and simmer 10 minutes. Add shrimp, pepper strips, and peas. Cover and simmer 10 minutes or until rice is tender and liquid is absorbed. *Makes 6 servings*

Favorite recipe from **USA Rice Council**

Paella

Oriental Seafood Stir-Fry

1/2 cup water
3 tablespoons REALEMON® Lemon Juice from Concentrate
3 tablespoons soy sauce
1 tablespoon brown sugar
1 tablespoon cornstarch
3/4 cup sliced fresh mushrooms
3/4 cup diced red bell pepper
1 medium onion, cut into wedges
2 ounces fresh pea pods
1 tablespoon vegetable oil
1/2 pound imitation crab blend, flaked
Shredded napa, hot cooked pasta or rice noodles

Combine water, ReaLemon® brand, soy sauce, sugar and cornstarch. In large skillet, cook and stir mushrooms, red pepper, onion and pea pods in oil until tender-crisp; remove. Add soy mixture; cook and stir until slightly thickened. Return vegetables along with crab blend to skillet; heat through. Serve with shredded napa, hot cooked pasta or rice noodles. Refrigerate leftovers.

Makes 4 servings

Oriental Seafood Stir-Fry

Hasty Bouillabaisse

5 green onions, thinly sliced
1/2 cup chopped green pepper
1 clove garlic, minced
2 tablespoons minced
    parsley
2 tablespoons olive or
    vegetable oil
1 can (14 1/2 ounces) stewed
    or whole tomatoes
1 cup red wine
3/4 teaspoon dried thyme
    leaves
1/4 teaspoon dried rosemary,
    crushed
1/4 teaspoon hot pepper sauce
1 can (16 ounces) mixed
    vegetables or peas and
    carrots, or 2 cans (8
    ounces each) other
    vegetables (beans, corn,
    carrots, peas, etc.)
1 can (7 ounces) tuna,
    drained and flaked
1 can (6 ounces) crabmeat,
    flaked and cartilage
    removed
1 can (6 ounces) minced
    clams, drained
1 can (4 1/4 ounces) shrimp,
    rinsed and drained

In large saucepan, cook onions,
green pepper, garlic and parsley in
oil over medium heat until tender.
Add tomatoes, wine and
seasonings. Simmer 10 minutes.
Add vegetables and seafood.
simmer 10 minutes more or until
heated through.

Makes 6 to 8 servings

Favorite recipe from **Canned Food
Information Council**

Hasty Bouillabaisse

Tuna Skillet

1/4 cup CRISCO® Shortening
2/3 cup chopped onion
1 small green pepper,
    slivered (about 1/2 cup)
1 can (10 3/4 ounces)
    condensed tomato soup
2 teaspoons soy sauce
2 to 3 tablespoons brown
    sugar
1 teaspoon grated lemon
    peel
3 tablespoons lemon juice
2 cans (6 1/2 or 7 ounces
    each) tuna, drained
    Hot cooked rice
    Red pepper rings
    (optional)

Melt Crisco® in large heavy skillet
over medium heat. Stir in onion
and green pepper. Cook until
almost tender, stirring
occasionally. Mix in tomato soup,
soy sauce, brown sugar, lemon
peel and lemon juice. Bring to
boiling; simmer for 5 minutes. Mix
in tuna, separating into small
pieces. Heat. Serve with hot
cooked rice. Garnish with red
pepper rings.

Makes 4 to 6 servings

Autumn Seafood Bake

Preheat oven to 350°F. Cut squash in half lengthwise; remove seeds. Place cut-side down in 3-quart baking dish. Add ½ inch water to dish. Bake 30 to 35 minutes or until squash is tender when pierced with a fork. Remove squash; pour water from dish. In large bowl combine Worcestershire, onion, celery, olives, shrimp and crabmeat; mix well. Add cheese and cereals, stirring until well combined. Fill each squash half with 1 cup mixture. Place in baking dish. Bake 15 to 20 minutes or until heated through.

Makes 6 servings

Autumn Seafood Bake

3 acorn squash (about
   4 pounds)
¼ cup white wine
   Worcestershire sauce
¼ cup chopped onion
¼ cup sliced celery
¼ cup sliced ripe olives
1 can (4¼ ounces) medium
   shrimp, rinsed and
   drained
1 can (6½ ounces)
   crabmeat, drained
1 cup (4 ounces) shredded
   Cheddar cheese
1½ cups Corn CHEX® brand
   cereal
1½ cups Wheat CHEX® brand
   cereal

Shrimp and Vegetable Stir-Fry

¾ pound raw medium
   shrimp, peeled and
   deveined
3 teaspoons cornstarch,
   divided
⅛ teaspoon ground ginger
   Dash garlic powder
½ pound fresh broccoli
5 cups water, divided
1 tablespoon sesame seed
   (optional)
4 tablespoons BUTTER
   FLAVOR CRISCO®,
   divided
½ teaspoon instant chicken
   bouillon granules
1 package (6 ounces) frozen
   pea pods, thawed
   Hot cooked rice

Mix shrimp, 1 teaspoon of the cornstarch, ginger and garlic powder in medium bowl. Cover and refrigerate until ready to use. Cut thin slices (¼ to ½ inch) off stalk ends of broccoli to remove tough part; discard thin slices. Cut large stalks in half or quarters and then into ¾-inch pieces; cut heads into flowerets. Heat 4 cups of the water to boiling in 2-quart saucepan. Add broccoli. Cover and cook 1 minute; remove from heat. Drain; rinse under cold water, drain again and set aside.

Cook sesame seed in small skillet over moderate heat until golden brown, stirring frequently. Remove from heat; set aside.

Melt 2 tablespoons Butter Flavor Crisco® in large skillet over moderate heat. Add shrimp mixture. Cook and stir until shrimp are opaque and white. Remove; set aside.

Blend remaining 1 cup cold water, 2 teaspoons cornstarch and bouillon granules in small bowl. Set aside.

In same large skillet melt remaining 2 tablespoons Butter Flavor Crisco®. Add broccoli. Cook and stir over moderate heat until tender. Add pea pods. Cook and stir 1 minute longer. Add cornstarch mixture. Cook and stir until mixture begins to bubble. Add shrimp. Cook and stir until mixture thickens and bubbles. Sprinkle with sesame seed before serving. Serve over rice, if desired.

Makes 4 to 6 servings

Lemon Fish Roll-Ups

1 cup cooked rice
1 (10-ounce) package frozen chopped broccoli, thawed and well drained
1 cup (4 ounces) shredded Cheddar cheese
⅓ cup margarine or butter, melted
⅓ cup REALEMON® Lemon Juice from Concentrate
½ teaspoon salt
¼ teaspoon pepper
8 fish fillets, fresh or frozen, thawed (about 2 pounds)
Paprika

Preheat oven to 375°F. In medium bowl, combine rice, broccoli and cheese. Combine margarine, ReaLemon® brand, salt and pepper; add ¼ cup margarine mixture to broccoli mixture. Place equal amounts of mixture on fillets; roll up. Place seam-side down in shallow baking dish; pour remaining margarine mixture over roll-ups. Bake 20 minutes or until fish flakes with fork. Garnish with paprika. Refrigerate leftovers.

Makes 8 servings

Lemon Fish Roll-Ups

Louisiana Tomato-Rice Gumbo

1 whole boned chicken
    breast, cut into pieces
2 tablespoons margarine
$^1/_2$ cup chopped onion
$^1/_2$ cup chopped green pepper
$^1/_2$ cup chopped celery
1 garlic clove, minced
1 package (10 ounces) frozen
    okra, thawed and sliced
1 can (16 ounces) crushed
    tomatoes
1 can ($13^3/_4$ ounces) chicken
    broth
1 small bay leaf
$^1/_2$ teaspoon sugar
$^1/_4$ teaspoon salt
$^1/_8$ teaspoon thyme leaves
    Dash of pepper
$^1/_2$ pound raw shrimp, cleaned
$1^1/_3$ cups Original MINUTE®
    Rice

Cook and stir chicken in hot margarine in large skillet until lightly browned. Stir in onion, green pepper, celery and garlic; cook until tender.

Add okra, tomatoes, broth and seasonings. Bring to a boil. Reduce heat; cover and simmer 5 minutes, stirring occasionally. Add shrimp and cook 5 minutes. Remove bay leaf. Stir in rice. Cover; remove from heat. Let stand 5 minutes.

Makes 8 servings

New Potato Stuffed Trout

$1^1/_2$ pounds red new potatoes,
    cooked
$^1/_2$ cup chopped fresh parsley
$^1/_4$ cup capers
$^1/_4$ cup black or Greek olives,
    sliced
3 tablespoons olive oil,
    divided
$^3/_4$ teaspoon salt
$^1/_2$ teaspoon freshly ground
    black pepper
4 CLEAR SPRINGS® Brand
    Idaho Rainbow Trout,
    whole, boned (8 ounces
    each)
4 teaspoons fresh lemon
    juice
    Salt and freshly ground
    pepper
$^1/_2$ cup white wine or
    vermouth
2 lemons, thinly sliced

Cut potatoes into large cubes. Combine with parsley, capers, olives, 2 tablespoons of the oil, $^3/_4$ teaspoon salt and $^1/_2$ teaspoon pepper in large bowl. Mix well; set aside. Sprinkle inside of each trout with lemon juice, salt and pepper. Stuff each trout with $^1/_4$ of potato mixture. Pour wine into baking pan. Place stuffed trout in pan. Brush trout with remaining 1 tablespoon oil. Top with lemon slices. Cover pan with foil and bake at 400°F for about 15 minutes until trout flakes easily with a fork. *Makes 4 servings*

Louisiana Tomato-Rice Gumbo

Rainbow Trout Santa Fe

2 tablespoons olive oil
4 CLEAR SPRINGS® Brand Idaho Rainbow Trout fillets (4 ounces each)
2 teaspoons butter
2 cloves garlic, minced
1/4 cup chopped green onion
1 small tomato, peeled, seeded and diced
1/2 cup fresh or frozen whole corn kernels
1/2 cup snow peas, cut in half diagonally
2 tablespoons chopped cilantro or parsley
1 to 1 1/2 teaspoons finely chopped jalapeño pepper*
1 teaspoon fresh lemon juice
1/4 teaspoon salt
Dash white pepper
1/4 cup heavy cream
Tortilla chips

Heat oil over medium-high heat in large skillet. Sauté trout 1 to 2 minutes on each side or until fish flakes easily; remove. Melt butter over medium heat. Sauté garlic and green onion, about 1 minute. Add tomato, corn, snow peas, cilantro, jalapeño, lemon juice, salt and pepper. Simmer about 2 to 3 minutes. Stir in cream; gently simmer about 1 minute more. Top trout with sauce. Serve immediately with tortilla chips.

Makes 4 servings

* Wear rubber gloves when working with jalapeño peppers and wash hands with warm soapy water. Avoid touching face or eyes.

Old-Fashioned Tuna Noodle Casserole

1/4 cup plain dry bread crumbs
3 tablespoons butter or margarine, melted and divided
1 tablespoon finely chopped parsley
1/2 cup chopped onion
1/2 cup chopped celery
1 cup water
1 cup milk
1 package LIPTON® Noodles & Sauce—Butter
2 cans (6 1/2 ounces each) tuna, drained and flaked

In small bowl, thoroughly combine bread crumbs, 1 tablespoon of the butter and the parsley; set aside.

In medium saucepan, cook onion and celery in remaining 2 tablespoons butter over medium heat, stirring occasionally, 2 minutes or until onion is tender. Add water and milk; bring to a boil. Stir in noodles & butter sauce. Continue boiling over medium heat, stirring occasionally, 8 minutes or until noodles are tender. Stir in tuna. Turn into greased 1-quart casserole, then top with bread crumb mixture. Broil until bread crumbs are golden.

Makes about 4 servings

Baja Fish and Rice Bake

Baja Fish and Rice Bake

3 tablespoons vegetable oil
¾ cup chopped onion
½ cup chopped celery
1 clove garlic, minced
½ cup rice, uncooked
3½ cups (two 14½-ounce cans)
    CONTADINA® Stewed
    Tomatoes, cut up
1 teaspoon lemon pepper
½ teaspoon salt
⅛ teaspoon cayenne pepper
1 pound fish fillets (any firm
    white fish)
¼ cup finely chopped fresh
    parsley
    Lemon slices (optional)

Preheat oven to 400°F. In large skillet, heat oil; sauté onion, celery and garlic. Stir in rice; sauté about 5 minutes, or until rice browns slightly. Add tomatoes with juice, lemon pepper, salt and cayenne pepper. Place fish in 12×7½×2-inch baking dish. Spoon rice mixture over fish. Cover with foil; bake 45 to 50 minutes or until rice is tender. Allow to stand 5 minutes before serving. Sprinkle with parsley. Garnish with lemon slices, if desired.   *Makes 6 servings*

Garlic Shrimp with Noodles

Garlic Shrimp with Noodles

4 tablespoons butter, divided
¼ cup finely chopped onion
2 cups water
1 package LIPTON® Noodles
   & Sauce—Butter & Herb
2 tablespoons olive oil
1 tablespoon finely chopped
   garlic
1 pound raw medium
   shrimp, cleaned
1 can (14 ounces) artichoke
   hearts, drained and
   halved
¼ cup finely chopped parsley
Pepper to taste

In medium saucepan, melt 2 tablespoons of the butter; add onion and cook until tender. Add water and bring to a boil. Stir in noodles & butter & herb sauce; continue boiling over medium heat, stirring occasionally, 8 minutes or until noodles are tender.

Meanwhile, in large skillet, heat remaining 2 tablespoons butter with olive oil; cook garlic over medium-high heat 30 seconds. Add shrimp and artichokes; cook, stirring occasionally, 3 minutes or until shrimp turn pink. Stir in parsley and pepper. To serve, combine shrimp mixture with hot noodles. Garnish, if desired, with watercress.

Makes about 4 servings

Microwave Directions: In 2-quart microwave-safe casserole, microwave 2 tablespoons of the butter with onion, uncovered, at HIGH (Full Power) 2 minutes or until tender. Stir in water and noodles & butter & herb sauce and microwave 11 minutes or until noodles are tender. Stir, then cover and set aside.

In 1-quart microwave-safe casserole or 9-inch glass pie plate, microwave remaining 2 tablespoons butter, olive oil and garlic at HIGH (Full Power) 2 minutes. Stir in shrimp and artichokes and microwave 3 minutes or until shrimp are almost pink, stirring once; stir in parsley and pepper. Combine shrimp mixture with noodles and microwave, covered, 1 minute or until heated through. Let stand, covered, 2 minutes.

Herb-Baked Fish & Rice

1½ cups hot chicken broth
½ cup uncooked regular rice
¼ teaspoon DURKEE® Italian Seasoning
¼ teaspoon DURKEE® Garlic Powder
1 package (10 ounces) frozen chopped broccoli, thawed and drained
1 can (2.8 ounces) DURKEE® French Fried Onions
1 tablespoon grated Parmesan cheese
1 pound unbreaded fish fillets, thawed if frozen
DURKEE® Paprika (optional)
½ cup (2 ounces) shredded Cheddar cheese

Preheat oven to 375°F. In 12×8-inch baking dish, combine hot broth, uncooked rice and seasonings. Bake, covered, for 10 minutes. Top with broccoli, *½ can* Durkee® French Fried Onions and the Parmesan cheese. Place fish fillets diagonally down center of dish; sprinkle fish lightly with paprika. Bake, covered, for 20 to 25 minutes or until fish flakes easily with fork. Top fish with Cheddar cheese and remaining onions; bake, uncovered, 3 minutes or until onions are golden brown.   *Makes 3 to 4 servings*

Microwave Directions: In 12×8-inch microwave-safe dish, prepare rice mixture as above, except reduce broth to 1¼ cups. Cook, covered, on HIGH 5 minutes, stirring halfway through cooking time. Stir in broccoli, *½ can* Durkee® French Fried Onions and Parmesan cheese. Arrange fish fillets in single layer on top of rice mixture; sprinkle fish lightly with paprika. Cook, covered, on MEDIUM (50%) 18 to 20 minutes or until fish flakes easily with fork and rice is done. Rotate dish halfway through cooking time. Top fish with Cheddar cheese and remaining onions; cook, uncovered, on HIGH 1 minute or until cheese melts. Let stand 5 minutes.

Herb-Baked Fish & Rice

PASTA PLUS

Italian Baked Frittata

1 cup broccoli flowerets
1/2 cup sliced mushrooms
1/2 red pepper, cut into rings
2 green onions, sliced into
   1-inch pieces
1 tablespoon BLUE BONNET®
   Margarine
8 eggs
1/4 cup GREY POUPON® Dijon
   Mustard or GREY POUPON®
   Country Dijon Mustard
1/4 cup water
1/2 teaspoon Italian seasoning
1 cup shredded Swiss cheese
   (4 ounces)

In 10-inch ovenproof skillet, over medium-high heat, cook broccoli, mushrooms, red pepper and onions in margarine until tender-crisp, about 5 minutes. Remove from heat.

In small bowl, with electric mixer at medium speed, beat eggs, mustard, water and Italian seasoning until foamy; stir in cheese. Pour mixture into skillet over vegetables. Bake at 375°F for 20 to 25 minutes or until set. Serve immediately.

Makes 4 servings

Chicken and Pasta Soup

1 (2 1/2-pound) chicken,
   cut up
1 (46-fluid ounce) can
   COLLEGE INN® Chicken
   Broth
1 (16-ounce) can cut green
   beans, drained
1 (6-ounce) can tomato paste
1 cup uncooked small shell
   macaroni
1 teaspoon dried basil leaves

In large saucepan, over medium-high heat, bring chicken and chicken broth to a boil; reduce heat. Cover; simmer 25 minutes or until chicken is tender. Remove chicken; cool slightly. Add remaining ingredients to broth. Heat to a boil; reduce heat. Cover; simmer 20 minutes or until macaroni is cooked. Meanwhile, remove chicken from bones and cut into bite-size pieces. Add to soup; cook 5 minutes more.

Makes 6 servings

Italian Baked Frittata

*Scandinavian
Salmon-Cheddar Pie*

Heat oven to 425°F. Beat eggs in large bowl; add milk, 2 tablespoons of the parsley, the butter, green onion, 1 tablespoon lemon juice, Worcestershire sauce and mustard; mix well. Fold in cheese and salmon; pour into cooled pie shell. Bake 20 to 25 minutes or until just set and crust is golden brown. Let stand 10 minutes before serving. Combine sour cream, cucumber, remaining 1 tablespoon parsley, dill, remaining 1 teaspoon lemon juice and pepper; mix well. Dollop each serving with sour cream mixture.

Makes 6 servings

Favorite recipe from **Wisconsin Milk Marketing Board** ©1993

Scandinavian Salmon-Cheddar Pie

3 large eggs
¼ cup milk
3 tablespoons chopped parsley, divided
2 tablespoons butter, melted
2 tablespoons minced green onion
1 tablespoon plus 1 teaspoon lemon juice
1 teaspoon Worcestershire sauce
½ teaspoon dry mustard
2 cups (8 ounces) shredded Wisconsin Cheddar cheese
½ pound fresh cooked, flaked salmon *or* 1 can (6½ ounce) salmon, drained, deboned and flaked
1 (9-inch) pie shell, baked and cooled
¾ cup dairy sour cream
¼ cup finely chopped cucumber
1 teaspoon dill weed
⅛ teaspoon ground white pepper

South-of-the-Border Lasagna

1 pound ground beef
½ pound Italian Sausage
1 large onion, chopped
3 tablespoons olive oil, divided
4 (10-ounce) cans spicy tomatoes with chili peppers, drained
3 teaspoons Italian seasoning
2 teaspoons cumin
2 teaspoons seasoned salt
12 corn tortillas, cut into strips
2 eggs
1 pound Wisconsin Ricotta cheese
4 cups (16 ounces) shredded Wisconsin Mozzarella cheese, divided

Preheat oven to 350°F. In skillet brown beef and sausage with onion in 1 tablespoon of the olive oil; drain. Mash tomatoes with fork and add Italian seasoning, cumin and seasoned salt; mix well. Add tomato mixture to beef mixture. Simmer 30 minutes. Meanwhile, grease 12×8×2-inch pan with 1 tablespoon of the olive oil, then line pan with a single layer of tortilla strips. Beat eggs and mix with ricotta cheese and 3 cups of the mozzarella cheese. Spoon ½ of beef mixture over tortilla strips. Add ½ of cheese mixture. Repeat layers of tortilla strips, meat mixture and cheese mixture. Top with final layer of tortilla strips brushed with remaining 1 tablespoon olive oil and sprinkle with remaining mozzarella cheese. Bake 30 minutes or until heated through. Let stand 20 minutes before serving.   *Makes 10 to 12 servings*

Favorite recipe from **Wisconsin Milk Marketing Board** © 1993

Pizza Casserole

1 (1-pound) loaf Italian
   bread, cut into 1-inch
   slices
4 eggs
1 (15-ounce) can tomato
   sauce
1¼ cups water
1½ teaspoons Italian
   seasoning
1 (3-ounce) package sliced
   pepperoni
1 (8-ounce) package FISHER®
   Pizza-Mate® Shredded
   Imitation Mozzarella
   Cheese

In greased 13×9-inch baking dish, arrange bread slices. In large bowl, beat eggs; mix in tomato sauce, water and Italian seasoning. Pour evenly over bread, moistening completely. Top with pepperoni and Pizza Mate® shreds. Cover; refrigerate 4 hours or overnight. Bake in preheated 350°F oven for 30 minutes or until hot. Refrigerate leftovers.
   Makes 8 to 10 servings

Pizza Casserole

Mushroom Frittata

1 teaspoon butter or
   margarine
1 medium zucchini,
   shredded
1 medium tomato, chopped
1 can (4 ounces) sliced
   mushrooms, drained
6 eggs, beaten
1/4 cup milk
2 teaspoons Dijon mustard
1/2 teaspoon LAWRY'S®
   Seasoned Salt
1/2 teaspoon LAWRY'S®
   Seasoned Pepper
2 cups (8 ounces) grated
   Swiss cheese

In large, ovenproof skillet, melt butter and sauté zucchini, tomato and mushrooms 1 minute. In large bowl, combine remaining ingredients; blend well. Pour egg mixture into skillet; cook 10 minutes over low heat. To brown top, place skillet under broiler 2 to 3 minutes. *Makes 4 servings*

Presentation: Serve directly from skillet or remove frittata to serving dish. Serve with additional Swiss cheese and fresh fruit.

Hint: Try serving frittata with prepared Lawry's® Spaghetti Sauce Seasoning Blend with Imported Mushrooms.

Tortellini with Three-Cheese Tuna Sauce

1 pound cheese-filled
   spinach and egg
   tortellini
2 green onions, thinly sliced
1 clove garlic, minced
1 tablespoon butter or
   margarine
1 cup low-fat ricotta cheese
1/2 cup low-fat milk
1 can (9 1/4 ounces)
   STARKIST® Tuna, drained
   and broken into chunks
1/2 cup shredded low-fat
   mozzarella cheese
1/4 cup grated Parmesan or
   Romano cheese
2 tablespoons chopped fresh
   basil *or* 2 teaspoons
   dried basil, crushed
1 teaspoon grated lemon
   peel
   Fresh tomato wedges for
   garnish (optional)

Cook tortellini in boiling salted water according to package directions. When tortellini is nearly done, in another saucepan sauté onions and garlic in butter for 2 minutes. Remove from heat. Whisk in ricotta cheese and milk. Add tuna, cheeses, basil and lemon peel. Cook over medium-low heat until mixture is heated and cheeses are melted.

Drain pasta; add to sauce. Toss well to coat; garnish with tomato wedges if desired. Serve immediately.
   Makes 4 to 5 servings

Preparation time: 25 minutes

*Tortellini with Three-Cheese
Tuna Sauce*

Vegetable & Cheese Pot Pie

2 tablespoons butter or
  margarine
½ cup sliced green onions
1¾ cups water
1 package LIPTON® Noodles
  & Sauce—Chicken Flavor
1 package (16 ounces) frozen
  mixed vegetables,
  partially thawed
1 cup shredded mozzarella
  cheese (4 ounces)
1 teaspoon prepared mustard
½ cup milk
1 tablespoon all-purpose
  flour
  Salt and pepper to taste
  Pastry for 9-inch single-
  crust pie
1 egg yolk
1 tablespoon water

Preheat oven to 425°F. In large saucepan, melt butter and cook green onions over medium heat 3 minutes or until tender. Add water and bring to a boil. Stir in noodles & chicken flavor sauce and vegetables, then continue boiling over medium heat, stirring occasionally, 7 minutes or until noodles are almost tender. Stir in cheese, mustard and milk blended with flour. Cook over medium heat, stirring frequently, 2 minutes or until thickened. Add salt and pepper.

Turn into greased 1-quart round casserole or soufflé dish, then top with pastry. Press pastry around edge of casserole to seal; trim excess pastry, then flute edges. (Use extra pastry to make decorative shapes.) Brush pastry with egg yolk beaten with water. With tip of knife, make small slits in pastry. Bake 12 minutes or until crust is golden brown.

Makes 4 servings

Bean Soup Santa Fe

1¼ cups dry black beans
½ cup dry pinto beans
6 cups water
1 can (14½ ounces) beef
  broth
1 can (14½ ounces) stewed
  tomatoes, undrained
1½ cups water
1 package (1.27 ounces)
  LAWRY'S® Spices &
  Seasonings for Fajitas
2 tablespoons LAWRY'S®
  Minced Onion with
  Green Onion Flakes
1 teaspoon dry parsley
  flakes

In Dutch oven, soak black beans and pinto beans in 6 cups water for 1 hour. Bring to a boil; reduce heat, cover and simmer 1 hour. Drain beans and rinse. Return to Dutch oven, add remaining ingredients. Bring to a boil; reduce heat, cover and simmer 1 hour.

Makes 4 servings

Vegetable & Cheese Pot Pie

Skillet Pasta Roma

½ pound Italian sausage,
    sliced or crumbled
1 large onion, coarsely
    chopped
1 large clove garlic, minced
2 cans (14½ ounces each)
    DEL MONTE® Chunky
    Pasta Style Stewed
    Tomatoes
1 can (8 ounces)
    DEL MONTE® Tomato
    Sauce
1 cup water
8 ounces uncooked rigatoni
    or spiral pasta
8 mushrooms, sliced
    (optional)
    Grated Parmesan cheese
    and parsley (optional)

In large skillet, brown sausage. Add onion and garlic. Cook until onion is soft; drain. Stir in stewed tomatoes, tomato sauce, water and pasta. Cover and bring to a boil; reduce heat. Simmer, covered, 25 to 30 minutes or until pasta is tender, stirring occasionally. Stir in mushrooms; simmer 5 minutes. Serve in skillet garnished with cheese and parsley, if desired.

Makes 4 servings

Prep time: 15 minutes
Cook time: 30 minutes

Ham and Cheese Casserole

1 package (10 ounces)
    BIRDS EYE® Pasta
    Primavera Style Recipe
    Vegetables in a Seasoned
    Sauce
1 package (8 ounces)
    PHILADELPHIA BRAND®
    Cream Cheese, cubed
⅓ cup milk
1½ cups (12 ounces) cooked
    cubed ham
⅓ cup cheese-flavored
    crackers, crushed

Heat oven to 350°F. Cook vegetable mixture, cream cheese and milk in medium saucepan on medium-high heat until cream cheese is melted, stirring occasionally. Stir in ham. Spoon into 1½-quart casserole; top with crackers. Bake 25 minutes.

Makes 4 servings

Prep time: 20 minutes
Cooking time: 25 minutes

Skillet Pasta Roma

Hearty Meatless Chili

1 envelope LIPTON® Recipe
  Secrets Onion, Onion-
  Mushroom or Beefy
  Mushroom Recipe Soup
  Mix
4 cups water
1 can (16 ounces) chick peas
  or garbanzo beans,
  rinsed and drained
1 can (16 ounces) red kidney
  beans, rinsed and drained
1 can (14½ ounces) whole
  peeled tomatoes, drained
  and chopped (reserve
  liquid)
1 cup uncooked lentils,
  rinsed
1 large stalk celery, coarsely
  chopped
1 tablespoon chili powder
2 teaspoons ground cumin
1 medium clove garlic,
  finely chopped
¼ teaspoon crushed red
  pepper
  Hot cooked brown or
  regular rice
  Shredded Cheddar cheese

In large saucepan or stockpot,
combine all ingredients except rice
and cheese. Bring to a boil, then
simmer covered 20 minutes or
until lentils are almost tender.
Remove cover and simmer, stirring
occasionally, an additional 30
minutes or until liquid is almost
absorbed and lentils are tender.
Serve, if desired, over rice and top
with shredded cheese.
          Makes 6 to 8 servings

Swiss-Bacon Onion Pie

1 cup fine cracker crumbs
  (about 26 crackers)
¼ cup (½ stick) butter,
  melted
6 slices bacon
1 cup chopped onions
2 eggs, slightly beaten
¾ cup dairy sour cream
½ teaspoon salt
  Dash pepper
2 cups (8 ounces) shredded
  Wisconsin Swiss cheese
½ cup (2 ounces) shredded
  Wisconsin Sharp
  Cheddar cheese

Combine cracker crumbs and
butter; press onto bottom and side
of 8-inch pie plate. Set aside. Cook
bacon until crisp. Remove bacon
and drain on paper towels;
crumble. Pour off all but 2
tablespoons bacon fat; add onion
and cook until tender but not
brown. Drain.

In large bowl, mix onion with
crumbled bacon, eggs, sour cream,
salt, pepper and Swiss cheese.
Pour mixture into crust. Sprinkle
top with Cheddar cheese.

Bake in preheated 375°F oven for
25 to 30 minutes, or until knife
inserted half-way between the
center and edge of filling comes
out clean. Let stand 5 to 10
minutes before serving.
          Makes 4 to 6 servings

Favorite recipe from **Wisconsin Milk
Marketing Board** ©1993

Light, Lean, & Low-Fat

Recipes from the Rice Council

Almond Brown Rice Stuffing (page 168)

The Good News Is...Rice

"The good news is..."

What a welcome phrase these days, especially when it brings easy-to-use information about health and fitness.

At the USA Rice Council the news keeps getting better. Now that we are urged to evaluate some old favorites in our diets to avoid health problems, we learn that rice not only maintains its position of esteem, it also is earning new praise. Here's a favorite we don't have to give up—a nutrition-savvy food that fits perfectly into our health-conscious lifestyles.

This versatile world-popular grain almost does it all. It is low in fat and calories and is cholesterol-free. And lately, consumers have discovered rice bran, another flavorful shortcut to great nutrition.

So, the good news is...
- All the recipes in this collection provide 30 percent or less of the calories from fat.
- Many of the recipes are low in sodium and cholesterol. Check the nutritional analysis included with each recipe.
- Most recipes can be prepared in 30 minutes or less.

Overall, these recipes demonstrate how rice remarkably combines with most other foods and can be served any time of day, from breakfast to formal dinner. Furthermore, rice comes in several types and forms. You'll never be bored!

THE THREE TYPES OF RICE

Long Grain: Long and slender, these grains are 4 to 5 times as long as they are wide. Cooked grains remain separate, light, and fluffy. The perfect choice for salad, side-dish, or main-dish recipes.

Medium Grain: Plump, but not round, when these are cooked, the grains are more moist and tender than long grain. Ideal for risottos, croquettes, molds, and desserts.

Short Grain: Almost round, the grains tend to cling together when cooked— just right for puddings.

FORMS OF RICE

Brown: Rice from which only the hull has been removed. When cooked, it has a slightly chewy texture and nut-like flavor. This is a natural source of rice bran.

Parboiled: Unmilled rice is soaked, steamed, and dried before milling. Nutrients stay within the grain. A favorite of chefs who like fluffy and separate results.

Precooked: Rice is cooked and dehydrated after milling. It takes less time to prepare than other forms.

Regular-Milled White Rice: The rice has been completely milled, removing the bran layers. Vitamins and minerals are added for enrichment.

Rice Bran: Previously used only by commercial bakers, rice bran now is available for home cooking. Rice bran is a sweet, nutty tasting product that ranges in color from tan to dark brown. When you add it to your favorite recipes—at only 16 calories per tablespoon—it boosts flavor, while adding important vitamins, minerals, and fiber. Great for toppings and as a replacement for up to ¼ of the flour called for in bread, muffin, or cookie recipes.

HOW TO PREPARE RICE:

1 cup uncooked rice	Liquid*	Cooking Time
Regular-milled long grain	1¾ to 2 cups	15 minutes
Regular-milled medium or short grain	1½ to 1¾ cups	15 minutes
Brown	2 to 2½ cups	45 to 50 minutes
Parboiled	2 to 2½ cups	20 to 25 minutes
Precooked	Follow package directions.	Follow package directions.
Flavored or seasoned mixes	Follow package directions.	Follow package directions.

Combine 1 cup rice, liquid (see chart above), 1 teaspoon salt (optional), and 1 tablespoon butter or margarine (optional) in 2- to 3-quart saucepan. Bring to a boil; stir once or twice. Reduce heat; cover and simmer. Cook according to time specified on chart. If rice is not quite tender or liquid is not absorbed, replace lid and cook 2 to 4 minutes longer. Fluff with fork.

Cooked rice may be stored in the refrigerator for up to one week or in the freezer for six months.

Liquids other than water that can be used include: chicken broth, beef broth, bouillon, consommé, tomato or vegetable juice (1 part water, 1 part juice), fruit juice, such as orange or apple (1 part water, 1 part juice).

MICROWAVE OVEN INSTRUCTIONS

Combine 1 cup rice, liquid (see chart), 1 teaspoon salt (optional), and 1 tablespoon butter or margarine (optional) in 2- to 3-quart deep microproof baking dish. Cover and cook on HIGH 5 minutes or until boiling. Reduce setting to MEDIUM (50% power) and cook 15 minutes (20 minutes for parboiled rice and 30 minutes for brown rice). Fluff with fork.

A Fit Beginning

Wake up to these light and healthy favorites!

Brunch Rice

1 teaspoon margarine
¾ cup shredded carrots
¾ cup diced green pepper
¾ cup (about 3 ounces) sliced
    fresh mushrooms
6 egg whites, beaten
2 eggs, beaten
½ cup skim milk

½ teaspoon salt
¼ teaspoon ground black
    pepper
3 cups cooked brown rice
½ cup (2 ounces) shredded
    Cheddar cheese
6 corn tortillas, warmed
    (optional)

Heat margarine in large skillet over medium-high heat until hot. Add carrots, green pepper, and mushrooms; cook 2 minutes. Combine egg whites, eggs, milk, salt, and black pepper in small bowl. Reduce heat to medium and pour egg mixture over vegetables. Continue stirring 1½ to 2 minutes. Add rice and cheese; stir to gently separate grains. Heat 2 minutes. Serve immediately or spoon mixture into warmed corn tortillas.

Makes 6 servings

To microwave: Heat margarine in 2- to 3-quart microproof baking dish. Add carrots, green pepper, and mushrooms; cover and cook on HIGH 4 minutes. Combine egg whites, eggs, milk, salt, and black pepper in small bowl; pour over vegetables. Cook on HIGH 4 minutes, stirring with fork after each minute to cut cooked eggs into small pieces. Stir in rice and cheese; cook on HIGH about 1 minute or until thoroughly heated. Serve immediately or spoon mixture into warmed corn tortillas.

Each serving provides 212 calories, 11.4 grams protein, 6.5 grams fat, 27.0 grams carbohydrate, 2.5 grams dietary fiber, 353 milligrams sodium, and 79 milligrams cholesterol.

Brunch Rice

Breakfast in a Cup

3 cups cooked rice
1 cup (4 ounces) shredded
    Cheddar cheese, divided
1 can (4 ounces) diced green
    chiles
1 jar (2 ounces) diced
    pimientos, drained

⅓ cup skim milk
2 eggs, beaten
½ teaspoon ground cumin
½ teaspoon salt
½ teaspoon ground black
    pepper
Vegetable cooking spray

Combine rice, ½ cup cheese, chiles, pimientos, milk, eggs, cumin, salt, and pepper in large bowl. Evenly divide mixture into 12 muffin cups coated with cooking spray. Sprinkle with remaining ½ cup cheese. Bake at 400° F. for 15 minutes or until set. *Makes 12 servings*

Each serving provides 123 calories, 5.2 grams protein, 4.2 grams fat, 15.8 grams carbohydrate, 0.4 gram dietary fiber, 368 milligrams sodium, and 45 milligrams cholesterol.

Tip: Breakfast Cups may be stored in the freezer in freezer bag or tightly sealed container. To reheat frozen Breakfast Cups, microwave each cup on HIGH 1 minute.

Rice Bran Granola Cereal

2 cups uncooked old-fashioned
    rolled oats
1 cup crisp rice cereal
¾ cup rice bran
¾ cup raisins
⅓ cup slivered almonds

1 tablespoon ground cinnamon
⅓ cup honey
1 tablespoon margarine,
    melted
Vegetable cooking spray

Combine oats, cereal, bran, raisins, almonds, and cinnamon in large bowl; stir in honey and margarine. Spread mixture on baking sheet coated with cooking spray. Bake in preheated 350° F. oven for 8 to 10 minutes. Let cool. Serve as a topping for yogurt and/or fresh fruit. Store in a tightly covered container. *Makes 10 (½ cup) servings*

Each serving provides 199 calories, 5.0 grams protein, 6.6 grams fat, 34.5 grams carbohydrate, 4.4 grams dietary fiber, 57 milligrams sodium, and 0 milligram cholesterol.

Tip: Can be served as a cereal (with milk), or as a snack.

Strawberry-Banana Smoothie

2 cups fresh or frozen
    unsweetened strawberries,
    hulled
2 bananas, sliced
1 container (8 ounces) low-fat
    vanilla yogurt

½ cup skim milk
¼ cup rice bran
3 tablespoons lemon juice
1 to 2 tablespoons honey

Cover and freeze strawberries and sliced bananas until firm, about 4 hours or overnight. Combine strawberries, bananas, yogurt, milk, bran, lemon juice, and honey in blender; process until smooth. Serve immediately in chilled glasses.
Makes 4 (1-cup) servings

Each serving provides 168 calories, 5.6 grams protein, 2.4 grams fat, 35.3 grams carbohydrate, 4.0 grams dietary fiber, 55 milligrams sodium, and 3 milligrams cholesterol.

Praline Pancakes

1½ cups skim milk
2 tablespoons margarine,
    melted
2 teaspoons brandy
1 teaspoon vanilla extract
1 cup all-purpose flour
2 tablespoons sugar
1 teaspoon baking powder

¼ teaspoon salt
⅛ teaspoon ground cinnamon
1 cup cooked rice, cooled
⅓ cup pecans, coarsely chopped
4 egg whites, stiffly beaten
    Vegetable cooking spray
    Reduced-calorie syrup
    (optional)

Combine milk, margarine, brandy, vanilla, flour, sugar, baking powder, salt, and cinnamon in large bowl; stir until smooth. Stir in rice and pecans. Fold in beaten egg whites. Pour scant ¼ cup batter onto hot griddle coated with cooking spray. Cook over medium heat until bubbles form on top and underside is lightly browned. Turn to brown other side. Serve warm drizzled with syrup.
Makes 12 (4-inch) pancakes

Each pancake provides 176 calories, 4.0 grams protein, 4.4 grams fat, 17.6 grams carbohydrate, .6 gram dietary fiber, 193.5 milligrams sodium, and .5 milligram cholesterol.

Strawberry-Banana Smoothies

Light Previews

Start out your party or meal in a light way with these tempting recipes!

Cucumber Canapés

1 cup cooked rice, cooled to room temperature
1 large tomato, peeled and diced
½ cup chopped parsley
⅓ cup sliced green onions
¼ cup chopped mint
2 cloves garlic, minced

3 tablespoons plain nonfat yogurt*
1 tablespoon lemon juice
1 tablespoon olive oil
¼ teaspoon ground white pepper
2 to 3 large cucumbers, peeled

Combine rice, tomato, parsley, onions, mint, garlic, yogurt, lemon juice, oil, and pepper in large bowl. Cover and chill. Cut each cucumber crosswise into ½-inch slices; hollow out center of each slice, leaving bottom intact. Fill each cucumber slice with scant tablespoon rice mixture. *Makes about 3 dozen canapés*

Substitute low-fat sour cream for yogurt, if desired.

Each serving (1 canapé) provides 17 calories, 0.5 gram protein, 0.5 gram fat, 2.9 grams carbohydrate, 0.3 gram dietary fiber, 26 milligrams sodium, and 0 milligram cholesterol.

Tip: Use ½ teaspoon measuring spoon to scoop seeds from cucumber.

Cucumber Canapés

Carrot-Rice Soup

1 pound carrots, peeled and
   chopped
1 medium onion, chopped
1 tablespoon margarine
4 cups chicken broth, divided
¼ teaspoon dried tarragon
   leaves

¼ teaspoon ground white
   pepper
2¼ cups cooked rice
¼ cup light sour cream
   Snipped parsley or mint for
   garnish

Cook carrots and onion in margarine in large saucepan or Dutch oven
over medium-high heat 2 to 3 minutes or until onion is tender. Add
2 cups broth, tarragon, and pepper. Reduce heat; simmer 10 minutes.
Combine vegetables and broth in food processor or blender; process until
smooth. Return to saucepan. Add remaining 2 cups broth and rice;
thoroughly heat. Dollop sour cream on each serving of soup. Garnish
with parsley. *Makes 6 servings*

Each serving provides 183 calories, 6.4 grams protein, 3.2 grams fat, 31.6 grams
carbohydrate, 3.2 grams dietary fiber, 860 milligrams sodium, and 0 milligram
cholesterol.

Pumpkin and Rice Soup

1 medium onion, chopped
1 clove garlic, minced
1 tablespoon vegetable oil
4 cups chicken broth
1 can (16 ounces) pumpkin
½ to 1 cup finely grated fresh
   pumpkin* (optional)

½ teaspoon ground coriander
¼ to ½ teaspoon red pepper
   flakes
¼ teaspoon ground nutmeg
3 cups hot cooked rice
   Cilantro sprigs for garnish

Cook onion and garlic in oil in large saucepan or Dutch oven over
medium heat until onion is tender. Stir in broth, pumpkin, fresh
pumpkin, coriander, pepper flakes, and nutmeg. Bring to a boil. Reduce
heat; simmer, uncovered, 5 to 10 minutes. Top each serving with ½ cup
rice. Garnish with cilantro sprigs. *Makes 6 servings*

**Substitute fresh acorn, butternut, hubbard, or other winter squash for fresh
pumpkin, if desired.*

Each serving provides 215 calories, 7.2 grams protein, 3.8 grams fat, 37.6 grams
carbohydrate, 2.2 grams dietary fiber, 913 milligrams sodium, and 0 milligram
cholesterol.

Carrot-Rice Soup

Cheddar-Rice Patties

2 cups cooked rice
1 cup (4 ounces) shredded
 low-fat Cheddar cheese
½ cup minced onion
3 tablespoons all-purpose
 flour
½ teaspoon salt
¼ teaspoon ground black
 pepper

3 egg whites
⅛ teaspoon cream of tartar
 Vegetable cooking spray
 Applesauce or apple wedges
 (optional)
 Low-fat sour cream
 (optional)

Combine rice, cheese, onion, flour, salt, and pepper in medium bowl.
Beat egg whites with cream of tartar in small bowl until stiff but not dry.
Fold beaten egg whites into rice mixture. Coat large skillet with cooking
spray and place over medium heat until hot. Spoon 2 to 3 tablespoons
batter into skillet for each patty; push batter into diamond shape using
spatula. Cook patties, turning once, until golden brown on both sides.
Serve warm with applesauce, apple wedges or sour cream.

Makes about 1 dozen (4 servings)

Each serving (3 patties) provides 233 calories, 14.2 grams protein, 6.4 grams fat,
29.3 grams carbohydrate, 2.2 grams dietary fiber, 550 milligrams sodium, and
18 milligrams cholesterol.

Tip: This recipe makes a great lunch item and is a favorite with kids!

Rice Cake De-Light

4 rice cakes
¼ cup light cream cheese,
 softened

¼ cup low-calorie fruit
 preserves

Top rice cakes with cream cheese, then with preserves.

Makes 4 servings

Variations: For Summer Fruit Rice Cakes, arrange on top of cakes with
cream cheese, 1 can (11 ounces) drained mandarin orange segments,
1 sliced kiwifruit, and ½ cup sliced strawberries.
For Rice Cake Treats, top rice cakes with 2 tablespoons smooth peanut
butter and 2 small sliced bananas.

Each serving provides 78 calories, 2.2 grams protein, 2.6 grams fat, 11.6 grams
carbohydrate, 0.1 gram dietary fiber, 84 milligrams sodium, and 8 milligrams
cholesterol.

Mexican Rice Cakes

½ cup pinto beans, mashed
¼ teaspoon garlic powder
1 teaspoon lime juice
4 rice cakes

¼ cup picante sauce
¼ cup (1 ounce) shredded
   Cheddar cheese
¼ cup sliced jalapeño peppers*

Combine mashed beans with garlic powder and lime juice in small bowl.
Spread mixture evenly on each rice cake; top with picante sauce, cheese,
then peppers. Place rice cakes on baking sheet. Bake at 400° F. for
10 minutes. Serve immediately. *Makes 4 servings*

To microwave: Prepare rice cakes as directed on microproof baking sheet
or plate. Cook, uncovered, on HIGH 1½ minutes; rotate after 1 minute.
Serve immediately.

Substitute chopped green chiles for jalapeño peppers, if desired.

Each serving provides 106 calories, 4.8 grams protein, 2.7 grams fat, 15.9 grams
carbohydrate, 1.2 grams dietary fiber, 211 milligrams sodium, and 7 milligrams
cholesterol.

Tortilla Rice Soup

⅓ cup sliced green onions
   Vegetable cooking spray
4 cups chicken broth
2 cups cooked rice
1 can (10½ ounces) diced
   tomatoes with green
   chiles,* undrained
1 cup cooked chicken breast
   cubes

1 can (4 ounces) chopped
   green chiles
   Salt to taste (optional)
1 tablespoon lime juice
   Tortilla chips
½ cup chopped tomato
½ avocado, cut into small cubes
4 lime slices for garnish
   Cilantro sprigs for garnish

Cook onions in Dutch oven or large saucepan coated with cooking spray
over medium-high heat until tender. Add broth, rice, tomatoes, chicken,
and chiles. Reduce heat; cover and simmer 20 minutes. Stir in salt and
lime juice. Just before serving, pour into soup bowls; top with tortilla
chips, chopped tomato, and avocado. Garnish with lime slices and
cilantro sprigs. *Makes 4 servings*

*Look for diced tomatoes with green chiles in the Mexican food section of your
supermarket.*

Each serving provides 307 calories, 19.5 grams protein, 8.3 grams fat, 37.8 grams
carbohydrate, 2.4 grams dietary fiber, 1403 milligrams sodium, and 31 milligrams
cholesterol.

Mushroom and Rice Soup

2 cups (about 8 ounces) sliced
  fresh mushrooms
1 cup (about 4 ounces)
  chopped fresh mushrooms
1 cup sliced green onions
2 tablespoons olive oil
6 cups chicken broth
2 jars (7 ounces each) whole
  straw mushrooms,
  undrained
1 cup water
¾ teaspoon cracked black
  pepper
¾ teaspoon dried thyme leaves
3 cups cooked rice
1 tablespoon dry sherry

Cook sliced and chopped mushrooms and onions in oil in Dutch oven over medium-high heat until tender crisp. Add broth, straw mushrooms, water, pepper, and thyme. Reduce heat; simmer, uncovered, 5 to 7 minutes. Stir in rice and sherry; simmer 1 to 2 minutes. *Makes 10 servings*

Each serving provides 142 calories, 5.9 grams protein, 3.8 grams fat, 20.4 grams carbohydrate, 1.1 grams dietary fiber, 861 milligrams sodium, and 0 milligram cholesterol.

Chicken Pâté

1½ cups cooked chicken
½ cup cooked rice
2 tablespoons brandy
1 tablespoon chopped onion
1 tablespoon chopped chives
1 teaspoon Worcestershire
  sauce
½ teaspoon salt
½ teaspoon poultry seasoning
½ teaspoon rubbed sage
Vegetable cooking spray
  (optional)
Lettuce leaves
Paprika
Sliced red onion rings for
  garnish
Sliced ripe olives for garnish
Chutney
Miniature rice cakes or
  melba rounds

Combine chicken, rice, brandy, onion, chives, Worcestershire sauce, salt, poultry seasoning, and sage in food processor or blender; process until smooth. Shape mixture into round shape or fill small decorative mold coated with cooking spray. Cover and chill 1 to 2 hours or until ready to serve. Serve pâté on lettuce leaves. Sprinkle with paprika and garnish with red onion rings and olives. Serve with chutney on rice cakes or melba rounds. *Makes 2 cups*

Each serving (2 tablespoons) provides 38 calories, 4.0 grams protein, 1.0 gram fat, 2.0 grams carbohydrate, 0.1 gram dietary fiber, 112 milligrams sodium, and 12 milligrams cholesterol.

Turning a New Leaf

What better way to begin a healthy eating plan than by turning a new leaf with these tasty salads!

Curried Tuna Salad

3 cups hot cooked rice
½ cup frozen peas
1 to 2 cans (6½ ounces each) tuna, packed in water, drained and flaked
¾ cup chopped celery
¼ cup sliced green onions
1 tablespoon drained capers (optional)

¼ cup lemon juice
2 tablespoons olive oil
¼ teaspoon curry powder
¼ teaspoon hot pepper sauce
Shredded romaine lettuce
2 medium tomatoes, cut into wedges, for garnish

Combine hot rice and peas in large bowl; toss lightly. Add tuna, celery, onions, and capers. Combine lemon juice, oil, curry powder, and pepper sauce in small jar with lid. Pour over rice mixture; toss lightly. Cover and chill 30 minutes. Serve on shredded lettuce and garnish with tomato wedges.

Makes 6 servings

Each serving provides 245 calories, 13.1 grams protein, 5.8 grams fat, 34.6 grams carbohydrate, 2.6 grams dietary fiber, 551 milligrams sodium, and 13 milligrams cholesterol.

Curried Tuna Salad

Black Bean and Rice Salad

2 cups cooked rice, cooled to
    room temperature
1 cup cooked black beans*
1 medium tomato, seeded and
    chopped
½ cup (2 ounces) shredded
    Cheddar cheese (optional)

1 tablespoon snipped parsley
¼ cup prepared light Italian
    dressing
1 tablespoon lime juice
    Lettuce leaves

green onion

Combine rice, beans, tomato, cheese, and parsley in large bowl. Pour dressing and lime juice over rice mixture; toss lightly. Serve on lettuce leaves.

Makes 4 servings

Substitute canned black beans, drained, for the cooked beans, if desired.

Each serving provides 210 calories, 7.4 grams protein, 0.7 gram fat, 43.1 grams carbohydrate, 3.2 grams dietary fiber, 560 milligrams sodium, and 0 milligram cholesterol.

Gazpacho Salad

3 cups cooked rice, cooled to
    room temperature
2 large tomatoes, cut into
    wedges
1 cup (about 4 ounces) sliced
    fresh mushrooms
1 medium green pepper, cut
    into strips
⅓ cup sliced green onions
1 tablespoon snipped parsley
    or cilantro

2 tablespoons vegetable oil
2 tablespoons white vinegar
1 tablespoon snipped basil
    leaves*
1 clove garlic, minced
¼ teaspoon salt
¼ teaspoon ground black
    pepper
    Lettuce leaves

Combine rice, tomatoes, mushrooms, green pepper, onions, and parsley in large bowl. Combine oil, vinegar, basil, garlic, salt, and black pepper in small jar with lid. Pour over rice mixture; toss lightly. Serve on lettuce leaves.

Makes 6 servings

Substitute ¼ teaspoon dried basil for fresh basil, if desired.

Each serving provides 189 calories, 3.6 grams protein, 5.0 grams fat, 32.4 grams carbohydrate, 1.6 grams dietary fiber, 494 milligrams sodium, and 0 milligram cholesterol.

Black Bean and Rice Salad

Grilled Chicken Salad

¾ pound boned and skinned
   chicken breast
½ teaspoon salt
½ teaspoon ground black
   pepper
1½ cups diagonally sliced small
   zucchini
3 cups cooked rice, cooled to
   room temperature
1 can (14 ounces) artichoke
   hearts, drained

¾ cup fresh snow peas,
   blanched*
½ medium red pepper, cut into
   1-inch cubes
⅓ cup light Italian salad
   dressing
1 teaspoon chopped fresh basil
   leaves
Lettuce leaves

Season chicken with salt and black pepper. Grill or broil chicken breast. Add zucchini during last 5 minutes of grilling or broiling. Cover and chill chicken and zucchini; cut chicken in ¾-inch cubes. Combine rice, chicken, zucchini, artichokes, snow peas, and red pepper in large bowl. Blend dressing and basil in small bowl. Pour over salad; toss lightly. Serve on lettuce leaves. *Makes 4 servings*

Substitute frozen snow peas, thawed, for fresh snow peas, if desired.

Each serving provides 416 calories, 34.3 grams protein, 3.8 grams fat, 60.2 grams carbohydrate, 3.0 grams dietary fiber, 1227 milligrams sodium, and 72 milligrams cholesterol.

Marinated Vegetable Salad

1 cup (about 4 ounces) sliced
   fresh mushrooms
¾ cup halved cherry tomatoes
½ cup avocado chunks
   (optional)
½ cup sliced ripe olives
⅓ cup chopped red onion
3 tablespoons red wine vinegar

2 tablespoons olive oil
1 tablespoon snipped parsley
½ teaspoon sugar
¼ teaspoon salt
¼ teaspoon dried basil leaves
3 cups cooked rice, cooled
   Red onion rings for garnish

Combine mushrooms, tomatoes, avocado, olives, and onion in shallow dish. Combine vinegar, oil, parsley, sugar, salt, and basil in jar with lid. Pour over vegetables. Cover and chill 2 to 3 hours. Add rice; toss lightly. Garnish with red onion rings. *Makes 8 servings*

Each serving provides 148 calories, 2.6 grams protein, 4.6 grams fat, 24.3 grams carbohydrate, 1.1 grams dietary fiber, 443 milligrams sodium, and 0 milligram cholesterol.

Grilled Chicken Salad

Refreshing Turkey Salad

3 cups cooked rice, cooled to
    room temperature
2 cups diced cantaloupe
1½ cups cooked turkey breast
    cubes
¼ cup packed mint leaves
¼ cup packed parsley

1 clove garlic, halved
1 container (8 ounces) plain
    nonfat yogurt
Lettuce leaves
Assorted fresh fruit for
    garnish (optional)

Combine rice, cantaloupe, and turkey in large bowl. Finely chop mint, parsley, and garlic in food processor. Add yogurt and blend. Add to rice mixture; toss lightly. Cover and chill 2 hours. Serve on lettuce leaves. Garnish with fresh fruit. *Makes 4 servings*

Each serving provides 332 calories, 24.2 grams protein, 1.2 grams fat, 54.5 grams carbohydrate, 1.6 grams dietary fiber, 667 milligrams sodium, and 45 milligrams cholesterol.

Shrimp and Strawberry Salad

3 cups cooked rice
½ pound peeled, deveined
    cooked small shrimp
¾ cup thinly sliced celery
⅔ cup cholesterol free, reduced
    calorie mayonnaise
½ cup low-fat strawberry
    yogurt

1 teaspoon dry mustard
1 teaspoon lemon juice
½ teaspoon salt
1½ cups sliced fresh strawberries
    Romaine lettuce

Combine rice, shrimp, and celery in large bowl. Combine mayonnaise, yogurt, mustard, lemon juice, and salt in medium bowl; mix well. Add yogurt mixture to rice mixture and stir well. Fold in strawberries. Cover and chill until serving time. Arrange lettuce on individual serving plates; top with salad. *Makes 6 servings*

Each serving provides 274 calories, 10.4 grams protein, 9.2 grams fat, 36.6 grams carbohydrate, 1.8 grams dietary fiber, 833 milligrams sodium, and 69 milligrams cholesterol.

Paella Salad

2 cups cooked rice (cooked in chicken broth and ⅛ teaspoon saffron*)
1 cup cooked chicken breast cubes
1 cup peeled, deveined cooked shrimp
1 medium tomato, seeded and diced
½ cup chopped onion
⅓ cup cooked green peas
⅓ cup sliced ripe olives
3 tablespoons white wine vinegar
1 tablespoon olive oil
1 clove garlic, minced
½ teaspoon salt
½ teaspoon ground white pepper
Lettuce leaves

Combine rice, chicken, shrimp, tomato, onion, peas, and olives in large bowl. Combine vinegar, oil, garlic, salt, and pepper in jar with lid. Pour over rice mixture; toss lightly. Serve on lettuce leaves.

Makes 4 servings

Substitute ground turmeric for the saffron, if desired.

Each serving provides 288 calories, 23.5 grams protein, 7.0 grams fat, 31.3 grams carbohydrate, 1.9 grams dietary fiber, 770 milligrams sodium, and 99 milligrams cholesterol.

Santa Fe Salad

2 cups cooked brown rice, cooled
1 can (16 ounces) black beans or pinto beans, rinsed and drained
1 can (17 ounces) whole kernel corn, drained
¼ cup minced onion
¼ cup white vinegar
2 tablespoons vegetable oil
2 tablespoons snipped cilantro
2 jalapeño peppers, minced
2 teaspoons chili powder
1 teaspoon salt

Combine rice, beans, corn, and onion in medium bowl. Combine vinegar, oil, cilantro, peppers, chili powder, and salt in small jar with lid. Pour over rice mixture; toss lightly. Cover and chill 2 to 3 hours so flavors will blend. Stir before serving.

Makes 4 servings

Each serving provides 425 calories, 15.9 grams protein, 9.2 grams fat, 75.5 grams carbohydrate, 8.1 grams dietary fiber, 934 milligrams sodium, and 0 milligram cholesterol.

Stir-Fry Beef Salad

1 pound boneless beef sirloin steak	3 tablespoons cider vinegar
2 tablespoons olive oil, divided	1 tablespoon soy sauce
1 tablespoon grated fresh ginger root	1 tablespoon honey
1 clove garlic, minced	3 cups hot cooked rice
1 small red onion, chopped	½ pound fresh spinach, torn into bite-size pieces
1 cup (about 4 ounces) fresh mushrooms, quartered	1 medium tomato, seeded and coarsely chopped

Partially freeze steak; slice across the grain into ⅛-inch strips. Set aside. Heat 1 tablespoon oil, ginger root, and garlic in large skillet or wok over high heat until hot. Stir-fry beef (half at a time) 1 to 2 minutes. Remove beef; keep warm. Add remaining 1 tablespoon oil; heat until hot. Add onion and mushrooms; cook 1 to 2 minutes. Stir in vinegar, soy sauce, and honey. Bring mixture to a boil. Add beef and rice; toss lightly. Serve over spinach. Top with tomato; serve immediately.   *Makes 6 servings*

Each serving provides 334 calories, 22.9 grams protein, 10.3 grams fat, 36.9 grams carbohydrate, 2.8 grams dietary fiber, 602 milligrams sodium, and 53 milligrams cholesterol.

Turkey Ensalada con Queso

2 cups cooked rice, cooled to room temperature	2 tablespoons snipped parsley
1½ cups cooked turkey breast cubes	¼ cup cholesterol free, reduced calorie mayonnaise
½ cup (2 ounces) jalapeño Monterey Jack cheese cut into ½-inch cubes	¼ cup plain nonfat yogurt
	Lettuce leaves
1 can (4 ounces) diced green chiles	Tomato wedges for garnish

Combine rice, turkey, cheese, chiles, and parsley in large bowl. Blend mayonnaise and yogurt; add to rice mixture and toss lightly. Serve on lettuce leaves; garnish with tomato wedges.   *Makes 4 servings*

Each serving provides 307 calories, 23.4 grams protein, 7.9 grams fat, 34.0 grams carbohydrate, 0.9 gram dietary fiber, 581 milligrams sodium, and 59 milligrams cholesterol.

Stir-Fry Beef Salad

Summer Fruit Salad

2 cups cooked rice, cooled to
    room temperature
½ cup quartered strawberries
½ cup grape halves
2 kiwifruit, sliced into
    quarters
½ cup pineapple tidbits

½ cup banana slices
¼ cup pineapple juice
2 tablespoons plain nonfat
    yogurt
1 tablespoon honey
Lettuce leaves

Combine rice and fruit in large bowl. Blend pineapple juice, yogurt, and
honey in small bowl. Pour over rice mixture; toss lightly. Serve on lettuce
leaves. *Makes 4 servings*

Each serving provides 239 calories, 4.1 grams protein, 1.1 grams fat, 54.0 grams
carbohydrate, 3.1 grams dietary fiber, 396 milligrams sodium, and 1 milligram
cholesterol.

Chinese Chicken Salad

3 cups cooked rice, cooled
1 cup cooked chicken breast
    cubes
1 cup sliced celery
1 can (8 ounces) sliced water
    chestnuts, drained
1 cup fresh bean sprouts*
½ cup (about 2 ounces) sliced
    fresh mushrooms
¼ cup sliced green onions

¼ cup diced red pepper
3 tablespoons lemon juice
2 tablespoons reduced-sodium
    soy sauce
2 tablespoons sesame oil
2 teaspoons grated fresh
    ginger root
¼ to ½ teaspoon ground white
    pepper
Lettuce leaves

Combine rice, chicken, celery, water chestnuts, bean sprouts, mushrooms,
onions, and red pepper in large bowl. Combine lemon juice, soy sauce,
oil, ginger root, and white pepper in small jar with lid. Pour over rice
mixture; toss lightly. Serve on lettuce leaves. *Makes 6 servings*

*Substitute canned bean sprouts, rinsed and drained, for fresh bean sprouts,
if desired.*

Each serving provides 248 calories, 11.6 grams protein, 5.8 grams fat, 37.1 grams
carbohydrate, 1.5 grams dietary fiber, 593 milligrams sodium, and 20 milligrams
cholesterol.

Summer Fruit Salad

Sesame Pork Salad

3 cups cooked rice
1½ cups slivered cooked pork*
¼ pound fresh snow peas, trimmed and julienned
1 medium cucumber, peeled, seeded, and julienned
1 medium red pepper, julienned
½ cup sliced green onions

2 tablespoons sesame seeds, toasted (optional)
¼ cup chicken broth
3 tablespoons rice or white wine vinegar
3 tablespoons soy sauce
1 tablespoon peanut oil
1 teaspoon sesame oil

Combine rice, pork, snow peas, cucumber, pepper, onions, and sesame seeds in large bowl. Combine broth, vinegar, soy sauce, and oils in small jar with lid. Pour over rice mixture; toss lightly. Serve at room temperature or slightly chilled. *Makes 6 servings*

Substitute 1½ cups slivered cooked chicken for pork, if desired.

Each serving provides 269 calories, 13.8 grams protein, 8.4 grams fat, 33.5 grams carbohydrate, 1.6 grams dietary fiber, 867 milligrams sodium, and 32 milligrams cholesterol.

Rice Salad Milano

3 cups hot cooked rice
2 tablespoons vegetable oil
2 tablespoons lemon juice
1 clove garlic, minced
½ teaspoon salt (optional)
½ teaspoon dried rosemary leaves
½ teaspoon dried oregano leaves

½ teaspoon ground black pepper
1 small zucchini, julienned*
1 medium tomato, seeded and chopped
2 tablespoons grated Parmesan cheese

Place rice in large bowl. Combine oil, lemon juice, garlic, salt, rosemary, oregano, and pepper in small jar with lid. Pour over rice; toss lightly. Cover; let cool. Add remaining ingredients. Serve at room temperature or chilled. *Makes 6 servings*

To julienne, slice zucchini diagonally. Cut slices into matchstick-size strips.

Each serving provides 189 calories, 3.9 grams protein, 5.4 grams fat, 30.8 grams carbohydrate, 0.9 gram dietary fiber, 620 milligrams sodium, and 1 milligram cholesterol.

Sesame Pork Salad

Specialties of the House

Bring on the family or dinner guests and treat them to the specialties of the house using our versatile rice recipes.

Stuffed Chicken Breasts

4 boneless, skinless chicken breast halves (about 1 pound), pounded to ¼-inch thickness
½ teaspoon ground black pepper, divided
¼ teaspoon salt
1 cup cooked brown rice (cooked in chicken broth)
¼ cup minced tomato
¼ cup (1 ounce) finely shredded mozzarella cheese
3 tablespoons toasted rice bran* (optional)
1 tablespoon chopped fresh basil
Vegetable cooking spray

Season insides of chicken breasts with ¼ teaspoon pepper and salt. Combine rice, tomato, cheese, bran, basil, and remaining ¼ teaspoon pepper. Spoon rice mixture on top of pounded chicken breasts; fold over and secure sides with wooden toothpicks soaked in water. Wipe off outsides of chicken breasts with paper towel. Coat a large skillet with cooking spray and place over medium-high heat until hot. Cook stuffed chicken breasts 1 minute on each side or just until golden brown. Transfer chicken to shallow baking pan. Bake at 350°F. for 8 to 10 minutes.

Makes 4 servings

To toast rice bran, spread on baking sheet and bake at 325°F. for 7 to 8 minutes.

Each serving provides 223 calories, 30.0 grams protein, 5.2 grams fat, 12.1 grams carbohydrate, 1.0 gram dietary fiber, 337 milligrams sodium, and 79 milligrams cholesterol.

Stuffed Chicken Breasts

Turkey and Rice Quiche

3 cups cooked rice, cooled to
    room temperature
1½ cups chopped cooked turkey
1 medium tomato, seeded and
    finely diced
¼ cup sliced green onions
¼ cup finely diced green pepper
1 tablespoon chopped fresh
    basil or 1 teaspoon
    dried basil

½ teaspoon seasoned salt
⅛ to ¼ teaspoon ground red
    pepper
½ cup skim milk
3 eggs, beaten
    Vegetable cooking spray
½ cup (2 ounces) shredded
    Cheddar cheese
½ cup (2 ounces) shredded
    mozzarella cheese

Combine rice, turkey, tomato, onions, green pepper, basil, salt, red
pepper, milk, and eggs in 13×9×2-inch pan coated with cooking spray.
Top with cheeses. Bake at 375°F. for 20 minutes or until knife inserted
near center comes out clean. To serve, cut quiche into 8 squares; cut each
square diagonally into 2 triangles.   *Makes 8 servings (2 triangles each)*

Each serving provides 231 calories, 16.1 grams protein, 7.4 grams fat, 23.9 grams
carbohydrate, 0.8 gram dietary fiber, 527 milligrams sodium, and 111 milligrams
cholesterol.

Vegetable Pork Stir-Fry

¾ pound pork tenderloin
1 tablespoon vegetable oil
1½ cups (about 6 ounces) sliced
    fresh mushrooms
1 large green pepper, cut into
    strips
1 zucchini, thinly sliced
2 ribs celery, cut into diagonal
    slices

1 cup thinly sliced carrots
1 clove garlic, minced
1 cup chicken broth
2 tablespoons reduced-sodium
    soy sauce
1½ tablespoons cornstarch
3 cups hot cooked rice

Slice pork across the grain into ⅛-inch strips. Brown pork strips in oil in
large skillet over medium-high heat. Push meat to side of skillet. Add
mushrooms, pepper, zucchini, celery, carrots, and garlic; stir-fry about
3 minutes. Combine broth, soy sauce, and cornstarch. Add to skillet and
cook, stirring, until thickened; cook 1 minute longer. Serve over rice.
Makes 6 servings

Each serving provides 257 calories, 16.8 grams protein, 4.4 grams fat, 36.3 grams
carbohydrate, 2.1 grams dietary fiber, 732 milligrams sodium, and 37 milligrams
cholesterol.

Sherried Beef

¾ pound boneless beef top
    round steak
1 cup water
¼ cup dry sherry
3 tablespoons soy sauce
2 large carrots, cut into
    diagonal slices

1 large green pepper, cut into
    strips
1 medium onion, cut into
    chunks
2 tablespoons vegetable oil,
    divided
1 tablespoon cornstarch
2 cups hot cooked rice

Partially freeze steak; slice across the grain into ⅛-inch strips. Combine water, sherry, and soy sauce. Pour over beef in dish; marinate 1 hour. Stir-fry vegetables in 1 tablespoon oil in large skillet over medium-high heat. Remove from skillet; set aside. Drain beef; reserve marinade. Brown beef in remaining 1 tablespoon oil. Combine cornstarch with marinade in bowl. Add vegetables and marinade to beef. Cook, stirring, until sauce is thickened; cook 1 minute longer. Serve over rice. *Makes 4 servings*

Each serving provides 365 calories, 23.9 grams protein, 10.9 grams fat, 41.5 grams carbohydrate, 3.3 grams dietary fiber, 1080 milligrams sodium, and 48 milligrams cholesterol.

Curried Black Beans and Rice with Sausage

1 tablespoon olive oil
1 medium onion, minced
1 tablespoon curry powder
½ pound smoked turkey
    sausage, thinly sliced
¾ cup chicken broth

2 cans (16 ounces each) black
    beans, drained
1 tablespoon white wine
    vinegar (optional)
3 cups cooked rice

Heat oil in large heavy skillet over medium heat. Cook onion and curry powder, stirring well, until tender. Stir in sausage and broth; simmer 5 minutes. Stir in beans; cook until hot, stirring constantly. Remove from heat and stir in vinegar. Spoon over rice. *Makes 10 servings*

To microwave: Combine oil, onion, and curry powder in 2- to 3-quart microproof baking dish. Cook on HIGH 2 minutes or until onion is tender. Add sausage, broth, and beans; cover with plastic wrap and cook on HIGH 5 to 6 minutes, stirring after 3 minutes, or until thoroughly heated. Continue as directed above.

Each serving provides 267 calories, 14.1 grams protein, 5.4 grams fat, 41.0 grams carbohydrate, 4.7 grams dietary fiber, 481 milligrams sodium, and 16 milligrams cholesterol.

Shrimp La Louisiana

1 tablespoon margarine
1½ cups uncooked rice*
1 medium onion, chopped
1 green pepper, chopped
2¾ cups beef broth
¼ teaspoon salt
¼ teaspoon ground black
    pepper

¼ teaspoon hot pepper sauce
1 pound medium shrimp,
    peeled and deveined
1 can (4 ounces) sliced
    mushrooms, drained
3 tablespoons snipped parsley
¼ cup sliced green onions for
    garnish (optional)

Melt margarine in 3-quart saucepan. Add rice, onion, and green pepper. Cook 2 to 3 minutes. Add broth, salt, black pepper, and pepper sauce; bring to a boil. Cover and simmer 15 minutes. Add shrimp, mushrooms, and parsley. Cook 5 minutes longer or until shrimp turn pink. Garnish with green onions. *Makes 8 servings*

Recipe based on regular-milled long grain white rice. If using other types of rice, refer to chart on page 125 for adjustments of liquid and time.

Each serving provides 206 calories, 14.1 grams protein, 2.5 grams fat, 31.0 grams carbohydrate, 1.0 gram dietary fiber, 527 milligrams sodium, and 96 milligrams cholesterol.

Rice-Stuffed Fish Fillets with Mushroom Sauce

3 cups cooked rice
¼ cup diced pimientos
2 tablespoons snipped parsley
1 teaspoon grated lemon peel
¼ teaspoon salt
¼ teaspoon ground white
    pepper

1 pound white fish fillets*
Vegetable cooking spray
2 teaspoons margarine, melted
½ teaspoon seasoned salt
¼ teaspoon paprika
    Lemon slices for garnish
    Mushroom Sauce (recipe
    follows)

Combine rice, pimientos, parsley, lemon peel, salt, and pepper in large bowl. Place fillets in shallow baking dish coated with cooking spray. Spoon rice mixture on lower portion of each fillet. Fold over to enclose rice mixture; fasten with wooden toothpicks soaked in water. Brush fillets with margarine; sprinkle with seasoned salt and paprika. Bake at 400° F. for 10 to 15 minutes or until fish flakes easily with fork. Prepare Mushroom Sauce while fillets are baking. Transfer fillets to serving platter; garnish platter with lemon slices. Serve fillets with Mushroom Sauce. *Makes 4 servings*

Haddock, orange roughy, sole, or turbot may be used.

continued

Mushroom Sauce

2 cups (about 8 ounces) sliced
fresh mushrooms
½ cup sliced green onions
1 teaspoon margarine
½ cup water

⅓ cup white wine
1 tablespoon white wine
Worcestershire sauce
½ cup cholesterol free, reduced
calorie mayonnaise

Cook mushrooms and onions in margarine in large skillet until tender.
Add water, wine, and Worcestershire sauce; bring to a boil. Reduce sauce
slightly. Stir in mayonnaise; keep warm.

Each serving provides 440 calories, 27.0 grams protein, 14.0 grams fat, 49.6 grams
carbohydrate, 1.8 grams dietary fiber, 1666 milligrams sodium, and 66 milligrams
cholesterol.

Curried Scallops in Rice Ring

Vegetable cooking spray
1½ pounds bay scallops
1 tablespoon margarine
1 medium onion, chopped
1 teaspoon all-purpose flour
½ teaspoon salt
1 bottle (8 ounces) clam juice
1 cup evaporated skim milk

1 red apple, cored and chopped
½ teaspoon curry powder
6 cups hot cooked rice
1 tablespoon snipped parsley
1 tablespoon diced pimiento
Chutney, chopped peanuts,
grated coconut, and raisins
for condiments (optional)

Coat large skillet with cooking spray and place over medium heat until
hot. Add scallops; cook until scallops are almost done, 2 to 3 minutes.
Remove scallops from skillet; keep warm. Melt margarine in skillet; add
onion and cook 1 to 2 minutes or until tender. Stir in flour and salt; cook,
stirring, 2 minutes over medium-high heat. Gradually add clam juice and
milk, stirring constantly until thickened. Stir in scallops, apple, and curry
powder. Keep warm. Combine rice, parsley, and pimiento; pack into
2-quart ring mold coated with cooking spray. Unmold onto serving
platter and fill center of ring with curried scallops. Serve with chutney,
chopped peanuts, grated coconut, and raisins.   *Makes 6 servings*

Each serving provides 440 calories, 28.4 grams protein, 3.6 grams fat, 70.7 grams
carbohydrate, 2.2 grams dietary fiber, 1315 milligrams sodium, and 39 milligrams
cholesterol.

Baked Stuffed Snapper

1 red snapper (1½ pounds)
2 cups hot cooked rice
1 can (4 ounces) sliced
    mushrooms, drained
½ cup diced water chestnuts
¼ cup thinly sliced green
    onions
¼ cup diced pimiento

2 tablespoons chopped parsley
1 tablespoon grated lemon peel
½ teaspoon salt
⅛ teaspoon ground black
    pepper
Vegetable cooking spray
1 tablespoon margarine,
    melted

Clean and butterfly fish. Combine rice, mushrooms, water chestnuts, onions, pimiento, parsley, lemon peel, salt, and pepper; toss lightly. Fill cavity of fish with rice mixture; enclose filling with wooden toothpicks soaked in water. Place fish in 13×9×2-inch baking dish coated with cooking spray; brush fish with margarine. Bake fish at 400°F. for 18 to 20 minutes or until fish flakes easily with fork. Wrap remaining rice in foil and bake in oven with fish. *Makes 4 servings*

Each serving provides 349 calories, 38.7 grams protein, 5.6 grams fat, 33.3 grams carbohydrate, 1.2 grams dietary fiber, 947 milligrams sodium, and 63 milligrams cholesterol.

Skillet Sauerbraten

¾ pound boneless beef sirloin
    steak
⅔ cup crushed gingersnaps
    (about 10 cookies)
½ teaspoon salt
1 tablespoon vegetable oil
1 medium onion, sliced

3 ribs celery, sliced
2 carrots, thinly sliced
1½ cups beef broth
⅓ cup cider vinegar
2 tablespoons cornstarch
2 tablespoons water
3 cups hot cooked brown rice

Partially freeze steak; slice diagonally across grain into ⅛-inch strips. Combine gingersnap crumbs and salt in medium bowl. Dredge slices into crumb mixture; set aside. Heat oil in large skillet over medium-high heat until hot. Add half of steak slices, stirring to brown both sides. Cook 2 minutes or until done. Reserve and keep warm. Repeat with remaining steak slices. Add onion, celery, and carrots to hot skillet; cook 5 minutes or until tender crisp. Add broth and vinegar; reduce heat and simmer 5 minutes. Combine cornstarch with water. Add to skillet, stirring constantly, until thickened; cook 1 minute longer. Add reserved steak slices; pour mixture over rice. *Makes 6 servings*

Each serving provides 309 calories, 18.8 grams protein, 8.0 grams fat, 40.1 grams carbohydrate, 3.2 grams dietary fiber, 470 milligrams sodium, and 51 milligrams cholesterol.

Baked Stuffed Snapper

Barbecued Shrimp with Spicy Rice

1 pound large shrimp, peeled
   and deveined
4 wooden* or metal skewers

Vegetable cooking spray
⅓ cup prepared barbecue sauce
Spicy Rice (recipe follows)

Thread shrimp on skewers. To broil in oven, place on broiler rack coated with cooking spray. Broil 4 to 5 inches from heat 4 minutes. Brush with barbecue sauce. Turn and brush with remaining barbecue sauce. Broil 2 to 4 minutes longer or until shrimp are done. To cook on outdoor grill, cook skewered shrimp over hot coals 4 minutes. Brush with barbecue sauce. Turn and brush with remaining barbecue sauce. Grill 4 to 5 minutes longer or until shrimp are done. Serve with Spicy Rice.

Makes 4 servings

Soak wooden skewers in water before using to prevent burning.

Spicy Rice

½ cup sliced green onions
½ cup minced carrots
½ cup minced red pepper
1 jalapeño or serrano pepper,
   minced
1 tablespoon vegetable oil

2 cups cooked rice (cooked in
   chicken broth)
2 tablespoons snipped cilantro
1 tablespoon lime juice
1 teaspoon soy sauce
Hot pepper sauce to taste

Cook onions, carrots, red pepper, and jalapeño pepper in oil in large skillet over medium-high heat until tender crisp. Stir in rice, cilantro, lime juice, soy sauce, and pepper sauce; cook until thoroughly heated. Serve with Barbecued Shrimp.

To microwave: Combine onions, carrots, red pepper, jalapeño pepper, and oil in 2-quart microproof baking dish. Cook on HIGH 2 to 3 minutes or until vegetables are tender crisp. Add rice, cilantro, lime juice, soy sauce, and pepper sauce. Cook on HIGH 3 to 4 minutes, stirring after 2 minutes, or until thoroughly heated. Serve with Barbecued Shrimp.

Each serving provides 285 calories, 22.6 grams protein, 5.2 grams fat, 35.5 grams carbohydrate, 1.9 grams dietary fiber, 839 milligrams sodium, and 175 milligrams cholesterol.

Barbecued Shrimp with Spicy Rice

Rice and Roast Beef Sandwiches

1 small red onion, sliced into thin rings
1 teaspoon olive oil
3 cups cooked brown rice
½ cup whole kernel corn
½ cup sliced ripe olives (optional)
½ cup barbecue sauce
2 tablespoons lime juice
½ teaspoon ground cumin
½ teaspoon garlic salt
4 whole-wheat pita rounds, halved and warmed
8 lettuce leaves
1 cup sliced, cooked lean roast beef
1 large tomato, seeded and chopped

Cook onion in oil in large skillet over medium-high heat until tender. Add rice, corn, olives, barbecue sauce, juice, cumin, and garlic salt; toss until heated. Line each pita half with lettuce leaf, ½ cup hot rice mixture, and roast beef; top with tomato.   *Makes 8 (½ pita) sandwiches*

Each serving provides 235 calories, 9.3 grams protein, 4.6 grams fat, 37.8 grams carbohydrate, 4.9 grams dietary fiber, 279 milligrams sodium, and 14 milligrams cholesterol.

Oriental Fried Rice

3 cups cooked brown rice, cold
½ cup slivered cooked roast pork
½ cup finely chopped celery
½ cup fresh bean sprouts*
⅓ cup sliced green onions
1 egg, beaten
Vegetable cooking spray
¼ teaspoon black pepper
2 tablespoons soy sauce

Combine rice, pork, celery, bean sprouts, onions, and egg in large skillet coated with cooking spray. Cook, stirring, 3 minutes over high heat. Add pepper and soy sauce. Cook, stirring, 1 minute longer.   *Makes 6 servings*

To microwave: Combine rice, pork, celery, bean sprouts, and onions in shallow 2-quart microproof baking dish coated with cooking spray. Cook on HIGH 2 to 3 minutes. Add egg, pepper, and soy sauce. Cook on HIGH 1 to 2 minutes or until egg is set, stirring to separate grains.

*Substitute canned bean sprouts, rinsed and drained, for fresh, if desired.

Each serving provides 156 calories, 7.3 grams protein, 3.4 grams fat, 23.9 grams carbohydrate, 2.0 grams dietary fiber, 310 milligrams sodium, and 45 milligrams cholesterol.

Tip: When preparing fried rice always begin with cold rice. The grains separate better if cold and it's a great way to use leftover rice.

On the Side

Just when you thought there wasn't another way to prepare rice . . . a collection of great go-alongs.

Almond Brown Rice Stuffing

⅓ cup slivered almonds
2 teaspoons margarine
2 medium tart apples, cored
    and diced
½ cup chopped onion
½ cup chopped celery

½ teaspoon poultry seasoning
¼ teaspoon dried thyme leaves
¼ teaspoon ground white
    pepper
3 cups cooked brown rice
    (cooked in chicken broth)

Cook almonds in margarine in large skillet over medium-high heat until brown. Add apples, onion, celery, poultry seasoning, thyme, and pepper; cook until vegetables are tender crisp. Stir in rice; cook until thoroughly heated. Serve or use as stuffing for poultry or pork roast. Stuffing may be baked in covered baking dish at 375°F. for 15 to 20 minutes.

Makes 6 servings

To microwave: Combine almonds and margarine in 2- to 3-quart microproof baking dish. Cook on HIGH 2 to 3 minutes or until browned. Add apples, onion, celery, poultry seasoning, thyme, and pepper. Cover with waxed paper and cook on HIGH 2 minutes. Stir in rice; cook on HIGH 2 to 3 minutes, stirring after 1½ minutes, or until thoroughly heated. Serve as directed above.

Variations: For Mushroom Stuffing, add 2 cups (about 8 ounces) sliced mushrooms; cook with apples, onion, celery, and seasonings.
For Raisin Stuffing, add ½ cup raisins; cook with apples, onion, celery, and seasonings.

Each serving provides 198 calories, 4.4 grams protein, 6.3 grams fat, 32.5 grams carbohydrate, 4.3 grams dietary fiber, 30 milligrams sodium, and 0 milligram cholesterol.

Almond Brown Rice Stuffing

Arroz Blanco

1 tablespoon margarine	1 cup uncooked rice*
½ cup chopped onion	2 cups chicken broth
2 cloves garlic, minced	

Melt margarine in 2- to 3-quart saucepan over medium heat. Add onion and garlic; cook until onion is tender. Add rice and broth. Bring to a boil; stir. Reduce heat; cover and simmer 15 minutes or until rice is tender and liquid is absorbed. Fluff with fork. *Makes 6 servings*

To microwave: Combine margarine, onion, and garlic in deep 2- to 3-quart microproof baking dish. Cover and cook on HIGH 2 minutes. Stir in rice and broth; cover and cook on HIGH 5 minutes. Reduce setting to MEDIUM (50% power) and cook 15 minutes or until rice is tender and liquid is absorbed. Let stand 5 minutes. Fluff with fork.

Recipe based on regular-milled long grain white rice. If using other types of rice, refer to chart on page 125 for adjustments of liquid and time.

Each serving provides 149 calories, 4.1 grams protein, 2.6 grams fat, 26.3 grams carbohydrate, 0.5 gram dietary fiber, 283 milligrams sodium, and 0 milligram cholesterol.

Tip: Prepare a double batch of Arroz Blanco to have one batch ready for Rice with Tomato and Chiles (page 172) or Green Rice (below) later in the week.

Green Rice

2 Anaheim chiles	¼ cup snipped cilantro
1 jalapeño pepper	1 recipe Arroz Blanco (see
1 tablespoon margarine or	above)
olive oil	¼ teaspoon dried oregano
¼ cup sliced green onions	leaves

Chop chiles and pepper in food processor until minced but not liquid. Melt margarine in large skillet over low heat. Add chiles and cook 1 minute over medium heat. Stir in onions and cilantro; cook 15 to 30 seconds. Add rice mixture and oregano; heat. *Makes 6 servings*

To microwave: Prepare chiles and pepper as directed. Combine chiles, onions, cilantro, and margarine in 2- to 3-quart microproof baking dish. Cook on HIGH 2 to 3 minutes. Add rice mixture and oregano; cover with waxed paper and cook on HIGH 3 minutes, stirring after 2 minutes.

Each serving provides 170 calories, 4.3 grams protein, 4.5 grams fat, 27.3 grams carbohydrate, 0.9 gram dietary fiber, 306 milligrams sodium, and 0 milligram cholesterol.

Clockwise from top: Arroz Blanco, Green Rice, Rice with Tomato and Chiles (page 172)

Rice with Tomato and Chiles

1 green pepper, diced
½ cup chopped onion
1 jalapeño pepper, chopped
1 tablespoon olive oil
1 recipe Arroz Blanco (see page 170)
1 can (14½ ounces) whole tomatoes, drained and chopped

⅛ teaspoon dried oregano leaves
2 tablespoons snipped cilantro for garnish

Cook green pepper, onion, and jalapeño pepper in oil in large skillet over medium-high heat until tender crisp. Stir in rice mixture, tomatoes, and oregano; cook 5 minutes longer. Garnish with cilantro.

Makes 6 servings

To microwave: Combine green pepper, onion, jalapeño pepper, and oil in 2- to 3-quart microproof baking dish. Cook on HIGH 3 to 4 minutes. Add rice mixture, tomatoes, and oregano; cover with waxed paper and cook on HIGH 3 to 4 minutes, stirring after 2 minutes. Garnish with cilantro.

Each serving provides 191 calories, 5.0 grams protein, 5.1 grams fat, 31.2 grams carbohydrate, 1.5 grams dietary fiber, 396 milligrams sodium, and 0 milligram cholesterol.

Tip: To reduce the heat level of jalapeño peppers, scrape and discard the seeds and membranes before chopping.

Harvest Rice

1 cup thinly sliced carrots
1 tablespoon vegetable oil
2 medium apples, cored and chopped
1 cup sliced green onions

3 cups cooked brown rice
½ cup raisins
1 tablespoon sesame seeds, toasted
½ teaspoon salt

Cook carrots in oil in large skillet over medium-high heat until tender crisp. Add apples and onions; cook 5 minutes. Stir in rice, raisins, sesame seeds, and salt. Cook, stirring, until thoroughly heated.

Makes 6 servings

continued

To microwave: Combine carrots and oil in 2-quart microproof baking dish. Cook on HIGH 2 to 3 minutes or until tender crisp. Add apples and onions; continue cooking on HIGH 3 to 4 minutes. Stir in rice, raisins, sesame seeds, and salt. Cover with waxed paper and cook on HIGH 3 to 4 minutes, stirring after 2 minutes, or until thoroughly heated.

Each serving provides 209 calories, 3.8 grams protein, 4.1 grams fat, 41.1 grams carbohydrate, 4.6 grams dietary fiber, 210 milligrams sodium, and 0 milligram cholesterol.

Apricot and Walnut Brown Rice Stuffing

½ cup chopped onion
½ cup chopped celery
1 teaspoon margarine
3 cups cooked brown rice
⅔ cup coarsely chopped dried apricots
¼ cup coarsely chopped walnuts

¼ cup raisins, plumped
2 tablespoons snipped parsley
½ teaspoon dried thyme leaves
¼ teaspoon salt
¼ teaspoon rubbed sage
¼ teaspoon ground black pepper
½ cup chicken broth

Cook onion and celery in margarine in large skillet over medium-high heat until tender crisp. Add rice, apricots, walnuts, raisins, parsley, thyme, salt, sage, pepper, and broth; transfer to 2-quart baking dish. Bake in covered baking dish at 375° F. for 15 to 20 minutes. (Stuffing may be baked inside poultry.) *Makes 6 servings*

To microwave: Reduce chicken broth to ¼ cup. Combine onion, celery, and margarine in 2- to 3-quart microproof baking dish. Cook on HIGH 2 to 3 minutes or until onion is tender. Add rice, apricots, walnuts, raisins, parsley, thyme, salt, sage, pepper, and ¼ cup broth. Cover with waxed paper and cook on HIGH 2 to 3 minutes, stirring after 1½ minutes, or until thoroughly heated.

Each serving provides 183 calories, 4.9 grams protein, 4.7 grams fat, 31.4 grams carbohydrate, 3.2 grams dietary fiber, 185 milligrams sodium, and 0 milligram cholesterol.

Tip: To plump raisins, cover with 1 cup boiling water. Let stand 1 to 2 minutes; drain.

Antipasto Rice

1½ cups water
½ cup tomato juice
1 cup uncooked rice*
1 teaspoon dried basil leaves
1 teaspoon dried oregano
    leaves
½ teaspoon salt (optional)
1 can (14 ounces) artichoke
    hearts, drained and
    quartered

1 jar (7 ounces) roasted red
    peppers, drained and
    chopped
1 can (2¼ ounces) sliced ripe
    olives, drained
2 tablespoons snipped parsley
2 tablespoons lemon juice
½ teaspoon ground black
    pepper
2 tablespoons grated Parmesan
    cheese

Combine water, tomato juice, rice, basil, oregano, and salt in 2- to 3-quart saucepan. Bring to a boil; stir once or twice. Reduce heat; cover and simmer 15 minutes or until rice is tender and liquid is absorbed. Stir in artichokes, red peppers, olives, parsley, lemon juice, and black pepper. Cook 5 minutes longer or until thoroughly heated. Sprinkle with cheese.

Makes 8 servings

To microwave: Combine water, tomato juice, rice, basil, oregano, and salt in deep 2- to 3-quart microproof baking dish. Cover and cook on HIGH 5 minutes. Reduce setting to MEDIUM (50% power) and cook 15 minutes or until rice is tender and liquid is absorbed. Add artichokes, red peppers, olives, parsley, lemon juice, and black pepper. Cook on HIGH 2 to 3 minutes or until mixture is thoroughly heated. Sprinkle with cheese.

*Recipe based on regular-milled long grain white rice. For medium grain rice, use 1¼ cups water and cook for 15 minutes. For parboiled rice, use 1¾ cups water and cook for 20 to 25 minutes. For brown rice, use 1¾ cups water and cook for 45 to 50 minutes.

Each serving provides 131 calories, 3.7 grams protein, 1.6 grams fat, 26.5 grams carbohydrate, 1.3 grams dietary fiber, 522 milligrams sodium, and 1 milligram cholesterol.

Oriental Rice Pilaf

½ cup chopped onion
1 clove garlic, minced
1 tablespoon sesame oil
1¾ cups beef broth
1 cup uncooked rice*
1 tablespoon reduced-sodium soy sauce

⅛ to ¼ teaspoon red pepper flakes
⅓ cup thinly sliced green onions
⅓ cup diced red pepper
2 tablespoons sesame seeds, toasted

Cook onion and garlic in oil in 2- to 3-quart saucepan over medium heat until onion is tender. Add broth, rice, soy sauce, and pepper flakes. Bring to a boil; stir once or twice. Reduce heat; cover and simmer 15 to 20 minutes or until rice is tender and liquid is absorbed. Stir green onions, red pepper, and sesame seeds into cooked rice; cover and let stand 5 minutes. Fluff with fork. *Makes 6 servings*

* Recipe based on regular-milled long grain white rice. If using other types of rice, refer to chart on page 125 for adjustments of liquid and time.

Each serving provides 168 calories, 4.6 grams protein, 4.2 grams fat, 28.1 grams carbohydrate, 0.9 gram dietary fiber, 312 milligrams sodium, and 7 milligrams cholesterol.

Southwestern Vegetable Rice

2 cups chicken broth
1 cup uncooked rice*
⅔ cup diced green pepper
⅔ cup chopped tomato
½ cup chopped onion

1 tablespoon margarine
1 teaspoon chili powder
1 teaspoon ground cumin
¼ teaspoon ground red pepper

Combine all ingredients in 2- to 3-quart saucepan. Bring to a boil; stir once or twice. Reduce heat; cover and simmer 15 minutes or until rice is tender and liquid is absorbed. Fluff with fork. *Makes 6 servings*

To microwave: Combine all ingredients in deep 2- to 3-quart microproof baking dish. Cover and cook on HIGH 5 minutes. Reduce setting to MEDIUM (50% power); cook 15 minutes or until rice is tender and liquid is absorbed. Fluff with fork.

*Recipe based on regular-milled long grain white rice. If using other types of rice, refer to chart on page 125 for adjustments of liquid and time.

Each serving provides 158 calories, 4.4 grams protein, 2.9 grams fat, 28.2 grams carbohydrate, 1.3 grams dietary fiber, 290 milligrams sodium, and 0 milligram cholesterol.

Oriental Rice Pilaf

Health Nut Brown Rice

½ cup shredded carrot
½ cup shredded zucchini
3 tablespoons sunflower
   kernels
3 tablespoons sliced almonds
¼ teaspoon red pepper flakes
   (optional)

1 teaspoon margarine
3 cups cooked brown rice
   (cooked in chicken broth)
2 tablespoons snipped parsley

Cook carrot, zucchini, sunflower kernels, almonds, and pepper flakes in margarine in large skillet over medium-high heat until almonds are browned. Add rice and parsley; stir until heated. *Makes 6 servings*

To microwave: Combine carrot, zucchini, sunflower kernels, almonds, pepper flakes, and margarine in 2-quart microproof baking dish. Cook on HIGH 3 to 4 minutes or until almonds are lightly browned. Add rice and parsley; cook on HIGH 3 to 4 minutes, stirring after 2 minutes, or until heated.

Each serving provides 182 calories, 5.9 grams protein, 5.8 grams fat, 26.9 grams carbohydrate, 2.1 grams dietary fiber, 273 milligrams sodium, and 0 milligram cholesterol.

Risotto with Peas and Mushrooms

½ cup chopped onion
2 teaspoons margarine
1 cup uncooked rice
⅓ cup dry white wine
1 cup chicken broth
4 cups water
1 cup frozen peas, thawed

1 jar (2½ ounces) sliced
   mushrooms, drained
¼ cup grated Parmesan cheese
¼ teaspoon ground white
   pepper
⅓ cup 2% low-fat milk

Cook onion in margarine in large skillet over medium-high heat until soft. Add rice; stir 2 to 3 minutes. Add wine; stir until absorbed. Stir in broth. Cook, uncovered, stirring constantly, until broth is absorbed. Continue stirring and adding water, one cup at a time; allow each cup to be absorbed before adding another, until rice is tender and has a creamy consistency, 20 to 25 minutes. Stir in remaining ingredients. Stir until creamy, 1 to 2 minutes. Serve immediately. *Makes 6 servings*

Each serving provides 205 calories, 6.7 grams protein, 5.6 grams fat, 31.3 grams carbohydrate, 1.8 grams dietary fiber, 316 milligrams sodium, and 4 milligrams cholesterol.

Tip: Medium grain rice will yield the best consistency for risottos, but long grain rice can be used.

Stuffed Squash

6 small acorn squash, about
    ½ pound each
2 cups cooked rice
1 medium tart apple, cored
    and diced
½ cup finely chopped green
    onions
½ cup chopped celery
½ cup chopped dates

¼ cup rice bran (optional)
¼ cup chopped walnuts
2 tablespoons lemon juice
2 tablespoons margarine,
    melted
½ teaspoon ground cinnamon
¼ teaspoon ground nutmeg
4 gingersnap cookies, crushed
    (optional)

To microwave: Pierce squash with meat fork in two places. Cook on
HIGH 12 to 14 minutes or until just tender, turning squash over after
6 minutes. (Do not overcook.) Let stand 5 minutes. Cut in half and scoop
out seeds. Combine rice and remaining ingredients except cookies in large
bowl; mix lightly. Spoon rice mixture into squash halves; place on round
microproof dish. Cover tightly with vented plastic wrap. Cook on HIGH
4 to 6 minutes or until thoroughly heated. Sprinkle with gingersnap
crumbs before serving.   *Makes 6 servings*

Each serving provides 341 calories, 6.3 grams protein, 7.5 grams fat, 68.6 grams
carbohydrate, 5.8 grams dietary fiber, 324 milligrams sodium, and 0 milligram
cholesterol.

Pesto Rice and Vegetables

1½ cups packed basil, arugula,
    watercress, or spinach
    leaves
1 clove garlic
⅓ cup grated Parmesan cheese
1 tablespoon olive oil

Vegetable cooking spray
1½ cups broccoli flowerets
1 cup sliced carrots
3 cups cooked brown or white
    rice

Finely mince basil and garlic in food processor. Add cheese and oil. Pulse
until combined; scrape bowl as necessary. Coat large skillet with cooking
spray; place over medium-high heat until hot. Cook vegetables until
tender crisp. Stir in rice and basil mixture. Serve immediately.

Makes 6 servings

To microwave: Prepare basil mixture as directed above. Combine broccoli
and carrots in 2-quart microproof baking dish. Cover and cook on HIGH
2 minutes; stir. Cook on HIGH 1 to 1½ minutes longer or until vegetables
are tender crisp. Stir in rice and basil mixture. Cover and cook on HIGH
1½ to 2½ minutes, stirring every minute, or until hot. Serve immediately.

Each serving provides 166 calories, 5.4 grams protein, 4.6 grams fat, 26.4 grams
carbohydrate, 3.0 grams dietary fiber, 102 milligrams sodium, and 4 milligrams
cholesterol.

Barbecue
& More

From Your Favorite Brand Name Companies

and many more

*Charcoal Beef Kabobs (page 186) and Chili
Tomato Grilled Chicken (page 219)*

Barbecue Basics

CHOOSING A GRILL

Before you purchase a grill, consider where you grill, what you'll be cooking, the seasons you'll be grilling and the size of your budget. A small portable grill is fine if you usually barbecue smaller cuts of meat for a few people. For larger cuts of meat, bigger groups of people and year-round grilling, a large covered grill is worth the expense. Basic types of grills include: gas, brazier, covered cooker, water smoker and portable.

Gas Grill: Fast starts, accurate heat control, even cooking and year-round use make this the most convenient type of grill. Bottled gas is fed into burners under a bed of lava rock or ceramic coals—no charcoal is required.

Brazier: Simple models have hollowed fire bowls set on three or four legs. More elaborate braziers have half-hoods, covers, rotisseries and wheels.

Covered Cooker: Square, rectangular or kettle-shaped, this versatile grill does everything a brazier does. The cover also lets you roast, steam, smoke or cook whole meals in any season of the year. Draft controls on the lid and the base help control temperature.

Water Smoker: This is a heavy, dome-covered grill with two pans—one for charcoal and, above it, one for water. When the grill is covered, steam slowly cooks the food. Hickory chips or other aromatic wood can be added. The water smoker doubles as an open brazier when you remove the water pan and place the charcoal pan directly under the food.

Portable Grills: These include the familiar hibachi and small picnic grills on collapsible legs.

BARBECUE TOOLS AND ACCESSORIES

These tools will help make your barbecue cooking safer and more convenient.

Long-Handled Tongs, Basting Brush and Spatula: Moving hot coals and food around the grill, as well as basting and turning foods, can be dangerous. Select tools with long handles and hang them where you are working. You may want to purchase two pairs of tongs, one for coals and one for food.

Meat Thermometer: There is no better way to judge the doneness of meat than with a good quality meat thermometer that has been kept clean and in working order. Always remember to insert the thermometer into the center of the largest muscle of the meat, with the point away from bone, fat and rotisserie rod.

Heavy-Duty Mitts: You will prevent many burns by safeguarding your hands with big, thick mitts. Keep them close to the barbecue so they are always there when you need them.

Aluminum Foil Drip Pans: A drip pan placed beneath grilling meats will prevent flare-ups. The pan should be 1½ inches deep and extend about 3 inches beyond either end of the meat. The juices that collect in the drip pan may be used for a sauce or gravy.

Water Spritzer: For safety's sake, it's a good idea to keep a water-filled spray bottle near the barbecue for dousing flare-ups.

Other Tools and Accessories: A charcoal chimney or electric charcoal starter is useful for starting the fire without lighter fluid. Hinged wire baskets facilitate the turning of some foods, such as fish fillets. Long skewers made of noncorrosive metal or bamboo are indispensable for kabobs. Bamboo skewers should be soaked in water at least 20 minutes before grilling to prevent the bamboo from flaring up.

HOW TO LIGHT A CHARCOAL FIRE

The number of coals needed to barbecue foods depends on the size and type of grill and type and amount of food to be cooked. Certain weather conditions, such as wind, cold and high humidity, will require more coals to be used.

Arrange coals in a pyramid shape in center of grill 20 to 30 minutes before cooking. To start with lighter fluid, soak coals with about ½ cup of lighter fluid. Wait 1 minute, then light with a match.

To start with an electric starter, place starter in center of coals. Plug in 8 to 10 minutes or until ash begins to form around edges of coals. Unplug starter and remove. The electric starter will be very hot and should be placed in a safe, heat-resistant place to cool.

To start with a chimney starter, remove grid from grill and place chimney starter in the base of the grill. Crumble a few sheets of newspaper and place in bottom of chimney starter. Place coals on top of newspaper, then light the newspaper. The coals will be ready for grilling in 20 to 30 minutes. Carefully remove chimney starter. Be sure to wear mitts. This method does not use starter fluid.

When coals are ready, they will be ash gray during daylight and will glow at night. Spread coals into a single layer with tongs. To lower cooking temperature, spread coals farther apart or raise the grid, if possible. To make fire hotter, move coals closer together and tap off ash.

ARRANGING COALS FOR COOKING

For **direct cooking**, arrange the coals in a single layer directly under the food. Use this method for quick-cooking foods, such as hamburgers, steaks and fish.

For **indirect cooking**, arrange coals to one side of the grill. Place a drip pan under the food at the other side. For more heat, divide the coals on either side of the drip pan. Use this method for slow-cooking foods, such as roasts and whole chicken.

CHECKING CHARCOAL TEMPERATURE

To check the temperature of the coals, cautiously hold the palm of your hand about 4 inches above the coals. Count the number of seconds you can hold your hand in that position before the heat forces you to pull it away.

Seconds	Coal Temperature
2	hot, 375°F or more
3	medium-hot, 350°F to 375°F
4	medium, 300°F to 350°F
5	low, 200°F to 300°F

MARINATING TIPS

- Marinades add unique flavors to foods and help tenderize less-tender cuts of meat. Turn marinating foods occasionally to let the flavor infuse evenly.

Heavy-duty plastic bags are great to hold foods as they marinate.
- After food is removed from a marinade, the marinade may be used as a basting or dipping sauce. When using as a basting sauce, allow food to cook on the grill at least 5 minutes after the last application of marinade. When using as a dipping sauce, place marinade in a small saucepan and bring to a full boil. These precautions are necessary to prevent the cooked food from becoming contaminated with bacteria now present in the marinade from the raw food.
- Basting sauces containing sugar, honey or tomato products should be applied only during the last 15 to 30 minutes of grilling. This will prevent the food from charring. Basting sauces made from seasoned oils and butters may be brushed on throughout grilling.

BARBECUE TIPS

- Cleanup is easier if the grill rack is coated with vegetable oil or vegetable oil cooking spray before grilling.
- For barbecue safety, position the grill on a heat-proof surface, away from trees and bushes that could catch a spark and out of the path of traffic. Also, make sure the grill's vents are not clogged with ashes before starting a fire.
- To avoid flare-ups and charred food when grilling, remove visible fat from meat.
- If you partially cook foods in the microwave or on the range, immediately finish cooking the food on the grill. Do not refrigerate partially cooked foods or let them sit at room temperature before you complete cooking on the grill.
- Always serve cooked food from the grill on a clean plate, not one that held the raw food.
- In hot weather, food should never sit out for over 1 hour. Remember, keep hot foods hot and cold foods cold.
- For the best kabobs, parboil solid or starchy vegetables, such as carrots or potatoes, before using.
- Use long-handled tongs or spatula to turn meat. A fork or knife punctures meat and lets the juices escape.
- Use a meat thermometer to accurately determine the doneness of large cuts of meat or poultry cooked on the rotisserie or covered grill.
- For additional flavor, toss water-soaked wood chips, such as hickory or mesquite, onto hot coals before adding food. Adding wood chips to the coals will create smoke, so make sure the grill is in a well-ventilated area away from any open windows.
- Watch foods carefully during grilling. Total cooking time will vary with the type of food, position on the grill, weather, temperature of the coals and degree of doneness you desire.
- If you plan on grilling for more than 45 minutes, add 10 to 12 new coals around edges of coals just before you begin to cook. When the new coals are ready, move them to the center of the fire.

For the Barbecue Novice

These easy-to-prepare, easy-to-grill recipes will make your guests and family think you're an experienced barbecue chef!

SCANDINAVIAN BURGERS

    1 pound lean ground beef
    ¾ cup shredded zucchini
    ⅓ cup shredded carrot
    2 tablespoons finely minced onion
    1 tablespoon fresh chopped dill *or*
        1 teaspoon dried dill weed
    ½ teaspoon salt
        Dash freshly ground pepper
    1 egg, beaten
    ¼ cup beer
    4 whole-wheat buns or rye rolls (optional)

Preheat grill. Combine ground beef, zucchini, carrot, onion and seasonings in medium bowl; mix lightly. Stir in egg and beer. Shape into four patties.

Grill 8 minutes or to desired doneness, turning once. Serve on whole-wheat buns or rye rolls, if desired.   *Makes 4 servings*

GRILLED SMOKED SAUSAGE

    1 cup apricot or pineapple preserves
    1 tablespoon lemon juice
    1½ pounds smoked sausage

Heat preserves and strain; reserve fruit pieces. Combine strained preserve liquid with lemon juice. Grill whole sausage, on uncovered grill, over low KINGSFORD® Briquets 5 minutes. Brush with glaze; continue to grill and glaze sausage about 5 minutes longer, turning occasionally. Garnish with fruit pieces.
                                    Makes 6 servings

Top to bottom: Scandinavian Burgers, Grilled Smoked Sausage

Charcoal Beef Kabobs

CHARCOAL BEEF KABOBS

½ cup vegetable oil
¼ cup lemon juice
1½ tablespoons (½ package) HIDDEN
  VALLEY RANCH® Salad Dressing Mix
2 pounds beef top round or boneless
  sirloin steak, cut into 1-inch cubes
1 or 2 red, yellow or green peppers, cut
  into 1-inch squares
16 pearl onions *or* 1 medium onion, cut
  into wedges
8 cherry tomatoes

Combine oil, lemon juice and dry salad dressing mix. Pour over beef cubes in shallow dish. Cover and refrigerate 1 hour or longer. Drain beef; reserve marinade. Thread beef cubes, peppers and onion onto skewers. Grill kabobs, on uncovered grill, over medium-hot KINGSFORD® Briquets 15 minutes, brushing often with reserved marinade and turning to brown all sides. A few minutes before serving, add cherry tomatoes to ends of skewers.

Makes 4 servings

PACIFIC COAST BARBECUED SALMON

4 fresh or frozen salmon steaks, 1 inch thick (about 8 ounces each)
½ cup butter or margarine
2 tablespoons fresh lemon juice
1 tablespoon Worcestershire sauce

Thaw salmon steaks, if frozen. In saucepan, combine butter, lemon juice and Worcestershire sauce; simmer 5 minutes, stirring frequently. Brush salmon steaks with butter mixture. Place steaks in well-greased wire grill basket.

Grill steaks, on uncovered grill, over medium-hot KINGSFORD® Briquets 6 to 9 minutes or until lightly browned. Baste steaks with butter mixture and turn; grill 6 to 9 minutes longer, basting often, until fish flakes easily when tested with fork. *Makes 4 servings*

SALSA-MARINATED CHUCK STEAK

1 pound boneless beef chuck shoulder steak, cut 1 inch thick
½ cup medium salsa
⅓ cup fresh lime juice
2 tablespoons hoisin sauce*
2 teaspoons grated fresh ginger

Combine salsa, lime juice, hoisin sauce and ginger. Place beef chuck shoulder steak in plastic bag; add ½ salsa mixture, turning to coat steak. Close bag securely; marinate in refrigerator 6 to 8 hours (or overnight, if desired), turning at least once. Remove steak from marinade; discard marinade. Place steak on grid over medium coals. Grill to desired doneness (rare to medium), 14 to 20 minutes, turning once and brushing occasionally with reserved ½ salsa mixture. Carve steak into thin slices. *Makes 4 servings*

*Hoisin sauce is available in the Oriental section of the supermarket.

*Favorite Recipe from **National Live Stock and Meat Board***

Pacific Coast Barbecued Salmon

GRILLED RAINBOW TROUT WITH ITALIAN BUTTER

2 tablespoons butter or margarine,
   softened
1 tablespoon finely chopped red bell
   pepper
½ teaspoon dried Italian seasonings
4 CLEAR SPRINGS® Brand Idaho
   Rainbow Trout fillets (4 ounces each)
2 tablespoons grated Parmesan cheese
   (optional)

Cream butter, pepper and seasonings; chill and set aside. Over hot coals, place trout fillets, flesh side down, on oiled grid and cook about 2 minutes. Gently turn trout with spatula; continue cooking 2 minutes longer. Serve immediately with a dollop of Italian Butter and a sprinkle of Parmesan cheese.

Makes 4 servings

ISLANDER'S BEEF BARBECUE

3- to 3½-pound boneless beef chuck roast
¾ cup apricot-pineapple jam
2 tablespoons soy sauce
1 teaspoon ground ginger
1 teaspoon grated lemon peel

Slice roast across grain into ¼-inch-thick slices. Combine remaining ingredients in bowl; mix well. Grill beef slices, on uncovered grill, over medium-hot KINGSFORD® Briquets 8 to 10 minutes. Turn and baste often with jam mixture. *Makes 4 to 6 servings*

Note: If time permits, pierce meat several times with fork and marinate in jam mixture 1 to 4 hours in refrigerator. Drain meat; reserve jam mixture. Continue as directed above.

BEEF KABOBS ITALIANO

1 (8-ounce) can tomato sauce
⅓ cup REALEMON® Lemon Juice from
   Concentrate
2 tablespoons brown sugar
2 teaspoons WYLER'S® or STEERO®
   Beef-Flavor Instant Bouillon
1½ teaspoons thyme leaves
1 pound beef sirloin steak (about 1½ inch
   thick), cut into cubes
1 large green bell pepper, cut into bite-size
   pieces
2 medium onions, quartered and
   separated into bite-size pieces
8 ounces medium fresh mushrooms (about
   2 cups)
½ pint cherry tomatoes

In shallow dish or plastic bag, combine tomato sauce, ReaLemon® brand, sugar, bouillon and thyme; mix well. Add meat. Cover; marinate in refrigerator 6 hours or overnight. Skewer meat with vegetables. Grill or broil as desired, basting frequently with marinade. Refrigerate leftovers. *Makes 4 servings*

CHICKEN ITALIANO

½ cup WISH-BONE® Italian Dressing
2½ to 3 pounds chicken pieces*

In large shallow baking dish, pour Italian dressing over chicken. Cover and marinate in refrigerator, turning occasionally, 4 hours or overnight. Remove chicken; reserve marinade.

Grill or broil chicken, turning and basting frequently with reserved marinade, until done.
Makes about 4 servings

*Use 1 (2½- to 3-pound) beef London broil or beef round steak for chicken pieces.

Grilled Rainbow Trout with Italian Butter

ALL-AMERICAN CHEESEBURGERS

1 pound lean ground beef
1 tablespoon WYLER'S® or STEERO®
    Beef-Flavor Instant Bouillon
¼ cup chopped onion
4 slices BORDEN® Process American
    Cheese Food
4 hamburger buns, split, buttered and
    toasted
    Lettuce
4 slices tomato

In medium bowl, combine beef, bouillon and onion; mix well. Shape into 4 patties. Grill or broil to desired doneness. Top with cheese food slices; heat until cheese food begins to melt. Top bottom halves of buns with lettuce, tomato and meat patties. Serve open-face or with bun tops. Refrigerate leftovers.

Makes 4 servings

VARIATIONS

Santa Fe Burgers: Add 3 tablespoons salsa or taco sauce to ground beef. On warm tortilla, spread refried beans; top with shredded lettuce, cooked burger, cheese food slice, salsa and sour cream.

Kansas City Burgers: Add ½ cup thawed frozen hash browns and 2 tablespoons barbecue sauce to ground beef. Place each cooked burger on bun; top with cheese food slice, cooked, crumbled bacon and sliced green onion.

Manhattan Burgers: Add ¼ cup pizza sauce, 2 tablespoons chopped mushrooms and 3 tablespoons chopped pepperoni to ground beef. Place each cooked burger on grilled Italian bread; top with cheese food slice, pepperoni and green pepper.

Clockwise from left: Santa Fe Burger, Kansas City Burger, Manhattan Burger

Parmesan Seasoned Turkey

PARMESAN SEASONED TURKEY

  2 tablespoons butter or margarine, melted
1½ teaspoons grated Parmesan cheese
    Dash coarsely ground black pepper
    Dash crushed red pepper
    Dash onion powder
  4 slices BUTTERBALL® Slice 'N Serve
    Breast of Turkey, cut ⅜ inch thick

Combine butter, cheese, peppers and onion powder in small dish. Brush both sides of turkey with seasoned butter. Grill over medium coals 6 to 8 minutes or until hot. Turn over halfway through heating.

Makes 4 servings

GRILLED HAKE FILLETS

  2 pounds hake fillets, fresh or frozen
¼ cup French dressing
  1 tablespoon lemon juice
  1 tablespoon grated onion
  2 teaspoons salt
    Dash pepper

Thaw fish, if frozen. Cut into serving-size portions. Mix remaining ingredients in small bowl until blended. Baste fish with sauce. Arrange fish on well-greased grid. Grill, 4 inches from moderately hot coals, 15 to 18 minutes or until fish flakes easily when tested with fork. Turn and baste with remaining sauce halfway through cooking.

Makes 6 servings

*Favorite Recipe from **National Fisheries Institute***

Sizzling Meats

Try your hand with these saucy ribs, tasty burgers, eye-catching kabobs and succulent steaks grilled to flavorful perfection.

HOT AND SPICY SPARERIBS

1 rack pork spareribs, 3 pounds
2 tablespoons butter or margarine
1 medium onion, finely chopped
2 cloves garlic, minced
1 can (15 ounces) tomato sauce
⅔ cup cider vinegar
⅔ cup firmly packed brown sugar
2 tablespoons chili powder
1 tablespoon prepared mustard
½ teaspoon pepper

Melt butter in large skillet over low heat; add onion and garlic and sauté until tender. Add remaining ingredients, except ribs, and bring to a boil. Reduce heat and simmer 20 minutes, stirring occasionally.

Place large piece of aluminum foil over coals beneath grill to catch drippings. Baste meatiest side of ribs with sauce. Place ribs on grill, meatiest side down, about 6 inches above low coals; baste top side. Close grill hood. Cook about 20 minutes; turn ribs and baste. Cook 45 minutes more or until done, basting every 10 to 15 minutes with sauce.

Makes 3 servings

*Favorite Recipe from **National Pork Producers Council***

ORIENTAL STEAK KABOBS

1 cup (8 ounces) WISH-BONE® Italian, Robusto Italian or Lite Italian Dressing
¼ cup soy sauce
2 tablespoons brown sugar
½ teaspoon ground ginger
1 green onion, thinly sliced
1 pound boneless beef round, cut into 1-inch pieces
12 large mushrooms
2 cups broccoli florets
1 medium red pepper, cut into chunks

In large shallow baking dish, combine Italian dressing, soy sauce, brown sugar, ginger and onion. Add beef and vegetables; turn to coat. Cover and marinate in refrigerator, stirring occasionally, 4 hours or overnight. Remove beef and vegetables; reserve marinade.

Onto large skewers, thread beef with vegetables. Grill or broil, turning and basting frequently with reserved marinade, 10 minutes or until beef is done.

Makes about 4 servings

Hot and Spicy Spareribs

HONEY-GARLIC AMERICA'S CUT

4 America's Cut boneless center pork loin
   chops, 1¼ to 1½ inches thick
¼ cup lemon juice
¼ cup honey
2 tablespoons soy sauce
1 tablespoon dry sherry
2 cloves garlic, minced

Place chops in heavy plastic bag. Combine
remaining ingredients in small bowl. Pour over
chops, turning bag to coat. Close bag;
refrigerate 4 to 24 hours.

Prepare covered grill with drip pan in center
banked by medium-hot coals. Remove chops
from marinade; reserve marinade. Grill chops
12 to 15 minutes, turning once and basting
occasionally with reserved marinade.

Makes 4 servings

*Favorite Recipe from **National Pork Producers Council***

SPICY LAMB BURGERS

¼ cup chopped onion
1 teaspoon curry powder
1 tablespoon butter or margarine, melted
¼ cup finely chopped almonds
¼ cup crushed pineapple, drained
1½ pounds ground lamb
½ cup dry bread crumbs
2 eggs
⅛ teaspoon pepper
6 pita breads

Cook onion and curry powder in butter until
onion is tender. Stir in almonds and crushed
pineapple. Mix thoroughly with lamb, bread
crumbs, eggs and pepper. Shape meat mixture
into 6 patties. Grill patties, on uncovered grill,
over medium-hot MATCH LIGHT® Charcoal
Briquets about 5 minutes on each side, or until
done. Grill pita breads on edge of grill. Serve
lamb burgers in pita breads.

Makes 6 servings

Honey-Garlic America's Cut

Greek Burgers

GREEK BURGERS

Yogurt Sauce (recipe follows)
1 pound ground beef
2 tablespoons red wine
2 teaspoons ground cumin
1 tablespoon chopped fresh oregano *or*
    1 teaspoon dried oregano leaves
½ teaspoon salt
    Dash ground red pepper
    Dash ground black pepper
4 pita breads
    Lettuce
    Chopped tomatoes

Prepare Yogurt Sauce. Soak 4 bamboo skewers in water at least 20 minutes before using. Combine meat, wine and seasonings in medium bowl; mix lightly. Divide mixture into eight equal portions; form each portion into an oval, each about 4 inches long. Cover; chill 30 minutes.

Preheat grill. Insert skewers lengthwise through centers of ovals, placing 2 on each skewer. Grill about 8 minutes or to desired doneness, turning once. Fill pita breads with lettuce, meat and chopped tomatoes. Serve with Yogurt Sauce.   *Makes 4 servings*

YOGURT SAUCE

2 cups plain yogurt
1 cup chopped red onion
1 cup chopped cucumber
¼ cup chopped fresh mint *or*
    1½ tablespoons dried mint leaves
1 tablespoon chopped fresh marjoram or
    1 teaspoon dried marjoram leaves

Combine ingredients in small bowl. Cover; chill up to 4 hours before serving.

GRILLED LAMB FAJITAS

    3 tablespoons olive oil
    3 tablespoons tequila or orange juice
    2 tablespoons fresh lime juice
    1 teaspoon ground cumin
    1 teaspoon chili powder
    1 teaspoon dried oregano leaves, crushed
    ½ teaspoon salt
    ¼ teaspoon black pepper
    ¼ teaspoon red pepper flakes, crushed
    ¼ cup chopped fresh cilantro
 1½ pounds lean American lamb leg steaks,
        cut 1 inch thick
    6 green onions
    3 fresh poblano or ancho chilies (optional)
    1 red pepper, halved and seeded
    1 green pepper, halved and seeded
    1 yellow pepper, halved and seeded
   12 medium flour tortillas, warmed
        Salsa

For marinade, in small bowl combine oil, tequila, lime juice, cumin, chili powder, oregano, salt, black pepper, red pepper flakes and cilantro. Place lamb in glass dish. Pour marinade over lamb; cover and refrigerate 4 to 6 hours.

Ignite coals in barbecue; allow to burn until bright red and covered with gray ash. Drain lamb; discard marinade. Grill lamb, onions, chilies and red, green and yellow peppers 4 inches from coals. Cook steaks 5 to 6 minutes per side for medium-rare or to desired degree of doneness. Turn vegetables frequently until cooked. Slice lamb steaks and vegetables into ¼-inch-thick slices. Serve on tortillas, top with salsa and roll up.

Makes 12 servings

Favorite Recipe from American Lamb Council

Grilled Lamb Fajitas

Barbecued Beef Short Ribs

BARBECUED BEEF SHORT RIBS

    6 pounds beef chuck ribs, cut into 1-rib pieces
    1 cup water
    ¾ cup soy sauce
    ⅔ cup dry sherry
    ½ cup packed dark brown sugar
    6 cloves garlic, minced
    1 tablespoon ground red pepper
    1 tablespoon grated fresh ginger
    2 teaspoons Chinese five spice powder

Trim excess fat from ribs. In large roasting pan, arrange ribs in single layer. For marinade, in medium saucepan combine remaining ingredients. Cook over medium heat on range top until sugar is dissolved. Remove from heat; cool slightly. Pour marinade over ribs. Cover and marinate in refrigerator 1 hour, turning ribs once.

Cover roasting pan with foil. Arrange medium-hot KINGSFORD® Briquets around drip pan. Place roasting pan on grid; cover grill and cook ribs 45 minutes. Remove ribs from roasting pan and place directly on grid; reserve marinade. Continue cooking, in covered grill, 45 to 60 minutes longer or until ribs are tender, turning occasionally. Brush ribs again with reserved marinade just before serving.

Makes 8 servings

BUTTERFLIED LEG OF LAMB WITH ORANGE SAUCE

    3½- to 4-pound butterflied lamb leg
    ⅔ cup orange juice
    ½ cup orange marmalade
    1 teaspoon butter or margarine
    ½ teaspoon grated fresh ginger
    ¼ teaspoon dry mustard
    2 tablespoons lemon juice
    1 tablespoon cornstarch

Thread 2 long metal skewers through butterflied lamb leg to secure and facilitate turning the roast. Grill lamb, on covered grill, over medium coals to desired doneness. Allow 40 to 60 minutes total cooking time.

Meanwhile, combine orange juice, marmalade, butter, ginger and mustard in small saucepan. Cook over medium-low heat until marmalade is melted, stirring occasionally. Combine lemon juice and cornstarch; stir into orange juice mixture and cook until thickened. Remove from heat; reserve. Turn leg several times during cooking, brushing with ⅓ cup reserved sauce during last 10 minutes of cooking. Remove skewers and separate leg into three sections along natural seams. Carve each section across grain into thin slices. Serve remaining sauce with carved lamb.

Makes 10 to 12 servings

*Favorite Recipe from **National Live Stock and Meat Board***

TEXAS BARBECUE BEEF BRISKET

1 boneless beef brisket (6 to 8 pounds)
2 teaspoons paprika
1 teaspoon freshly ground black pepper, divided
1 tablespoon butter or margarine
1 medium onion, grated
1½ cups catsup
1 tablespoon fresh lemon juice
1 tablespoon Worcestershire sauce
1 teaspoon hot pepper sauce

Trim external fat on beef brisket to ¼ inch. Combine paprika and ½ teaspoon of the black pepper; rub evenly over surface of beef brisket. Place brisket, fat side down, in 11½×9-inch disposable foil pan. Add 1 cup water. Cover pan tightly with aluminum foil. Place in center of grid over very low coals (use a single layer of coals with space in between each); cover cooker. Cook 5 hours, turning brisket over every 1½ hours; use baster to remove fat from pan as it accumulates. Add ½ cup water, if needed, to pan during cooking. (Add just enough briquets during cooking to keep coals at a very low temperature.) Remove brisket from pan; place on grid, fat side down, directly over very low coals. Reserve pan drippings. Cover; continue cooking 30 minutes.

Meanwhile, skim fat from pan drippings; reserve 1 cup drippings. Melt butter in medium saucepan over medium heat. Add onion; cook until tender-crisp. Add reserved pan drippings, remaining ½ teaspoon black pepper, the catsup, lemon juice, Worcestershire sauce and hot pepper sauce; simmer 15 minutes. Carve brisket into thin slices across grain; serve with sauce. Garnish with fresh peppers and lemon and lime slices.   *Makes 18 to 24 servings*

Note: For a smoky flavor, soak oak, pecan, mesquite or hickory chips in water 30 minutes and add to very low coals.

*Favorite Recipe from **National Live Stock and Meat Board***

PEANUT PORK SATÉ

1 cup (8 ounces) WISH-BONE® Sweet 'n Spicy French or Lite Sweet 'n Spicy French Dressing
¼ cup peanut butter
1 tablespoon dry sherry
2 teaspoons soy sauce
½ to 1 teaspoon crushed red pepper
1 (1-inch) piece fresh ginger, peeled and cut into pieces *or* ½ teaspoon ground ginger
1 medium clove garlic
¼ cup water
1½ pounds pork tenderloin, sliced diagonally into ¼-inch strips*

In blender or food processor, blend sweet 'n spicy French dressing, peanut butter, sherry, soy sauce, pepper, ginger and garlic until smooth.

In large shallow baking dish, blend ½ cup dressing mixture with water; add pork and turn to coat. Cover and marinate in refrigerator, stirring occasionally, 4 hours or overnight. Cover and refrigerate remaining dressing mixture for use as basting sauce. Remove pork from marinade; discard marinade.

Onto 12-inch skewers thread pork strips, weaving back and forth. Grill or broil, turning and basting occasionally with reserved dressing mixture, 12 minutes or until pork is done.   *Makes about 6 servings*

*Use 1½ pounds boneless beef flank or round steak, sliced diagonally into ¼-inch strips for the pork strips.

Texas Barbecue Beef Brisket

Grilled Steaks with Vegetables

GRILLED STEAKS WITH VEGETABLES

  2 beef Porterhouse steaks, cut 1 to
        1½ inches thick (about 1 pound each)
  2 cloves garlic, finely minced, divided
1½ teaspoons dried basil leaves, divided
  ½ teaspoon coarse ground black pepper
  1 tablespoon olive oil
  1 large zucchini, cut into 2×½-inch pieces
  1 small onion, cut into thin wedges
1¼ cups sliced fresh mushrooms
  ¼ teaspoon salt
  6 cherry tomatoes, cut into halves

Season steaks with 1 clove of the garlic,
¾ teaspoon of the basil and the pepper. Place
steaks on grid over medium coals. Grill to
desired doneness, turning once. (Steaks cut

1 inch thick require about 16 minutes for rare;
20 minutes for medium. Steaks cut 1½ inches
thick require about 22 minutes for rare;
30 minutes for medium.) After turning steaks,
heat oil in large heavy skillet on grid over
coals. Add remaining clove garlic, the zucchini
and onion; cook and stir 4 to 5 minutes. Add
mushrooms, salt and remaining ¾ teaspoon
basil; continue cooking 2 minutes, stirring
frequently. Add tomatoes; heat through.

Makes 4 to 6 servings

Favorite Recipe from **National Live Stock and Meat Board**

SNAPPY BEEF ROAST

  1 boneless beef chuck eye roast or
        boneless chuck cross rib roast (3½ to
        4 pounds)
  ½ cup catsup
  3 tablespoons fresh lemon juice
  2 tablespoons vegetable oil
1½ tablespoons Worcestershire sauce
  2 large cloves garlic, minced
  1 teaspoon ground cumin
  1 teaspoon salt
  ½ teaspoon ground red pepper

Combine catsup, lemon juice, vegetable oil,
Worcestershire sauce, garlic, cumin, salt and
red pepper. Brush mixture evenly over surface
of beef chuck eye roast; place in large plastic
bag. Close bag securely; refrigerate 12 hours
(or overnight, if desired).

Insert meat thermometer in roast so bulb is
centered in thickest part, not resting in fat.
Cook in covered grill using indirect heat.
Arrange coals on lower grid around outside
edges; place drip pan between coals. When
coals are ash-gray (about 30 minutes), place
roast, fat side up, on grid above drip pan.
Cover cooker, leaving all vents open. Cook
roast to desired doneness, about 25 to
30 minutes per pound. Remove from grill when
meat thermometer registers 135°F for rare or
155°F for medium. Allow roast to stand 15 to
20 minutes in warm place before carving.
(Roast will continue to rise about 5°F in
temperature to 140°F for rare and 160°F for
medium.) Carve roast into thin slices.

Makes 12 to 16 servings

Favorite Recipe from **National Live Stock and Meat Board**

LAMB SHASLEK
(Shish Kebab)

½ cup fresh lemon juice
3 tablespoons virgin olive oil
⅓ cup minced onion
4 cloves garlic, minced
1 tablespoon cracked pepper
1 teaspoon coarse salt
1½- pound fresh American lamb sirloin
    roast, cut into 2-inch cubes
1 small red onion, cut into 8 wedges
1 small white onion, cut into 8 wedges
1 lemon, cut into 8 wedges, for garnish

For marinade, in small bowl combine lemon juice, oil, minced onion, garlic, pepper and salt. In glass dish, place lamb and red and white onions. Pour marinade over lamb and onions; cover and refrigerate 6 to 24 hours. Stir lamb occasionally. Drain lamb and onions; discard marinade. Thread red onion, lamb and white onion onto skewers, ending with lemon wedge.

Ignite coals in barbecue; allow to burn until bright red and covered with gray ash. Grill lamb shaslek 4 inches from coals 5 to 6 minutes per side for medium-rare or until desired degree of doneness.

Makes 4 servings

*Favorite Recipe from **American Lamb Council***

Lamb Shaslek

Raspberry-Glazed Lamb Ribs

RASPBERRY-GLAZED LAMB RIBS

   2 Denver ribs of American lamb (about
      6 ounces), 8 ribs each
 ½ teaspoon salt
 ¼ teaspoon pepper
 ¼ teaspoon paprika
 ½ cup red wine vinegar or raspberry
      vinegar
 ½ cup white wine
 ½ cup raspberry jam, seedless
   1 tablespoon shallots, minced
   1 tablespoon cornstarch
   1 tablespoon water

One hour before grilling, rub salt, pepper and
paprika into lamb ribs. In medium saucepan,
combine vinegar, white wine, raspberry jam
and shallots. Stir over medium heat until jam is
melted. Stir together cornstarch and water; add
to raspberry mixture and stir sauce until
smooth and clear.

Preheat grill. Move hot white coals to each side
of grill. Place foil drip pan in center. Place
lamb ribs in center of pan. Cover and cook
50 to 60 minutes, turning every 10 minutes.
Brush on glaze during last 10 to 15 minutes of
grilling.   *Makes 2 servings*

Favorite Recipe from American Lamb Council

TEXAS-STYLE STEAK ON HOT BREAD

 ½ cup olive or vegetable oil
 ¼ cup lime juice
 ¼ cup red wine vinegar
   1 medium onion, finely chopped
   1 large clove garlic, minced
   1 teaspoon chili powder
 ½ teaspoon salt
 ¼ teaspoon ground cumin
 1½ pounds beef skirt or flank steak
   1 round loaf French or sourdough bread
   1 cup Mexican-style salsa
   1 cup guacamole

Combine oil, lime juice, vinegar, onion, garlic,
chili powder, salt and cumin in large glass dish.
Pound steak to ¼-inch thickness. Place steak in
marinade; turn to coat. Cover and refrigerate
overnight or several hours, turning several
times. Drain steak; discard marinade. Grill
steak, on covered grill, over medium-hot
KINGSFORD® with Mesquite Charcoal
Briquets 4 to 8 minutes on each side or until
done. Cut bread into 1-inch slices and toast on
grill. Heat salsa. Arrange steak, sliced into
¾-inch diagonal strips, on toasted bread. Top
with hot salsa and guacamole.

Makes 4 to 6 servings

CAMPERS' PIZZA

¼ pound ground beef (80% lean)
1 medium onion, chopped
½ teaspoon salt
1 can (8 ounces) refrigerated crescent rolls
1 can (8 ounces) pizza sauce
1 can (4 ounces) mushroom stems and
    pieces, drained and chopped
1 can (2½ ounces) sliced pitted ripe
    olives, drained
⅓ cup coarsely chopped green bell pepper
1 cup (4 ounces) shredded mozzarella
    cheese
1 teaspoon dried oregano leaves

Brown ground beef and onion in well-seasoned 11- to 12-inch cast-iron skillet over medium coals. Remove to paper towels; season with salt. Pour off drippings from pan. Separate crescent dough into triangles; place in skillet, points toward center, to form circle. Press edges together to form bottom crust and 1-inch rim up side of pan. Spread half of pizza sauce over dough; spoon ground beef mixture over sauce. Top with mushrooms, olives and green pepper. Pour remaining sauce over all; sprinkle with cheese and oregano. Place pan in center of grid over medium coals. Place cover on grill; cook 20 to 30 minutes or until crust is lightly browned. *Makes 4 servings*

Note: If cooked over open grill or coals, cover pan securely with foil.

*Favorite Recipe from **National Live Stock and Meat Board***

Campers' Pizza

BARBECUED PORK LEG

1 fresh pork leg, skinned, boned, trimmed
  of fat, rolled and tied (14 to
  16 pounds)
Sam's Mop Sauce (recipe follows)
K.C. MASTERPIECE® Hickory
  Barbecue Sauce

Arrange medium-hot KINGSFORD® Briquets
around drip pan. Place prepared pork leg over
drip pan; cover grill and cook pork 4 to
4½ hours or until thermometer inserted into
thickest portion registers 170°F. Baste pork
with Sam's Mop Sauce every 30 minutes,
patting a thin coating of sauce on meat with
cotton swab mop or pastry brush. Let stand,
covered with foil, 10 minutes before serving.

Meanwhile, in saucepan, combine half the
remaining mop sauce with an equal amount of
barbecue sauce. Heat through and serve with
slices of pork.   *Makes about 20 servings*

Note: The final weight of the fresh pork leg for
grilling should be 8 to 10 pounds. To save time,
you can have the butcher prepare the fresh
pork leg for you.

SAM'S MOP SAUCE

  1 lemon
  1 cup water
  1 cup cider vinegar
  1 tablespoon butter or margarine
  1 tablespoon olive oil
  ½ teaspoon ground red pepper
1½ to 3 teaspoons hot pepper sauce
1½ to 3 teaspoons Worcestershire sauce
1½ teaspoons black pepper

With vegetable peeler, remove peel from
lemon; squeeze juice from lemon. In heavy
saucepan, combine lemon peel, juice and
remaining ingredients. Bring to boil. Place
saucepan on grill to keep warm, if space
permits.   *Makes 2¼ cups*

Barbecued Pork Leg

Beef Fajitas

BEEF FAJITAS

½ cup REALEMON® Lemon Juice from
    Concentrate
¼ cup vegetable oil
2 cloves garlic, finely chopped
2 teaspoons WYLER'S® or STEERO®
    Beef-Flavor Instant Bouillon
1 (1- to 1½-pound) beef top round steak
10 (6-inch) flour tortillas, warmed
    according to package directions
    Picante sauce, shredded lettuce,
    shredded cheddar cheese, sliced green
    onions for garnish

In shallow dish or plastic bag, combine
ReaLemon® brand, oil, garlic and bouillon; add
meat. Cover; marinate in refrigerator 6 hours
or overnight. Remove meat from marinade;
grill or broil as desired, basting frequently with
marinade. Slice meat diagonally into thin
strips; place on tortillas. Top with one or more
garnishes; fold tortillas. Serve immediately.
Refrigerate leftovers.   *Makes 10 fajitas*

HONEY MUSTARD PORK TENDERLOIN

¼ cup vegetable oil
2 tablespoons brown sugar
2 tablespoons honey
2 tablespoons REALEMON® Lemon Juice
    from Concentrate
1 tablespoon Dijon-style mustard
2 teaspoons WYLER'S® or STEERO®
    Beef- or Chicken-Flavor Instant
    Bouillon
1 (¾- to 1-pound) pork tenderloin

In shallow dish or plastic bag, combine all
ingredients except meat; add meat. Cover;
marinate in refrigerator 6 hours or overnight.
Remove meat from marinade; grill or broil as
desired, basting frequently with marinade.
Refrigerate leftovers.

Makes 2 to 4 servings

Kamaaina Spareribs

KAMAAINA SPARERIBS

    4 pounds lean pork spareribs
      Salt and pepper
    1 can (20 ounces) DOLE® Crushed
         Pineapple in Juice, drained
    1 cup catsup
    ½ cup packed brown sugar
    ⅓ cup red wine vinegar
    ¼ cup soy sauce
    1 teaspoon ground ginger
    ½ teaspoon dry mustard
    ¼ teaspoon garlic powder

Have butcher cut across rib bones to make
strips 1½ inches wide. Preheat oven to 350°F.
Place ribs close together in single layer in
baking pan. Sprinkle with salt and pepper to
taste. Cover tightly with aluminum foil. Bake
1 hour. Uncover; pour off and discard drippings.

In bowl, combine remaining ingredients.
Spoon sauce over ribs. Place ribs over hot
coals. Grill 15 minutes or until ribs are tender
and glazed.   *Makes 6 servings*

BARBECUED SAUSAGE KABOBS

    1 pound ECKRICH® Smoked Sausage, cut
        into 1-inch pieces
    1 cup dried apricots
    1 can (12 ounces) beer
    ½ red bell pepper, cut into 1¼-inch squares
    ½ green bell pepper, cut into 1¼-inch
        squares
    1 Spanish onion, cut into wedges
    ¼ pound fresh medium mushrooms
    ¾ cup apricot preserves
    2 tablespoons chili sauce
    1 tablespoon prepared mustard
    1 teaspoon Worcestershire sauce

Simmer sausage and apricots in beer in large
saucepan over low heat 10 minutes. Add
peppers to sausage mixture; remove from heat.
Let stand 10 minutes. To assemble kabobs,
thread on skewers sausage, onion, red and
green peppers, mushrooms and apricots.
Combine preserves, chili sauce, mustard and
Worcestershire sauce in small saucepan. Heat
over medium heat, stirring until blended.
Brush kabobs with sauce. Grill or broil,
4 inches from heat, 10 minutes, turning and
brushing with more sauce after 5 minutes.
Brush with remaining sauce and serve.
                         Makes 4 servings

CURRIED BEEF AND FRUIT KABOBS

1- to 1¼-pound beef top round or boneless
    beef sirloin steak, cut 1 inch thick
1 cup plain yogurt
2 teaspoons fresh lemon juice
1½ teaspoons curry powder
⅛ to ¼ teaspoon ground red pepper
1 ripe mango* (about 1 pound)
    Salt to taste

Partially freeze beef top round steak to firm;
slice into ⅛- to ¼-inch-thick strips. Combine
yogurt, lemon juice, curry powder and red
pepper. Place beef strips and marinade in
plastic bag, turning to coat. Close bag securely
and marinate in refrigerator 30 minutes,
turning occasionally. Meanwhile, soak eight
12-inch bamboo skewers in water 20 minutes.
Peel mango and cut into ¾-inch pieces.
Remove beef from marinade; discard
marinade. Thread an equal amount of beef
strips (weaving back and forth) and mango
pieces on each skewer. Place kabobs on grid
over medium coals. Grill 4 to 5 minutes,
turning once. Season with salt to taste.

Makes 4 servings

*Peaches, nectarines, plums or pineapple may
be substituted for mango. Peel and cut fruit
into ¾-inch pieces.

Note: Kabobs may also be cooked covered over
medium coals. Grill 3 to 4 minutes, turning
once.

*Favorite Recipe from **National Live Stock and Meat Board***

BIRTHDAY BURGERS

¾ cup boiling water
¼ cup bulgur (cracked wheat)
⅓ cup whole natural almonds
1 pound lean ground beef or ground turkey
¼ cup chopped green onions
1 teaspoon garlic salt
1 teaspoon dried basil leaves
4 hamburger buns
    Lettuce
    Tomato slices
    Red onion slices

Pour water over bulgur; let stand until cool.
Place almonds in single layer on baking sheet.
Bake at 350°F, 12 to 15 minutes, stirring
occasionally, until lightly toasted. Cool; chop
coarsely. Drain bulgur well. Combine bulgur,
almonds, ground beef, green onions, garlic salt
and basil; mix well. Shape into 4 patties. Grill
or broil until desired doneness. Serve on
hamburger buns with lettuce, tomatoes and red
onions.　　　　　*Makes 4 servings*

*Favorite Recipe from **Almond Board of California***

Birthday Burgers

Fired-Up Poultry

Grilled chicken, Cornish hens and turkey taste great! Kabobs, burgers and boneless pieces cook in minutes. Quarters, halves and whole poultry need a slower heat and longer cooking time.

ZINGY BARBECUED CHICKEN

   1 broiler-fryer chicken, cut into parts
   ½ cup grapefruit juice
   ½ cup apple cider vinegar
   ½ cup vegetable oil
   ¼ cup chopped onion
   1 egg
   ½ teaspoon celery salt
   ½ teaspoon ground ginger
   ⅛ teaspoon pepper

In blender container, place all ingredients except chicken; blend 30 seconds. In small saucepan, pour blended sauce mixture and heat about 5 minutes, until slightly thick. Remove from heat; dip chicken in sauce one piece at a time, turning to thoroughly coat. Reserve sauce.

Place chicken on prepared grill, skin side up, about 8 inches from heat. Grill, turning every 10 minutes, for about 50 minutes or until fork tender and juices run clear. Brush generously with reserved sauce during last 20 minutes of grilling. Watch chicken carefully as egg in sauce may cause chicken to become too brown. *Makes 4 servings*

*Favorite Recipe from **National Broiler Council***

GRILLED TURKEY WITH VEGETABLE PIZZAZZ

   1½ pounds turkey breast, cut into 2-inch
        pieces
   2 medium zucchini, cut into 1-inch chunks
   12 large mushrooms
   1 medium red pepper, cut into 1½-inch
        pieces
   12 jumbo pimiento-stuffed olives
   1 tablespoon vegetable oil
   1 cup pizza sauce
   1 tablespoon dried basil leaves

Thread turkey, zucchini, mushrooms, pepper and olives alternately on skewers; brush thoroughly with oil. Mix pizza sauce and basil; reserve. Grill kabobs, on uncovered grill, over medium-hot MATCH LIGHT® Charcoal Briquets about 10 minutes, turning occasionally. Baste with reserved pizza sauce and continue to grill about 15 minutes, basting and turning 2 to 3 times, until turkey is tender and vegetables are cooked.

Makes 6 servings

Zingy Barbecued Chicken

SWEET AND SPICY CHICKEN BARBECUE

1½ cups DOLE® Pineapple Orange Juice
1 cup orange marmalade
⅔ cup teriyaki sauce
½ cup packed brown sugar
½ teaspoon ground cloves
½ teaspoon ground ginger
4 frying chickens (about 2 pounds each), halved or quartered
Salt and pepper
DOLE® Pineapple Slices, drained
4 teaspoons cornstarch

In saucepan, combine juice, marmalade, teriyaki sauce, brown sugar, cloves and ginger. Heat until sugar dissolves; let cool. Sprinkle chicken with salt and pepper to taste. Place in glass baking dish. Pour juice mixture over chicken; turn to coat all sides. Marinate, covered, 2 hours in refrigerator, turning often.

Preheat oven to 350°F. Light charcoal grill. Drain chicken; reserve marinade. Bake chicken in oven 20 minutes. Arrange chicken on lightly greased grid 4 to 6 inches above glowing coals. Grill, turning and basting often with reserved marinade, 20 to 25 minutes or until meat near bone is no longer pink. Grill pineapple slices 3 minutes or until heated through.

In small saucepan, dissolve cornstarch in remaining marinade. Cook over medium heat until sauce boils and thickens. To serve, arrange chicken and pineapple on plate; spoon sauce over tops.   *Makes 8 servings*

JALAPEÑO GRILLED CHICKEN

1 broiler-fryer chicken, quartered
2 tablespoons vegetable oil
¼ cup chopped onion
1 clove garlic, minced
1 cup catsup
2 tablespoons vinegar
1 tablespoon brown sugar
1 tablespoon minced jalapeño peppers
½ teaspoon salt
½ teaspoon dry mustard

In saucepan, heat oil to medium temperature. Add onion and garlic; cook, stirring occasionally, about 5 minutes or until onion is tender. Add catsup, vinegar, brown sugar, jalapeño peppers, salt and mustard. Cook, stirring occasionally, until mixture is blended. Place chicken, skin side up, on prepared grill about 8 inches from heat. Grill, turning every 8 to 10 minutes, about 50 minutes. Brush chicken with sauce; grill, turning and basting with sauce every 5 minutes, about 25 minutes more or until chicken is fork tender.

Makes 4 servings

*Favorite Recipe from **Delmarva Poultry Industry, Inc.***

Sweet and Spicy Chicken Barbecue

Turkey Fajitas

TURKEY FAJITAS

⅓ cup REALEMON® Lemon Juice from
    Concentrate
2 tablespoons vegetable oil
1 tablespoon WYLER'S® or STEERO®
    Chicken-Flavor Instant Bouillon
3 cloves garlic, finely chopped
2 fresh turkey breast tenderloins (about
    1 pound), pierced with fork
8 (8-inch) flour tortillas, warmed
    according to package directions
  Shredded lettuce and cheese, sliced ripe
    olives and green onions, salsa,
    guacamole and sour cream for garnish

In shallow dish or plastic bag, combine
ReaLemon® brand, oil, bouillon and garlic; add
turkey. Cover; marinate in refrigerator 4 hours
or overnight, turning occasionally. Remove
turkey from marinade; reserve marinade. Grill
or broil as desired, 6 inches from heat,
10 minutes per side or until no longer pink,
basting frequently with reserved marinade. Let
stand 10 minutes. Slice turkey; place on
tortillas. Top with one or more of the garnishes;
fold tortillas. Serve immediately. Refrigerate
leftovers. *Makes 4 servings*

STUFFED GRILLED GAME HENS

4 (1 to 1½ pounds each) Cornish game
    hens, thawed
½ cup orange juice
½ cup vegetable oil
1 garlic clove, minced
⅛ teaspoon pepper
1⅓ cups Original MINUTE® Rice
1 (8-ounce) container PHILADELPHIA
    BRAND® Soft Cream Cheese
¼ cup golden raisins
¼ cup chopped fresh parsley
2 tablespoons orange juice
1 shallot, minced
1½ teaspoons grated orange peel
½ teaspoon salt
⅛ teaspoon pepper
    Whole cooked carrots (optional)

Remove giblets; discard or save for another
use. Rinse hens; pat dry.

Marinate hens in combined ½ cup orange
juice, oil, garlic and ⅛ teaspoon pepper in
refrigerator 30 minutes, basting occasionally.

Prepare coals for grilling.

Prepare rice according to package directions.
Mix together rice and remaining ingredients
except carrots in medium bowl. Remove hens
from marinade, reserving marinade for
basting. Stuff hens with rice mixture; close
openings with skewers.

Place aluminum drip pan in center of charcoal
grate under grilling rack. Arrange hot coals
around drip pan.

Place hens, breast side up, on greased grill
directly over drip pan. Grill, covered, 1 hour
and 15 minutes to 1 hour and 30 minutes or
until tender, brushing frequently with reserved
marinade.

Serve with whole carrots, if desired.

Makes 4 servings

TASTY TACO CHICKEN GRILL

1 broiler-fryer chicken, cut into parts
1 small onion, minced
1 can (8 ounces) Spanish-style tomato
    sauce
1 can (4 ounces) taco sauce
¼ cup molasses
2 tablespoons vinegar
1 tablespoon vegetable oil
1 teaspoon salt
½ teaspoon oregano leaves
⅛ teaspoon pepper
½ cup shredded Monterey Jack cheese

In small saucepan, make sauce by mixing
together onion, tomato sauce, taco sauce,
molasses, vinegar, oil, salt, oregano and
pepper; bring sauce to a boil. Remove from
heat and cool 2 minutes. In large shallow dish,
place chicken; pour sauce over chicken. Cover
and marinate in refrigerator at least 1 hour.

Drain chicken; reserve sauce. Place chicken on
prepared grill, skin side up, about 8 inches
from heat. Grill, turning every 10 minutes,
about 50 minutes or until fork tender and
juices run clear. Brush generously with
reserved sauce during last 20 minutes of
grilling. When chicken is done, place on
platter; sprinkle with cheese.

Makes 4 servings

*Favorite recipe from **National Broiler Council***

TURKEY BURGERS

1 pound ground fresh turkey
¼ cup BENNETT'S® Chili Sauce
1 teaspoon WYLER'S® or STEERO®
    Chicken-Flavor Instant Bouillon

Combine ingredients; shape into patties. Grill,
broil or pan-fry until no longer pink in center.
Refrigerate leftovers.   *Makes 4 servings*

Stuffed Grilled Game Hens

BUFFALO TURKEY KABOBS

⅔ cup HELLMANN'S® or BEST FOODS® Real, Light or Cholesterol Free Reduced Calorie Mayonnaise, divided
1 teaspoon hot pepper sauce
1½ pounds boneless turkey breast, cut into 1-inch cubes
2 red bell peppers *or* 1 red and 1 yellow bell pepper, cut into 1-inch squares
2 medium onions, cut into wedges
¼ cup (1 ounce) crumbed blue cheese
2 tablespoons milk
1 medium stalk celery, minced
1 medium carrot, minced

In medium bowl, combine ⅓ cup of the mayonnaise and the hot pepper sauce. Stir in turkey. Cover and marinate in refrigerator 20 minutes. Drain turkey; discard marinade. On 6 skewers, thread turkey, peppers and onions. Grill or broil, 5 inches from heat, brushing with remaining mayonnaise mixture and turning frequently, 12 to 15 minutes. Meanwhile, in small bowl blend remaining ⅓ cup mayonnaise with blue cheese and milk. Stir in celery and carrot. Serve with kabobs.

Makes 6 servings

Note: For best results, use Real Mayonnaise. If using Light or Cholesterol Free Reduced Calorie Mayonnaise, use sauce the same day.

SPICY THAI CHICKEN

¾ cup canned cream of coconut
3 tablespoons lime juice
3 tablespoons soy sauce
8 sprigs cilantro
3 large cloves garlic
3 large green onions, cut up
3 anchovy fillets
1 teaspoon TABASCO® Brand Pepper Sauce
2 whole boneless skinless chicken breasts, cut into halves (about 1½ pounds)

In blender container or food processor, combine cream of coconut, lime juice, soy sauce, cilantro, garlic, green onions, anchovies and Tabasco® sauce. Cover; process until smooth. Place chicken in large shallow dish or plastic bag; add marinade. Cover; refrigerate at least 2 hours, turning chicken occasionally.

Drain chicken; reserve marinade. Place chicken on grill about 5 inches from source of heat. Brush generously with marinade. Grill 5 minutes. Turn chicken; brush with reserved marinade. Grill 5 minutes longer or until chicken is cooked. Heat any remaining marinade to a boil; serve as dipping sauce for chicken.

Makes 4 servings

GRILLED CHICKEN POLYNESIAN TREAT

12 broiler-fryer chicken thighs
2 tablespoons butter or margarine
1 small onion, minced
¾ cup vinegar
¼ cup soy sauce
¼ cup plum jam
¼ teaspoon salt
1 bay leaf
3 large pineapples, cut lengthwise into halves
2 large green peppers, sliced into rings

In small saucepan, melt butter over medium heat; add onion. Stir and cook about 3 minutes or until onion is clear and soft. Add vinegar, soy sauce and plum jam. Bring mixture to a boil, stirring constantly. Remove from heat and stir in salt and bay leaf. In large shallow dish, place chicken thighs; pour hot sauce over chicken. Cover and marinate in refrigerator at least 1 hour.

Remove chicken from sauce; reserve sauce. Place chicken thighs on prepared grill, skin side up, about 8 inches from heat. Grill about 15 minutes or until brown on one side. Turn and continue grilling 15 minutes longer. Chicken is done when fork tender and juices run clear. Brush generously with reserved sauce during entire grilling time. Serve chicken thighs in scooped out pineapple halves and top with green pepper rings. *Makes 6 servings*

Favorite Recipe from **National Broiler Council**

Buffalo Turkey Kabobs

COOL GRILLED CHICKEN SALAD

1 pound boneless, skinless chicken breasts
¼ cup lemon juice
2 tablespoons olive or vegetable oil
1 teaspoon dried tarragon leaves, crushed
¾ teaspoon LAWRY'S® Garlic Salt
1 quart salad greens, torn into bite-size pieces
6 medium red potatoes, cooked, cooled and cut into chunks
1 cup shredded carrot

Rinse chicken and place in resealable plastic bag. In small bowl, combine lemon juice, oil, tarragon and Garlic Salt; blend well. Pour marinade over chicken; seal bag and refrigerate 30 to 45 minutes or overnight. Drain chicken; reserve marinade. Grill or broil chicken 4 minutes on each side, basting with reserved marinade, until golden and cooked through. Cool and cut into strips. Line individual plates with salad greens. Arrange potato chunks, carrot and chicken on top.

Makes 4 main-dish servings

Hint: For a more colorful salad, add sliced tomatoes or shredded red cabbage.

SPICY BARBECUED WINGETTES

13 PERDUE OVEN STUFFER Roaster Wingettes
⅔ cup cider vinegar
⅓ cup vegetable oil
½ teaspoon hot pepper sauce
¼ teaspoon crushed dried red pepper
1 clove garlic, minced or pressed

Rinse wingettes and pat dry; place in shallow dish. In small saucepan over medium heat, stir together remaining ingredients. Cook about 5 minutes or until mixture is hot; pour over wingettes. Cover; refrigerate several hours or overnight.

Prepare outdoor grill for cooking or preheat broiler. Remove wingettes from marinade; reserve marinade. Grill 6 inches from source of heat or broil indoors 25 to 35 minutes, turning and basting frequently with reserved marinade. Let stand 5 minutes before serving.

Makes 6 servings

CHICKEN KABOBS WITH PEANUT SAUCE

2 whole broiler-fryer chicken breasts, halved, boned, skinned, cut into 1-inch pieces
¼ cup finely chopped onion
2 tablespoons white wine
2 tablespoons soy sauce
1 tablespoon brown sugar
1 tablespoon vegetable oil
½ teaspoon ground coriander
1 clove garlic, crushed
2 cans (8 ounces each) pineapple chunks in natural juice, drained
2 red or green peppers, halved, cored, cut into 1-inch pieces
Peanut Sauce (recipe follows)

In shallow, nonmetallic dish, mix together onion, wine, soy sauce, brown sugar, oil, coriander and garlic. Add chicken, stirring to coat. Cover and marinate in refrigerator, stirring occasionally, 1 hour. Drain chicken; reserve marinade. On each of 8 skewers, thread chicken, pineapple and peppers. Place chicken on prepared grill about 8 inches from heat. Grill, turning and basting frequently with reserved marinade, about 20 minutes or until chicken is fork tender. Serve with Peanut Sauce. *Makes 4 servings*

Peanut Sauce: In saucepan, place ½ cup chunky peanut butter, ¼ cup finely chopped onion, ¼ cup canned cream of coconut, ¼ cup water, 2 tablespoons soy sauce, 1 tablespoon brown sugar and ¼ tablespoon crushed red pepper flakes. Heat, stirring, until mixture boils. *Makes about 1¼ cups*

Favorite Recipe from **Delmarva Poultry Industry, Inc.**

Cool Grilled Chicken Salad

Grilled Cornish Game Hens

GRILLED CORNISH GAME HENS

- 2 Cornish game hens (1 to 1½ pounds each)
- 3 tablespoons olive oil
- ⅓ cup lemon juice
- 1 tablespoon black peppercorns, coarsely crushed
- ½ teaspoon salt
  Fresh rosemary sprigs (optional)

Split hens lengthwise. Rinse hen halves; pat dry with paper toweling.

For marinade, in small bowl combine olive oil, lemon juice, peppercorns and salt. Place hen halves in large plastic bag. Set in bowl. Pour marinade over hens. Close bag and refrigerate several hours or overnight, turning hen halves occasionally to coat with marinade.

Arrange medium-hot KINGSFORD® Briquets around drip pan. Just before grilling, add a rosemary sprig to coals. Remove hens from marinade; reserve marinade. Place hens, skin side up, over drip pan. Cover grill and cook 45 minutes or until thigh moves easily and juices run clear. Baste with reserved marinade occasionally. Garnish with rosemary sprigs, if desired.   *Makes 4 servings*

BARBECUED CHICKEN

1 cup chicken broth
¼ cup catsup
2 tablespoons vinegar
2 tablespoons Worcestershire sauce
2 tablespoons finely chopped onion
1 teaspoon dry mustard
½ teaspoon garlic salt
½ teaspoon salt
¼ teaspoon pepper
1 broiler-fryer chicken (2 to 3 pounds),
    quartered

Combine all ingredients, except chicken, in small saucepan. Bring to boil; cool slightly. Place chicken in shallow glass dish. Pour warm sauce over chicken; cover and refrigerate at least 2 hours. Drain chicken; reserve marinade. Grill chicken, skin side up, on uncovered grill, over hot KINGSFORD® Briquets 40 to 55 minutes, basting often with reserved marinade and turning frequently, until chicken is fork tender. *Makes 4 to 5 servings*

CHICKEN VEGETABLE KABOBS

½ cup WISH-BONE® Italian Dressing
¼ cup dry white wine
1 pound boneless chicken breasts, cubed
1 medium zucchini, cut into ½-inch pieces
1 large green pepper, cut into chunks

In large shallow baking dish, blend Italian dressing with wine. Add chicken and vegetables and turn to coat. Cover and marinate in refrigerator, turning occasionally, at least 2 hours. Remove chicken and vegetables; reserve marinade.

Onto skewers; thread chicken and vegetables. Grill or broil, turning and basting frequently with reserved marinade, until chicken is done. *Makes about 4 servings*

CHILI TOMATO GRILLED CHICKEN

6 broiler-fryer chicken quarters
2 tablespoons vegetable oil
½ cup finely chopped onion
1 clove garlic, minced
1 chicken bouillon cube
½ cup hot water
1 bottle (8 ounces) taco sauce *or* 1 can
    (8 ounces) tomato sauce
1 teaspoon salt
¼ teaspoon dried oregano leaves
2 tablespoons vinegar
1 tablespoon prepared mustard
3 teaspoons mild chili powder, divided

In small skillet, place oil and heat to medium temperature. Add onion and garlic; stir and cook about 3 minutes or until clear and soft. Dissolve bouillon cube in hot water; add bouillon to skillet, along with taco sauce, salt, oregano, vinegar and mustard. Dip chicken into sauce mixture; then sprinkle 2 teaspoons of the chili powder on all sides of chicken. Add remaining 1 teaspoon of chili powder to sauce; bring to a boil and remove from heat. Redip each quarter in sauce. Place chicken on prepared grill, skin side up, about 8 inches from heat. Grill, turning every 15 minutes, for about 60 minutes or until fork tender and juices run clear. Brush generously with sauce during last 30 minutes of grilling.
Makes 6 servings

Favorite Recipe from **National Broiler Council**

Grilled Seafood

Fish and shellfish cook quickly and deliciously on the grill. In just minutes you can serve your guests fork-tender fish and melt-in-the-mouth scallops or shrimp.

SALMON STEAKS IN ORANGE-HONEY MARINADE

⅓ cup orange juice
⅓ cup soy sauce
3 tablespoons peanut oil
3 tablespoons catsup
1 tablespoon honey
½ teaspoon ground ginger
1 clove garlic, crushed
4 salmon steaks (about 6 ounces each)

In 1-quart measure, mix all ingredients except salmon steaks. Place salmon steaks in shallow glass dish. Pour marinade over salmon steaks; cover and marinate in refrigerator 1 hour. Drain salmon; reserve marinade. Grill salmon, on uncovered grill, 6 inches above hot KINGSFORD® Briquets 5 minutes. Carefully turn salmon steaks. Brush with reserved marinade and grill 5 minutes longer or until salmon flakes easily when tested with fork.

Makes 4 servings

SEAFOOD KABOBS

⅓ cup pineapple juice
⅓ cup REALEMON® Lemon Juice from Concentrate
2 tablespoons vegetable oil
1 to 2 tablespoons brown sugar
1 teaspoon grated orange rind
¼ teaspoon ground cinnamon
¾ pound large raw shrimp, peeled and deveined
½ pound sea scallops
1 cup melon chunks or balls
1 medium avocado, peeled, seeded and cut into chunks

In large shallow dish or plastic bag, combine juices, oil, sugar, rind and cinnamon; add seafood and melon. Cover; marinate in refrigerator 4 hours or overnight. Place shrimp, scallops, melon and avocado on skewers. Grill or broil 3 to 6 minutes or until shrimp are pink and scallops are opaque, basting frequently with marinade. Refrigerate leftovers.

Makes 4 servings

Top to bottom: Salmon Steaks in Orange-Honey Marinade, Seafood Kabobs

MAGIC GRILLED FISH

6 (½-inch-thick) firm-fleshed fish fillets
(8 to 10 ounces each), such as redfish,
pompano, tilefish, red snapper, or
salmon or tuna steaks
¾ cup (1½ sticks) unsalted butter, melted
3 tablespoons plus 2 teaspoons CHEF
PAUL PRUDHOMME 'S BLACKENED
REDFISH MAGIC®

Heat grill as hot as possible and have flames
reaching above grid before putting fish on grill.
Add dry wood chunks to glowing coals to make
fire hotter.

Dip each fillet in melted butter so that both
sides are well coated, then sprinkle Blackened
Redfish Magic generously and evenly on both
sides of fillets, patting it in by hand. Place
fillets directly over flame on very hot grill and
pour 1 teaspoon of the melted butter on top of
each. (Be careful; butter may flare up.) Cook,
uncovered, directly in flames until underside
looks blackened, about 2 minutes. (Time will
vary according to each fillet's thickness and
heat of grill.) Turn fish over and grill until
cooked through, about 2 minutes more. Serve
piping hot with assorted grilled vegetables.

Makes 6 servings

Note: Do not prepare this recipe indoors.

Magic Grilled Fish

Shrimp and Steak Kabobs

SHRIMP AND STEAK KABOBS

½ cup vegetable oil
¼ cup REALEMON® Lemon Juice from Concentrate
1 teaspoon dried oregano leaves
½ teaspoon dried basil leaves
1 clove garlic, finely chopped
½ pound medium raw shrimp, peeled and deveined
½ pound boneless beef sirloin, cut into cubes
Zucchini, onion and red or yellow bell pepper chunks

In shallow dish or plastic bag, combine oil, ReaLemon® brand, oregano, basil and garlic; add shrimp and meat. Cover; marinate in refrigerator 3 to 4 hours. Skewer shrimp and meat with vegetables. Grill or broil as desired, basting frequently with marinade.

Makes 16 appetizer or 4 main-dish servings

Tip: One-half pound of scallops can be substituted for sirloin.

LAKESIDE LOBSTER TAILS

4 (1-pound) cleaned lobster tails with shells
Herb Wine Sauce (recipe follows)
Lemon wedges (optional)

Prepare coals for grilling. Cut lobster tails through center of back with knife or kitchen shears; split open. Place lobster, shell side down, on greased grill over hot coals (coals will be glowing). Grill, covered, 5 to 8 minutes on each side or until shell is bright red and lobster meat is white. Serve with Herb Wine Sauce. Garnish with lemon wedges, if desired.

Makes 4 servings

HERB WINE SAUCE

1 (8-ounce) container PHILADELPHIA BRAND® Soft Cream Cheese with Herb & Garlic
¼ cup dry white wine
2 green onions, thinly sliced
½ teaspoon salt

Stir together ingredients in small bowl until well blended.

SWORDFISH WITH LEEK CREAM

4 (1 to 1½ pounds total) swordfish steaks
2 tablespoons olive oil
  Leek Cream (recipe follows)

Prepare coals for grilling. Brush fish with oil. Place fish on greased grill over hot coals (coals will be glowing). Grill, uncovered, 3 to 4 minutes on each side or until fish flakes easily when tested with fork. Serve with Leek Cream.   *Makes 4 servings*

LEEK CREAM

1 leek, cut into 1-inch strips
2 tablespoons PARKAY® Margarine
1 (3-ounce) package PHILADELPHIA BRAND® Cream Cheese, cubed
3 tablespoons dry white wine
2 tablespoons chopped fresh parsley
½ teaspoon garlic salt
¼ teaspoon pepper

Sauté leeks in margarine in medium skillet until tender. Add remaining ingredients; stir over low heat until cream cheese is melted.

DEVILED TROUT FILLETS

2 pounds trout fillets, fresh or frozen
½ cup chili sauce
2 tablespoons vegetable oil
2 tablespoons prepared mustard
2 tablespoons cream-style prepared horseradish
1 tablespoon Worcestershire sauce
½ teaspoon salt

Thaw fish, if frozen. Place fish on well-greased grid. Mix remaining ingredients in small bowl until blended. Spread sauce evenly over fish. Grill, 6 inches from medium hot coals, 5 to 8 minutes or until fish begins to flake when tested with a fork.   *Makes 6 servings*

*Favorite recipe from **National Fisheries Institute***

SHRIMP IN FOIL

1 pound medium raw shrimp, peeled and deveined
1 cup sliced fresh mushrooms
¼ cup sliced green onions
2 tablespoons margarine or butter
¼ cup REALEMON® Lemon Juice from Concentrate
½ to 1 teaspoon dried dill weed
½ teaspoon salt
⅛ teaspoon pepper
2 tablespoons chopped parsley

On 4 large heavy-duty aluminum foil squares, place equal amounts of shrimp, mushrooms and green onions. Melt margarine; add ReaLemon® brand, dill weed, salt and pepper. Pour equal amounts over shrimp. Sprinkle with parsley. Fold and seal foil securely around shrimp. Grill 8 minutes or until shrimp are pink or bake in preheated 400° oven 12 to 15 minutes. Refrigerate leftovers.
          Makes 4 servings

GRILLED SALMON WITH CUCUMBER SAUCE

¾ cup HELLMANN'S® or BEST FOODS® Real, Light or Cholesterol Free Reduced Calorie Mayonnaise
¼ cup snipped fresh dill *or* 1 tablespoon dried dill weed
1 tablespoon lemon juice
6 salmon steaks (4 ounces each), ¾ inch thick
1 small cucumber, seeded and chopped
½ cup chopped radishes
  Lemon wedges

In medium bowl combine mayonnaise, dill and lemon juice; reserve ½ cup for sauce. Brush fish steaks with remaining mayonnaise mixture. Grill 6 inches from heat, turning and brushing frequently with mayonnaise mixture, 6 to 8 minutes or until fish is firm but moist. Stir cucumber and radishes into reserved mayonnaise mixture. Serve fish with cucumber sauce and lemon wedges.
          Makes 6 servings

Swordfish with Leek Cream

SEAFOOD-VEGETABLE KABOBS

2 dozen large sea scallops
1 dozen medium shrimp, shelled and
  deveined
2 red or yellow peppers, cut into 2-inch
  pieces
1 can (8½ ounces) artichoke hearts,
  drained
¼ cup olive or vegetable oil
¼ cup lime juice

Combine all ingredients in bowl; toss gently.
Thread scallops, shrimp, peppers and
artichokes onto skewers; reserve marinade.
Lightly oil grid. Grill kabobs, on uncovered
grill, over low KINGSFORD® Briquets 6 to
8 minutes or until scallops turn opaque and
shrimp turn pink. Turn kabobs twice during
grilling; brush with reserved marinade.

Makes 6 servings

EASY BROILED ALBACORE

1 tablespoon vegetable oil
2 tablespoons lime juice
1 teaspoon Worcestershire sauce
1½ teaspoons dry mustard
1½ pounds skinned albacore tuna steaks or
  loin cuts, 1 inch thick
2 tablespoons grated lime peel

Combine oil, lime juice, Worcestershire sauce
and mustard in small bowl to make basting
sauce. Arrange albacore on well-greased grid.
Baste with sauce. Grill, 4 to 5 inches from
medium-hot coals, 6 to 8 minutes, turning fish
halfway through cooking time and basting
frequently. Albacore should be pink in center
when removed from heat. Top with lime peel.

Makes 4 servings

Favorite Recipe from **National Fisheries Institute**

Seafood-Vegetable Kabobs

Grilled Rainbow Trout with Caponata Relish

GRILLED RAINBOW TROUT WITH CAPONATA RELISH

2 tablespoons olive oil
1 to 2 cloves garlic, crushed
1 cup peeled and chopped eggplant or
   sliced mushrooms
½ cup chopped bell peppers (mix of green
   and yellow peppers)
½ cup chopped tomatoes
2 tablespoons sliced ripe olives
1 tablespoon capers
1 teaspoon balsamic or red wine vinegar
4 CLEAR SPRINGS® Brand Idaho
   Rainbow Trout fillets (4 ounces each)

In small saucepan, heat oil over medium heat;
sauté garlic 1 minute. Add eggplant and
peppers; stir quickly to coat. Sauté 5 minutes
until softened. Add tomatoes, olives, capers
and vinegar. Continue cooking 5 minutes
longer; hold on very low heat. Over hot coals,
place trout fillets, flesh side down, on oiled
grid and cook about 2 minutes. Gently turn
trout with spatula; continue cooking 2 minutes
longer or until fish flakes easily with fork.
Serve immediately topped with 2 tablespoons
of caponata relish.   *Makes 4 servings*

TERIYAKI FISH FILLETS

1 can (20 ounces) DOLE® Pineapple
   Chunks in Juice
1 clove garlic, pressed
2 tablespoons slivered fresh ginger root
1 tablespoon minced green onion
5 teaspoons teriyaki sauce
1 teaspoon white vinegar
1 pound sole fillets
2 teaspoons cornstarch
1 teaspoon minced fresh ginger root
1 teaspoon sesame oil

Measure 2 tablespoons juice from pineapple
can; mix with garlic, slivered ginger, onion,
3 teaspoons teriyaki sauce and the vinegar.
Arrange fish in shallow dish. Pour marinade
over fish. Refrigerate 10 minutes. Drain fish;
reserve marinade. Arrange fish on oiled grid.
Brush with reserved marinade. Grill or broil
6 inches from heat 5 to 6 minutes or until fish
flakes easily with fork.

In saucepan, combine remaining 2 teaspoons
teriyaki sauce, undrained pineapple and
remaining ingredients. Cook, stirring, until
sauce boils and thickens. Serve with fish.
          Makes 4 servings

Salads & Extras

Potato, vegetable, fruit and gelatin—all the great salad combinations for outdoor eating are here. The extras are the sauces and marinades that add flavor to barbecued foods.

RANCH PICNIC POTATO SALAD

[handwritten: add cucumber]
[handwritten: needs more salt]

6 medium potatoes (about 3½ pounds), cooked, peeled and sliced
½ cup chopped celery
¼ cup sliced green onions
2 tablespoons chopped parsley
¼ teaspoon salt
⅛ teaspoon black pepper
1 tablespoon Dijon-style mustard
1 cup prepared HIDDEN VALLEY RANCH® Original Ranch® Salad Dressing
2 hard-cooked eggs, finely chopped
Paprika
Lettuce (optional)

In large bowl, combine potatoes, celery, onions, parsley, salt and pepper. In small bowl, stir mustard into salad dressing; pour over potatoes and toss lightly. Cover and refrigerate several hours. Sprinkle with eggs and paprika. Serve in lettuce-lined bowl, if desired.
Makes 8 servings

CALIFORNIA SALAD

1 DOLE® Fresh Pineapple
1 head DOLE® Iceberg Lettuce
2 DOLE® Bananas, peeled, sliced
8 ounces seedless DOLE® Grapes
2 DOLE® Carrots, sliced
1 tomato, cut into wedges
½ cucumber, sliced
2 stalks DOLE® Celery, sliced
¼ cup DOLE® Whole Natural Almonds, toasted
Date Dressing (recipe follows)

Twist crown from pineapple. Cut pineapple lengthwise into quarters. Remove fruit with curved knife. Trim off core and cut fruit into thin wedges. Line serving platter with lettuce leaves. Arrange half the pineapple and remaining fruits and vegetables on lettuce. Reserve remaining pineapple for another use. Sprinkle with almonds. Serve with Date Dressing.
Makes 6 servings

Date Dressing: In 1-quart measure, combine ⅔ cup vegetable oil, ¼ cup raspberry vinegar, 1 tablespoon sugar, 2 teaspoons soy sauce, 1 teaspoon *each* curry powder and dry mustard and ½ teaspoon garlic salt. Stir in ⅓ cup DOLE® Chopped Dates.

Top to bottom: Ranch Picnic Potato Salad, California Salad

Classic Spinach Salad

CLASSIC SPINACH SALAD

½ pound fresh spinach leaves (about
    10 cups)
1 cup sliced mushrooms
1 medium tomato, cut into wedges
⅓ cup seasoned croutons
¼ cup chopped red onion
4 slices bacon, crisp-cooked and crumbled
½ cup WISH-BONE® Lite Classic Dijon
    Vinaigrette Dressing
1 hard-cooked egg, sliced

In large salad bowl, combine spinach,
mushrooms, tomato, croutons, red onion and
bacon. Add lite classic Dijon vinaigrette
dressing and toss gently. Garnish with egg.
    Makes about 6 side-dish servings

DOLE® SUMMER VEGETABLE SALAD

1 head DOLE® Lettuce
2 tomatoes
1 cucumber
½ DOLE® Red Bell Pepper
¼ DOLE® Red Onion
1 cup sliced DOLE® Celery
1 cup snow peas, ends and strings removed
1 cup sliced DOLE® Cauliflower
    Dill Dressing (recipe follows)

Tear lettuce into bite-size pieces. Cut tomatoes
into wedges. Slice cucumber, red pepper and
red onion. Toss all vegetables in salad bowl
with Dill Dressing.   *Makes 4 servings*

Dill Dressing: In 1-quart measure, combine
½ cup *each* dairy sour cream and mayonnaise,
1 tablespoon vinegar, 1 teaspoon *each* dried
dill weed and onion powder, 1 teaspoon Dijon-
style mustard, ¾ teaspoon garlic salt and
cracked pepper to taste. Refrigerate, covered,
until ready to serve.

BARLEY WITH CORN AND RED PEPPER

½ cup WISH-BONE® Italian Dressing*
1 medium red pepper, chopped
½ cup chopped onion
1 cup uncooked pearled barley
1¾ cups chicken broth
1¼ cups water
2 tablespoons finely chopped coriander
    (cilantro) or parsley
1 tablespoon lime juice
½ teaspoon ground cumin
⅛ teaspoon pepper
1 can (7 ounces) whole kernel corn,
    drained

In large saucepan, heat Italian dressing; add red pepper and onion. Cook over medium heat, stirring occasionally, 5 minutes or until tender. Stir in barley and cook, stirring constantly, 1 minute. Stir in broth, water, coriander, lime juice, cumin and pepper. Simmer covered 50 minutes or until barley is done. (Do not stir while simmering.) Stir in corn.   *Makes about 6 servings*

*Also terrific with WISH-BONE® Robusto Italian, Herbal Italian, Lite Italian, Blended Italian or Lite Classic Dijon Vinaigrette Dressing.

Country Cole Slaw

COUNTRY COLE SLAW

1 cup HELLMANN'S® or BEST FOODS®
    Real, Light or Cholesterol Free
    Reduced Calorie Mayonnaise
3 tablespoons lemon juice
2 tablespoons sugar
1 teaspoon salt
6 cups shredded cabbage
1 cup shredded carrots
½ cup chopped or thinly sliced green
    pepper

In medium bowl, combine mayonnaise, lemon juice, sugar and salt. Stir in cabbage, carrots and green pepper. Cover; chill.
           Makes about 10 servings

RAITA
(Cucumber and Yogurt Salad)

3 medium cucumbers, peeled, seeded and
    thinly sliced
1 tablespoon minced onion
2 cups plain yogurt
½ teaspoon pepper
¼ teaspoon cumin
2 tablespoons cilantro, chopped

Mix together all ingredients. Chill for 2 to 24 hours to develop flavors.
           Makes 4 to 6 servings
*Favorite Recipe from the **National Pork Producers Council***

Barley with Corn and Red Pepper

In small saucepan over medium heat, melt 3 tablespoons of the butter. Whisk in flour until smooth, about 1 minute. Reserve.

In 10-inch skillet over high heat, melt remaining 8 tablespoons butter. When it comes to a hard sizzle, add almonds, Seafood Magic and celery. Cook, stirring frequently at first and constantly near end of cooking time, about 8 minutes or until almonds are browned. Stir in honey and cook, stirring frequently, about 1 minute. Stir in lemon peel and stock. Cook, stirring occasionally, about 8 minutes. Add nutmeg; cook 3 minutes, stirring occasionally. Whisk in reserved butter mixture until it is incorporated and sauce is slightly thickened, 30 to 60 seconds. Remove from heat.

Makes about 2½ cups

Note: This glaze is wonderful on grilled seafood, chicken and pork. Brush it on right before meat is ready to come off the grill and bring some to the table for dipping.

ONION-MOLASSES BARBECUE SAUCE

    4 tablespoons margarine
    2 tablespoons walnut or vegetable oil
    2 tablespoons olive oil
    3 cups chopped onions
    3 tablespoons CHEF PAUL
        PRUDHOMME'S POULTRY MAGIC®
    ¾ cup light molasses
    1 cup cider vinegar
    ¼ cup freshly squeezed orange juice
    ½ teaspoon dried dill weed
    ½ cup chicken stock or water

In 10-inch skillet over high heat, melt margarine with walnut oil and olive oil. When it comes to a hard sizzle, add onions and Poultry Magic. Stir to mix well and cook, stirring frequently, about 8 minutes or until onions are browned. Stir in molasses, mixing well. Add vinegar, orange juice and dill weed. Stir well and cook about 12 minutes, stirring frequently. Stir in stock and cook about 2 minutes more for flavors to blend.

Makes about 3 cups

Note: This sauce was created for anything that can be grilled. Just mop it on generously near the end of cooking time.

Top to bottom: Honey Almond Grilling Glaze, Onion-Molasses Barbecue Sauce

HONEY ALMOND GRILLING GLAZE

    11 tablespoons unsalted butter, in all
    2 tablespoons all-purpose flour
    1 cup slivered almonds
    2 tablespoons CHEF PAUL
        PRUDHOMME'S SEAFOOD MAGIC®
    1 cup chopped celery
    1 cup honey
    1 teaspoon grated fresh lemon peel
    1 cup chicken stock or water
    ⅛ teaspoon ground nutmeg

ORANGE-BERRY SALAD

½ cup prepared HIDDEN VALLEY
    RANCH® Original Ranch® Salad
    Dressing
2 tablespoons orange juice
1 teaspoon grated orange peel
½ cup heavy cream, whipped
1 can (11 ounces) mandarin orange
    segments
2 packages (3 ounces each) strawberry- or
    raspberry-flavored gelatin
1 can (16 ounces) whole-berry cranberry
    sauce
½ cup walnut pieces
    Mint sprigs
    Whole fresh strawberries and
    raspberries

In large bowl, whisk together salad dressing, orange juice and peel. Fold in whipped cream; cover and refrigerate. Drain oranges, reserving juice. Add water to juice to measure 3 cups; pour into large saucepan and bring to boil. Stir in gelatin until dissolved. Cover and refrigerate until partially set. Fold orange segments, cranberry sauce and walnuts into gelatin. Pour into lightly oiled 6-cup ring mold. Cover and refrigerate until firm; unmold. Garnish with mint and fresh strawberries and raspberries. Serve with chilled dressing.

Makes 8 servings

Orange-Berry Salad

Refreshing Coolers

The coolers, mocktails and cocktails featured here are wonderful for sipping during a relaxing summer afternoon or evening.

THE MAIDEN MARY

2½ cups Florida grapefruit juice
2 cups tomato juice
1 cup clam juice
2 teaspoons Worcestershire sauce
Dash hot pepper sauce
Ice cubes

In 2-quart pitcher, combine grapefruit juice, tomato juice, clam juice, Worcestershire and hot pepper sauce; blend well. Add ice cubes. Pour into serving glasses. Garnish as desired.

Makes 4 servings

Favorite Recipe from Florida Department of Citrus

ORANGE FANTASIA

1½ cups Florida orange juice
1 cup (½ pint) orange sherbet
Cracked ice (optional)

Pour orange juice into blender container; add orange sherbet. Cover and process at medium speed until smooth. Or, sherbet may be softened slightly, added to orange juice and beaten with rotary beater until smooth. If desired, pour over cracked ice. Garnish as desired. *Makes 2½ cups or 2 servings*

Favorite Recipe from Florida Department of Citrus

LEMONADE

½ cup sugar
½ cup REALEMON® Lemon Juice from Concentrate
3¼ cups cold water
Ice cubes

In large pitcher, dissolve sugar in ReaLemon® brand; add water. Serve over ice. Garnish as desired. *Makes about 1 quart*

Sparkling Lemonade: Substitute club soda for cold water.

Slushy Lemonade: In blender container, combine ReaLemon® brand and sugar with ½ cup water. Gradually add 4 cups ice cubes, blending until smooth. Serve immediately.

Pink Lemonade: Stir in 1 to 2 teaspoons grenadine syrup *or* 1 to 2 drops red food coloring.

Minted Lemonade: Stir in 2 to 3 drops peppermint extract.

Low Calorie: Omit sugar. Add 4 to 8 envelopes sugar substitute *or* 1½ teaspoons liquid sugar substitute.

Left to right: The Maiden Mary, Orange Fantasia, Lemonade

Top to bottom: Strawberry-Banana Shake, Banana Shake

BANANA SHAKE

2 ripe bananas, cut up (about 2 cups)
⅓ cup REALEMON® Lemon Juice from Concentrate
1 cup cold water
1 (14-ounce) can EAGLE® Brand Sweetened Condensed Milk (NOT evaporated milk)
2 cups ice cubes

In blender container, combine all ingredients except ice; blend well. Gradually add ice; blend until smooth. Garnish as desired. Refrigerate leftovers. (Mixture stays thick and creamy in refrigerator.)

Makes about 5 cups

Strawberry-Banana Shake: Reduce bananas to ½ cup; add 1½ cups fresh strawberries *or* 1 cup frozen unsweetened strawberries, partially thawed. Proceed as above.

Mixer Method: Omit ice cubes. In large mixer bowl, mash bananas; gradually beat in ReaLemon® brand, sweetened condensed milk and 2½ cups cold water. Chill before serving.

PINA COLADA MOCKTAIL

1 can (6 ounces) frozen limeade concentrate, thawed
6 cups DOLE® Pine-Passion-Banana Juice, chilled
2 bottles (28 ounces each) mineral water, chilled
1 can (15 ounces) real cream of coconut
Lime slices for garnish
DOLE® Orange slices for garnish
Mint sprigs for garnish

Reconstitute limeade according to label directions in large punch bowl. Add remaining ingredients.

Makes 24 servings

MAI TAI SLUSH

1½ cups DOLE® Pineapple Juice
1 pint lemon sherbet
2 ounces rum
2 tablespoons triple sec
1 cup crushed ice
Lime slices for garnish (optional)

Combine pineapple juice, sherbet, rum and triple sec in blender. Add ice; blend until slushy. Garnish with lime slices, if desired.

Makes 2 servings

Mai Tai Slush

Double Berry Coco Punch

DOUBLE BERRY COCO PUNCH

Ice Ring (recipe follows) (optional) *or*
  block of ice
2 (10-ounce) packages frozen strawberries
  in syrup, thawed
1 (15-ounce) can COCO LOPEZ® Cream
  of Coconut
1 (48-ounce) bottle cranberry juice
  cocktail, chilled
2 cups light rum (optional)
1 (32-ounce) bottle club soda, chilled

Prepare ice ring in advance, if desired. In
blender container, purée strawberries and
cream of coconut until smooth. In large punch
bowl, combine strawberry mixture, cranberry
juice and rum, if desired. Just before serving,
add club soda and ice ring.

Ice Ring: Fill ring mold with water to within
1 inch of top rim; freeze. Arrange strawberries,
cranberries, mint leaves, lime slices or other
fruits on top of ice. Carefully pour small
amount of cold water over fruits; freeze.

Makes about 4 quarts

ORANGE AND SPICE ICED TEA

6 cups cold water, divided
3 cinnamon sticks (2 inches each)
½ teaspoon whole cloves
10 tea bags
1 can (6 ounces) Florida frozen
  concentrated orange juice, thawed,
  undiluted
¼ cup sugar
1 Florida orange, sliced

In medium saucepan, combine 3 cups cold
water, cinnamon sticks and cloves. Bring to
boiling; remove from heat. Add tea bags. Brew
5 minutes. Remove tea bags; discard. Strain
mixture. Add remaining 3 cups cold water,
orange juice concentrate and sugar; mix well.
Chill. Serve in tall glasses over ice cubes.

Garnish with fresh orange slices.

Makes six 8-ounce servings

Favorite Recipe from **Florida Department of Citrus**

LEMONY LIGHT COOLER

3 cups dry white wine or white grape juice, chilled
½ to ¾ cup sugar
½ cup REALEMON® Lemon Juice from Concentrate
1 (32-ounce) bottle club soda, chilled
Strawberry, plum, peach or orange slices or other fresh fruit

In pitcher, combine wine, sugar and ReaLemon® brand; stir until sugar dissolves. Just before serving, add club soda and fruit; serve over ice.   *Makes about 7 cups*

Tip: Recipe can be doubled.

Left to right: City Slicker, The Rattlesnake

CITY SLICKER

¾ cup DOLE® Pineapple Juice
Ice cubes
Ginger ale
Dash ground ginger
Cucumber slice, cherry tomato and lemon slice for garnish

Pour pineapple juice over ice cubes in glass. Fill with ginger ale. Add ginger and stir. Garnish with cucumber slice, cherry tomato and lemon slice.   *Makes 1 serving*

THE RATTLESNAKE

3 cups DOLE® Pineapple Juice
⅓ cup tomato juice
1 tablespoon powdered sugar
½ to 1 teaspoon liquid hot pepper sauce
8 ice cubes
Lime wedges or slices (optional)
Dried red pepper, ripe olive and lime peel for garnish

In pitcher, combine pineapple juice, tomato juice, sugar and hot pepper sauce; blend well. Pour over ice cubes in glass. Squeeze lime juice into each drink, if desired. Garnish with dried red pepper, ripe olive and lime peel.
Makes 4 servings

Lemony Light Cooler

LITE QUENCHER

3 cups DOLE® Pineapple Juice, chilled
3 cups mineral water, chilled
1 cup assorted sliced DOLE® fresh fruit
½ cup mint sprigs
1 lime, sliced, for garnish

Combine all ingredients in pitcher.

Makes 8 servings

APPLE GRAPE PUNCH

Ice Ring (recipe follows) (optional) *or*
    block of ice
1 quart apple juice, chilled
3 cups red grape juice, chilled
1 (8-ounce) bottle REALIME® Lime Juice
    from Concentrate, chilled
1 cup vodka (optional)
½ cup sugar

Prepare ice ring in advance, if desired. In punch bowl, combine juices, vodka, if desired, and sugar; stir until sugar dissolves. Just before serving, add ice ring.

Ice Ring: Combine 1 (8-ounce) bottle ReaLime® brand and ¾ cup sugar; stir until sugar dissolves. Add 3 cups water; mix well. Pour 3 cups mixture into ring mold; freeze. Arrange apple slices and grapes on top of ice. Carefully pour remaining mixture over fruits; freeze. *Makes about 2 quarts*

Bloody Marys

BLOODY MARY

3 cups tomato juice, chilled
¾ cup vodka
4 teaspoons REALEMON® Lemon Juice
    from Concentrate
2 teaspoons Worcestershire sauce
½ teaspoon celery salt
⅛ teaspoon hot pepper sauce
    Dash pepper

In pitcher, combine ingredients; stir. Serve over ice; garnish as desired.

Makes about 1 quart

Tip: For nonalcoholic Bloody Mary, omit vodka. Proceed as above.

BLOODY MARY GARNISHES
Onion & Olive Pick: Dip cocktail onions in chopped parsley; alternate on toothpick with pimiento-stuffed olives.

Green Onion Firecracker: With small scissors or very sharp knife, cut tips of green onion to end of dark green onion portion. Chill in ice water until curled.

Apple Grape Punch

Light & Easy
Chinese
With Quick Wok Cooking

Clockwise from top right: Wonton Soup (page 246), Easy Wonton Chips (page 248) and Beef Soup with Noodles (page 248)

EASY COOKING, CHINESE-STYLE

Chinese cooking, as we know it, is actually a combination of cooking techniques and seasonings from all the regions of China. Northern or Beijing cooking features wheat noodles, dumplings, sweet-sour sauces, garlic and green onions. The coastal areas around Shanghai are known for their fabulous seafood and delectable sauces. Szechuan and Hunan cooking use a blend of seasonings to create dishes that have a combination hot, sour, sweet, salty taste all in one bite. Southern or Cantonese cooking, which is mildly seasoned and frequently served in Chinese-American restaurants, emphasizes cooking with soy sauce, ginger and sherry. We have taken the best from these regions to create the delectable recipes in this book.

These recipes have been developed with the health-conscious cook in mind. While this is not a diet book, many of the recipes have been lightened by omitting fat-laden cooking techniques and reducing fat, cholesterol and calories. For example, deep-fat frying techniques are not included in the book; instead recipes are modified to be stir-fried, baked or pan-fried in a small amount of oil. Also, egg whites have been substituted for whole eggs whenever possible, and ground chicken and turkey are used in place of pork for some recipes.

These recipes were designed to be easy with no-fuss cooking techniques, clear step-by-step directions and readily available ingredients. Before you begin, read the recipe thoroughly. Then do any marinating, soaking and chopping before cooking. The final dish will be sure to be a hit!

Cooking Techniques

Although a variety of familiar cooking techniques are used in preparing Chinese dishes, stir-frying, the most popular technique, is featured throughout this book. Before you begin, take a few minutes to read the following information. Stir-frying is easily mastered, and these helpful guidelines will enhance your enjoyment of these wonderful dishes.

Stir-frying involves the rapid cooking of ingredients in a small amount of oil over medium-high to high heat for a few minutes. In addition to saving time, the quick cooking preserves the nutrients, flavors, textures and colors of the food. Stir-frying can be divided into two separate steps—preparing the ingredients and cooking the ingredients.

It is essential to have all the ingredients prepared in advance. This means all cleaning, cutting, measuring, combining, etc. Stir-frying proceeds so quickly that there is no time to do anything else once cooking begins. When cutting meats and vegetables, make the pieces a uniform shape and size to ensure even cooking. Otherwise, one ingredient may overcook, while others are undercooked.

When you're ready to begin, place a wok or large skillet over medium-high or high heat. Preheating the pan prevents the food from sticking. When a drop of water added to the pan sizzles, the pan is sufficiently hot. Next add the oil, swirling to coat the inside of the pan; heat until the oil is hot, about 30 seconds. Now the ingredients can be added.

Stir-fry the meat first and remove. Then add the vegetables, beginning with those that take the longest to cook. Briskly toss and stir with a flat metal or wooden spatula. Be sure to keep the food in constant motion. This ensures that all surfaces are quickly coated with hot oil to seal in the flavorings, and also prevents overcooking or burning. To maintain the characteristic Chinese tender-crisp quality, serve stir-fried dishes immediately.

The best oils to use for stir-frying are vegetable oils that can withstand intense heat without smoking. Peanut oil, corn oil and soybean oil are excellent choices.

Helpful Hints

• When removing stir-fried meat, poultry or seafood from the wok, always place the meat in a clean dish, not one that held the raw or marinated food.

• Any foods that need to be marinated over 20 minutes should be marinated in the refrigerator.

• Resealable heavy-duty plastic food storage bags are great to use for marinating foods.

• Always have all the ingredients prepared— sliced, measured, marinated, combined—before you begin stir-frying, and have them located close to the wok.

• Stir any cornstarch mixtures before adding them to the hot wok. The cornstarch needs to be dissolved in the liquid to prevent it from lumping.

• Partially freeze beef, pork or poultry to make it easier to slice into thin strips.

• For a no-fuss stir-fry, use vegetables, such as sliced mushrooms, broccoli or cauliflower florets, spinach or bean sprouts, from the deli bar of the supermarket or frozen mixed vegetables, such as a broccoli and cauliflower combination.

• Use fresh flour tortillas from the supermarket dairy case in place of mandarin pancakes.

• Use roasted whole chicken from the deli department of your local supermarket or vacuum-packed precooked chicken breasts when a recipe calls for cooked chicken.

• Freeze leftover broth in clean ice cube trays. Once the broth is frozen, remove the cubes and store them in a resealable freezer bag to prevent evaporation. Remove cubes as needed; they can be quickly defrosted in a microwave oven.

• Use packaged preshredded coleslaw mix or cabbage for egg roll fillings or any other recipes that call for shredded cabbage.

• Use chicken tenders for recipes that call for stir-frying strips of chicken. Turkey tenders, cutlets and tenderloin can be substituted for chicken cubes or strips.

Glossary of Chinese Ingredients

All of the recipes in this book were developed with Chinese ingredients that are generally available in large supermarkets. If you are unable to locate them in your store, you may also look for them in gourmet food stores and Oriental markets.

Bamboo shoots: tender, ivory-colored shoots of tropical bamboo plants, used separately as a vegetable and to add crispness and a slight sweetness to dishes. They are available fresh or in cans and should be rinsed with water before using. Store opened, canned bamboo shoots submerged in water in a covered container in the refrigerator. Every 2 to 3 days, drain and discard the water and replace it with fresh cold water. Bamboo shoots may be kept up to 2 weeks.

Bean sprouts: small white shoots of the pea-like mung bean plant, used separately as a vegetable and included in a wide variety of dishes. They are available fresh or in cans. Canned bean sprouts should be rinsed before use to eliminate any metallic taste. Store opened, canned bean sprouts submerged in water in a covered container in the refrigerator for up to 5 days. Store fresh bean sprouts in a plastic bag in the refrigerator for about 1 week.

Bean threads (also called cellophane noodles or Chinese rice vermicelli): dry, hard, white, fine noodles made from powdered mung beans. They have little flavor of their own, but readily absorb the flavors of other foods.

Bok choy: a member of the cabbage family, has white stalks and green, crinkled leaves. The woody stems take longer to cook than the delicate leaf tips. Store in a plastic bag in the refrigerator for up to 4 days.

Chili oil, hot: vegetable or sesame oil that has had hot red chilies steeped in it. This red-colored oil adds heat and flavor to Chinese dishes.

Egg noodles, Chinese: a thin pasta usually made of flour, egg, water and salt. The noodles can be purchased fresh, frozen or dried.

Egg roll wrappers: commercially prepared dough made of flour and water, rolled very thin and cut into 7- or 8-inch squares. They are available fresh or frozen.

Five-spice powder, Chinese: cocoa-colored powder that is a ready-mixed blend of five ground spices, usually anise seed, fennel seed, cloves, cinnamon and ginger or pepper. It has a slightly sweet, pungent flavor and should be used sparingly.

Ginger (also called ginger root): a knobby, gnarled root with a brown skin and whitish or light green interior. It has a fresh, pungent flavor and is used as a basic seasoning in many Chinese recipes. Ginger is available fresh and needs to be peeled before using. Store it wrapped in plastic in the refrigerator for about 2 weeks or in a resealable freezer bag in the freezer for up to 4 weeks. (You may cut off what you need and return the remainder to the freezer.) Or, store peeled ginger covered with dry sherry in an airtight container in the refrigerator for up to 6 months. The sherry absorbs some of the ginger flavor and may be used for cooking.

Hoisin sauce: a thick, dark brown sauce made of soybeans, flour, sugar, spices, garlic, chilies and salt. It has a sweet, spicy flavor and is called for in numerous Chinese recipes. It is available as a prepared sauce.

Mushrooms, dried: dehydrated black or brown mushrooms from the Orient, with caps from 1 to 3 inches in diameter. They have a strong distinctive flavor and are included in many different kinds of recipes. Chinese dried mushrooms must be soaked in warm water before using and are usually called for thinly sliced. Store in an airtight container in a cool, dark place.

Napa cabbage: a member of the cabbage family, has elongated tightly furled leaves, wide white ribs and soft pale green tips. Store in a closed plastic bag in the refrigerator for up to 5 days.

Oyster sauce: a thick, brown, concentrated sauce made of ground oysters, soy sauce and brine. It imparts very little fish flavor and is used as a seasoning to intensify other flavors. It is available as a prepared sauce.

Peanut oil: a golden-colored oil pressed from peanuts that has a light and slightly nutty flavor. This oil has a high smoke point that makes it ideal for using in stir-fried recipes. Store it tightly covered in a cool, dark place for up to 6 months after opening.

Plum sauce: a thick, piquant, chutney-like sauce frequently served with duck or pork dishes. It is available as a prepared sauce or can be homemade.

Sesame oil: an amber-colored oil pressed from toasted sesame seeds. It has a strong, nut-like flavor and is best used sparingly. Sesame oil is generally used as a flavoring, not as a cooking oil because of its low smoke point. Store it tightly covered in a cool, dark place for up to 2 months after opening.

Snow peas (also called pea pods or Chinese peas): flat, green pods that are picked before the peas have matured. They add crispness, color and flavor to foods, require very little cooking and are frequently used in stir-fried dishes. Snow peas are available fresh or frozen. Store fresh snow peas in a plastic bag in the refrigerator for 3 to 4 days.

Soy sauce: a pungent, brown, salty liquid made of fermented soybeans, wheat, yeast, salt and sometimes sugar. It is an essential ingredient in Chinese cooking. There are several types of soy sauce (light, dark, heavy), as well as Japanese-style soy sauce. The Japanese-style sauce is somewhere between the light and dark varieties. All types of soy sauce are available in bottles.

Stir-fry sauce: a prepared sauce that can be added as an instant seasoning to stir-fried dishes.

Sweet and sour sauce: a combination of sugar, vinegar and other flavorings. It is available as a prepared sauce or can be homemade.

Szechuan peppercorns: a reddish-brown pepper with a strong, pungent aroma and flavor. Its potent flavor has a time-delayed action and may not be noticed immediately. It is usually sold whole or crushed in small packages and should be used sparingly. Store it in an airtight container in a cool, dark place for up to 1 year.

Tofu (also called bean curd): puréed soybeans pressed to form a white, custard-like cake, used as a vegetable and as an excellent source of protein. Tofu can be used in all kinds of recipes because it readily absorbs the flavor of other foods. Tofu is available fresh. Store opened tofu submerged in water in a covered container in the refrigerator for up to 3 days. Drain and discard the water and replace it with fresh cold water daily. Tofu may also be stored tightly wrapped in plastic in the refrigerator for a few days.

Water chestnuts: walnut-sized bulbs from an aquatic plant. The bulb has a tough, brown skin and crisp, white interior. Water chestnuts are served separately as a vegetable and are used to add crisp texture and a delicate, sweet flavor to dishes. They are available fresh or in cans. Store opened, canned water chestnuts submerged in water in a covered container in the refrigerator for up to 1 week. Store fresh, unpeeled water chestnuts in a plastic bag in the refrigerator for up to 1 week.

Wonton wrappers: commercially prepared dough made of flour and water, rolled very thin and cut into 3- to 4-inch squares. They are available fresh or frozen.

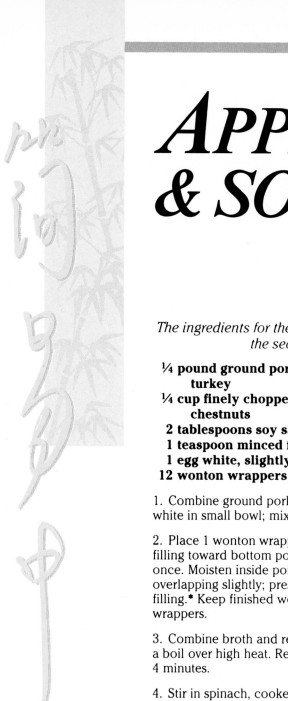

APPETIZERS & SOUPS

WONTON SOUP

The ingredients for the wontons may be doubled. Use one batch now and freeze the second batch for a quick soup at a later date.

¼ **pound ground pork, chicken or turkey**
¼ **cup finely chopped water chestnuts**
2 **tablespoons soy sauce, divided**
1 **teaspoon minced fresh ginger**
1 **egg white, slightly beaten**
12 **wonton wrappers**

1 **can (46 ounces) chicken broth**
1½ **cups sliced fresh spinach leaves**
1 **cup thinly sliced cooked pork (optional)**
½ **cup diagonally sliced green onions**
1 **tablespoon Oriental sesame oil**
Shredded carrot for garnish

1. Combine ground pork, water chestnuts, 1 tablespoon soy sauce, ginger and egg white in small bowl; mix well.

2. Place 1 wonton wrapper with a point toward edge of counter. Mound 1 teaspoon of filling toward bottom point. Fold bottom point over filling, then roll wrapper over once. Moisten inside points with water. Bring side points together below the filling, overlapping slightly; press together firmly to seal. Repeat with remaining wrappers and filling.* Keep finished wontons covered with plastic wrap, while filling remaining wrappers.

3. Combine broth and remaining 1 tablespoon soy sauce in large saucepan. Bring to a boil over high heat. Reduce heat to medium; add wontons. Simmer, uncovered, 4 minutes.

4. Stir in spinach, cooked pork and onions; remove from heat. Stir in sesame oil. Ladle into soup bowls. Garnish with shredded carrot.

Makes 4 to 6 appetizer servings (about 7 cups)

Note: For information on storing unused water chestnuts, see page 245.

*Wontons may be made ahead to this point; cover and refrigerate up to 8 hours or freeze up to 3 months. Proceed as directed in step 3, if using refrigerated wontons. Increase simmer time to 6 minutes, if using frozen wontons.

Clockwise from top right: Wonton Soup, Easy Wonton Chips (page 248) and Beef Soup with Noodles (page 248)

EASY WONTON CHIPS

These chips are so easy to make and are a great accompaniment to soups or dips.

1 tablespoon soy sauce
2 teaspoons peanut or vegetable oil

½ teaspoon sugar
¼ teaspoon garlic salt
12 wonton wrappers

1. Preheat oven to 375°F.

2. Combine soy sauce, oil, sugar and garlic salt in small bowl; mix well.

3. Cut each wonton wrapper diagonally in half. Place wonton wrappers on 15×10-inch jelly-roll pan coated with nonstick cooking spray. Brush soy sauce mixture lightly but evenly over both sides of each wonton wrapper.

4. Bake 4 to 6 minutes or until crisp and lightly browned, turning after 3 minutes. Transfer to cooling rack; cool completely. *Makes 2 dozen chips*

BEEF SOUP WITH NOODLES

2 tablespoons soy sauce
1 teaspoon minced fresh ginger
¼ teaspoon crushed red pepper flakes
1 boneless beef top sirloin steak, cut 1 inch thick (about ¾ pound)
1 tablespoon peanut or vegetable oil
2 cups sliced fresh mushrooms
2 cans (about 14 ounces each) beef broth

3 ounces (1 cup) fresh snow peas, cut diagonally into 1-inch pieces
1½ cups hot cooked fine egg noodles (2 ounces uncooked)
1 green onion, cut diagonally into thin slices
1 teaspoon Oriental sesame oil (optional)
Red bell pepper strips for garnish
Easy Wonton Chips (see above) (optional)

1. Combine soy sauce, ginger and crushed red pepper in small bowl. Spread mixture evenly over both sides of steak. Marinate at room temperature 15 minutes.

2. Heat deep skillet over medium-high heat. Add peanut oil; heat until hot. Drain steak; reserve soy sauce mixture (there will only be a small amount of mixture). Add steak to skillet; cook 4 to 5 minutes per side.* Let stand on cutting board 10 minutes.

3. Add mushrooms to skillet; stir-fry 2 minutes. Add broth, snow peas and reserved soy sauce mixture; bring to a boil, scraping up browned meat bits. Reduce heat to medium-low. Stir in noodles.

4. Cut steak across the grain into ⅛-inch slices; cut each slice into 1-inch pieces. Stir into soup; heat through. Stir in onion and sesame oil. Ladle into soup bowls. Garnish with red pepper strips. Serve with Easy Wonton Chips.
Makes 4 main-dish or 6 appetizer servings (about 6 cups)

*Cooking time is for medium-rare doneness. Adjust time for desired doneness.

CHINATOWN STUFFED MUSHROOMS

24 large fresh mushrooms (about 1 pound)
½ pound ground pork or turkey
1 clove garlic, minced
¼ cup fine dry bread crumbs
¼ cup thinly sliced green onions

3 tablespoons soy sauce, divided
1 teaspoon minced fresh ginger
1 egg white, slightly beaten
⅛ teaspoon crushed red pepper flakes (optional)

1. Remove stems from mushrooms; finely chop enough stems to equal 1 cup. Reserve remaining stems for use in salads, soups or stews, if desired. Cook pork with chopped stems and garlic in medium skillet over medium-high heat until pork is no longer pink, stirring to separate pork. Spoon off fat.

2. Stir in bread crumbs, onions, 2 tablespoons soy sauce, ginger, egg white and crushed red pepper; mix well.

3. Brush mushrooms lightly on all sides with remaining 1 tablespoon soy sauce; spoon about 2 teaspoons stuffing into each mushroom cap.* Place stuffed mushrooms on rack of foil-lined broiler pan. Broil 4 to 5 inches from heat 5 to 6 minutes until hot.

Makes 2 dozen appetizers

*Mushrooms may be made ahead to this point; cover and refrigerate up to 24 hours. Increase broiling time by 1 to 2 minutes for the chilled mushrooms.

ORIENTAL CHICKEN WINGS

These wings are an Oriental version of the popular Buffalo Wings.

12 chicken wings *or* 24 chicken drumettes
¼ cup *plus* 2 teaspoons soy sauce, divided
2 tablespoons dry sherry

2 cloves garlic, minced
2 teaspoons brown sugar
½ cup lite or fat-free mayonnaise
1 teaspoon rice vinegar
½ teaspoon Oriental sesame oil

1. Cut off chicken wing tips at joint; discard tips or save for making chicken broth. Cut each remaining wing portion at other joint to make 2 pieces. Place in large plastic bag.

2. Combine ¼ cup soy sauce, sherry, garlic and brown sugar in cup; pour over chicken wings. Close bag securely; turn to coat. Marinate in refrigerator at least 4 hours or up to 24 hours.

3. Combine mayonnaise, vinegar, sesame oil and remaining 2 teaspoons soy sauce in small bowl. Cover and refrigerate until ready to serve.

4. Drain chicken wings; reserve marinade. Place wings on rack of broiler pan. Brush with half of reserved marinade. Broil 6 inches from heat 10 minutes. Turn wings over; brush with remaining marinade. Broil 10 minutes or until chicken is browned and cooked through. Serve mayonnaise mixture as a dipping sauce for wings.

Makes 2 dozen appetizers

SPICY CHICKEN BUNDLES

1 pound ground chicken or turkey
2 teaspoons minced fresh ginger
2 cloves garlic, minced
¼ teaspoon crushed red pepper
  flakes
3 tablespoons soy sauce
1 tablespoon cornstarch
1 tablespoon peanut or vegetable
  oil

⅓ cup finely chopped water
  chestnuts
⅓ cup thinly sliced green onions
¼ cup chopped peanuts
12 large lettuce leaves, such as
  romaine
Chinese hot mustard (optional)

1. Combine chicken, ginger, garlic and crushed red pepper in medium bowl.

2. Blend soy sauce into cornstarch in cup until smooth.

3. Heat wok or large skillet over medium-high heat. Add oil; heat until hot. Add chicken mixture; stir-fry 2 to 3 minutes until chicken is no longer pink.

4. Stir soy sauce mixture and add to wok. Stir-fry 30 seconds or until sauce boils and thickens. Add water chestnuts, onions and peanuts; heat through.*

5. Divide filling evenly among lettuce leaves; roll up. Secure with wooden toothpicks. Serve warm or at room temperature. Do not let filling stand at room temperature more than 2 hours. Serve with hot mustard. *Makes 12 appetizers*

Note: For information on storing unused water chestnuts, see page 245.

*Filling may be made ahead to this point; cover and refrigerate up to 4 hours. Just before rolling in lettuce, reheat chicken filling until warm. Proceed as directed in step 5.

SPRING ROLLS

Flour tortillas make these no-cook Spring Rolls so easy to prepare!

1 cup preshredded cabbage or
  coleslaw mix
½ cup finely chopped cooked ham
¼ cup finely chopped water
  chestnuts

¼ cup thinly sliced green onions
3 tablespoons plum sauce, divided
1 teaspoon Oriental sesame oil
3 flour tortillas (6 to 7 inches)

1. Combine cabbage, ham, water chestnuts, onions, 2 tablespoons plum sauce and sesame oil in medium bowl; mix well.

2. Spread remaining 1 tablespoon plum sauce evenly over tortillas. Spread about ½ cup cabbage mixture on each tortilla to within ¼ inch of edge; roll up.

3. Wrap each tortilla tightly in plastic wrap. Refrigerate at least 1 hour or up to 24 hours before serving.

4. Cut each tortilla diagonally into 4 pieces. *Makes 12 appetizers*

Note: For information on storing unused water chestnuts, see page 245.

Top to bottom: Spicy Chicken Bundles and Spring Rolls

HOT AND SOUR SOUP

Leftovers from Roasted Pork, Chinese Barbecued Pork or Crispy Roasted Chicken are ideal to use for this spicy soup.

1 package (1 ounce) dried black
    Chinese mushrooms*
4 ounces firm tofu, drained
4 cups chicken broth
3 tablespoons white vinegar
2 tablespoons soy sauce
½ to 1 teaspoon hot chili oil
¼ teaspoon ground white pepper
1 cup shredded cooked pork,
    chicken or turkey

½ cup drained canned bamboo
    shoots, cut into thin strips
3 tablespoons water
2 tablespoons cornstarch
1 egg white, slightly beaten
¼ cup thinly sliced green onions or
    chopped cilantro
1 teaspoon Oriental sesame oil

1. Place mushrooms in small bowl; cover with warm water. Soak 20 minutes to soften. Drain; squeeze out excess water. Discard stems; slice caps. Press tofu lightly between paper towels; cut into ½-inch squares or triangles.

2. Combine broth, vinegar, soy sauce, chili oil and pepper in medium saucepan. Bring to a boil over high heat. Reduce heat to medium. Simmer 2 minutes.

3. Stir in mushrooms, tofu, pork and bamboo shoots; heat through.

4. Blend water into cornstarch in cup until smooth. Stir into soup. Cook and stir 4 minutes or until soup boils and thickens.

5. Remove from heat. Stirring constantly in one direction, slowly pour egg white in a thin stream into soup. Stir in onions and sesame oil. Ladle into soup bowls.

Makes 4 to 6 appetizer servings (about 6 cups)

Note: For information on storing unused bamboo shoots and tofu, see pages 244 and 245.

*Or, substitute 2 cups sliced fresh mushrooms. Omit soaking mushrooms in step 1.

ORIENTAL SALSA

Here's an Oriental twist to a Tex-Mex favorite.

1 cup diced, unpeeled cucumber
½ cup chopped red bell pepper
½ cup thinly sliced green onions
⅓ cup coarsely chopped cilantro
1 clove garlic, minced
1 tablespoon rice vinegar

2 teaspoons soy sauce
½ teaspoon Oriental sesame oil
¼ teaspoon crushed red pepper
    flakes
Easy Wonton Chips (page 248)
    or Chinese crackers

1. Combine all ingredients except Easy Wonton Chips in medium bowl until well blended.

2. Cover and refrigerate until serving time. Serve with Easy Wonton Chips for dipping. Or, use salsa as an accompaniment to broiled fish, chicken or pork.

Makes 1½ cups salsa

CHILLED SHRIMP IN CHINESE MUSTARD SAUCE

1 cup water
½ cup dry white wine
2 tablespoons soy sauce
½ teaspoon Szechuan or black peppercorns

1 pound large raw shrimp, peeled, deveined
¼ cup sweet and sour sauce
2 teaspoons Chinese hot mustard

1. Combine water, wine, soy sauce and peppercorns in medium saucepan. Bring to a boil over high heat. Add shrimp; reduce heat to medium. Cover and simmer 2 to 3 minutes until shrimp are opaque. Drain well. Cover and refrigerate until chilled.

2. Combine sweet and sour sauce and hot mustard in small bowl; mix well. Serve as a dipping sauce for shrimp.
Makes 6 appetizer servings

EGG ROLLS

¼ cup soy sauce
2 tablespoons dry sherry
4 teaspoons cornstarch
    Peanut or vegetable oil
6 cups chopped or shredded cabbage *or* preshredded coleslaw mix or cabbage (about 12 ounces)
1 cup chopped fresh mushrooms
⅔ cup thinly sliced green onions

½ pound ground beef, pork or turkey
3 cloves garlic, minced
¼ teaspoon crushed red pepper flakes
12 egg roll wrappers *or* 24 wonton wrappers
    Sweet and sour sauce for dipping
    Chinese hot mustard (optional)

1. Blend soy sauce and sherry into cornstarch in cup until smooth.

2. Heat wok or large skillet over medium-high heat. Add 1 tablespoon oil; heat until hot. Add cabbage, mushrooms and onions; stir-fry 2 minutes (cabbage will still be crisp). Remove; set aside.

3. Add beef, garlic and crushed red pepper to wok; cook until beef is no longer pink, stirring to separate beef. Spoon off fat.

4. Stir soy sauce mixture and add to wok. Stir-fry 2 minutes or until sauce boils and thickens. Return cabbage mixture; heat through, mixing well.*

5. Place each egg roll wrapper with one point toward edge of counter. Spoon filling across and just below center of wrapper; use heaping ⅓ cup filling for each egg roll wrapper or 2 teaspoons filling for each wonton wrapper.

6. To form egg roll, fold bottom point of wrapper up over filling. Fold side points over filling, forming an envelope shape. Moisten inside edges of top point with water and roll egg roll toward that point, pressing firmly to seal. Repeat with remaining wrappers and filling.

7. Pour ½ inch oil into large skillet. Heat oil to 375°F. Fry egg rolls, 2 or 3 at a time, or mini-egg rolls, 6 to 8 at time, 2 minutes per side or until crisp and golden brown. Drain on paper towels. Serve with sweet and sour sauce and hot mustard.
Makes about 12 egg rolls or 24 mini-egg rolls

*Egg roll filling may be made ahead to this point; cover and refrigerate up to 24 hours. When ready to use, heat mixture until hot. Proceed as directed in step 5.

Light & Easy Chinese   253

SHRIMP TOAST

Shrimp Toast, a perennial favorite of Chinese cuisine, can be easily prepared at home following this delicious recipe.

½ pound raw shrimp, peeled, deveined
2 tablespoons chopped green onion
2 tablespoons finely chopped water chestnuts
2 tablespoons soy sauce

1 teaspoon Oriental sesame oil
1 egg white, slightly beaten
6 slices white sandwich bread, crusts removed
Red and yellow bell peppers for garnish

1. Finely chop shrimp. If using food processor, process with on/off pulses, about 10 times or until shrimp are finely chopped.

2. Combine shrimp, onion, water chestnuts, soy sauce and sesame oil in medium bowl; mix well. Stir in egg white; mix well.*

3. Toast bread lightly on both sides. Cut toast diagonally into quarters. Spread shrimp mixture evenly over toast to edges.

4. Place toast on foil-lined baking sheet or broiler pan. Broil 6 inches from heat 4 minutes or until lightly browned. Garnish with peppers.

Makes 2 dozen appetizers

Note: For information on storing unused water chestnuts, see page 245.

*The filling may be made ahead to this point; cover and refrigerate filling up to 24 hours. Proceed as directed in step 3.

CHICKEN AND CORN SOUP

1 can (17 ounces) cream-style corn
1 can (about 14 ounces) chicken broth
1½ cups shredded cooked chicken or turkey
1 tablespoon soy sauce

1 tablespoon dry sherry
1 teaspoon minced fresh ginger
⅛ teaspoon ground white pepper
1 teaspoon Oriental sesame oil (optional)
¼ cup thinly sliced green onions

1. Combine corn, broth, chicken, soy sauce, sherry, ginger and pepper in large saucepan. Bring to a boil over high heat. Reduce heat to medium-low.

2. Simmer, uncovered, 5 minutes; remove from heat. Stir in sesame oil. Sprinkle with onions. Ladle into soup bowls.

Makes 4 appetizer servings (about 5 cups)

Shrimp Toast

MEATS

PEPPER BEEF

This makes a colorful entrée.

1 tablespoon soy sauce
2 cloves garlic, minced
¼ teaspoon crushed red pepper
   flakes
1 boneless beef sirloin, tenderloin
   or rib eye steak, cut 1 inch
   thick (about 1 pound)
2 tablespoons peanut or vegetable
   oil, divided
1 small red bell pepper, cut into
   thin strips

1 small yellow or green bell
   pepper, cut into thin strips
1 small onion, cut into thin strips
¼ cup stir-fry sauce
2 tablespoons rice wine or dry
   white wine
¼ cup coarsely chopped cilantro
   Hot cooked white rice or Chinese
   egg noodles (optional)

1. Combine soy sauce, garlic and crushed red pepper in medium bowl. Cut beef across the grain into ⅛-inch slices; cut each slice into 1½-inch pieces. Toss beef with soy sauce mixture.

2. Heat wok or large skillet over medium-high heat. Add 1 tablespoon oil; heat until hot. Add half of beef mixture; stir-fry until beef is barely pink in center. Remove and reserve. Repeat with remaining beef mixture; remove and reserve.

3. Heat remaining 1 tablespoon oil in wok; add bell peppers and onion. Reduce heat to medium. Stir-fry 6 to 7 minutes until vegetables are crisp-tender. Add stir-fry sauce and wine; stir-fry 2 minutes or until heated through.

4. Return beef along with any accumulated juices to wok; heat through. Sprinkle with cilantro. Serve over rice.   *Makes 4 servings*

Pepper Beef

PORK WITH THREE ONIONS

⅓ cup teriyaki sauce
2 cloves garlic, minced
1 pound pork tenderloin
2 tablespoons peanut or vegetable oil, divided
1 small red onion, cut into thin wedges

1 small yellow onion, cut into thin wedges
1 teaspoon sugar
1 teaspoon cornstarch
2 green onions, cut into 1-inch pieces
Fried bean threads* (optional)

1. Combine teriyaki sauce and garlic in shallow bowl. Cut pork across the grain into ¼-inch slices; cut each slice in half. Toss pork with teriyaki mixture. Marinate at room temperature 10 minutes.

2. Heat large skillet over medium-high heat. Add 1 tablespoon oil; heat until hot. Drain pork; reserve marinade. Stir-fry pork 3 minutes or until no longer pink. Remove and reserve.

3. Heat remaining 1 tablespoon oil in skillet; add red and yellow onions. Reduce heat to medium. Cook 4 to 5 minutes until softened, stirring occasionally. Sprinkle with sugar; cook 1 minute more.

4. Blend reserved marinade into cornstarch in cup until smooth. Stir into skillet. Stir-fry 1 minute or until sauce boils and thickens.

5. Return pork along with any accumulated juices to skillet; heat through. Stir in green onions. Serve over bean threads. *Makes 4 servings*

*To fry bean threads, follow package directions.

FRAGRANT BEEF WITH GARLIC SAUCE

1 boneless beef top sirloin steak, cut 1 inch thick (about 1¼ pounds)

⅓ cup teriyaki sauce
10 large cloves garlic, peeled
½ cup beef broth

1. Place beef in large plastic bag. Pour teriyaki sauce over beef. Close bag securely; turn to coat. Marinate in refrigerator at least 30 minutes or up to 4 hours.

2. Combine garlic and broth in small saucepan. Bring to a boil over high heat. Reduce heat to medium. Simmer, uncovered, 5 minutes. Cover and simmer 8 to 9 minutes until garlic is softened. Transfer to blender or food processor; process until smooth.

3. Meanwhile, drain beef; reserve marinade. Place beef on rack of broiler pan. Brush with half of reserved marinade. Broil 5 to 6 inches from heat 5 minutes. Turn beef over; brush with remaining marinade. Broil 5 minutes.*

4. Slice beef thinly; serve with garlic sauce. *Makes 4 servings*

*Broiling time is for medium-rare doneness. Adjust time for desired doneness.

Pork with Three Onions

ORANGE BEEF

1 boneless beef sirloin or
    tenderloin steak, cut 1 inch
    thick (about 1 pound)
2 cloves garlic, minced
1 teaspoon grated *fresh* orange
    peel
2 tablespoons soy sauce
2 tablespoons orange juice

1 tablespoon dry sherry
1 tablespoon cornstarch
1 tablespoon peanut or vegetable
    oil
2 cups hot cooked white rice
    (optional)
Orange slices for garnish

1. Cut beef across the grain into ⅛-inch slices; cut each slice into 2-inch pieces. Toss with garlic and orange peel in medium bowl.

2. Blend soy sauce, orange juice and sherry into cornstarch in cup until smooth.

3. Heat wok or large skillet over medium-high heat. Add oil; heat until hot. Add beef mixture; stir-fry 2 to 3 minutes or until beef is barely pink in center. Stir soy sauce mixture and add to wok. Stir-fry 30 seconds or until sauce boils and thickens. Serve over rice. Garnish with orange slices.

Makes 4 servings

MONGOLIAN HOT POT

With this fondue-like dish, each person cooks their own dinner in a simmering broth. When all the food is cooked, spinach is added to the broth. Then the broth is served over bean threads in soup bowls.

2 ounces bean threads
1 boneless beef sirloin or
    tenderloin steak, cut 1 inch
    thick (about ½ pound)
1 can (46 ounces) chicken broth
½ pound pork tenderloin, cut into
    ⅛-inch slices

½ pound medium raw shrimp,
    peeled, deveined
½ pound sea scallops, cut
    lengthwise into halves
½ pound small fresh mushrooms
    Dipping Sauce (recipe follows)
1 pound spinach leaves

1. Place bean threads in medium bowl; cover with warm water. Soak 15 minutes to soften; drain well. Cut bean threads into 1- to 2-inch lengths; set aside.

2. Cut beef across the grain into ⅛-inch slices; cut each slice into 1½-inch pieces.

3. Heat broth in electric skillet to a simmer (or, heat half of broth in fondue pot, keeping remaining broth hot for replacement).

4. Arrange beef, pork, shrimp, scallops and mushrooms on large platter.

5. Prepare Dipping Sauce.

6. To serve, select food from platter and cook it in simmering broth until desired doneness, using chop sticks or long-handled fork. Dip into dipping sauce before eating.

6. After all the food is cooked, stir spinach into broth and heat until wilted. (Cook spinach in two batches if using a fondue pot.) Place bean threads in individual soup bowls. Ladle broth mixture into bowls. Season with dipping sauce, if desired.

Makes 4 to 6 servings

Dipping Sauce: Combine ½ cup lite soy sauce, ¼ cup dry sherry and 1 tablespoon Oriental sesame oil in small bowl; divide into individual dipping bowls.

HONEY-GLAZED PORK

1 large *or* 2 small pork tenderloins
    (about 1¼ pounds total
    weight)
¼ cup soy sauce
2 cloves garlic, minced

3 tablespoons honey
2 tablespoons brown sugar
1 teaspoon minced fresh ginger
1 tablespoon toasted sesame
    seeds*

1. Place pork in large plastic bag. Combine soy sauce and garlic in small cup; pour over pork. Close bag securely; turn to coat. Marinate in refrigerator up to 2 hours.

2. Preheat oven to 400°F. Drain pork; reserve 1 tablespoon marinade. Combine honey, brown sugar, ginger and reserved marinade in small bowl.

3. Place pork in shallow, foil-lined roasting pan. Brush with half of honey mixture. Roast 10 minutes. Turn pork over; brush with remaining honey mixture and sprinkle with sesame seeds. Roast 10 minutes for small or 15 minutes for large tenderloin or until internal temperature reaches 155°F when tested with a meat thermometer inserted in thickest part of pork.

4. Let pork stand, tented with foil, on cutting board 5 minutes. (Temperature will rise to 160°F.) Pour pan juices into serving pitcher. Cut pork across the grain into ½-inch slices. Serve with pan juices. *Makes 4 servings*

*To toast sesame seeds, spread seeds in small skillet. Shake skillet over medium heat 2 minutes or until seeds begin to pop and turn golden.

MING DYNASTY BEEF STEW

2 pounds boneless beef chuck or
    veal shoulder, cut into 1½-inch
    pieces
1 teaspoon Chinese five-spice
    powder
½ teaspoon crushed red pepper
    flakes
2 tablespoons peanut or vegetable
    oil, divided
1 large onion, coarsely chopped

2 cloves garlic, minced
1 cup beef broth
1 cup regular or light beer
2 tablespoons soy sauce
1 tablespoon cornstarch
    Hot cooked Chinese egg noodles
    Grated lemon peel, chopped
      cilantro, *and/or* chopped
      peanuts for garnish

1. Sprinkle beef with five-spice powder and crushed red pepper. Heat large saucepan or Dutch oven over medium-high heat. Add 1 tablespoon oil; heat until hot. Add half of beef; brown on all sides. Remove and reserve. Repeat with remaining oil and beef.

2. Add onion and garlic to saucepan; cook 3 minutes, stirring occasionally. Add broth and beer; bring to a boil. Reduce heat to medium-low. Return beef along with any accumulated juices to saucepan; cover and simmer 1 hour and 15 minutes or until beef is fork tender.*

3. Blend soy sauce into cornstarch in cup until smooth. Stir into saucepan. Cook, uncovered, 2 minutes or until mixture thickens, stirring occasionally. Serve over noodles. Garnish as desired. *Makes 6 to 8 servings*

*Stew may be oven-braised if saucepan or Dutch oven is ovenproof. Cover and bake in 350°F oven 1 hour and 15 minutes or until beef is fork tender. Proceed as directed in step 3.

SPICY BEEF WITH NOODLES

This dish is perfect for make-ahead entertaining and is easy to transport. It is great for a buffet, since the flavors are best when served at room temperature.

1 package (1 ounce) dried black Chinese mushrooms*
6 tablespoons peanut or vegetable oil, divided
2 teaspoons minced fresh ginger
2 large cloves garlic, minced
½ teaspoon crushed red pepper flakes
2 tablespoons soy sauce
2 tablespoons rice vinegar
1 teaspoon Oriental sesame oil
1 boneless beef top sirloin steak, cut 1 inch thick (about 1 pound)

1 red bell pepper, cut into short, thin strips
5 ounces (1½ cups) fresh snow peas, cut lengthwise into thin strips
8 ounces vermicelli or thin spaghetti, broken in half *or* somen noodles, cooked and drained
Coarsely chopped roasted cashews (optional)

1. Place mushrooms in small bowl; cover with warm water. Soak 20 minutes to soften. Drain; squeeze out excess water. Discard stems; slice caps.

2. Combine 2 tablespoons peanut oil, ginger, garlic and crushed red pepper in small bowl. Spread 2 teaspoons oil mixture evenly over both sides of steak. Marinate at room temperature 15 minutes or cover and refrigerate up to 24 hours. Stir soy sauce, vinegar, 3 tablespoons peanut oil and sesame oil into remaining oil mixture; set aside.

3. Heat large, deep nonstick skillet over medium to medium-high heat until hot. Add steak; cook 4 to 5 minutes per side.** Let stand on cutting board 10 minutes.

4. Heat remaining 1 tablespoon peanut oil in skillet over medium heat. Add mushrooms, red bell pepper and snow peas; stir-fry 3 to 4 minutes until vegetables are crisp-tender.

5. Toss hot cooked vermicelli with reserved oil mixture in large bowl. Cut steak across the grain into ⅛-inch slices; cut each slice into 1½-inch pieces. Add steak along with any accumulated juices to noodle mixture. Add vegetables; toss well. Serve warm, at room temperature or chilled. Just before serving, sprinkle with cashews.

Makes 4 to 6 servings

*Or, substitute 4 ounces fresh shiitake mushrooms; discard stems and slice caps. Omit step 1.

**Cooking time is for medium-rare doneness. Adjust time for desired doneness.

Spicy Beef with Noodles

CANTON PORK STEW

1½ pounds lean pork shoulder or
    pork loin roast, cut into 1-inch
    pieces
1 teaspoon ground ginger
¼ teaspoon ground cinnamon
¼ teaspoon ground red pepper
1 tablespoon peanut or vegetable
    oil
1 large onion, coarsely chopped
3 cloves garlic, minced

1 can (about 14 ounces) chicken
    broth
¼ cup dry sherry
1 package (about 10 ounces)
    frozen baby carrots, thawed
1 large green bell pepper, cut into
    1-inch pieces
3 tablespoons soy sauce
1½ tablespoons cornstarch
    Cilantro for garnish

1. Sprinkle pork with ginger, cinnamon and ground red pepper; toss well. Heat large saucepan or Dutch oven over medium-high heat. Add oil; heat until hot.

2. Add pork to saucepan; brown on all sides. Add onion and garlic; cook 2 minutes, stirring frequently. Add broth and sherry. Bring to a boil over high heat. Reduce heat to medium-low. Cover and simmer 40 minutes.

3. Stir in carrots and green pepper; cover and simmer 10 minutes or until pork is fork tender. Blend soy sauce into cornstarch in cup until smooth. Stir into stew. Cook and stir 1 minute or until stew boils and thickens. Ladle into soup bowls. Garnish with cilantro.
Makes 6 servings

MEAT PATTIES WITH CHINESE GRAVY

1 pound lean ground beef
¼ cup fresh bread crumbs
3 tablespoons minced onion
3 tablespoons chopped cilantro,
    divided
2 tablespoons oyster sauce
2 cloves garlic, minced

1 cup beef broth
1 tablespoon cornstarch
¼ teaspoon sugar
¼ teaspoon crushed red pepper
    flakes (optional)
    Hot cooked white rice (optional)

1. Combine ground beef, bread crumbs, onion, 2 tablespoons cilantro, oyster sauce and garlic in medium bowl. Mix lightly, but thoroughly. Shape to form 4 oval patties, ½ inch thick.

2. Heat large nonstick skillet over medium heat. Add patties; cook 7 minutes. Turn patties over; cook 6 to 7 minutes.*

3. Remove patties to warm serving platter. Spoon off fat from skillet, if necessary. Blend broth into cornstarch in small bowl until smooth. Pour into skillet along with sugar and crushed red pepper. Cook and stir 1 minute or until sauce boils and thickens; pour over patties. Sprinkle with remaining 1 tablespoon cilantro. Serve with rice.
Makes 4 servings

*Cooking time is for medium doneness. Adjust time for desired doneness.

Canton Pork Stew

SWEET AND SOUR PORK

To lighten this dish, the pork is stir-fried, not deep-fat fried.

1 tablespoon soy sauce
2 cloves garlic, minced
1 lean boneless pork loin or
    tenderloin roast* (about 1
    pound)
1 can (8 ounces) pineapple chunks
    in juice, undrained
2 tablespoons peanut or vegetable
    oil, divided

2 medium carrots, diagonally cut
    into thin slices
1 large green bell pepper, cut into
    1-inch pieces
⅓ cup stir-fry sauce
1 tablespoon white wine or white
    vinegar
Hot cooked white rice (optional)

1. Combine soy sauce and garlic in medium bowl. Cut pork across the grain into 1-inch pieces; toss with soy sauce mixture.

2. Drain pineapple; reserve 2 tablespoons juice.

3. Heat wok or large skillet over medium-high heat. Add 1 tablespoon oil; heat until hot. Add pork mixture; stir-fry 4 to 5 minutes until pork is no longer pink. Remove and reserve.

4. Heat remaining 1 tablespoon oil in wok. Add carrots and green pepper; stir-fry 4 to 5 minutes until vegetables are crisp-tender. Add pineapple; heat through.

5. Add stir-fry sauce, reserved pineapple juice and vinegar; stir-fry 30 seconds or until sauce boils.

6. Return pork along with any accumulated juices to wok; heat through. Serve over rice.   *Makes 4 servings*

*Or, substitute 1 pound boneless skinless chicken breasts or thighs.

SESAME-GARLIC FLANK STEAK

1 beef flank steak (about
    1¼ pounds)
2 tablespoons soy sauce

2 tablespoons hoisin sauce
1 tablespoon Oriental sesame oil
2 cloves garlic, minced

1. Score steak lightly with a sharp knife in a diamond pattern on both sides; place in large plastic bag.

2. Combine remaining ingredients in small bowl; pour over steak. Close bag securely; turn to coat. Marinate in refrigerator at least 2 hours or up to 24 hours, turning once.

3. Drain steak; reserve marinade. Brush steak with some of the marinade. Grill or broil 5 to 6 inches from heat 5 minutes. Brush with marinade; turn steak over. Discard remaining marinade. Grill or broil 5 to 7 minutes until internal temperature reaches 135°F on meat thermometer inserted in thickest part of steak.*

4. Transfer steak to cutting board; carve across the grain into thin slices.
    Makes 4 servings

*Broiling time is for medium-rare doneness. Adjust time for desired doneness.

ORIENTAL BEEF WITH VEGETABLES

Start with one pound of ground meat to make this easy stir-fry your kids will love.

1 pound lean ground beef or
   ground turkey
1 large onion, coarsely chopped
2 cloves garlic, minced
2½ cups (8 ounces) frozen mixed
   vegetable medley, such as
   carrots, broccoli and red
   peppers, thawed

½ cup stir-fry sauce
1 can (3 ounces) chow mein
   noodles

1. Cook beef and onion in wok or large skillet over medium heat until beef is no longer pink, stirring to separate beef. Spoon off fat.

2. Add garlic; stir-fry 1 minute. Add vegetables; stir-fry 2 minutes or until heated through.

3. Add stir-fry sauce; stir-fry 30 seconds or until hot. Serve over chow mein noodles.

Makes 4 servings

ROASTED PORK

3 tablespoons hoisin sauce
1 tablespoon soy sauce
1 tablespoon dry sherry
2 cloves garlic, minced
½ teaspoon crushed Szechuan
   peppercorns or crushed red
   pepper flakes

2 whole pork tenderloin roasts
   (about 1¼ to 1½ pounds total
   weight)

1. Preheat oven to 350°F. Combine hoisin sauce, soy sauce, sherry, garlic and peppercorns in small bowl.

2. Brush one fourth of hoisin sauce mixture evenly over each roast. Place roasts on rack in shallow, foil-lined roasting pan. Cook roasts 15 minutes; turn and brush with remaining hoisin sauce mixture. Continue to cook until internal temperature reaches 155°F on meat thermometer inserted in thickest part of pork. (Timing will depend on thickness of pork; test at 30 minutes.)

3. Let pork stand, tented with foil, on cutting board 5 minutes. (Temperature of pork will rise to 160°F). Slice diagonally and serve warm. Or, for use in other recipes, cut into portions and refrigerate up to 3 days or freeze up to 3 months.

Makes 4 to 6 servings

Variation: For *Chinese Barbecued Pork,* add 1 teaspoon red food coloring to hoisin sauce mixture. Prepare roasts as directed in recipe. Roasts may be grilled over medium coals until an internal temperature reaches 155°F on meat thermometer. (Turn pork after 8 minutes; check temperature at 16 minutes.)

POULTRY

ALMOND CHICKEN

⅓ cup blanched whole almonds
1 pound boneless skinless chicken breasts or thighs
2 cloves garlic, minced
1 teaspoon minced fresh ginger
¼ teaspoon crushed red pepper flakes
¾ cup chicken broth
¼ cup soy sauce — *less*

4 teaspoons cornstarch
4 large ribs bok choy (about ¾ pound)
2 tablespoons peanut or vegetable oil, divided
2 medium carrots, thinly sliced
Chow mein noodles or hot cooked white rice

1. Preheat oven to 350°F. Spread almonds on baking sheet. Toast 6 to 7 minutes until golden brown, stirring once. Set aside.

2. Cut chicken into 1-inch pieces. Toss chicken with garlic, ginger and crushed red pepper in medium bowl. Marinate chicken at room temperature 15 minutes.

3. Blend broth and soy sauce into cornstarch in small bowl until smooth.

4. Cut woody stems from bok choy leaves; slice stems into ½-inch pieces. Cut tops of leaves crosswise into halves.

5. Heat wok or large skillet over medium-high heat. Add 1 tablespoon oil; heat until hot. Add chicken mixture; stir-fry 3 minutes or until chicken is no longer pink. Remove and reserve.

6. Heat remaining 1 tablespoon oil in wok; add bok choy stems and carrots. Stir-fry 5 minutes or until vegetables are crisp-tender. Stir broth mixture and add to wok along with bok choy leaves. Stir-fry 1 minute or until sauce boils and thickens.

7. Return chicken along with any accumulated juices to wok; heat through. Stir in almonds. Serve over chow mein noodles.   *Makes 4 servings*

Almond Chicken

GINGERED CHICKEN THIGHS

1 tablespoon peanut or vegetable oil
½ teaspoon hot chili oil
8 chicken thighs (1½ to 2 pounds)
2 cloves garlic, minced

¼ cup sweet and sour sauce
1 tablespoon soy sauce
2 teaspoons minced fresh ginger
Cilantro and strips of orange peel for garnish

1. Heat large nonstick skillet over medium-high heat. Add peanut oil and chili oil; heat until hot. Cook chicken, skin side down, 4 minutes or until golden brown.

2. Reduce heat to low; turn chicken skin side up. Cover and cook 15 to 18 minutes until juices run clear.

3. Spoon off fat. Increase heat to medium. Stir in garlic and cook 2 minutes. Combine sweet and sour sauce, soy sauce and ginger. Brush half of mixture over chicken; turn chicken over. Brush remaining mixture over chicken. Cook 5 minutes, turning once more, until sauce has thickened and chicken is browned. Transfer chicken to serving platter; pour sauce evenly over chicken. Garnish with cilantro and orange peel.

Makes 4 servings

PINEAPPLE-HOISIN HENS

Hoisin sauce is a sweet-spicy, thick, brown sauce that is frequently used in Chinese cooking.

2 cloves garlic
1 can (8 ounces) crushed pineapple in juice, undrained
2 tablespoons rice vinegar
2 tablespoons soy sauce
2 tablespoons hoisin sauce

2 teaspoons minced fresh ginger
1 teaspoon Chinese five-spice powder
2 large Cornish hens (about 1½ pounds each), split in half

1. Mince garlic in blender or food processor. Add pineapple with juice; process until fairly smooth. Add remaining ingredients except hens; process 5 seconds.

2. Place hens in large plastic bag; pour pineapple mixture over hens. Close bag securely; turn to coat. Marinate in refrigerator at least 2 hours or up to 24 hours, turning bag once.

3. Preheat oven to 375°F. Drain hens; reserve marinade. Place hens, skin side up, on rack in shallow, foil-lined roasting pan. Roast 35 minutes.

4. Brush hens lightly with some of the reserved marinade; discard remaining marinade. Roast 10 minutes or until hens are browned and juices run clear.

Makes 4 servings

Gingered Chicken Thighs

SHANGHAI CHICKEN WITH ASPARAGUS AND HAM

2 cups diagonally cut 1-inch
    asparagus pieces*
1 pound boneless skinless chicken
    breasts or thighs
1 tablespoon peanut or vegetable
    oil

1 medium onion, coarsely chopped
2 cloves garlic, minced
¼ cup stir-fry sauce
½ cup diced deli ham
    Hot cooked Chinese egg noodles
    or white rice (optional)

1. To blanch asparagus pieces, cook 3 minutes in boiling water to cover. Plunge asparagus into cold water. Drain well.

2. Cut chicken crosswise into 1-inch pieces.

3. Heat wok or large skillet over medium-high heat. Add oil; heat until hot.

4. Add onion and garlic; stir-fry 2 minutes. Add chicken; stir-fry 2 minutes. Add asparagus; stir-fry 2 minutes or until chicken is no longer pink.

5. Add stir-fry sauce; mix well. Add ham; stir-fry until heated through. Serve over noodles. *Makes 4 servings*

*Or, substitute thawed frozen asparagus. Omit step 1.

CRISPY ROASTED CHICKEN

Any remaining cooked chicken can be used to make another dish, such as Chinese Chicken Salad or Hot and Sour Soup.

1 roasting chicken or capon (about
    6½ pounds)
1 tablespoon peanut or vegetable
    oil

2 cloves garlic, minced
1 tablespoon soy sauce

1. Preheat oven to 350°F. Rinse chicken; pat dry. Place on rack in shallow, foil-lined roasting pan.

2. Combine oil and garlic in small cup; brush evenly over chicken. Roast 15 to 20 minutes per pound or until internal temperature reaches 170°F on meat thermometer inserted in thickest part of thigh.

3. Increase oven temperature to 450°F. Remove drippings from pan; discard. Brush chicken evenly with soy sauce. Roast 5 to 10 minutes until skin is very crisp and deep golden brown. Let stand on cutting board 10 minutes. Cover and refrigerate leftovers up to 3 days or freeze up to 3 months. *Makes 8 to 10 servings*

Shanghai Chicken with Asparagus and Ham

MOO GOO GAI PAN

1 package (1 ounce) dried black Chinese mushrooms
¼ cup lite soy sauce
2 tablespoons rice vinegar
3 cloves garlic, minced
1 pound boneless skinless chicken breasts
½ cup chicken broth
1 tablespoon cornstarch

2 tablespoons peanut or vegetable oil, divided
1 jar (7 ounces) straw mushrooms, drained
3 green onions, cut into 1-inch pieces
Hot cooked white rice or Chinese egg noodles (optional)

1. Place dried mushrooms in small bowl; cover with warm water. Soak 20 minutes to soften. Drain; squeeze out excess water. Discard stems; slice caps.

2. Combine soy sauce, vinegar and garlic in medium bowl. Cut chicken crosswise into ½-inch strips. Toss chicken with soy sauce mixture. Marinate at room temperature 20 minutes.

3. Blend broth into cornstarch in cup until smooth.

4. Heat wok or large skillet over medium-high heat. Add 1 tablespoon oil; heat until hot. Drain chicken; reserve marinade. Add chicken to wok; stir-fry chicken 3 minutes or until no longer pink. Remove and reserve.

5. Heat remaining 1 tablespoon oil in wok; add dried and straw mushrooms and onions. Stir-fry 1 minute.

6. Stir broth mixture and add to wok along with reserved marinade. Stir-fry 1 minute or until sauce boils and thickens.

7. Return chicken along with any accumulated juices to wok; heat through. Serve over rice.

Makes 4 servings

HONEY-LIME GLAZED CHICKEN

This sweet-sour sauce glazes the chicken beautifully!

1 broiler-fryer chicken, quartered (about 3½ pounds) *or* 3 pounds chicken parts

⅓ cup honey
2 tablespoons fresh lime juice
1½ tablespoons soy sauce

1. Preheat oven to 375°F. Arrange chicken, skin side up, in single layer in shallow casserole dish or 11×7-inch baking dish.

2. Combine remaining ingredients in small bowl; mix well. Brush one third of honey mixture over chicken; bake 15 minutes.

3. Brush one third of honey mixture over chicken; bake 15 minutes. Brush remaining honey mixture over chicken; bake 10 to 15 minutes until juices run clear. Transfer chicken to serving platter. If desired, spoon fat from juices in baking dish; serve with chicken.

Makes 4 servings

SZECHUAN CHICKEN SALAD WITH PEANUT DRESSING

1 pound boneless skinless chicken
   breast halves
1 can (about 14 ounces) chicken
   broth
1 tablespoon creamy peanut butter
1 tablespoon peanut or vegetable
   oil

1 tablespoon soy sauce
1 tablespoon rice vinegar
1 teaspoon Oriental sesame oil
¼ teaspoon ground red pepper
   Shredded lettuce
   Chopped cilantro or green
    onions (optional)

1. Place chicken in single layer in large skillet. Pour broth over chicken. Bring to a boil over high heat. Reduce heat to medium-low. Cover and simmer 10 to 12 minutes until chicken is no longer pink in center.

2. Meanwhile, mix peanut butter and peanut oil in small bowl until smooth. Stir in soy sauce, rice vinegar, sesame oil and ground red pepper.

3. Drain chicken; reserve broth. Stir 2 tablespoons of the reserved broth* into peanut butter mixture.

4. To serve salad warm, cut chicken crosswise into ½-inch slices and place on lettuce-lined plates. Spoon peanut dressing over chicken. Sprinkle with cilantro.

5. To serve salad at room temperature, cool chicken and shred or coarsely chop. Toss chicken with peanut dressing; cover and refrigerate. Just before serving, bring chicken mixture to room temperature (about 1 hour). Arrange chicken on lettuce-lined plates. Sprinkle with cilantro.
Makes 4 servings

*Strain remaining broth; cover and refrigerate or freeze for use in other recipes.

ORIENTAL CHICKEN KABOBS

1 pound boneless skinless chicken
   breasts
2 small zucchini or yellow squash,
   cut into 1-inch slices
8 large fresh mushrooms
1 large red, yellow or green bell
   pepper, cut into 1-inch pieces

¼ cup soy sauce
2 tablespoons dry sherry
2 teaspoons Oriental sesame oil
2 cloves garlic, minced
2 large green onions, cut into
   1-inch pieces

1. Cut chicken into 1½-inch pieces; place in large plastic bag. Add zucchini, mushrooms and red pepper to bag. Combine soy sauce, sherry, sesame oil and garlic in cup; pour over chicken and vegetables. Close bag securely; turn to coat. Marinate in refrigerator at least 30 minutes or up to 4 hours.

2. Drain chicken and vegetables; reserve marinade. Alternately thread chicken and vegetables with onions onto metal skewers.

3. Place kabobs on rack of broiler pan. Brush with half of reserved marinade. Broil 5 to 6 inches from heat 5 minutes. Turn kabobs over; brush with remaining marinade. Discard any remaining marinade. Broil 5 minutes or until chicken is no longer pink.
Makes 4 servings

ORANGE-GINGER BROILED CORNISH HENS

This easy-to-do entrée will impress your guests!

**2 large Cornish hens, split (about
1½ pounds each)
2 teaspoons peanut or vegetable
oil, divided**

**¼ cup orange marmalade
1 tablespoon minced fresh ginger**

1. Place hens, skin side up, on rack of foil-lined broiler pan. Brush with 1 teaspoon oil.

2. Broil 6 to 7 inches from heat 10 minutes. Turn hens skin side down; brush with remaining 1 teaspoon oil. Broil 10 minutes.

3. Combine marmalade and ginger in cup; brush half of mixture over hens. Broil 5 minutes.

4. Turn hens skin side up; brush with remaining marmalade mixture. Broil 5 minutes or until juices run clear and hens are browned and glazed.   *Makes 4 servings*

CHICKEN CHOP SUEY

Chop Suey originated in California and literally means "chopped up" leftovers.

**1 package (1 ounce) dried black
Chinese mushrooms
3 tablespoons soy sauce
1 tablespoon cornstarch
1 pound boneless skinless chicken
breasts or thighs
2 cloves garlic, minced
1 tablespoon peanut or vegetable
oil**

**½ cup thinly sliced celery
½ cup sliced water chestnuts
½ cup bamboo shoots
1 cup chicken broth
Hot cooked white rice or chow
mein noodles
Thinly sliced green onions
(optional)**

1. Place mushrooms in small bowl; cover with warm water. Soak 20 minutes to soften. Drain; squeeze out excess water. Discard stems; quarter caps.

2. Blend soy sauce into cornstarch in cup until smooth.

3. Cut chicken into 1-inch pieces; toss with garlic in small bowl. Heat wok or large skillet over medium-high heat. Add oil; heat until hot. Add chicken mixture and celery; stir-fry 2 minutes. Add water chestnuts and bamboo shoots; stir-fry 1 minute. Add broth and mushrooms; cook 3 minutes or until chicken is no longer pink in center, stirring frequently.

4. Stir soy sauce mixture and add to wok. Cook and stir 1 to 2 minutes until sauce boils and thickens. Serve over rice. Garnish with onions.   *Makes 4 servings*

Note: For information on storing unused bamboo shoots and water chestnuts, see pages 244 and 245.

Orange-Ginger Broiled Cornish Hen

CHICKEN CHOW MEIN

This light version of chow mein omits the deep-fat frying of the noodles.

**1 pound boneless skinless chicken
breasts or thighs
2 cloves garlic, minced
2 tablespoons peanut or vegetable
oil, divided
¼ cup soy sauce
2 tablespoons dry sherry
6 ounces (2 cups) fresh snow peas
or 1 package (6 ounces) frozen
snow peas, thawed, cut into
halves**

**3 large green onions, cut
diagonally into 1-inch pieces
6 ounces uncooked Chinese egg
noodles or vermicelli, cooked,
drained and rinsed
1 tablespoon Oriental sesame oil**

1. Cut chicken crosswise into ¼-inch slices; cut each slice into 1×¼-inch strips. Toss chicken with garlic in small bowl.

2. Heat wok or large skillet over medium-high heat. Add 1 tablespoon peanut oil; heat until hot. Add chicken mixture; stir-fry 3 minutes or until chicken is no longer pink. Transfer to bowl; toss with soy sauce and sherry.

3. Heat remaining 1 tablespoon peanut oil in wok. Add snow peas; stir-fry 2 minutes for fresh or 1 minute for frozen snow peas. Add onions; stir-fry 30 seconds. Add chicken mixture; stir-fry 1 minute.

4. Add noodles to wok; stir-fry 2 minutes or until heated through. Stir in sesame oil; serve immediately.   *Makes 4 servings*

HOISIN-ROASTED CHICKEN WITH VEGETABLES

**1 broiler-fryer chicken, cut up
(about 3 pounds)
3 tablespoons hoisin sauce
1 tablespoon dry sherry
1 tablespoon Oriental sesame oil
6 ounces medium or large fresh
mushrooms**

**2 small red or yellow onions, cut
into thin wedges
1 package (9 or 10 ounces) frozen
baby carrots, thawed**

1. Preheat oven to 375°F. Place chicken, skin side up, in shallow, lightly oiled, foil-lined roasting pan.

2. Combine hoisin sauce, sherry and sesame oil in small bowl. Brush half of mixture evenly over chicken; bake 20 minutes.

3. Scatter mushrooms, onions and carrots around chicken. Brush remaining hoisin sauce mixture over chicken and vegetables; bake 20 minutes or until juices from chicken run clear.   *Makes 4 to 6 servings*

Chicken Chow Mein

SESAME CHICKEN

1 pound boneless skinless chicken breasts or thighs
⅓ cup teriyaki sauce
2 teaspoons cornstarch
1 tablespoon peanut or vegetable oil

2 cloves garlic, minced
2 large green onions, cut into ½-inch slices
1 tablespoon toasted sesame seeds*
1 teaspoon Oriental sesame oil

1. Cut chicken into 1-inch pieces; toss chicken with teriyaki sauce in small bowl. Marinate at room temperature 15 minutes or cover and refrigerate up to 2 hours.

2. Drain chicken; reserve marinade. Blend reserved marinade into cornstarch in cup until smooth.

3. Heat wok or large skillet over medium-high heat. Add peanut oil; heat until hot. Add chicken and garlic; stir-fry 3 minutes or until chicken is no longer pink. Stir marinade mixture and add to wok along with onions and sesame seeds. Stir-fry 30 seconds or until sauce boils and thickens. Stir in sesame oil.   *Makes 4 servings*

*To toast sesame seeds, spread seeds in small skillet. Shake skillet over medium heat 2 minutes or until seeds begin to pop and turn golden.

CHINESE CURRIED CHICKEN

Coconut milk is available in cans in the ethnic food section of large supermarkets. If you prefer, substitute chicken broth for the coconut milk.

1 pound boneless skinless chicken breasts or thighs
1 tablespoon all-purpose flour
1 tablespoon curry powder
¼ teaspoon salt
¼ teaspoon ground red pepper
2 tablespoons peanut or vegetable oil, divided
1 large onion, chopped
2 cloves garlic, minced
1 can (14 ounces) coconut milk

3 tablespoons soy sauce
6 ounces (2 cups) fresh snow peas *or* 1 package (6 ounces) frozen snow peas, thawed
Hot cooked white rice or Chinese egg noodles
¼ cup chopped cilantro or thinly sliced green onions
2 tablespoons chopped peanuts or cashews

1. Cut chicken into 1-inch pieces. Combine flour, curry powder, salt and ground red pepper in medium plastic bag. Add chicken; shake to coat.

2. Heat large skillet over medium-high heat. Add 1 tablespoon oil; heat until hot. Add onion and garlic; cook 3 minutes, stirring occasionally.

3. Push onion mixture to edges of skillet. Add remaining 1 tablespoon oil and chicken mixture; stir-fry 2 to 3 minutes until chicken is no longer pink. Add coconut milk and soy sauce; reduce heat to medium-low. Simmer, uncovered, 10 minutes.

4. Stir in snow peas; cook 4 minutes for fresh or 2 minutes for frozen snow peas or until crisp-tender and sauce is slightly thickened. Serve over rice. Sprinkle with cilantro and peanuts.
     Makes 4 servings

KUNG PO CHICKEN

Kung Po Chicken is a Szechuan specialty. This version uses hot chili oil for the heat and is milder than recipes using dried chilies.

1 pound boneless skinless chicken breasts or thighs
2 cloves garlic, minced
1 teaspoon hot chili oil
¼ cup lite soy sauce
2 teaspoons cornstarch
1 tablespoon peanut or vegetable oil

⅓ cup roasted peanuts
2 green onions, cut into short, thin strips
Lettuce leaves (optional)
Plum sauce (optional)

1. Cut chicken into 1-inch pieces. Toss chicken with garlic and chili oil in medium bowl.

2. Blend soy sauce into cornstarch in cup until smooth.

3. Heat wok or large skillet over medium-high heat. Add peanut oil; heat until hot. Add chicken mixture; stir-fry 3 minutes or until chicken is no longer pink.

4. Stir soy sauce mixture and add to wok along with peanuts and onions. Stir-fry 1 minute or until sauce boils and thickens.

5. To serve, spread each lettuce leaf lightly with plum sauce. Add chicken mixture; roll up and serve immediately.
Makes 4 main-dish or 8 appetizer servings

CASHEW CHICKEN

1 pound boneless skinless chicken breasts or thighs
2 teaspoons minced fresh ginger
1 tablespoon peanut or vegetable oil
1 medium red bell pepper, cut into short, thin strips

⅓ cup teriyaki baste and glaze sauce
⅓ cup roasted or dry roasted cashews
Hot cooked white rice (optional)
Coarsely chopped cilantro (optional)

1. Cut chicken into ½-inch slices; cut each slice into 1½×½-inch strips. Toss chicken with ginger in small bowl.

2. Heat wok or large skillet over medium-high heat. Add oil; heat until hot. Add chicken mixture; stir-fry 2 minutes. Add red pepper; stir-fry 4 minutes or until chicken is no longer pink and red pepper is crisp-tender.

3. Add teriyaki sauce, stir-fry 1 minute or until sauce is hot. Stir in cashews. Serve over rice. Sprinkle with cilantro.
Makes 4 servings

SEAFOOD

EASY SEAFOOD STIR-FRY

Dried black mushrooms must be soaked before using.
They add a unique flavor to dishes.

1 package (1 ounce) dried black
   Chinese mushrooms*
1 cup chicken broth
3 tablespoons soy sauce
2 tablespoons dry sherry
4½ teaspoons cornstarch
2 tablespoons peanut or vegetable
   oil, divided
½ pound medium raw shrimp,
   peeled, deveined

½ pound bay scallops or halved
   sea scallops
2 cloves garlic, minced
6 ounces (2 cups) fresh snow peas,
   cut diagonally into halves
   Hot cooked noodles or white rice
¼ cup thinly sliced green onions
   (optional)

1. Place mushrooms in small bowl; cover with warm water. Soak 20 minutes to soften. Drain; squeeze out excess water. Discard stems; slice caps.

2. Blend broth, soy sauce and sherry into cornstarch in another small bowl until smooth.

3. Heat wok or large skillet over medium-high heat. Add 1 tablespoon oil; heat until hot. Add shrimp, scallops and garlic; stir-fry 3 minutes or until seafood is opaque. Remove and reserve.

4. Add remaining 1 tablespoon oil to wok. Add mushrooms and snow peas; stir-fry 3 minutes or until snow peas are crisp-tender.

5. Stir broth mixture and add to wok. Stir-fry 2 minutes or until sauce boils and thickens.

6. Return seafood along with any accumulated juices to wok; heat through. Serve over noodles. Garnish with onions. *Makes 4 servings*

*Or, substitute 1½ cups sliced fresh mushrooms. Omit step 1.

Easy Seafood Stir-Fry

GRILLED CHINESE SALMON

While salmon is not a traditional Chinese fish, this recipe gives it an Oriental twist.

3 tablespoons soy sauce
2 tablespoons dry sherry
2 cloves garlic, minced

1 pound salmon steaks or fillets
2 tablespoons finely chopped fresh cilantro

1. Combine soy sauce, sherry and garlic in shallow dish. Add salmon; turn to coat. Cover and refrigerate at least 30 minutes or up to 2 hours.

2. Drain salmon; reserve marinade. Arrange steaks (arrange fillets skin side down) on oiled rack of broiler pan or oiled grid over hot coals. Broil or grill 5 to 6 inches from heat 10 minutes. Baste with reserved marinade after 5 minutes of broiling; discard any remaining marinade. Sprinkle with cilantro. *Makes 4 servings*

STIR-FRIED CRAB

For best results use firm to extra-firm tofu for stir-fries and gently stir tofu into dish.

8 ounces firm tofu, drained
1 tablespoon soy sauce
¼ cup chicken broth
3 tablespoons oyster sauce
2 teaspoons cornstarch
1 tablespoon peanut or vegetable oil
6 ounces (2 cups) fresh snow peas, cut into halves *or* 1 package (6 ounces) frozen snow peas, separated, but not thawed

8 ounces thawed frozen cooked crabmeat or imitation crabmeat, broken into ½-inch pieces (about 2 cups)
2 tablespoons chopped cilantro or thinly sliced green onions

1. Press tofu lightly between paper towels; cut into ½-inch squares or triangles. Place in shallow dish. Drizzle soy sauce over tofu.

2. Blend broth and oyster sauce into cornstarch in cup until smooth.

3. Heat wok or large skillet over medium-high heat. Add oil; heat until hot. Add snow peas; stir-fry 3 minutes for fresh or 2 minutes for frozen snow peas. Add crabmeat; stir-fry 1 minute. Stir broth mixture and add to wok. Stir-fry 30 seconds or until sauce boils and thickens.

4. Stir in tofu mixture; heat through. Sprinkle with cilantro. *Makes 4 servings*

Note: For information on storing unused tofu, see page 245.

Grilled Chinese Salmon

GARLIC SKEWERED SHRIMP

For a prettier presentation, leave the tails on the shrimp.

**1 pound large raw shrimp, peeled,
   deveined**
2 tablespoons soy sauce
**1 tablespoon peanut or vegetable
   oil**

3 cloves garlic, minced
**¼ teaspoon crushed red pepper
   flakes (optional)**
**3 green onions, cut into 1-inch
   pieces**

1. Soak 4 (12-inch) bamboo skewers in water to cover 20 minutes.

2. Place shrimp in large plastic bag. Combine soy sauce, oil, garlic and crushed red pepper in cup; mix well. Pour over shrimp. Close bag securely; turn to coat. Marinate at room temperature 10 to 15 minutes.

3. Drain shrimp; reserve marinade. Alternately thread shrimp and onions onto skewers. Place on rack of broiler pan. Brush with reserved marinade; discard remaining marinade.

4. Broil shrimp 5 to 6 inches from heat 5 minutes. Turn shrimp over; broil 5 minutes or until shrimp are opaque.   *Makes 4 servings*

SHANGHAI STEAMED FISH

**1 cleaned whole sea bass, red
   snapper, carp or grouper
   (about 1½ pounds)**
¼ cup teriyaki sauce
2 teaspoons shredded fresh ginger

**2 green onions, cut into 4-inch
   pieces**
**1 teaspoon Oriental sesame oil
   (optional)**

1. Sprinkle inside cavity of fish with teriyaki sauce and ginger. Place onions in cavity in single layer.

2. Pour enough water into wok so that water is just below steaming rack. Bring water to a boil over high heat. Reduce heat to medium-low to maintain a simmer. Place fish on steaming rack in steamer. Cover and steam fish over simmering water about 10 minutes per inch of thickness measured at thickest part of fish. Fish is done when it flakes easily when tested with fork.

3. Carefully remove fish; discard onions. Cut fish into four serving-size portions. Sprinkle with sesame oil.   *Makes 4 servings*

Garlic Skewered Shrimp

BEIJING FILLET OF SOLE

These rolled stuffed fillets are easy-to-make and bake in just 30 minutes.

2 tablespoons soy sauce
1 tablespoon Oriental sesame oil
4 sole fillets (6 ounces each)
1¼ cups preshredded coleslaw mix
   or cabbage

½ cup crushed chow mein noodles
1 egg white, slightly beaten
2 teaspoons toasted sesame seeds*

1. Preheat oven to 350°F. Combine soy sauce and sesame oil in small bowl. Place sole in shallow dish. Lightly brush both sides of sole with soy sauce mixture.

2. Combine coleslaw mix, noodles, egg white and remaining soy sauce mixture in small bowl. Spoon evenly over sole. Roll up each fillet and place, seam side down, in shallow, foil-lined roasting pan. Sprinkle rolls with sesame seeds. Bake 25 to 30 minutes until fish flakes easily when tested with fork. *Makes 4 servings*

*To toast sesame seeds, spread seeds in small skillet. Shake skillet over medium heat 2 minutes or until seeds begin to pop and turn golden.

FIVE-SPICE SHRIMP WITH WALNUTS

1 pound medium or large raw
   shrimp, peeled, deveined
½ teaspoon Chinese five-spice
   powder
2 cloves garlic, minced
½ cup chicken broth
2 tablespoons soy sauce
2 tablespoons dry sherry
1 tablespoon cornstarch

1 tablespoon peanut or vegetable
   oil
1 large red bell pepper, cut into
   short, thin strips
⅓ cup walnut halves or quarters
   Hot cooked white rice (optional)
¼ cup thinly sliced green onions
   (optional)

1. Toss shrimp with five-spice powder and garlic in small bowl.

2. Blend broth, soy sauce and sherry into cornstarch in cup until smooth.

3. Heat wok or large skillet over medium-high heat. Add oil; heat until hot. Add shrimp mixture, red pepper and walnuts; stir-fry 3 to 5 minutes until shrimp are opaque and red pepper is crisp-tender.

4. Stir broth mixture and add to wok. Stir-fry 1 minute or until sauce boils and thickens. Serve over rice. Garnish with onions. *Makes 4 servings*

Beijing Fillet of Sole

HOT AND SOUR SHRIMP

The crushed red pepper creates the hot and the vinegar creates the sour in this scrumptious shrimp stir-fry.

½ package (½ ounce) dried black Chinese mushrooms
½ small unpeeled cucumber
1 tablespoon brown sugar
2 teaspoons cornstarch
3 tablespoons rice vinegar
2 tablespoons soy sauce
1 tablespoon peanut or vegetable oil

1 pound medium raw shrimp, peeled, deveined
2 cloves garlic, minced
¼ teaspoon crushed red pepper flakes
1 large red bell pepper, cut into short, thin strips
Hot cooked white rice or Chinese egg noodles (optional)

1. Place mushrooms in small bowl; cover with warm water. Soak 20 minutes to soften. Drain; squeeze out excess water. Discard stems; slice caps.

2. Cut cucumber in half lengthwise; scrape out seeds. Slice crosswise.

3. Combine brown sugar and cornstarch in small bowl. Blend in vinegar and soy sauce until smooth.

4. Heat wok or large skillet over medium-high heat. Add oil; heat until hot. Add shrimp, garlic and crushed red pepper; stir-fry 1 minute. Add mushrooms and red pepper strips; stir-fry 2 minutes or until shrimp are opaque.

5. Stir vinegar mixture and add to wok. Stir-fry 30 seconds or until sauce boils and thickens. Add cucumber; stir-fry until heated through. Serve over rice.

Makes 4 servings

HALIBUT WITH CILANTRO AND LIME

1 pound halibut, tuna or swordfish steaks
2 tablespoons fresh lime juice
¼ cup regular or lite teriyaki sauce
1 teaspoon cornstarch
½ teaspoon minced fresh ginger

1 tablespoon peanut or vegetable oil
½ cup slivered red or yellow onion
2 cloves garlic, minced
¼ cup coarsely chopped cilantro

1. Cut halibut into 1-inch pieces; sprinkle with lime juice.

2. Blend teriyaki sauce into cornstarch in cup until smooth. Stir in ginger.

3. Heat wok or large skillet over medium-high heat. Add oil; heat until hot. Add onion and garlic; stir-fry 2 minutes. Add halibut; stir-fry 2 minutes or until halibut is opaque.

4. Stir teriyaki sauce mixture and add to wok. Stir-fry 30 seconds or until sauce boils and thickens. Sprinkle with cilantro.

Makes 4 servings

BROILED HUNAN FISH FILLETS

3 tablespoons soy sauce
1 tablespoon finely chopped green
    onion
2 teaspoons Oriental sesame oil
1 teaspoon minced fresh ginger

1 clove garlic, minced
¼ teaspoon crushed red pepper
    flakes
1 pound red snapper, scrod or cod
    fillets

1. Combine soy sauce, onion, sesame oil, ginger, garlic and crushed pepper in cup.

2. Spray rack of broiler pan with nonstick cooking spray. Place fish on rack; brush with soy sauce mixture.

3. Broil 4 to 5 inches from heat 10 minutes or until fish flakes easily when tested with fork.
Makes 4 servings

ORANGE-ALMOND SCALLOPS

3 tablespoons orange juice
3 tablespoons soy sauce
1 clove garlic, minced
1 pound bay scallops or halved
    sea scallops
1 tablespoon cornstarch
2 tablespoons peanut or vegetable
    oil, divided

1 green bell pepper, cut into short,
    thin strips
1 can (8 ounces) sliced water
    chestnuts, drained and rinsed
⅓ cup toasted blanched almonds
    Hot cooked white rice (optional)
½ teaspoon finely grated orange
    peel

1. Combine orange juice, soy sauce and garlic in medium bowl. Add scallops; toss to coat. Marinate at room temperature 15 minutes or cover and refrigerate up to 1 hour.

2. Drain scallops; reserve marinade. Blend marinade into cornstarch in cup until smooth.

3. Heat wok or large skillet over medium-high heat. Add 1 tablespoon oil; heat until hot. Add scallops; stir-fry 2 minutes or until scallops are opaque. Remove and reserve.

4. Add remaining 1 tablespoon oil to wok. Add green pepper and water chestnuts. Stir-fry 3 minutes.

5. Return scallops along with any accumulated juices to wok. Stir marinade mixture and add to wok. Stir-fry 1 minute or until sauce boils and thickens. Stir in almonds. Serve over rice. Sprinkle with orange peel.
Makes 4 servings

VEGETABLES

MOO SHU VEGETABLES

½ package dried black Chinese
    mushrooms
    (6 to 7 mushrooms)
2 tablespoons peanut or vegetable
    oil
2 cloves garlic, minced
2 cups shredded napa cabbage or
    green cabbage *or* preshredded
    cabbage or coleslaw mix

1 red bell pepper, cut into short,
    thin strips
1 cup fresh or rinsed, drained
    canned bean sprouts
2 large green onions, cut into
    short, thin strips
¼ cup hoisin sauce
⅓ cup plum sauce
8 flour tortillas (6 to 7 inches),
    warmed

1. Place mushrooms in small bowl; cover with warm water. Soak 20 minutes to soften. Drain; squeeze out excess water. Discard stems; slice caps.

2. Heat wok or large skillet over medium-high heat. Add oil; heat until hot. Add garlic; stir-fry 30 seconds.

3. Add cabbage, mushrooms and red pepper; stir-fry 3 minutes. Add bean sprouts and onions; stir-fry 2 minutes. Add hoisin sauce; stir-fry 30 seconds or until mixture is hot.

4. Spread about 2 teaspoons plum sauce on each tortilla. Spoon heaping ¼ cup vegetable mixture over sauce. Fold bottom of tortilla up over filling, then fold sides over filling.
Makes 8 servings

Note: For information on storing unused bean sprouts, see page 244.

SESAME-HONEY VEGETABLE CASSEROLE

1 package (16 ounces) frozen
    mixed vegetable medley, such
    as baby carrots, broccoli,
    onions and red peppers,
    thawed and drained

3 tablespoons honey
1 tablespoon Oriental sesame oil
1 tablespoon soy sauce
2 teaspoons sesame seeds

1. Preheat oven to 350°F. Place vegetables in shallow, 1½-quart casserole dish or quiche pan.

2. Combine remaining ingredients; mix well. Drizzle evenly over vegetables. Bake 20 to 25 minutes or until vegetables are hot, stirring after 15 minutes.
Makes 4 to 6 servings

Moo Shu Vegetables

DRAGON TOFU

double

To quickly cut squash, stack several slices, then cut into 2×¼-inch strips.

¼ cup soy sauce
1 tablespoon creamy peanut butter
1 package (about 12 ounces) firm tofu, drained
1 medium zucchini squash
1 medium yellow squash
2 teaspoons peanut or vegetable oil

½ teaspoon hot chili oil
2 cloves garlic, minced
2 cups packed fresh torn spinach leaves
¼ cup coarsely chopped cashews or peanuts (optional)

1. Whisk soy sauce into peanut butter in small bowl. Press tofu lightly between paper towels; cut into ¾-inch squares or triangles. Place in single layer in shallow dish. Pour soy sauce mixture over tofu; stir gently to coat all surfaces. Let stand at room temperature 20 minutes.

2. Cut zucchini and yellow squash into ¼-inch slices; cut each slice into 2×¼-inch strips.

3. Heat nonstick skillet over medium-high heat. Add peanut oil and chili oil; heat until hot. Add garlic and squash; stir-fry 3 minutes. Add tofu mixture; cook 2 minutes or until tofu is heated through and sauce is slightly thickened, stirring occasionally.

4. Stir in spinach; remove from heat. Sprinkle with cashews.

Makes 2 main-dish or 4 side-dish servings

SZECHUAN EGGPLANT

1 pound Oriental eggplants or regular eggplant, peeled
2 tablespoons peanut or vegetable oil
2 cloves garlic, minced
¼ teaspoon crushed red pepper flakes *or* ½ teaspoon hot chili oil

3 green onions, cut into 1-inch pieces
¼ cup hoisin sauce
¼ cup chicken broth
Toasted sesame seeds* (optional)

1. Cut eggplants into ½-inch slices; cut each slice into 2×½-inch strips.

2. Heat wok or large nonstick skillet over medium-high heat. Add peanut oil; heat until hot. Add eggplant, garlic and crushed red pepper; stir-fry 7 minutes or until eggplant is very tender and browned.

3. Reduce heat to medium. Add onions, hoisin sauce and broth; stir-fry 2 minutes. Sprinkle with sesame seeds.

Makes 4 to 6 servings

*To toast sesame seeds, spread seeds in small skillet. Shake skillet over medium heat 2 minutes or until seeds begin to pop and turn golden.

Dragon Tofu

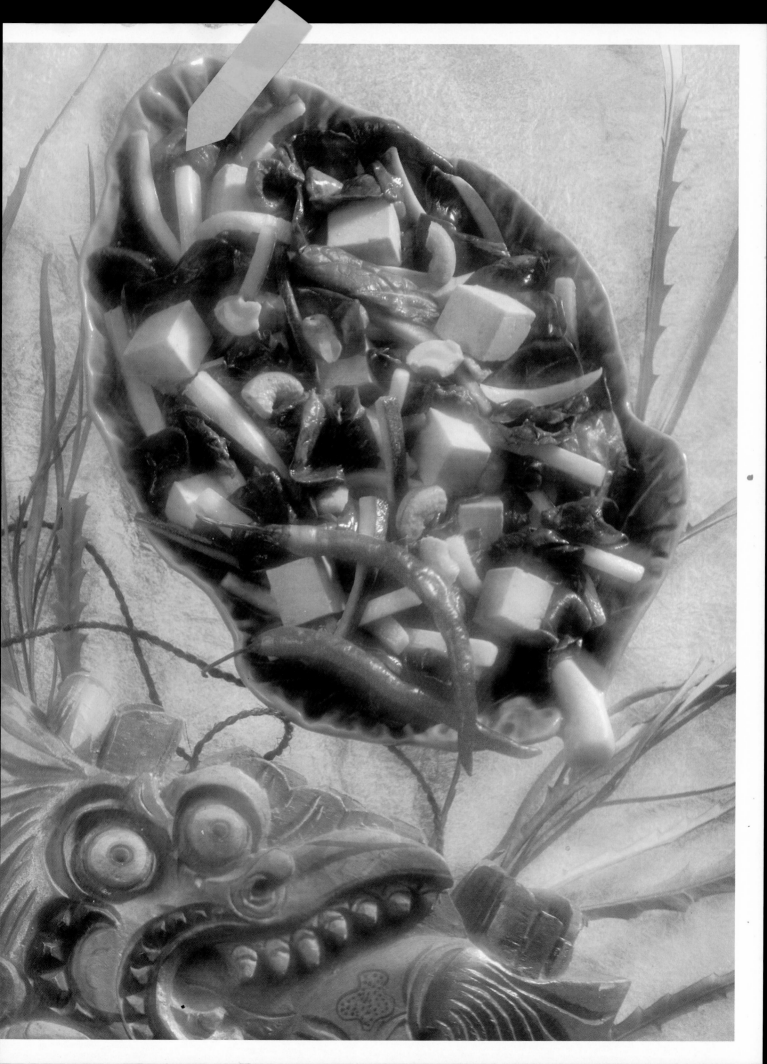

CHINESE SWEET AND SOUR VEGETABLES

3 cups broccoli florets
2 medium carrots, diagonally
   sliced
1 large red bell pepper, cut into
   short, thin strips
¼ cup water
2 teaspoons cornstarch
1 teaspoon sugar

⅓ cup unsweetened pineapple
   juice
1 tablespoon soy sauce
1 tablespoon rice vinegar
½ teaspoon Oriental sesame oil
¼ cup diagonally sliced green
   onions or chopped cilantro
   (optional)

1. Combine broccoli, carrots, and red pepper in large skillet with tight-fitting lid. Add water; bring to a boil over high heat. Reduce heat to medium. Cover and steam 4 minutes or until vegetables are crisp-tender.

2. Meanwhile, combine cornstarch and sugar in small bowl. Blend in pineapple juice, soy sauce and vinegar until smooth.

3. Transfer vegetables to colander; drain. Stir pineapple mixture and add to skillet. Cook and stir 2 minutes or until sauce boils and thickens.

4. Return vegetables to skillet; toss with sauce. Stir in sesame oil. Garnish with onions.
Makes 4 servings

THREE HAPPINESS MUSHROOMS

To save time, purchase pre-sliced fresh mushrooms and spinach leaves from the salad bar in your local supermarket.

1 package (1 ounce) dried black
   Chinese mushrooms
2 tablespoons peanut or vegetable
   oil
1 small yellow onion, cut into thin
   wedges
2 cloves garlic, minced

2 cups sliced fresh mushrooms
1 jar (7 ounces) straw mushrooms,
   drained
1 cup firmly packed fresh spinach
   leaves
3 tablespoons stir-fry sauce

1. Place dried mushrooms in small bowl; cover with warm water. Soak 20 minutes to soften. Drain; squeeze out excess water. Discard stems; slice caps.

2. Heat wok or large skillet over medium-high heat. Add oil; heat until hot. Add onion and garlic; stir-fry 6 minutes or until limp. Add dried, fresh and straw mushrooms; stir-fry 4 minutes.

3. Stir in spinach and stir-fry sauce; stir-fry 1 minute or until spinach is wilted and sauce is heated through.
Makes 4 servings

Chinese Sweet and Sour Vegetables

BUDDHA'S DELIGHT

1 package (1 ounce) dried black
  Chinese mushrooms
1 package (about 12 ounces) firm
  tofu, drained
1 tablespoon peanut or vegetable
  oil
2 cups diagonally cut 1-inch
  asparagus pieces *or* 1 package
  (10 ounces) frozen cut
  asparagus, thawed and
  drained

1 medium onion, cut into thin
  wedges
2 cloves garlic, minced
½ cup chicken broth
3 tablespoons hoisin sauce
¼ cup coarsely chopped cilantro or
  thinly sliced green onions

1. Place mushrooms in small bowl; cover with warm water. Soak 20 minutes to soften. Drain, squeezing out excess water over fine strainer into measuring cup; reserve. Discard mushroom stems; slice caps.

2. Press tofu lightly between paper towels; cut into ¾-inch squares or triangles.

3. Heat wok or large skillet over medium-high heat. Add oil; heat until hot. Add asparagus, onion wedges and garlic; stir-fry 4 minutes for fresh or 3 minutes for frozen asparagus.

4. Add mushrooms, ¼ cup reserved mushroom liquid,* broth and hoisin sauce. Reduce heat to medium-low. Simmer, uncovered, until asparagus is crisp-tender, 2 to 3 minutes for fresh or 1 minute for frozen asparagus.

5. Stir in tofu; heat through, stirring occasionally. Ladle into shallow bowls. Sprinkle with cilantro.   *Makes 2 main-dish or 4 side-dish servings*

*Remaining mushroom liquid may be covered and refrigerated up to 3 days or frozen up to 3 months. It may be used in soups and stews.

ORIENTAL SALAD SUPREME

¼ cup peanut or vegetable oil
¼ cup rice vinegar
2 tablespoons brown sugar
½ medium unpeeled cucumber,
  halved and sliced

6 cups torn romaine or leaf lettuce
1 cup chow mein noodles
¼ cup peanut halves or coarsely
  chopped cashews (optional)

1. Combine oil, vinegar and brown sugar in small bowl; whisk until sugar dissolves.* Toss with cucumbers. Marinate, covered, in the refrigerator up to 4 hours.

2. Just before serving, toss dressing with remaining ingredients.   *Makes 4 servings*

*At this point, dressing may be tossed with remaining ingredients and served immediately.

Buddha's Delight

SZECHUAN-GRILLED MUSHROOMS

1 pound large fresh mushrooms
2 tablespoons soy sauce
2 teaspoons peanut or vegetable oil
1 teaspoon Oriental sesame oil

1 clove garlic, minced
½ teaspoon crushed Szechuan peppercorns or crushed red pepper flakes

1. Place mushrooms in large plastic bag. Add remaining ingredients to bag. Close bag securely; shake to coat mushrooms with marinade. Marinate at room temperature 15 minutes or cover and refrigerate up to 8 hours. (Mushrooms will absorb marinade.)

2. Thread mushrooms onto skewers. Grill or broil mushrooms 5 inches from heat 10 minutes or until lightly browned, turning once. Serve immediately.

Makes 4 servings

Variation: For *Szechuan-Grilled Mushrooms and Onions*, add 4 green onions, cut into 1½-inch pieces, to marinade. Alternately thread onto skewers with mushrooms. Proceed as directed in step 2.

STIR-FRIED SPINACH WITH GARLIC

2 teaspoons peanut or vegetable oil
1 large clove garlic, minced
6 cups packed fresh spinach leaves (about 8 ounces)

2 teaspoons soy sauce
1 teaspoon rice vinegar
¼ teaspoon sugar
1 teaspoon toasted sesame seeds*

1. Heat wok or large skillet over medium-high heat. Add oil; heat until hot. Add garlic; cook 1 minute.

2. Add spinach, soy sauce, vinegar and sugar; stir-fry 1 to 2 minutes until spinach is wilted. Sprinkle with sesame seeds.

Makes 2 servings

*To toast sesame seeds, spread seeds in small skillet. Shake skillet over medium heat 2 minutes or until seeds begin to pop and turn golden.

MARINATED CUCUMBERS

Serve as a salad or a condiment with pork or chicken dishes.

1 large cucumber (about 12 ounces)
2 tablespoons rice vinegar
2 tablespoons peanut or vegetable oil

2 tablespoons soy sauce
1½ teaspoons sugar
1 clove garlic, minced
¼ teaspoon crushed red pepper flakes

1. Score cucumber lengthwise with tines of fork. Cut in half lengthwise; scrape out and discard seeds. Cut crosswise into ⅛-inch slices; place in medium bowl.

2. Combine remaining ingredients in cup; pour over cucumber. Toss to coat. Cover and refrigerate at least 4 hours or up to 2 days.

Makes 4 to 6 servings

MA PO TOFU

This lighter version of a Szechuan specialty omits the pork and adds vegetables.

1 package (about 12 ounces) firm
    tofu, drained
2 tablespoons soy sauce
2 teaspoons minced fresh ginger
1 cup chicken broth, divided
1 tablespoon cornstarch

1½ cups broccoli florets
1 teaspoon hot chili oil
2 teaspoons Oriental sesame oil
¼ cup coarsely chopped cilantro or
    green onion tops

1. Press tofu lightly between paper towels; cut into ¾-inch squares or triangles. Place in shallow dish; sprinkle with soy sauce and ginger.

2. Blend ¼ cup broth into cornstarch in cup until smooth. Combine remaining ¾ cup broth, broccoli and chili oil in 10-inch skillet. Bring to a boil over high heat. Reduce heat to medium. Cover and cook 3 minutes or until broccoli is crisp-tender.

3. Stir broth mixture and add to skillet. Cook and stir 1 minute or until sauce boils and thickens. Stir in tofu mixture. Simmer, uncovered, until tofu is hot. Stir in sesame oil. Sprinkle with cilantro. *Makes 2 main-dish or 4 side-dish servings*

ROASTED VEGETABLES WITH NOODLES

Oven roasting gives these vegetables a browned appearance.

5 tablespoons soy sauce, divided
3 tablespoons peanut or vegetable
    oil
2 tablespoons rice vinegar
2 cloves garlic, minced
½ pound large fresh mushrooms
4 ounces shallots
1 medium zucchini squash, cut
    into 1-inch pieces, each cut
    into halves
1 medium yellow crookneck
    squash, cut into 1-inch pieces,
    each cut into halves

1 red bell pepper, cut into 1-inch
    pieces
1 yellow bell pepper, cut into
    1-inch pieces
2 small Oriental eggplants, cut
    into ½-inch slices *or* 2 cups
    cubed eggplant
8 ounces Chinese egg noodles or
    vermicelli, hot cooked,
    drained
1 tablespoon Oriental sesame oil
1 teaspoon sugar

1. Preheat oven to 425°F. Combine 2 tablespoons soy sauce, peanut oil, vinegar and garlic in small bowl; mix well.

2. Combine vegetables in shallow roasting pan (do not line pan with foil). Toss with soy sauce mixture to coat well.

3. Roast vegetables 20 minutes or until browned and tender, stirring well after 10 minutes.

4. Place noodles in large bowl. Toss hot noodles with remaining 3 tablespoons soy sauce and sesame oil.

5. Toss roasted vegetables with noodle mixture; serve warm or at room temperature.
Makes 6 servings

THE MUFFIN COOKBOOK

Muffins for All Occasions

Clockwise from top right: Orange Coconut Muffin (page 352), Tropical Treat Muffin (page 349), Whole Wheat Herb Muffin (page 316), Taffy Apple Muffin (page 332), Pineapple Carrot Raisin Muffin (page 342), Crunch Top Blueberry Muffin (page 332) and Herbed Parmesan Muffin (page 319)

GREAT-START
MUFFINS

Muffins are a great way to start the day! The aroma of freshly baked muffins will be sure to entice the family out of bed. Muffins complement eggs, fruit or a morning beverage. They can be easily eaten while dressing or commuting to work or school. Pictured here are Nutty Banana Jam Muffins and Peanut Orange Breakfast Puffs. See page 306 for recipes.

Nutty Banana Jam Muffins

These muffins have a sweet surprise in the center.

1¼ cups ground walnuts
1½ cups sugar
¾ cup margarine, softened
2 extra-ripe, medium DOLE®
    Bananas, peeled
1 egg
2 cups all-purpose flour

2 teaspoons baking powder
1½ teaspoons ground cinnamon
½ teaspoon ground nutmeg
¼ teaspoon salt
1 ripe, small DOLE® Banana, peeled
3 tablespoons raspberry jam

Line 18 (2½-inch) muffin cups with paper liners. In shallow dish, combine ¾ cup walnuts with ½ cup sugar; set aside.

In large bowl, beat remaining ½ cup nuts with remaining 1 cup sugar and margarine until light and fluffy. Puree 2 medium bananas in blender (1 cup). Beat pureed bananas and egg into sugar-margarine mixture. In medium bowl, combine flour, baking powder, cinnamon, nutmeg and salt. Beat dry ingredients into banana mixture until well mixed.

Mash small banana in small bowl; stir in raspberry jam. For each muffin, roll 1 heaping tablespoon dough in walnut-sugar mixture to coat. Place in lined muffin cup. Make a dimple in center of dough with back of spoon. Spoon 1 teaspoon jam mixture into center. Roll 1 more heaping tablespoon dough in walnut-sugar mixture. Drop over jam mixture. Repeat with remaining dough and jam mixture.

Bake in 400° oven 15 to 20 minutes or until wooden pick inserted in center comes out clean. Cool slightly in pan; cool slightly on wire rack. Serve warm.

Makes 18 muffins

Peanut Orange Breakfast Puffs

2 cups sifted all-purpose flour
1 tablespoon baking powder
1 teaspoon salt
¼ cup sugar

1 egg, beaten
1 cup milk
¼ cup peanut oil
½ cup chopped salted peanuts

Topping:
¼ cup sugar
1 teaspoon grated orange peel

¼ cup butter or margarine, melted

In large bowl, sift together flour, baking powder, salt and ¼ cup sugar. In small bowl, combine egg, milk and peanut oil. Add liquid all at once to flour mixture, stirring only until moistened. Fold in chopped peanuts. Fill oiled 2½-inch muffin cups ⅔ full. Bake in preheated 425° oven 15 to 20 minutes or until tops are lightly browned. Meanwhile, in small bowl, blend ¼ cup sugar and orange peel until crumbly. When muffins are baked, remove from muffin cups and immediately dip tops in melted butter, then in orange-sugar mixture. Serve warm.

Makes 12 muffins

Favorite recipe from **Oklahoma Peanut Commission**

Banana Blueberry Muffins

2 extra-ripe, medium DOLE®
  Bananas, peeled
2 eggs
1 cup packed brown sugar
½ cup margarine, melted
1 cup blueberries

1 teaspoon vanilla
2¼ cups all-purpose flour
2 teaspoons baking powder
½ teaspoon ground cinnamon
½ teaspoon salt

Puree bananas in blender (1 cup). In medium bowl, combine bananas, eggs, sugar and margarine until well blended. Stir in blueberries and vanilla. In large bowl, combine flour, baking powder, cinnamon and salt. Stir banana mixture into flour mixture until evenly moistened. Spoon batter into well greased 2½-inch muffin cups. Bake in 350° oven 25 to 30 minutes or until wooden pick inserted in center comes out clean. Serve warm.

Makes 12 muffins

Banana Blueberry Muffins

Sausage Corn Muffins

½ pound ECKRICH® Smoked Sausage	1 tablespoon baking powder
1 cup unsifted all-purpose flour	1 cup buttermilk
¾ cup yellow cornmeal	¼ cup vegetable oil
¼ cup sugar	2 eggs, beaten
	Honey Butter (recipe follows)

Preheat oven to 375°. Cut sausage into quarters lengthwise, then cut crosswise into ¼-inch pieces. Lightly brown sausage in medium skillet over medium heat. Drain on paper towels. Combine flour, cornmeal, sugar and baking powder in medium bowl. Add buttermilk, oil, eggs and sausage. Stir only until blended. Fill paper-lined 2½-inch muffin cups ⅔ full. Bake 12 to 15 minutes or until wooden pick inserted near center comes out clean. Serve with Honey Butter.   *Makes 15 muffins*

Honey Butter: Blend ½ cup softened butter or margarine and ¼ cup honey in small bowl.

Sausage Corn Muffins

Morning Muffins

2¾ cups QUAKER® Crunchy Bran
    Cereal finely crushed to 1 cup
1½ cups all-purpose flour
⅓ cup packed brown sugar
4 teaspoons baking powder

1 teaspoon ground cinnamon
1 cup chopped pitted prunes
1¼ cups 2% low-fat milk
⅓ cup vegetable oil
1 egg

Heat oven to 400°. Grease or paper-line 12 (2½-inch) muffin cups. In large bowl, combine cereal, flour, brown sugar, baking powder and cinnamon. Stir in prunes. In small bowl, combine milk, oil and egg. Add to flour mixture, stirring just until moistened. Fill muffin cups almost full. Bake 25 minutes or until wooden pick inserted in center comes out clean. Cool in pan on wire rack 5 minutes. Remove from pan. Cool on wire rack. *Makes 12 muffins*

Tips

To freeze muffins: Wrap securely in foil or place in freezer bag. Seal, label and freeze.

To reheat frozen muffins: Unwrap muffins; wrap in paper towel. Microwave at HIGH (100%) about 45 seconds per muffin.

Nutrition information: Each serving (1 muffin)
Calories 230, Dietary Fiber 3 g

Lemony Apple Oat Muffins

1¼ cups unsifted flour
½ cup packed light brown sugar
1½ teaspoons baking powder
1 teaspoon baking soda
1 teaspoon ground cinnamon
½ teaspoon salt
¼ teaspoon ground nutmeg
1 egg
½ cup BORDEN® *or* MEADOW
    GOLD® Milk

¼ cup vegetable oil
2 tablespoons REALEMON® Lemon
    Juice from Concentrate
¾ cup quick-cooking oats
1 cup finely chopped all-purpose
    apples
½ cup chopped nuts
    Lemon Glaze (recipe follows)

Preheat oven to 400°. In small bowl, combine flour, sugar, baking powder, baking soda, cinnamon, salt and nutmeg. In medium bowl, beat egg; stir in milk, oil, then ReaLemon® brand. Add oats; mix well. Add flour mixture, apples and nuts; stir only until moistened (batter will be thick). Spoon into greased or paper-lined 2½-inch muffin cups. Bake 20 minutes or until golden. Spoon Lemon Glaze over muffins. Remove from pans; serve warm. *Makes about 12 muffins*

Lemon Glaze: In small bowl, combine ½ cup confectioners' sugar, 1 tablespoon ReaLemon® brand and 1 tablespoon melted margarine or butter. Makes about ¼ cup.

Cranberry Banana Muffins

*Tart cranberries and ripened, sweet bananas provide an extra twist
to the traditional oat bran muffin.*

2 cups QUAKER OAT BRAN™ Hot Cereal, uncooked	½ cup finely chopped cranberries
½ cup packed brown sugar	⅔ cup cranberry juice cocktail
¼ cup all-purpose flour	½ cup mashed ripe banana (about 1 medium)
2 teaspoons baking powder	2 egg whites, slightly beaten
½ teaspoon salt (optional)	3 tablespoons vegetable oil
½ teaspoon ground cinnamon	

Heat oven to 400°. Paper-line 12 (2½-inch) muffin cups. In large bowl, combine oat bran, brown sugar, flour, baking powder, salt and cinnamon. Gently stir in cranberries. In small bowl, combined cranberry juice, banana, egg whites and oil. Stir into flour mixture, mixing just until moistened. Fill muffin cups almost full. Bake 20 to 22 minutes or until golden brown and wooden pick inserted in center comes out clean. Remove from pan. *Makes 12 muffins*

Tips

To freeze muffins: Wrap securely in foil or place in freezer bag. Seal, label and freeze.

To reheat frozen muffins: Unwrap muffins. Microwave at HIGH (100%) about 30 seconds per muffin.

Nutrition information: Each serving (1 muffin)
Calories 150, Protein 4 g, Carbohydrate 24 g, Fat 5 g (polyunsaturated 2 g, monounsaturated 2 g, saturated 0 g), Oat Bran 14 g, Dietary Fiber 2 g, Sodium 85 mg, Cholesterol 0 mg
Percentage of calories from fat: 28%, Diabetic exchanges: 1 Starch/Bread; 1 Fat; ½ Fruit

Cheesy Bacon 'n Apple Muffins

2 cups sifted all-purpose flour	½ cup finely chopped unpeeled apple
¼ cup sugar	¾ cup (3 ounces) shredded aged Cheddar cheese
4 teaspoons baking powder	⅔ cup crisp bacon crumbles (about 8 slices)
¾ teaspoon salt	
1 cup milk	
⅓ cup butter, melted	
1 egg, slightly beaten	

In large bowl, sift together flour, sugar, baking powder and salt. In small bowl, combine milk, butter and egg; stir into dry ingredients just until moistened. Fold in apple, cheese and bacon crumbles. Spoon into buttered muffin cups, filling ⅔ full. Bake in preheated 400° oven 15 to 20 minutes or until golden brown. Remove from pan. Cool on wire rack. *Makes 18 muffins*

Favorite recipe from **Wisconsin Milk Marketing Board** © 1993

Cranberry Banana Muffins

Blueberry Yogurt Muffins

Blueberry Yogurt Muffins

Try these moist, flourless yogurt muffins sweetened with the natural taste of honey and blueberry.

2 cups QUAKER OAT BRAN™ Hot Cereal, uncooked
¼ cup packed brown sugar
2 teaspoons baking powder
1 carton (8 ounces) plain low fat yogurt

2 egg whites, slightly beaten
¼ cup skim milk
¼ cup honey
2 tablespoons vegetable oil
1 teaspoon grated lemon peel
½ cup fresh or frozen blueberries

Heat oven to 425°. Paper-line 12 (2½-inch) muffin cups. In large bowl, combine oat bran, brown sugar and baking powder. In small bowl, combine yogurt, egg whites, skim milk, honey, oil and lemon peel. Stir into oat bran mixture, mixing just until moistened. Fold in blueberries. Fill muffin cups almost full. Bake 18 to 20 minutes or until golden brown and wooden pick inserted in center comes out clean. Remove from pan. *Makes 12 muffins*

Tips

To freeze muffins: Wrap securely in foil or place in freezer bag. Seal, label and freeze.

To reheat frozen muffins: Unwrap muffins. Microwave at HIGH (100%) about 30 seconds per muffin.

Nutrition information: Each serving (1 muffin)
Calories 130, Protein 5 g, Carbohydrate 21 g, Fat 4 g (polyunsaturated 2 g, monounsaturated 1 g, saturated 1 g), Oat Bran 14 g, Dietary Fiber 2 g, Sodium 100 mg, Cholesterol 0 mg
Percentage of calories from fat: 25%, Diabetic exchanges: 1 Starch/Bread; ½ Fruit; ½ Fat

Orange Glazed Muffins

1½ cups all-purpose flour
½ cup KRETSCHMER® Original or Honey Crunch Wheat Germ
¼ cup granulated sugar
1 tablespoon baking powder
1 tablespoon grated orange peel

½ teaspoon salt (optional)
⅔ cup milk
⅓ cup margarine, melted
2 eggs
½ cup powdered sugar
1 tablespoon orange juice

Heat oven to 400°. Grease or paper-line 12 (2½-inch) muffin cups. In large bowl, combine flour, wheat germ, granulated sugar, baking powder, orange peel and salt. In small bowl, combine milk, margarine and eggs. Add to flour mixture, stirring just until moistened. Fill muffin cups ⅔ full. Bake 20 to 25 minutes or until light golden brown and wooden pick inserted in center comes out clean. Remove from pan. Cool on wire rack. In small bowl, combine powdered sugar and orange juice. Drizzle over slightly cooled muffins. *Makes 12 muffins*

SAVORY
M U F F I N S

Savory muffins have a hearty flavor and make a
delightful side dish to any meal. Herbs, cheese, vegetables,
fruits and grains are used to create
wonderful tasting muffins. Serve with soup
and a salad for a light lunch or as an accompaniment for
dinner. Pictured here are Whole Wheat
Herb Muffins and Wisconsin Blue Cheese Muffins.
See page 316 for recipes.

Whole Wheat Herb Muffins

1 cup all-purpose flour
1 cup whole wheat flour
⅓ cup sugar
2 teaspoons baking powder
½ teaspoon baking soda
½ teaspoon salt
½ teaspoon dried basil leaves
¼ teaspoon dried marjoram leaves
¼ teaspoon dried oregano leaves
⅛ teaspoon dried thyme leaves
¾ cup raisins
1 cup buttermilk
2 tablespoons butter or margarine, melted
1 egg, beaten
2 tablespoons wheat germ

Preheat oven to 400°. Grease 12 (2½-inch) muffin cups. In large bowl, combine flours, sugar, baking powder, baking soda, salt, herbs and raisins. In small bowl, combine buttermilk, butter and egg. Stir into flour mixture just until moistened. Spoon into muffin cups. Sprinkle wheat germ on tops. Bake 15 to 20 minutes or until lightly browned and wooden pick inserted in center comes out clean. Remove from pan.   *Makes 12 muffins*

Wisconsin Blue Cheese Muffins

Blue cheese lovers beware! This muffin could be addicting. The golden exterior and the nuggets of melted cheese make these muffins hard to resist.

2 cups all-purpose flour
3 tablespoons sugar
1 tablespoon baking powder
¼ teaspoon salt
1 cup Wisconsin Blue Cheese, crumbled
1 egg, beaten
1 cup milk
¼ cup butter, melted

Preheat oven to 400°. Butter 2½-inch muffin cups. In large bowl, combine flour, sugar, baking powder, salt and cheese. In small bowl, combine egg, milk and butter until blended. Stir into flour mixture just until moistened. Spoon into muffin cups, filling ¾ full. Bake 20 to 25 minutes or until golden brown. Remove from pan; serve warm.   *Makes 10 muffins*

Favorite recipe from **Wisconsin Milk Marketing Board** © **1993**

Country Corn Muffins

2 (8½-ounce) packages corn muffin mix
10 slices bacon, cooked and crumbled
¾ cup BAMA® Strawberry or Blackberry Preserves

Preheat oven to 400°. Prepare muffin mix according to package directions; stir in bacon. Fill paper-lined 2½-inch muffin cups ⅓ full. Drop 2 level teaspoons preserves in center of each. Add remaining batter to fill cups ¾ full. Bake 15 to 20 minutes or until golden brown. Remove from pans. Serve warm.   *Makes 12 to 18 muffins*

Tex-Mex Pumpkin Corn Muffins

1 cup yellow cornmeal
1 cup all-purpose flour
2 tablespoons sugar
4 teaspoons baking powder
½ teaspoon salt
½ teaspoon chili powder
2 eggs
1 cup LIBBY'S® Solid Pack
   Pumpkin

1 cup milk
2 tablespoons vegetable oil
1 can (4 ounces) chopped green
   chilies
¾ cup (3 ounces) shredded Cheddar
   cheese

In large bowl, combine cornmeal, flour, sugar, baking powder, salt and chili powder. In small bowl, beat eggs; mix in pumpkin, milk, oil and chiles. Add pumpkin mixture to flour mixture; stir just until moistened. Spoon into 18 greased or paper-lined 2½-inch muffin cups. Sprinkle with cheese. Bake in preheated 400° oven for 20 to 25 minutes or until wooden pick inserted in center comes out clean. Remove from pan. Serve warm. *Makes 18 muffins*

Note: Batter may be baked in any of the following well-greased pans, in preheated 425° oven for 20 to 25 minutes or until wooden pick inserted in center comes out clean. To avoid sticking, be sure cheese is not too close to edges of pan.
   One 10-inch cast iron skillet
   Two 9-inch divided metal pans
   Corn-stick pans (omit cheese on top)

Tex-Mex Pumpkin Corn Muffins with Corn Stick and Corn Bread variations

Popover Pan Muffins

2 cups all-purpose flour
¾ cup sugar
2 teaspoons pumpkin pie spice
¾ teaspoon baking powder
¾ teaspoon baking soda
¾ teaspoon salt

3 eggs
¾ cup almond oil
2 teaspoons vanilla
1 cup grated zucchini
½ cup chopped toasted almonds
½ cup seedless raisins

Preheat oven to 375°. Grease 6 popover pans.* In large bowl, combine flour, sugar, pumpkin pie spice, baking powder, baking soda and salt. In small bowl, beat eggs with oil and vanilla. Add to flour mixture with zucchini, almonds and raisins. Stir just until moistened. Spoon into popover pans. Bake in center of oven 25 minutes.

Makes 6 popover pan muffins

*To make standard-size muffins, divide batter among 18 (2½-inch) muffin cups. Bake in a preheated 375° oven 20 minutes.

Makes 18 muffins

Favorite recipe from **Almond Board of California**

Popover Pan Muffins

Apple-Cranberry Muffins

1¾ cups plus 2 tablespoons all-purpose flour
½ cup sugar
1½ teaspoons baking powder
½ teaspoon baking soda
½ teaspoon salt
1 egg

¾ cup milk
¾ cup sweetened applesauce
¼ cup butter or margarine, melted
1 cup fresh cranberries, coarsely chopped
½ teaspoon ground cinnamon

In medium bowl, combine 1¾ cups of the flour, ¼ cup of the sugar, the baking powder, baking soda and salt. In small bowl, combine egg, milk, applesauce and butter; mix well. Add egg mixture to flour mixture, stirring just until moistened. Batter will be lumpy. In small bowl, toss cranberries with remaining 2 tablespoons flour; fold into batter. Spoon batter into 12 greased 2½-inch muffin cups. In another small bowl, combine remaining ¼ cup sugar and the cinnamon. Sprinkle over muffins. Bake in preheated 400° oven 20 to 25 minutes or until wooden pick inserted in center comes out clean. Remove from pan; cool on wire rack.

Makes 12 muffins

Favorite recipe from **Western New York Apple Growers Association, Inc.**

Herbed Parmesan Muffins

Serve these muffins with an Italian-style meal or a minestrone soup.

2 cups all-purpose flour
¾ cup grated Parmesan cheese
2 teaspoons sugar
2 teaspoons baking powder
2 teaspoons mixed Italian-style herb seasoning*
½ teaspoon baking soda

½ teaspoon salt
½ cup chopped fresh basil, parsley or cilantro leaves
1¼ cups buttermilk
¼ cup olive or vegetable oil
1 egg

Preheat oven to 400°. Grease bottoms only of 12 (2½-inch) or 36 miniature muffin cups. In large bowl, combine flour, Parmesan, sugar, baking powder, herb seasoning, baking soda, salt and basil. In small bowl, combine buttermilk, oil and egg until blended. Stir into flour mixture just until moistened. Spoon into muffin cups. Bake 15 to 20 minutes for regular-size muffins, 12 to 15 minutes for miniature muffins or until golden and wooden pick inserted in center comes out clean. Remove from pan. Serve warm.

Makes 12 regular-size or 36 miniature muffins

*Italian-style herb seasoning is a blend of marjoram, thyme, rosemary, savory, sage, oregano and basil.

Spiced Brown Bread Muffins

Quick to make, serve these with a hearty stew.

2 cups whole wheat flour
⅔ cup all-purpose flour
⅔ cup packed brown sugar
2 teaspoons baking soda

1 teaspoon pumpkin pie spice
2 cups buttermilk
¾ cup raisins

Preheat oven to 350°. Grease 6 (4-inch) muffin cups. In large bowl, combine flours, sugar, baking soda and pumpkin pie spice. Stir in buttermilk just until flour mixture is moistened. Fold in raisins. Spoon into muffin cups. Bake 35 to 40 minutes or until wooden pick inserted in center comes out clean. Remove from pan.

Makes 6 giant muffins

Turkey Ham, Cheese & Pepper Muffins

Serve these savory muffins baked in miniature muffin cups as an appetizer. Larger muffins are a perfect accompaniment to salad or soup.

¼ cup butter or margarine
½ cup minced sweet onion
¼ cup minced green bell pepper
1 clove garlic, minced or pressed
2 cups all-purpose flour
1 tablespoon baking powder
1 teaspoon salt
½ teaspoon coarsely ground black pepper

1 cup milk
2 eggs
1 cup (4 ounces) finely diced turkey ham
½ cup diced Cheddar cheese
¼ cup roasted shelled sunflower seeds

Preheat oven to 375°. Generously grease or paper-line 12 (2½-inch) or 36 miniature muffin cups. In heavy skillet, over medium-high heat, melt butter. Add onion, green pepper and garlic; cook and stir 5 to 7 minutes or until onion is translucent.

In large bowl, combine flour, baking powder, salt and pepper. In small bowl, combine milk and eggs until blended. Add milk mixture, vegetables with drippings, turkey and cheese to flour mixture. Stir mixture just until moistened. Spoon into muffin cups. Sprinkle sunflower seeds over tops. Bake 25 to 30 minutes for regular-size muffins, 15 to 20 minutes for miniature muffins or until wooden pick inserted in center comes out clean. Remove from pan.

Makes 12 regular-size muffins or 36 miniature muffins

Spiced Brown Bread Muffins

Top: Fruited Corn Muffins Bottom: Orange Spice Muffins

Orange Spice Muffins

⅓ cup packed brown sugar
¼ cup margarine or butter, softened
1 egg, beaten
¾ cup BORDEN® *or* MEADOW
    GOLD® Milk
½ cup orange juice
1 tablespoon grated orange peel

3 cups biscuit baking mix
1 (9-ounce) package NONE SUCH®
    Condensed Mincemeat,
    crumbled
Cinnamon and Sugar Topping
    (recipe follows)

Preheat oven to 375°. In large bowl, beat sugar and margarine until fluffy. Add egg, milk, orange juice and peel; mix well. Stir in biscuit mix and mincemeat only until moistened (do not overmix). Fill greased or paper-lined 2½-inch muffin cups ¾ full. Sprinkle Cinnamon and Sugar Topping evenly over muffins. Bake 18 to 22 minutes or until golden brown. Remove from pan. Serve warm.   *Makes about 18 muffins*

Cinnamon and Sugar Topping: In small bowl, combine 2 tablespoons sugar and 2 teaspoons ground cinnamon.

Fruited Corn Muffins

2 (8½-ounce) packages *or*
   1 (18-ounce) package corn
   muffin mix

1 (9-ounce) package NONE SUCH®
   Condensed Mincemeat, finely
   crumbled

Preheat oven to 400°. Prepare muffin mix according to package directions, stirring in mincemeat. Fill greased or paper-lined 2½-inch muffin cups ½ full. Bake 15 to 18 minutes or until golden brown. Remove from pan. Serve warm.

Makes about 18 muffins

Mandarin Muffins

1 can (8¼ ounces) DOLE® Crushed
   Pineapple
   Milk
2 cups all-purpose flour
⅓ cup packed brown sugar
2 tablespoons toasted wheat germ
1 tablespoon baking powder

½ teaspoon salt
1 egg, beaten
¾ cup finely shredded carrot
⅓ cup vegetable oil
½ teaspoon vanilla
2 tablespoons granulated sugar
½ teaspoon ground cinnamon

Drain pineapple well, reserving syrup. (Press pineapple with back of spoon to remove as much syrup as possible.) Add enough milk to syrup to measure ¾ cup liquid.

In large bowl, combine flour, brown sugar, wheat germ, baking powder and salt. Make well in center. In medium bowl, combine egg, carrot, oil, vanilla, milk-syrup mixture and pineapple. Add pineapple mixture all at once to dry ingredients, stirring just until moistened. Batter should be lumpy. Fill paper-lined 2½-inch muffin cups ⅔ full. In small bowl, combine granulated sugar and cinnamon; sprinkle over tops of muffins. Bake in 400° oven 20 to 25 minutes or until wooden pick inserted in center comes out clean. Remove from pan. *Makes 15 muffins*

Herb Cheese Muffins

Herbed cream cheese is soft and spreadable, available in the deli section of your supermarket. These muffins are great served with any chicken breast or fish dish.

1½ cups all-purpose flour
2 teaspoons baking powder
½ teaspoon salt
¼ teaspoon freshly ground black
   pepper
⅔ cup milk

1 package (4 ounces) soft
   spreadable herbed cream
   cheese
1 egg, beaten
2 teaspoons minced fresh chives

Preheat oven to 375°. Grease or paper-line 12 (2½-inch) muffin cups. In large bowl, combine flour, baking powder, salt and black pepper. In small bowl, combine milk, cream cheese, egg and chives until blended. Stir into flour mixture just until moistened. Spoon into muffin cups. Bake 15 to 20 minutes or until wooden pick inserted in center comes out clean. Remove from pan. Serve warm.

Makes 12 muffins

Cheddar Pepper Muffins

Cheddar Pepper Muffins

*These are especially light, and when eaten hot, the cheese inside
the muffins is stringy.*

2 cups all-purpose flour
1 tablespoon sugar
1 tablespoon baking powder
1 teaspoon coarsely cracked black
   pepper
½ teaspoon salt

1¼ cups milk
¼ cup vegetable oil
1 egg
1 cup (4 ounces) shredded sharp
   Cheddar cheese

Preheat oven to 400°. Generously grease 12 (2½-inch) muffin cups. In large bowl,
combine flour, sugar, baking powder, pepper and salt. In small bowl, combine milk,
oil and egg until blended. Stir into flour mixture just until moistened. Fold in ¾ cup
of the cheese. Spoon into muffin cups. Sprinkle remaining cheese over tops. Bake 15
to 20 minutes or until light golden brown. Let cool in pan on wire rack 5 minutes.
Remove from pan and serve warm. *Makes 12 muffins*

Treasure Bran Muffins

1¼ cups wheat bran cereal
1 cup milk
¼ cup vegetable oil
1 egg, beaten
1¼ cups all-purpose flour
½ cup sugar
1 tablespoon baking powder

½ teaspoon salt
½ cup raisins
1 (8-ounce) package
   PHILADELPHIA BRAND®
   Cream Cheese*, softened
¼ cup sugar
1 egg, beaten

In large bowl, combine cereal and milk. Let stand 2 minutes. In small bowl, combine
oil and 1 egg; stir into cereal mixture. In medium bowl, combine flour, ½ cup sugar,
baking powder and salt. Add to cereal mixture, stirring just until moistened. Fold in
raisins. Spoon into greased and floured 2½-inch muffin cups, filling each ⅔ full.

In small bowl, combine cream cheese, ¼ cup sugar and 1 egg, mixing until well
blended. Drop rounded measuring tablespoonfuls of cream cheese mixture onto
batter. Bake at 375° 25 minutes. Remove from pan. *Makes 12 muffins*

*Light PHILADELPHIA BRAND® Neufchâtel Cheese may be substituted.

Cheddar Almond Muffins

Topping

2 tablespoons butter, melted
1 teaspoon Worcestershire sauce
½ teaspoon garlic salt

⅓ cup chopped blanched slivered
  almonds

Muffins

2 cups sifted all-purpose flour
¼ cup sugar
1 tablespoon baking powder
1 teaspoon salt
¾ cup (3 ounces) shredded Cheddar
  cheese

1 cup milk
1 egg
3 tablespoons butter, melted

To make topping: In bowl, blend together butter, Worcestershire sauce and garlic salt. Stir in almonds; set aside.

To make muffins: Into large bowl, sift together flour, sugar, baking powder and salt. Stir in cheese. In small bowl, beat together milk and egg; stir in remaining butter. Add to dry ingredients just until moistened, about 25 strokes. Spoon into buttered muffin cups, filling ⅔ full. Sprinkle about 1 teaspoon of the almond mixture over each muffin, pressing almonds into batter slightly. Bake in preheated 400° oven 20 to 25 minutes or until golden brown. Remove from muffin cups; serve warm.

Makes 12 muffins

Variations

Parmesan Almond Muffins: Follow above directions, except substitute ½ cup grated Parmesan cheese for the Cheddar cheese.

Pineapple Muffins: Omit almond topping. Follow muffin directions, except fold in ½ cup (8½ oz. can) drained crushed pineapple.

Favorite recipe from **Wisconsin Milk Marketing Board** © 1993

Favorite Corn Muffins

1 cup all-purpose flour
¾ cup cornmeal
¼ cup wheat bran cereal
2 teaspoons baking powder
1½ teaspoons salt

½ teaspoon baking soda
1 cup dairy sour cream
2 eggs
¼ cup honey
¼ cup butter, melted

In large bowl, combine flour, cornmeal, bran, baking powder, salt and baking soda. In medium bowl, beat sour cream, eggs, honey and butter until blended. Add to flour mixture, stirring just until moistened. Spoon batter into generously buttered 2½-inch muffin cups. Bake in preheated 425° oven 15 to 20 minutes or until wooden pick inserted in center comes out clean. Cool in pan on wire rack 5 minutes. Remove from pan. Serve warm.

Makes 12 muffins

Favorite recipe from **Wisconsin Milk Marketing Board** © 1993

Cheesy Green Onion Muffins

Cheesy Green Onion Muffins

1 package (3 ounces) cream cheese	2 eggs, beaten
1¾ cups all-purpose flour	1¼ cups milk
4 teaspoons baking powder	⅓ cup vegetable oil
1 tablespoon sugar	½ cup chopped green onions with
1 teaspoon salt	tops
3 cups RICE CHEX® Brand Cereal, crushed to 1 cup	

Preheat oven to 400°. Grease 18 (2½-inch) muffin cups. Cut and separate cream cheese into ¼-inch cubes; set aside. In large bowl, combine flour, baking powder, sugar and salt. In medium bowl, combine cereal, eggs, milk, oil and onions. Add all at once to flour mixture, stirring just until moistened. Fold in cheese. Spoon into muffin cups. Bake 20 to 25 minutes or until wooden pick inserted in center comes out clean. Remove from pan. *Makes 18 muffins*

Calico Bell Pepper Muffins

Calico Bell Pepper Muffins

This is a rather moist batter, but results in a light and tender muffin. This is especially good with roasted or grilled chicken.

¼ cup *each* finely chopped red,
    yellow and green bell pepper
¼ cup butter or margarine
2 cups all-purpose flour
2 tablespoons sugar

1 tablespoon baking powder
¾ teaspoon salt
½ teaspoon dried basil leaves
1 cup milk
2 eggs

Preheat oven to 400°. Grease or paper-line 12 (2½-inch) muffin cups. In small skillet, over medium-high heat, cook peppers in butter until color is bright and pepper is tender crisp about 3 minutes. Set aside.

In large bowl, combine flour, sugar, baking powder, salt and basil. In small bowl, combine milk and eggs until blended. Add milk mixture and peppers with dripping to flour mixture. Stir just until moistened. Spoon into muffin cups. Bake 15 minutes or until golden and wooden pick inserted in center comes out clean. Remove from pan.
Makes 12 muffins

Bacon Topped Chili Corn Bread Muffins

Serve these muffins with a "Tex-Mex" style meal; they would be great with a taco salad.

4 slices bacon, diced
1½ cups stone ground yellow
    cornmeal
½ cup all-purpose flour
¼ cup instant minced onion
1 tablespoon sugar
2 teaspoons baking powder
1 teaspoon baking soda
½ teaspoon salt

1 cup buttermilk
1 can (4 ounces) chopped green
    chilies, drained
2 eggs
3 tablespoons bacon drippings,
    melted butter or margarine,
    or oil
1 cup (4 ounces) ½-inch cubes
    Monterey Jack cheese

Preheat oven to 400°. Grease 12 (2½-inch) muffin cups. In heavy skillet, over medium-high heat, cook bacon until crisp. Drain and reserve drippings. Reserve bacon bits.

In large bowl, combine cornmeal, flour, minced onion, sugar, baking powder, baking soda and salt. In small bowl, combine buttermilk, chilies, eggs and bacon drippings until blended. Stir into flour mixture just until moistened. Fold in cheese. Spoon into muffin cups. Sprinkle bacon bits over tops. Bake 15 to 20 minutes or until lightly browned. Remove from pan.
Makes 12 muffins

SNACK-TIME
M U F F I N S

Muffins make a great between-meal treat whether it's for a coffee break, after-school snack or late-night munchie. The muffins in this chapter range from sweet to hearty. There's sure to be one to please everyone. Pictured here are Crunch Top Blueberry Muffins, Pineapple Carrot Raisin Muffins and Taffy Apple Muffins. See pages 332 and 342 for recipes.

Crunch Top Blueberry Muffins

Crunch Topping (recipe follows)
2 cups all-purpose flour
⅔ cups sugar
1 tablespoon baking powder
½ teaspoon salt

½ teaspoon ground nutmeg
1½ cups blueberries*
¾ cup milk
½ cup butter or margarine, melted
2 eggs, beaten

Preheat oven to 400°. Grease or paper-line 6 (4-inch) muffin cups. Prepare Crunch Topping; set aside.

In large bowl, combine flour, sugar, baking powder, salt and nutmeg. Add 1 tablespoon of the flour mixture to the blueberries, tossing to coat. In small bowl, combine milk, butter and eggs until blended. Stir into flour mixture just until moistened. Fold in blueberries. Spoon evenly into muffin cups. Sprinkle Crunch Topping over tops. Bake 30 to 35 minutes or until wooden pick inserted in center comes out clean. Remove from pan. Cool on wire rack.   *Makes 6 giant muffins*

Crunch Topping: In medium bowl, combine ½ cup uncooked rolled oats, ½ cup all-purpose flour, ¼ cup packed brown sugar and 1 teaspoon ground cinnamon. With fork, blend in ¼ cup softened butter or margarine until mixture is crumbly.

*If you are using frozen blueberries, do not thaw. Baking time may need to be increased by up to 10 minutes.

Taffy Apple Muffins

These apple studded miniature muffins are baked, then dipped in a honey-brown sugar glaze and rolled in chopped walnuts.

2 cups all-purpose flour
½ cup granulated sugar
1 tablespoon baking powder
½ teaspoon salt
¼ teaspoon ground nutmeg
½ cup milk
¼ cup butter or margarine, melted

2 eggs
1 teaspoon vanilla
1 cup chopped apple
½ cup honey
½ cup packed dark brown sugar
¾ cup finely chopped walnuts

Preheat oven to 400°. Grease 36 miniature muffin cups. In large bowl, combine flour, granulated sugar, baking powder, salt and nutmeg. In small bowl, combine milk, butter, eggs and vanilla until blended. Stir into flour mixture just until moistened. Fold in apple. Spoon into muffin cups. Bake 10 to 12 minutes or until lightly browned and wooden pick inserted in center comes out clean. Remove from pan.

Meanwhile, in small saucepan, heat honey and brown sugar over medium-high heat to a boil; stir to dissolve sugar. Dip warm muffins into hot glaze, then into chopped nuts. Spear with popsicle sticks or wooden skewers, if desired.

Makes 36 miniature muffins

Sweet Surprise Muffins

1¾ cups unsifted flour
¼ cup sugar
2 teaspoons baking powder
1 teaspoon ground cinnamon
¾ teaspoon salt
2 eggs

¾ cup BORDEN® or MEADOW
    GOLD® Milk
¼ cup margarine or butter, melted
½ cup chopped nuts
¾ cup BAMA® Blackberry or
    Strawberry Preserves

Preheat oven to 400°. In small bowl, combine flour, sugar, baking powder, cinnamon and salt. In medium bowl, beat eggs; stir in milk and margarine. Add dry ingredients; stir only until moistened (batter will be slightly lumpy). Stir in nuts. Fill paper-lined 2½-inch muffin cups ⅓ full; drop 2 level teaspoons preserves into center of each. Add remaining batter to fill cups ⅔ full. Bake 20 minutes or until golden brown. Remove from pans; serve warm.   *Makes about 12 muffins*

Sweet Surprise Muffins and Fruit Blossom Muffins (see page 339)

Honey Fig Whole Wheat Muffins

Honey Fig Whole Wheat Muffins

Healthy tasting, these muffins are stuffed with figs, nuts and wheat germ.

1 cup whole wheat flour
½ cup all-purpose flour
½ cup wheat germ
2 teaspoons baking powder
1 teaspoon ground cinnamon
½ teaspoon salt
½ teaspoon ground nutmeg

½ cup milk
½ cup honey
¼ cup butter or margarine, melted
1 egg
1 cup chopped dried figs
½ cup chopped walnuts

Preheat oven to 375°. Grease or paper-line 12 (2½-inch) muffin cups. In large bowl, combine flours, wheat germ, baking powder, cinnamon, salt and nutmeg. In small bowl, combine milk, honey, butter and egg until well blended. Stir into flour mixture just until moistened. Fold in figs and nuts. Spoon into muffin cups. Bake 20 minutes or until lightly browned on edges and wooden pick inserted in center comes out clean. Remove from pan. *Makes 12 muffins*

Banana Chocolate Chip Muffins

2 extra-ripe, medium DOLE®
   Bananas, peeled
2 eggs
1 cup packed brown sugar
½ cup margarine, melted
1 teaspoon vanilla

2¼ cups all-purpose flour
2 teaspoons baking powder
½ teaspoon ground cinnamon
½ teaspoon salt
1 cup chocolate chips
½ cup chopped walnuts

Puree bananas in blender (1 cup). In medium bowl, beat pureed bananas, eggs, sugar, margarine and vanilla until well blended. In large bowl, combine flour, baking powder, cinnamon and salt. Stir in chocolate chips and nuts. Make well in center of dry ingredients. Pour in banana mixture. Mix until just blended. Spoon into well greased 2½-inch muffin cups. Bake in 350° oven 25 to 30 minutes. Remove from pan. *Makes 12 muffins*

Sour Cream Lemon Streusel Muffins

A buttery wheat germ streusel crowns these lemon-flavored muffins. They are good served plain or with butter and strawberry jam.

2 cups all-purpose flour
½ cup sugar
1 tablespoon baking powder
1 teaspoon grated lemon peel
½ teaspoon salt
1 cup chopped walnuts

½ cup sour cream
½ cup milk
½ cup butter or margarine, melted
1 egg, beaten
1 tablespoon sugar

Preheat oven to 400°. Grease or paper-line 12 (2½-inch) or 6 (4-inch) muffin cups. In large bowl, combine flour, ½ cup sugar, baking powder, lemon peel, salt and walnuts. In small bowl, combine sour cream, milk, butter and egg until blended. Stir into flour mixture just until moistened. Spoon into muffin cups. Sprinkle remaining 1 tablespoon sugar over tops. Bake 15 to 20 minutes for regular-size muffins, 20 to 25 minutes for giant-size muffins or until wooden pick inserted in center comes out clean. Remove from pan. Cool on wire rack.

Makes 12 regular-size muffins or 6 giant muffins

Banana Scotch Muffins

1 ripe, large DOLE® Banana, peeled
1 egg, beaten
½ cup sugar
¼ cup milk
¼ cup vegetable oil
1 teaspoon vanilla

1 cup all-purpose flour
1 cup quick-cooking rolled oats
1 teaspoon baking powder
½ teaspoon baking soda
½ teaspoon salt
½ cup butterscotch chips

Puree banana in blender (⅔ cup). In medium bowl, combine pureed banana, egg, sugar, milk, oil and vanilla. In large bowl, combine flour, oats, baking powder, baking soda and salt. Stir banana mixture into dry ingredients with butterscotch chips until just blended. Spoon into well greased 2½-inch muffin cups. Bake in 400° oven 12 to 15 minutes. Remove from pan.

Makes 12 muffins

Sour Cream Lemon Streusel Muffins

Sesame Crunch Banana Muffins

A satisfying muffin with a spicy nut topping.

2 ripe, medium DOLE® Bananas, peeled
1 cup milk
1 egg
¼ cup vegetable oil
1 teaspoon vanilla

1½ cups quick-cooking rolled oats
½ cup all-purpose flour
½ cup whole wheat flour
1 tablespoon baking powder
½ teaspoon salt
Sesame Crunch (recipe follows)

Puree bananas in blender (1 cup). In large bowl, combine pureed bananas, milk, egg, oil and vanilla; set aside. In large bowl, combine oats, flours, baking powder and salt. Stir in banana mixture just until dry ingredients are moistened (batter will be lumpy). Fill 12 greased 2½-inch muffin cups about ¾ full. Sprinkle 2 teaspoons Sesame Crunch over batter in each cup. Bake in 400° oven 20 to 25 minutes or until golden on top and wooden pick inserted in center comes out clean. Cool slightly in pan before turning out onto wire rack. Serve warm. *Makes 12 muffins*

Sesame Crunch: In small bowl, combine ¼ cup chopped nuts, 2 tablespoons *each* brown sugar and sesame seeds, 1 tablespoon whole wheat flour and ¼ teaspoon *each* ground cinnamon and nutmeg. Cut in 2 tablespoons margarine until crumbly.

Sesame Crunch Banana Muffins

Fruit Blossom Muffins

⅔ cups BAMA® Blackberry Jam or
   Orange Marmalade
½ cup orange juice
1 egg, slightly beaten
2 cups biscuit baking mix
⅔ cup chopped pecans

¼ cup sugar
1 tablespoon flour
½ teaspoon ground cinnamon
¼ teaspoon ground nutmeg
2 to 3 teaspoons cold margarine or
   butter

Preheat oven to 400°. In medium bowl, combine jam, orange juice and egg. Add biscuit mix; stir only until moistened (batter will be slightly lumpy). Stir in nuts. Fill greased or paper-lined 2½-inch muffin cups ⅔ full. In small bowl, combine sugar, flour and spices; cut in margarine until crumbly. Sprinkle over batter. Bake 15 to 20 minutes or until golden brown. Remove from pans; serve warm.

Makes about 12 muffins

Apple Spice Muffins

1½ cups all-purpose flour
½ cup KRETSCHMER® Original
   Wheat Germ
½ cup sugar
1 tablespoon baking powder
1¼ teaspoons ground cinnamon
½ teaspoon salt (optional)

1 cup peeled, chopped apple
1 cup 2% low-fat milk
¼ cup vegetable oil
1 egg
⅓ cup chopped nuts
2 tablespoons margarine or butter,
   melted

Heat oven to 400°. Grease bottoms only or paper-line 12 (2½-inch) muffin cups. In large bowl, combine flour, wheat germ, ¼ cup of the sugar, the baking powder, ¾ teaspoon of the cinnamon and the salt. Stir in apple. In small bowl, combine milk, oil and egg. Add to flour mixture, stirring just until moistened. Fill muffin cups almost full. In small bowl, combine remaining ¼ cup sugar, ½ teaspoon cinnamon, the nuts and margarine. Sprinkle over muffins. Bake 20 to 25 minutes or until golden brown and wooden pick inserted in center comes out clean. Remove from pan.

Makes 12 muffins

Tips

To freeze muffins: Wrap securely in foil or place in freezer bag. Seal, label and freeze.

To reheat frozen muffins: Unwrap muffins. Microwave at HIGH (100%) about 30 seconds per muffin.

Nutrition information: Each serving (1 muffin)
Calories 210, Carbohydrate 26 g, Protein 5 g, Fat 10 g, Sodium 150 mg, Calcium 95 mg, Cholesterol 25 mg, Dietary Fiber 1 g

Backpack Banana Muffins

2 extra-ripe, large DOLE® Bananas, peeled
1 cup whole bran cereal (not flakes)
¼ cup milk
2 eggs
1 cup packed brown sugar

½ cup margarine, melted
1 teaspoon vanilla
1¼ cups all-purpose flour
2 teaspoons baking powder
1 teaspoon ground cinnamon
½ teaspoon salt

Puree bananas in blender (1¼ cups). In small bowl, mix bran and milk to soften slightly. Add cereal mixture to blender along with eggs, sugar, margarine and vanilla. Blend and stir until well mixed. In large bowl, combine remaining ingredients. Pour in banana mixture. Stir until just blended. Pour into greased 2½-inch muffin cups. Bake in 350° oven 25 to 30 minutes. Remove from pan.   *Makes 12 muffins*

Cinnamon Chip Muffins

2 cups all-purpose biscuit baking mix
¼ cup sugar
1 egg
⅔ cup milk

1 cup HERSHEY'S MINI CHIPS Semi-Sweet Chocolate
¼ cup finely chopped nuts (optional)
Sugar-Cinnamon Topping (recipe follows)

Heat oven to 400°. Grease or paper-line 12 muffin cups (2½ inches in diameter). In large bowl, stir together baking mix, sugar, egg and milk; with spoon, beat 30 seconds. Stir in small chocolate chips and nuts, if desired. Fill muffin cups ¾ full with batter. Sprinkle each with about ½ teaspoon Sugar-Cinnamon Topping. Bake 15 to 17 minutes or until very lightly browned. Serve warm.

Makes about 12 muffins

Sugar-Cinnamon Topping: In small bowl, stir together 2 tablespoons sugar and 2 teaspoons ground cinnamon.

Cheesy Peperoni Bites

½ pound SWIFT PREMIUM® *or*
  MARGHERITA® Deli Sandwich
  Peperoni, unsliced
1 cup all-purpose flour
1 cup yellow cornmeal
4 teaspoons baking powder
¼ teaspoon salt

⅛ teaspoon ground red pepper
2 eggs, slightly beaten
1 cup milk
¼ cup vegetable oil
½ cup (2 ounces) shredded
  Monterey Jack cheese
¼ cup drained diced green chilies

Preheat oven to 400°. Cut five ⅛-inch-thick slices from peperoni; cut each slice into 8 wedges. Set aside. Cut remaining peperoni into ¼-inch cubes. Combine flour, cornmeal, baking powder, salt and pepper in large mixing bowl. Combine eggs, milk and oil in small bowl; add to flour mixture, stirring just until dry ingredients are moistened. Fold in cheese, chilies and cubed peperoni. Spoon batter into greased mini-muffin cups, filling each almost to top. Top each muffin with 1 wedge of reserved peperoni, pressing halfway into batter. Bake 10 to 12 minutes or until golden brown. Remove from pans immediately and serve warm or at room temperature.   *Makes about 3½ dozen muffins*

Cheesy Peperoni Bites

Pineapple Carrot Raisin Muffins

Pineapple Carrot Raisin Muffins

2 cups all-purpose flour
1 cup sugar
2 teaspoons baking powder
½ teaspoon ground cinnamon
¼ teaspoon ground ginger
½ cup shredded carrots
½ cup DOLE® Raisins

½ cup chopped walnuts
1 can (8 ounces) DOLE® Crushed
  Pineapple
2 eggs
½ cup margarine, melted
1 teaspoon vanilla

In large bowl, combine flour, sugar, baking powder, cinnamon and ginger. Stir in carrots, raisins and nuts. In small bowl, combine undrained pineapple, eggs, margarine and vanilla. Stir into dry ingredients until just blended. Spoon into greased 2½-inch muffin cups. Bake in 375° oven 20 to 25 minutes. Remove from pan; cool on wire rack.   *Makes 12 muffins*

Cherry Blossom Muffins

1 egg
⅔ cup BAMA® Cherry or Strawberry
    Preserves
¼ cup BORDEN® or MEADOW
    GOLD® Milk
½ cup sugar
2 cups biscuit baking mix

⅔ cup chopped pecans
1 tablespoon flour
¾ teaspoon ground cinnamon
2 tablespoons cold margarine or
    butter
Additional chopped pecans

Preheat oven to 400°. In medium bowl, beat egg; stir in preserves, milk and *¼ cup* sugar. Add biscuit mix; stir only until moistened (batter will be slightly lumpy). Stir in *⅔ cup* nuts. Fill greased or paper-lined 2½-inch muffin cups ¾ full. In small bowl, combine remaining *¼ cup* sugar, flour and cinnamon. Cut in margarine until crumbly; sprinkle over batter. Top with additional nuts. Bake 15 to 20 minutes or until golden brown. Remove from pans; serve warm.   *Makes about 12 muffins*

Apple-Walnut Muffins

2 cups all-purpose flour
⅔ cup sugar
2¼ teaspoons baking powder
¾ teaspoon salt
¼ teaspoon ground cinnamon
1 egg

⅔ cup milk
3 tablespoons vegetable oil
1 teaspoon grated lemon peel
¾ teaspoon vanilla
1 cup chopped DIAMOND® Walnuts
¾ cup coarsely grated pared apple

In medium bowl, sift flour with sugar, baking powder, salt and cinnamon. In small bowl, beat egg; add milk, oil, lemon peel and vanilla. Stir into dry ingredients, mixing just until flour is moistened. Fold in walnuts and apple. Spoon batter into 12 greased 2½-inch muffin cups. Bake in preheated 400° oven 20 to 25 minutes or until golden brown and wooden pick inserted in center comes out clean.

Makes 12 muffins

DESSERT
M U F F I N S

These individual treats are a great way to complete a meal.
A compact dessert—they can be packed for
picnics or used as a delicious ending for family meals.
The muffins in this chapter will satisfy your sweet tooth.
Pictured here are Streusel Raspberry Muffins.
See page 346 for recipe.

Streusel Raspberry Muffins

The juicy tartness of raspberries is balanced by the topping of caramelized, crunchy pecan streusel.

Pecan Streusel Topping (recipe
   follows)
1½ cups all-purpose flour
½ cup sugar
2 teaspoons baking powder
½ cup milk
½ cup butter or margarine, melted
1 egg, beaten
1 cup fresh or individually frozen,
   whole unsugared raspberries

Preheat oven to 375°. Grease or paper-line 12 (2½-inch) muffin cups. Prepare Pecan Streusel Topping; set aside.

In large bowl, combine flour, sugar and baking powder. In small bowl, combine milk, butter and egg until blended. Stir into flour mixture just until moistened. Spoon ½ of the batter into muffin cups. Divide raspberries among cups, then top with remaining batter. Sprinkle Pecan Streusel Topping over tops. Bake 25 to 30 minutes or until golden and wooden pick inserted in center comes out clean. Remove from pan.
Makes 12 muffins

Pecan Streusel Topping: In small bowl, combine ¼ cup *each* chopped pecans, packed brown sugar and all-purpose flour. Stir in 2 tablespoons melted butter or margarine until mixture resembles moist crumbs.

Chocolate Chip Fruit Muffins

1 package (about 15 ounces)
   banana quick bread mix
2 eggs
1 cup milk
¼ cup vegetable oil
1 cup HERSHEY'S Semi-Sweet
   Chocolate Chips, MINI CHIPS
   Semi-Sweet Chocolate or Milk
   Chocolate Chips
½ cup dried fruit bits

Heat oven to 400°. Grease or paper-line 18 muffin cups (2½ inches in diameter). In large bowl, stir together quick bread mix, eggs, milk and oil; beat with spoon 30 seconds. Stir in chocolate chips and fruit bits. Fill muffin cups ¾ full with batter. Bake 18 to 20 minutes or until lightly browned. Serve warm.
Makes about 18 muffins

Two Tone Muffins

Two Tone Muffins

2 cups all-purpose flour	¾ cup orange juice
½ cup sugar	⅓ cup almond oil or vegetable oil
1 tablespoon baking powder	1 egg, beaten
1 teaspoon salt	¼ cup cocoa powder
¾ cup roasted diced almonds	1 teaspoon grated orange peel

Preheat oven to 400°. Paper-line 12 (2½-inch) muffin cups. In large bowl, combine flour, sugar, baking powder and salt. Stir in almonds, reserving some for garnish. In small bowl, combine orange juice, oil and egg. Stir into flour mixture just until moistened. Transfer ½ of the batter into another small bowl; stir in cocoa and set aside. Stir orange peel into remaining batter. Carefully spoon orange batter into one side of each cup. Fill other side with cocoa batter. Sprinkle reserved almonds over tops. Bake 20 minutes or until wooden pick inserted in center comes out clean. Remove from pan. Serve warm. *Makes 12 muffins*

Favorite recipe from **Almond Board of California**

Tropical Treat Muffins

Tropical Treat Muffins

Chewy and sweet, dried papaya chunks, chopped banana chips, macadamia nuts and coconut give these muffins an exotic but healthy character.

2 cups all-purpose flour
⅓ cup sugar
1 tablespoon baking powder
1 teaspoon grated lemon peel
½ teaspoon salt
¾ cup (4 ounces) dried papaya, finely diced
½ cup coarsely chopped banana chips

½ cup chopped macadamia nuts
¼ cup flaked coconut
½ cup milk
½ cup butter or margarine, melted
¼ cup sour cream
1 egg, beaten
1 tablespoon sugar

Preheat oven to 400°. Grease or paper-line 12 (2½-inch) or 6 (4-inch) muffins cups. In large bowl, combine flour, ⅓ cup sugar, baking powder, lemon peel and salt. In small bowl, combine papaya, banana chips, nuts and coconut. Stir in 1 tablespoon of the flour mixture until well coated. In another small bowl, combine milk, butter, sour cream and egg until blended. Stir into flour mixture just until moistened. Fold in fruit mixture. Spoon into muffin cups. Sprinkle remaining 1 tablespoon sugar over tops. Bake 15 to 20 minutes for regular-size muffins, 25 to 30 minutes for giant muffins or until wooden pick inserted in center comes out clean. Remove from pan. Cool on wire rack.   *Makes 12 regular-size or 6 giant muffins*

Apple Date Nut Muffins

1½ cups all-purpose flour
⅔ cup packed brown sugar
½ cup uncooked rolled oats
1 tablespoon baking powder
1 teaspoon ground cinnamon
½ teaspoon salt
⅛ teaspoon ground nutmeg
⅛ teaspoon ground ginger

Dash ground cloves
1 cup coarsely chopped pared apples
½ cup chopped walnuts
½ cup chopped pitted dates
½ cup butter or margarine, melted
¼ cup milk
2 eggs

Preheat oven to 400°. Grease well or paper-line 12 (2½-inch) muffin cups. In large bowl, combine flour, brown sugar, oats, baking powder, cinnamon, salt, nutmeg, ginger and cloves. Mix in apples, nuts and dates. In small bowl, combine butter, milk and eggs until blended. Pour into flour mixture, stirring just until moistened. Spoon into muffin cups. Bake 20 to 25 minutes or until wooden pick inserted in center comes out clean. Remove from pan.   *Makes 12 muffins*

Chocolate Spice Surprise Muffins

⅓ cup packed light brown sugar
¼ cup margarine or butter, softened
1 egg
1 cup BORDEN® or MEADOW GOLD® Milk
2 cups biscuit baking mix
⅓ cup unsweetened cocoa

1 (9-ounce) package NONE SUCH® Condensed Mincemeat, crumbled
18 solid milk chocolate candy drops
½ cup confectioners' sugar
1 tablespoon water

Preheat oven to 375°. In large bowl, beat brown sugar and margarine until fluffy. Add egg and milk; mix well. Stir in biscuit mix, cocoa and mincemeat until moistened. Fill greased or paper-lined 2½-inch muffin cups ¾ full. Top with candy drop; press into batter. Bake 15 to 20 minutes. Cool in pan on wire rack 5 minutes. Remove from pan. Meanwhile, in small bowl, mix confectioners' sugar and water; drizzle over warm muffins. *Makes about 18 muffins*

Chocolate Spice Surprise Muffins

Walnut Streusel Muffins

3 cups all-purpose flour
1½ cups packed brown sugar
¾ cup butter or margarine
1 cup chopped DIAMOND® Walnuts
2 teaspoons baking powder
1 teaspoon ground nutmeg

1 teaspoon ground ginger
½ teaspoon baking soda
½ teaspoon salt
1 cup buttermilk or sour milk*
2 eggs, beaten

In medium bowl, combine 2 cups of the flour and the sugar; cut in butter to form fine crumbs. In small bowl, combine ¾ cup of the crumbs and ¼ cup of the walnuts; set aside. Into remaining crumb mixture, stir in remaining 1 cup flour, the baking powder, spices, baking soda, salt and remaining ¾ cup walnuts. In another small bowl, combine buttermilk and eggs; stir into dry ingredients just to moisten. Spoon into 18 greased or paper-lined 2¾-inch muffin cups, filling about ⅔ full. Top each with a generous spoonful of reserved crumb-nut mixture. Bake in preheated 350° oven 20 to 25 minutes or until wooden pick inserted in center comes out clean. Cool in pans on wire rack 10 minutes. Loosen and remove from pans. Serve warm.

Makes 18 muffins

*To sour milk: Use 1 tablespoon vinegar plus milk to equal 1 cup. Stir; let stand 5 minutes.

Cranberry Muffins and Creamy Orange Spread

2 cups all-purpose flour
7 tablespoons sugar
2 teaspoons baking powder
½ teaspoon salt
¾ cup milk
½ cup PARKAY® Margarine, melted
1 egg, beaten

¾ cup coarsely chopped cranberries
1 (8-ounce) package
 PHILADELPHIA BRAND®
 Cream Cheese*, softened
1 tablespoon orange juice
1 teaspoon grated orange peel

In large bowl, combine flour, 4 tablespoons sugar, baking powder and salt; mix well. In medium bowl, combine milk, margarine and egg. Pour into flour mixture, mixing just until moistened. In small bowl, combine 2 tablespoons sugar and cranberries; fold into batter. Spoon into greased 2½-inch muffin cups, filling each ⅔ full. Bake at 400° 20 to 25 minutes or until golden brown. Remove from pan.

In small bowl, combine cream cheese, remaining 1 tablespoon sugar, orange juice and peel until well blended. Cover and chill. Serve with muffins.

Makes 12 muffins

*Light PHILADELPHIA BRAND® Neufchâtel Cheese may be substituted.

Orange Coconut Muffins

¾ cup all-purpose flour
¾ cup whole wheat flour
⅔ cup toasted wheat germ
½ cup sugar
½ cup coconut
1½ teaspoons baking soda

½ teaspoon salt
1 cup dairy sour cream
2 eggs
1 can (11 ounces) mandarin
    oranges, drained
½ cup chopped nuts

In large bowl, combine flours, wheat germ, sugar, coconut, baking soda and salt. In small bowl, blend sour cream, eggs and oranges. Stir into flour mixture just until moistened. Fold in nuts. Spoon into buttered 2½-inch muffin cups, filling ¾ full. Bake in preheated 400° oven 18 to 20 minutes or until wooden pick inserted in center comes out clean. Remove from pan. Cool on wire rack.

Makes about 12 muffins

Favorite recipe from **Wisconsin Milk Marketing Board** © 1993

Black Cherry Muffins

2 cups all-purpose flour
1 tablespoon baking powder
¼ teaspoon salt
1 cup pitted black cherries, coarsely
    chopped
6 tablespoons butter or margarine,
    softened

⅔ cup sugar
2 eggs
1 teaspoon vanilla
½ cup milk

Preheat oven to 400°. Grease or paper-line 12 (2½-inch) muffin cups. In small bowl, combine flour, baking powder and salt. Toss 1 tablespoon of the flour mixture with the cherries; set aside. In large bowl, beat butter and sugar until light and fluffy. Add eggs and vanilla; beat 3 minutes. Alternately beat in flour mixture and the milk. Fold in cherries. Spoon into muffin cups. Bake 20 to 25 minutes or until golden and wooden pick inserted in center comes out clean. Remove from pan. Cool on wire rack.

Makes 12 muffins

Orange Coconut Muffins

BORDEN® *NEW*
Great American
P I E S

Featuring Main-Dish & Dessert Pies

Cherry Cheese Pie (page 395)

SAVORY

MAIN

DISHES

★ ★ ★ ★

Chicken Primavera Pasta Pie

★★★★

Makes one 10-inch pie

Pasta Crust
 2 **cups frozen broccoli, carrot and cauliflower combination, thawed and drained**
1½ **cups diced cooked chicken**
 ¼ **cup unsifted flour**
 2 **eggs, beaten**
 1 **cup Borden® or Meadow Gold® Half-and-Half**
 ⅓ **cup grated Parmesan cheese**
 2 **teaspoons Wyler's® or Steero® Chicken-Flavor Instant Bouillon**
 1 **clove garlic, finely chopped**
 ½ **teaspoon basil leaves**
 ½ **teaspoon oregano leaves**

Preheat oven to 350°. Prepare Pasta Crust; set aside. In large bowl, toss vegetables and chicken with flour to coat; add remaining ingredients. Mix well. Spoon into prepared crust. Cover tightly with aluminum foil; bake 25 to 30 minutes or until set. Uncover; let stand 5 minutes. Garnish as desired. Refrigerate leftovers.

Pasta Crust: Cook ½ (1-pound) package Creamette® Spaghetti as package directs; drain. In large bowl, combine hot spaghetti, 2 beaten eggs, ⅓ cup grated Parmesan cheese and 2 tablespoons margarine or butter, melted. Spoon into well-greased 10-inch pie plate; press on bottom and up side to rim to form crust.

Top to bottom: Chicken Primavera Pasta Pie, California Salmon Pie (page 358) and Tuna Melt Turnovers (page 358)

California Salmon Pie
★ ★ ★ ★

Makes one 9-inch pie

1 (9-inch) unbaked pastry
    shell
4 eggs
1 (15½-ounce) can salmon,
    drained and flaked
1 (9-ounce) package frozen
    artichoke hearts, cooked,
    drained and chopped *or*
    1 (14-ounce) can
    artichoke hearts, drained
    and chopped
¼ cup chopped green onions
¼ cup grated Parmesan cheese
2 tablespoons margarine or
    butter, melted
3 tablespoons ReaLemon®
    Lemon Juice from
    Concentrate
1½ teaspoons Wyler's® or
    Steero® Chicken-Flavor
    Instant Bouillon
1 (8-ounce) container
    Borden® or Meadow
    Gold® Sour Cream, at
    room temperature
1½ teaspoons dill weed

Preheat oven to 425°. In large bowl, beat eggs; add salmon, artichokes, green onions, cheese, margarine, *1 tablespoon* ReaLemon® brand and *1 teaspoon* bouillon. Pour into pastry shell. Bake 25 minutes. In small bowl, combine sour cream, remaining *2 tablespoons* ReaLemon® brand, remaining *½ teaspoon* bouillon and dill weed. Spread over salmon filling; bake 5 minutes longer or until set. Serve warm or chilled. Garnish as desired. Refrigerate leftovers.

Tuna Melt Turnovers
★ ★ ★ ★

Makes 4 to 6 servings

1 (15-ounce) package
    refrigerated pie crusts
1 (12½-ounce) can tuna,
    drained
2 hard-cooked eggs, chopped
⅓ cup Bennett's® Tartar Sauce
⅓ cup chopped celery
¼ cup finely chopped carrot
¼ cup chopped onion
2 tablespoons ReaLemon®
    Lemon Juice from
    Concentrate
6 slices Borden® Process
    American Cheese Food,
    quartered
    Additional ReaLemon®
    Lemon Juice from
    Concentrate
    Sesame seeds

Preheat oven to 425°. On large baking sheet, unfold pie crusts; press out fold lines. In medium bowl, combine tuna, eggs, tartar sauce, celery, carrot, onion and *2 tablespoons* ReaLemon® brand. On half of each crust, place 3 slices cheese food; top with half the tuna mixture to within 1 inch of the outside edge. Fold over and seal edges. Brush with additional ReaLemon® brand; sprinkle with sesame seeds. Bake 15 to 18 minutes or until golden brown. Cut into wedges to serve. Refrigerate leftovers.

Savory Shrimp Cheese Cups

★★★★

Makes 16 appetizers

¼ pound peeled cooked
   shrimp, finely chopped *or*
   1 (4¼-ounce) can
   Orleans® Shrimp, drained
   and soaked as label directs
1 (8-ounce) package cream
   cheese, softened
¼ cup Bennett's® Cocktail
   Sauce
⅛ teaspoon *each* basil leaves,
   garlic powder, marjoram
   leaves, oregano leaves and
   thyme leaves
1 (8-ounce) package
   refrigerated crescent rolls
   Additional Bennett's®
   Cocktail Sauce

Preheat oven to 375°. In small
mixer bowl, beat cheese, cocktail
sauce and seasonings until smooth.
Stir in shrimp. Unroll crescent roll
dough; separate into 4 rectangles.
Firmly press perforations together
to seal. Cut *each* rectangle
lengthwise then crosswise into 4
pieces; press onto bottom and ½
inch up side of muffin cups. Spoon
rounded tablespoon cheese mixture
into each prepared muffin cup.
Bake 10 minutes or until hot. Let
stand 5 minutes; remove from pan.
Garnish as desired. Serve warm
with additional cocktail sauce.
Refrigerate leftovers.

Hot Chicken Salad in Stuffing Crust

★★★★

Makes one 9-inch pie

4 cups herb-seasoned stuffing mix
½ cup margarine or butter, melted
3 eggs, beaten
2 cups diced cooked chicken
1 cup chopped celery
1 (8-ounce) can water chestnuts, drained and chopped
½ cup mayonnaise or salad dressing
1 (2-ounce) jar sliced pimiento, drained, optional
3 tablespoons ReaLemon® Lemon Juice from Concentrate
1½ teaspoons Wyler's® or Steero® Chicken-Flavor Instant Bouillon

Preheat oven to 350°. In medium bowl, combine stuffing mix and margarine; reserve ½ cup. To remaining stuffing, add eggs; mix well. Spoon into greased 9-inch pie plate; press on bottom and up side to rim to form crust. In large bowl, combine remaining ingredients except reserved stuffing; spoon into prepared crust. Top with reserved stuffing. Bake 40 to 45 minutes or until hot. Let stand 10 minutes. Garnish as desired. Refrigerate leftovers.

Turkey Cranberry Loaf Wedges

★★★★

Makes 6 servings

1 (12-ounce) container cranberry-orange sauce
1½ pounds ground fresh turkey
1½ cups fresh bread crumbs (3 slices)
¼ cup ReaLemon® Lemon Juice from Concentrate
1 egg
1 tablespoon Wyler's® or Steero® Chicken-Flavor Instant Bouillon *or* 3 Chicken-Flavor Bouillon Cubes
1 to 2 teaspoons poultry seasoning

Preheat oven to 350°. Reserve ½ cup cranberry-orange sauce. In large bowl, combine remaining ingredients; mix well. Turn into 9-inch pie plate. Bake 50 minutes or until set. Top with reserved sauce. Let stand 5 minutes before serving. Cut into wedges; garnish as desired. Refrigerate leftovers.

Top to bottom: Hot Chicken Salad in Stuffing Crust, Turkey Cranberry Loaf Wedges and Fruited Chicken Salad Tarts (page 362)

Fruited Chicken Salad Tarts

★ ★ ★ ★

Makes 12 tarts

- 1 cup mayonnaise or salad dressing
- ¼ cup ReaLime® Lime Juice from Concentrate
- 2 teaspoons Wyler's® or Steero® Chicken-Flavor Instant Bouillon
- 4 cups cubed cooked chicken
- 1 (11-ounce) can mandarin orange segments, drained
- 1 cup seedless grape halves
- 1 (8-ounce) can crushed pineapple, drained
- ½ cup slivered almonds, toasted
- 12 (3-inch) baked tart-size pastry crusts

In large bowl, combine mayonnaise, ReaLime® brand and bouillon; stir in remaining ingredients except tart crusts. Chill thoroughly. Serve in tart crusts. Refrigerate leftovers.

Seafood Pizza Primavera

Seafood Pizza Primavera

★ ★ ★ ★

Makes one 15×10-inch pie

- 2 (8-ounce) packages refrigerated crescent rolls
- 1 (8-ounce) container Borden® or Meadow Gold® Sour Cream
- ½ cup Bennett's® Chili, Cocktail *or* Hot Seafood Sauce
- ¼ pound peeled, cooked small shrimp *or* 1 (4¼-ounce) can Orleans® Shrimp, drained and soaked as label directs
- ¼ pound imitation crab blend, flaked *or* 1 (6-ounce) can Harris® or Orleans® Crab Meat, drained
- 1 cup chopped broccoli
- ½ cup sliced green onions
- ½ cup chopped green bell pepper
- ½ cup chopped red bell pepper

Preheat oven to 400°. Unroll crescent roll dough; press on bottom of 15×10-inch baking pan, pressing perforations together. Bake 10 minutes or until golden. Cool. Combine sour cream and sauce; spread over crust. Top with remaining ingredients. Chill. Cut into squares to serve. Refrigerate leftovers.

Taco Chili Pie

★ ★ ★ ★

Makes one 9-inch pie

1 pound lean ground beef
1 (16-ounce) can refried
  beans
¾ cup Bennett's® Chili Sauce
1 egg, beaten
2 teaspoons Wyler's® or
  Steero® Beef-Flavor
  Instant Bouillon
2 teaspoons chili powder
¼ to ½ teaspoon hot pepper
  sauce
1 (11.5-ounce) package
  refrigerated cornmeal
  twists

Preheat oven to 375°. In large skillet, brown meat; pour off fat. Stir in beans, ¼ *cup* chili sauce, egg, bouillon, chili powder and hot pepper sauce; simmer uncovered 10 minutes. Meanwhile, unroll cornmeal twists; *do not* separate dough. Press evenly on bottom and up side and rim of 9-inch pie plate to form crust, pressing perforations together. Turn filling into crust. Bake 20 minutes or until hot. Top with remaining ½ *cup* chili sauce; garnish as desired. Refrigerate leftovers.

Shrimp Cocktail Strata Tart

★ ★ ★ ★

Makes one 10-inch tart

- 2½ cups fresh bread crumbs (5 slices)
- 1 cup Borden® or Meadow Gold® Half-and-Half
- 4 eggs, beaten
- 2 (4¼-ounce) cans Orleans® Shrimp, drained and soaked as label directs *or* 2 (6-ounce) cans Crab Meat, rinsed and drained
- ½ cup Bennett's® Cocktail *or* Hot Seafood Sauce
- ¼ cup chopped green onions
- 2 tablespoons ReaLemon® Lemon Juice from Concentrate
- 1½ teaspoons Wyler's® or Steero® Chicken-Flavor Instant Bouillon
- ¼ teaspoon pepper Additional Bennett's® Cocktail *or* Hot Seafood Sauce

Preheat oven to 350°. In large bowl, combine crumbs and half-and-half; let stand 10 minutes. Add remaining ingredients except additional cocktail sauce; mix well. Pour into 10-inch oiled quiche dish or tart pan. Bake 30 to 35 minutes or until set. Cool. Garnish as desired. Serve warm or chilled with additional cocktail sauce. Refrigerate leftovers.

Traditional Quiche

★ ★ ★ ★

Makes one 9-inch quiche

- 1 (9-inch) unbaked pastry shell, pricked
- 12 slices bacon, cooked and crumbled
- 1½ cups (6 ounces) shredded Swiss cheese
- 4 eggs
- 2 cups (1 pint) Borden® or Meadow Gold® Half-and-Half
- ¼ teaspoon salt
- ⅛ teaspoon ground nutmeg Dash cayenne pepper

Preheat oven to 425°. Bake pastry shell 8 minutes; remove from oven. Sprinkle bacon and cheese on bottom of pastry shell. In medium bowl, beat eggs; add remaining ingredients. Pour into prepared pastry shell. Bake 15 minutes. *Reduce oven temperature to 350°;* bake 25 minutes or until center is set. Cool slightly. Serve warm or chilled. Refrigerate leftovers.

Shrimp Cocktail Strata Tart

Mediterranean Phyllo Pie
★★★★

Makes 8 to 10 servings

1 cup sliced fresh mushrooms
¾ cup olive oil or melted butter
1 (26-ounce) jar Classico® Di Napoli (Tomato & Basil) Pasta Sauce
2 cups chopped cooked chicken
1 (14-ounce) can artichoke hearts drained and chopped *or* 1 (9-ounce) package frozen artichoke hearts, thawed, drained and chopped
½ cup sliced pitted ripe olives
1 teaspoon Wyler's® or Steero® Chicken-Flavor Instant Bouillon
1 (16-ounce) package frozen phyllo pastry dough, thawed
¾ cup grated Parmesan or Romano cheese

In large skillet, cook mushrooms in *2 tablespoons* oil until tender. Add pasta sauce, chicken, artichokes, olives and bouillon. Bring to a boil; reduce heat and simmer uncovered 20 minutes, stirring occasionally. Preheat oven to 400°. Meanwhile, place 2 sheets pastry in bottom of greased 15×10-inch baking pan, pressing into corners. Brush with oil; working quickly, repeat using 2 sheets pastry until 14 sheets have been used. Sprinkle with *¼ cup* cheese. Spread chicken mixture over pastry; top with *¼ cup* cheese. Repeat layering with pastry sheets and oil until all pastry has been used. Trim edges of pastry even with edges of pan. Top with remaining *¼ cup* cheese. Bake 25 to 30 minutes or until golden. Refrigerate leftovers.

Tuna Pot Pie

Tuna Pot Pie
★★★★

Makes 4 to 6 servings

¼ cup margarine or butter
2 tablespoons flour
1½ cups Borden® or Meadow Gold® Half-and-Half or Milk
8 slices Borden® Process American Cheese Food
¼ cup ReaLemon® Lemon Juice from Concentrate
1 (12½-ounce) can tuna, drained
1 (10-ounce) package frozen green peas and carrots, thawed
1 (10-ounce) package refrigerated biscuits

Preheat oven to 400°. In medium saucepan, melt margarine; stir in flour until smooth, then half-and-half. Over medium heat, cook and stir until thickened. Add cheese food, stirring until melted. Stir in ReaLemon® brand. Add tuna and peas and carrots; heat through. Pour into 1½-quart baking dish; top with biscuits. Bake 20 to 25 minutes or until biscuits are done. Refrigerate leftovers.

Meatza Pizza Pie
★★★★

Makes one 9-inch pie

1 pound ground round
½ cup fresh bread crumbs (1 slice)
1 egg
2 teaspoons Wyler's® or Steero® Beef-Flavor Instant Bouillon
½ teaspoon Italian seasoning
½ cup Classico® Di Napoli (Tomato & Basil) Pasta Sauce
1 (2½-ounce) jar sliced mushrooms, drained
2 tablespoons chopped green bell pepper
2 tablespoons chopped onion
1 cup (4 ounces) shredded mozzarella cheese

Preheat oven to 350°. In medium bowl, combine meat, crumbs, egg, bouillon and seasoning; mix well. Press evenly on bottom and up side to rim of 9-inch pie plate to form crust. Bake 15 minutes; pour off fat. Spoon pasta sauce over crust. Top with mushrooms, green pepper, onion and cheese. Bake 10 minutes longer or until cheese melts. Garnish as desired. Refrigerate leftovers.

Pizza Calzones
★★★★

Makes 8 calzones

½ pound Italian sausage
1 (26-ounce) jar Classico® D'Abruzzi (Beef & Pork) Pasta Sauce
1 cup sliced fresh mushrooms
½ cup chopped green bell pepper
½ cup chopped onion
2 (8-ounce) packages refrigerated crescent rolls
1 egg, beaten
1 tablespoon water
1 cup (4 ounces) shredded mozzarella cheese

Preheat oven to 350°. In large skillet, brown sausage; pour off fat. Add ¾ *cup* pasta sauce, mushrooms, green pepper and onion; simmer uncovered 10 minutes. Meanwhile, unroll crescent roll dough; separate into 8 rectangles. Firmly press perforations together and flatten slightly. In small bowl, mix egg and water; brush on dough edges. Stir cheese into meat mixture. Spoon equal amounts of meat mixture on half of each rectangle to within ½ inch of edges. Fold dough over filling; press to seal edges. Arrange on baking sheet; brush with egg mixture. Bake 15 minutes or until golden brown. Heat remaining pasta sauce; serve with calzones. Refrigerate leftovers.

Top to bottom: Quick Classic Pizza (page 368), Pizza Calzones and Meatza Pizza Pie

Quick Classic Pizza
★ ★ ★ ★

Makes one 12-inch pizza

1 (12-inch) Italian bread shell
   or prepared pizza crust
1 cup (4 ounces) shredded
   mozzarella cheese
1 (14-ounce) jar Classico®
   Pasta Sauce, any flavor
   (1½ cups)
   Pizza toppings: chopped
   onion, peppers, sliced
   mushrooms, pepperoni,
   sliced olives, cooked
   sausage, cooked ground
   beef, cooked bacon

Preheat oven to 450°. Top bread
shell with half the cheese, pasta
sauce, desired toppings and
remaining cheese. Bake 10 to 12
minutes or until hot and bubbly. Let
stand 5 minutes. Serve warm.
Refrigerate leftovers.

Coney Dog Pie
★ ★ ★ ★

Makes 6 to 8 servings

1 (6- or 8½-ounce) package
   corn muffin mix
1 pound lean ground beef
1 (12-ounce) jar Bennett's®
   Chili Sauce
1 teaspoon Wyler's® or
   Steero® Beef-Flavor
   Instant Bouillon
1 teaspoon prepared mustard
1 pound frankfurters, cut into
   quarters

Preheat oven to 350°. Prepare
muffin mix as package directs. In
12-inch ovenproof skillet, brown
beef; pour off fat. Add chili sauce,
bouillon, mustard and frankfurters;
bring to a boil. Top with prepared
corn muffin batter. Bake 20 minutes
or until golden brown. Refrigerate
leftovers.

Coney Dog Pie

French Toast Strata Pie

★ ★ ★ ★

Makes one 10-inch pie

½ **pound bulk country sausage**
1 **all-purpose apple, cored,
    pared and thinly sliced**
5 **eggs**
2 **cups Borden® or Meadow
    Gold® Milk**
⅓ **cup Cary's®, Maple Orchards®
    or MacDonald's™ Pure
    Maple Syrup**
½ **teaspoon ground nutmeg**
½ **(1-pound) loaf French or
    Italian bread, cut into
    ½-inch slices**
    **Additional Cary's®,
    Maple Orchards® or
    MacDonald's™ Pure Maple
    Syrup**

In large skillet, thoroughly cook
sausage. Remove sausage from
skillet; drain and crumble. Add
apple slices to skillet; over medium
heat, cook covered 3 minutes. In
medium bowl, beat eggs; add milk,
⅓ cup pure maple syrup and
nutmeg. Mix well. In buttered 10-
inch pie plate, arrange about three-
fourths of the bread slices. Top with
sausage, apples and remaining bread
slices. Pour milk mixture evenly
over top. Cover; refrigerate
overnight. Bake uncovered at 350°
for 55 to 60 minutes or until set
and golden. Serve immediately with
additional pure maple syrup.
Refrigerate leftovers.

Fish & Chowder Pie
★ ★ ★ ★

Makes 6 to 8 servings

Pastry for 1-crust pie
½ pound white fish fillets, fresh or frozen, thawed, cut into small pieces
1 (15-ounce) can Snow's® or Doxsee® Condensed New England Clam Chowder
2 (6½-ounce) cans Snow's® or Doxsee® Chopped or Minced Clams, drained, reserving ¼ cup liquid
⅓ cup Borden® or Meadow Gold® Half-and-Half or Milk
1 (10-ounce) package frozen peas and carrots, thawed
¼ cup unsifted flour
½ teaspoon thyme leaves
⅛ to ¼ teaspoon pepper

Preheat oven to 400°. In 1½-quart baking dish, combine all ingredients except pastry. Top with pastry; cut slits near center. Seal and flute. Bake 1 hour or until golden brown. Let stand 10 minutes before serving. Refrigerate leftovers.

Clam Bake Pie
★ ★ ★ ★

Makes one 9-inch pie

Pastry for 2-crust pie
3 slices bacon
¼ cup chopped onion
¼ cup unsifted flour
1 (15-ounce) can Snow's® or Doxsee® Condensed New England Clam Chowder
1 (6½-ounce) can Snow's® or Doxsee® Chopped or Minced Clams, drained, reserving ¼ cup liquid
1 cup whole kernel corn
½ cup Borden® or Meadow Gold® Half-and-Half
2 tablespoons chopped parsley *or* 1 tablespoon parsley flakes

Place rack in lowest position in oven; preheat oven to 425°. In medium skillet, cook bacon until crisp; remove and crumble. In 2 tablespoons drippings, cook onion until tender; stir in flour until smooth. Add chowder, reserved clam liquid, corn and half-and-half; cook and stir until thickened. Stir in clams, bacon and parsley. Turn into pastry-lined 9-inch pie plate. Cover with top crust; cut slits near center. Seal and flute. Bake 30 minutes or until golden. Let stand 20 minutes before serving. Garnish as desired. Refrigerate leftovers.

Top to bottom: Fish & Chowder Pie and Clam Bake Pie

FESTIVE
FINALES

★ ★ ★ ★

Margarita Parfait Pie
★ ★ ★ ★

Makes one 9-inch pie

1¼ cups *finely* crushed
    Seyfert's® Pretzels
¼ cup sugar
½ cup plus 2 tablespoons
    margarine or butter,
    melted
1 (14-ounce) can Eagle®
    Brand Sweetened
    Condensed Milk (NOT
    evaporated milk)
¼ cup ReaLime® Lime Juice
    from Concentrate
¼ cup tequila
2 tablespoons triple sec or
    other orange-flavored
    liqueur
1 cup chopped fresh or
    frozen unsweetened
    strawberries, thawed
    and *well drained*
    Red food coloring,
    optional
1½ cups Borden® or Meadow
    Gold® Whipping
    Cream, whipped

Combine pretzel crumbs, sugar and margarine; press firmly on bottom and up side to rim of lightly buttered 9-inch pie plate to form crust. In large bowl, combine sweetened condensed milk, ReaLime® brand, tequila and triple sec; mix well. Divide mixture in half. Add strawberries and food coloring if desired to one half of mixture. Fold half the whipped cream into each mixture. Spoon mixtures alternately into prepared crust. With metal spatula, swirl through mixtures to marble. Freeze 4 hours or until firm. Remove from freezer 10 minutes before serving. Garnish as desired. Freeze ungarnished leftovers.

*Top to bottom:
Frozen Lemon Angel
Pie (page 374) and Margarita
Parfait Pie*

Frozen Lemon Angel Pie

★★★★

Makes one 9-inch pie

3 egg whites
½ teaspoon vanilla extract
¼ teaspoon cream of tartar
1½ cups sugar
2 cups (1 pint) Borden® or Meadow Gold® Whipping Cream
½ cup ReaLemon® Lemon Juice from Concentrate Yellow food coloring, optional

Preheat oven to 275°. In small mixer bowl, beat egg whites, vanilla and cream of tartar to soft peaks. Gradually add ½ *cup* sugar, beating until stiff but not dry. Spread on bottom and up side of *well-buttered* 9-inch pie plate to form crust. Bake 1 hour. Turn oven off; leave crust in oven 1 hour. Cool to room temperature. In large mixer bowl, combine cream, remaining *1 cup* sugar, ReaLemon® brand and food coloring if desired; beat until stiff. Spoon into prepared crust. Freeze 3 hours or until firm. Garnish as desired. Freeze ungarnished leftovers.

Pumpkin Caramel Tarts

★★★★

Makes 14 tarts

1 (15-ounce) package refrigerated pie crusts
12 Eagle™ Brand Caramels, unwrapped
1 (14-ounce) can Eagle® Brand Sweetened Condensed Milk (NOT evaporated milk)
1 (16-ounce) can pumpkin (about 2 cups)
2 eggs
3 tablespoons water
1 tablespoon vanilla extract
½ teaspoon ground cinnamon

Preheat oven to 425°. From each pie crust, cut 7 (4-inch) circles; press into 3-inch tart pans. In medium saucepan, over low heat, melt caramels with sweetened condensed milk, stirring constantly. Remove from heat; stir in remaining ingredients. Pour equal portions into crusts. Place on baking sheets. Bake 15 minutes. *Reduce oven temperature to 350°*; bake 20 to 25 minutes longer or until set. Cool. Garnish as desired. Refrigerate leftovers.

MICROWAVE TIP: In 2-quart glass measure with handle, combine caramels and sweetened condensed milk. Cook on 100% power (high) 3 minutes or until caramels melt, stirring after each minute. Proceed as above.

Apricot Walnut
Mince Pie

★★★★

Makes one 9-inch pie

1 **(9-inch) unbaked pastry
   shell**
1 **(6-ounce) package dried
   apricots**
1 **(27-ounce) jar None Such®
   Ready-to-Use Mincemeat
   (Regular *or* Brandy &
   Rum)**
1 **cup chopped walnuts**
1 **(16-ounce) container
   Borden® or Meadow
   Gold® Sour Cream, at
   room temperature**
1 **tablespoon sugar**
1 **teaspoon vanilla extract
   Walnut halves**

Place rack in lowest position in
oven; preheat oven to 400°. Chop
½ cup apricots; reserve remainder.
In medium bowl, combine
mincemeat, chopped apricots and
nuts; turn into pastry shell. Bake 25
minutes. Meanwhile, in medium
bowl, combine sour cream, sugar
and vanilla. Spread evenly over pie.
Bake 8 minutes longer or until set.
Cool. Garnish with reserved
apricots and walnut halves.
Refrigerate leftovers.

Sweet Potato Praline Pie
★ ★ ★ ★

Makes one 9-inch pie

1 (9-inch) unbaked pastry
   shell
1 pound sweet potatoes or
   yams, cooked and peeled
¼ cup margarine or butter
1 (14-ounce) can Eagle®
   Brand Sweetened
   Condensed Milk (NOT
   evaporated milk)
1 teaspoon vanilla extract
1 teaspoon ground cinnamon
1 teaspoon ground allspice
¼ teaspoon salt
2 eggs, beaten
   Praline Topping

Preheat oven to 350°. In large
mixer bowl, beat *hot* sweet
potatoes with margarine. Add
sweetened condensed milk, vanilla,
spices and salt; beat until smooth.
Stir in eggs. Pour into pastry shell.
Bake 50 to 55 minutes or until
center is set. Cool. Top with warm
Praline Topping. Serve warm or
chilled. Refrigerate leftovers.

TIP: 1 (16- to 18-ounce) can sweet
potatoes or yams, drained, can be
substituted for fresh. Melt
margarine. Proceed as above.

Praline Topping: In small
saucepan, combine ½ cup Borden®
or Meadow Gold® Whipping Cream,
⅓ cup firmly packed brown sugar
and ½ teaspoon vanilla extract.
Cook and stir until sugar dissolves.
Boil rapidly 5 to 8 minutes or until
thickened, stirring occasionally.
Remove from heat; stir in ½ cup
chopped toasted pecans. (Makes
about ⅔ cup)

California Nut Pie
★ ★ ★ ★

Makes one 9-inch pie

1 (9-inch) unbaked pastry
   shell, pricked
1 (14-ounce) can Eagle®
   Brand Sweetened
   Condensed Milk (NOT
   evaporated milk)
1 cup water
3 eggs
¼ cup amaretto liqueur or
   water
1 teaspoon vanilla extract
½ cup slivered almonds,
   toasted
½ cup chopped walnuts,
   toasted

Preheat oven to 425°. Bake pastry
shell 8 minutes. Meanwhile, in small
mixer bowl, beat sweetened
condensed milk, water, eggs,
liqueur and vanilla until well
blended. Stir in nuts. Pour into
prepared pastry shell. Bake 10
minutes. *Reduce oven temperature
to 350°;* bake 25 minutes longer or
until set. Cool. Serve warm or
chilled. Garnish as desired.
Refrigerate leftovers.

*Top to bottom: Sweet Potato Praline
Pie and California Nut Pie*

Velvety Lemon Lime Pie
★ ★ ★ ★

Makes one 9-inch pie

Almond Pastry Crust
1 (8-ounce) package cream cheese, softened
1 (14-ounce) can Eagle® Brand Sweetened Condensed Milk (NOT evaporated milk)
1 (8-ounce) container Borden® Lite-line® or Viva® Lemon Yogurt
⅓ cup ReaLime® Lime Juice from Concentrate
1 teaspoon grated lime or lemon rind, optional
Green or yellow food coloring, optional
1 (4-ounce) container frozen non-dairy whipped topping, thawed (1¾ cups)

Prepare Almond Pastry Crust. In large mixer bowl, beat cheese until fluffy. Gradually beat in sweetened condensed milk until smooth. Beat in yogurt and ReaLime® brand. Stir in rind and food coloring if desired. Fold in whipped topping. Pour into prepared pastry crust. Chill 3 hours or until set. Garnish as desired. Refrigerate leftovers.

Velvety Lemon Lime Pie

Almond Pastry Crust: Preheat oven to 425°. In medium bowl, combine 1⅓ cups unsifted flour, 2 tablespoons ground almonds and ½ teaspoon salt; cut in ½ cup shortening until crumbly. Adding 1 tablespoon at a time, sprinkle with 3 tablespoons cold water, stirring to form a ball. On floured surface, roll dough into 10-inch circle. Turn dough into 9-inch pie plate; trim and flute edge. Prick bottom and side with fork. Bake 10 to 15 minutes or until lightly browned. Cool.

Mince Cheesecake Pie
★ ★ ★ ★

Makes one 9-inch pie

1 (9-inch) unbaked pastry shell
1 (27-ounce) jar None Such® Ready-to-Use Mincemeat (Regular *or* Brandy & Rum)
1½ teaspoons grated orange rind
2 (3-ounce) packages cream cheese, softened
½ cup sugar
2 eggs
1 teaspoon vanilla extract

Place rack in lowest position in oven; preheat oven to 425°. Combine mincemeat and *1 teaspoon* rind; turn into pastry shell. Bake 15 minutes. Meanwhile, in small mixer bowl, beat cheese and sugar until fluffy. Add eggs, vanilla and remaining *½ teaspoon* rind; mix well. Pour over mincemeat. *Reduce oven temperature to 350°.* Bake 25 minutes longer or until set. Cool. Serve warm or chilled. Garnish as desired. Refrigerate leftovers.

Left to right: Mince Cheesecake Pie and Apple Almond Mince Pie

Apple Almond Mince Pie

★ ★ ★ ★

Makes one 9-inch pie

Pastry for 2-crust pie
3 **medium all-purpose apples, cored, pared and thinly sliced**
3 **tablespoons flour**
2 **tablespoons margarine or butter, melted**
1 **(27-ounce) jar None Such® Ready-to-Use Mincemeat (Regular *or* Brandy & Rum)**
½ **cup slivered almonds, toasted and chopped**
½ **teaspoon almond extract**
1 **egg *yolk* mixed with 2 tablespoons water, optional**

Place rack in lowest position in oven; preheat oven to 425°. Toss apples with flour and margarine; arrange in pastry-lined 9-inch pie plate. Combine mincemeat with almonds and extract. Spoon over apples. Cover with top crust; cut slits near center. Seal and flute. Brush egg mixture over crust if desired. Bake 10 minutes. *Reduce oven temperature to 375°*; bake 30 minutes longer or until golden. Serve warm. Garnish as desired. Refrigerate leftovers.

TIP: 1 (9-ounce) package None Such® Condensed Mincemeat, reconstituted as package directs, can be substituted for None Such® Ready-to-Use Mincemeat.

EXTRA EASY

★ ★ ★ ★

Black Forest Pie
★ ★ ★ ★

Makes one 9- or 10-inch pie

1 (9- or 10-inch) baked
  pastry shell
4 (1-ounce) squares
  unsweetened
  chocolate
1 (14-ounce) can Eagle®
  Brand Sweetened
  Condensed Milk (NOT
  evaporated milk)
1 teaspoon almond extract
1½ cups Borden® or Meadow
  Gold® Whipping
  Cream, whipped
1 (21-ounce) can cherry
  pie filling, chilled
  Toasted almonds,
  optional

In heavy saucepan, over medium-low heat, melt chocolate with sweetened condensed milk. Remove from heat; stir in extract. Pour into large bowl; cool or chill thoroughly. Beat until smooth. Gradually fold in whipped cream. Pour into prepared pastry shell. Chill 4 hours or until set. Top with pie filling. Garnish with almonds if desired. Refrigerate leftovers.

MICROWAVE TIP: In 1-quart glass measure with handle, combine chocolate and sweetened condensed milk. Cook on 100% power (high) 2 to 4 minutes, stirring after each minute until smooth. Proceed as above.

Top to bottom:
Black Forest Pie and
Lemon Cloud Pie (page 382)

Lemon Cloud Pie
★★★★

Makes one 9-inch pie

- 1 (9-inch) baked pastry shell or graham cracker crumb crust
- 1 (14-ounce) can Eagle® Brand Sweetened Condensed Milk (NOT evaporated milk)
- ½ cup ReaLemon® Lemon Juice from Concentrate
  Yellow food coloring, optional
- 1 cup (½ pint) Borden® or Meadow Gold® Whipping Cream, whipped

In medium bowl, stir together sweetened condensed milk, ReaLemon® brand and food coloring if desired. Fold in whipped cream. Pour into prepared pastry shell. Chill 3 hours or until set. Garnish as desired. Refrigerate leftovers.

Mince Almond Pie
★★★★

Makes one 9-inch pie

- 1 (9-inch) unbaked pastry shell
- 1 (27-ounce) jar None Such® Ready-to-Use Regular Mincemeat
- ¼ cup amaretto liqueur
- ¾ cup sliced almonds

Place rack in lowest position in oven; preheat oven to 400°. In medium bowl, combine mincemeat and amaretto; turn into pastry shell. Top with almonds. Bake 25 minutes or until bubbly. Serve warm or cooled.

TIP: 1 (9-ounce) package None Such® Condensed Mincemeat, crumbled, reconstituted with 1¼ cups water and ¼ cup amaretto liqueur as package directs, can be substituted for None Such® Ready-to-Use Mincemeat. Proceed as above.

Mince Almond Pie

Cherry Vanilla Ribbon Pie

★★★★

Makes one 9- or 10-inch pie

1 (9- or 10-inch) baked pastry
   shell
1 (8-ounce) package cream
   cheese, softened
1 (14-ounce) can Eagle®
   Brand Sweetened
   Condensed Milk (NOT
   evaporated milk)
¾ cup cold water
1 (4-serving size) package
   instant vanilla flavor
   pudding mix
1 cup (½ pint) Borden® or
   Meadow Gold® Whipping
   Cream, whipped
1 (21-ounce) can cherry pie
   filling, chilled

In large mixer bowl, beat cheese
until fluffy; gradually beat in
sweetened condensed milk until
smooth. On low speed, beat in
water and pudding mix until
smooth. Fold in whipped cream.
Spread half the pudding mixture
into prepared pastry shell; top with
half the cherry pie filling. Repeat.
Chill 2 hours or until set.
Refrigerate leftovers.

Microwave Banana Caramel Pie

★ ★ ★ ★

Makes 1 pie

¼ cup margarine or butter
1 (14-ounce) can Eagle®
   Brand Sweetened
   Condensed Milk (NOT
   evaporated milk)
1 teaspoon vanilla extract
1 cup (½ pint) Borden® or
   Meadow Gold® Whipping
   Cream
3 medium bananas
   ReaLemon® Lemon Juice
   from Concentrate
1 (6-ounce) packaged graham
   cracker crumb pie crust

In 2-quart glass measure with
handle, melt margarine on 100%
power (high) 1 minute. Stir in
sweetened condensed milk and
vanilla. Cook on 100% power
(high) 6 to 10 minutes, stirring
briskly after each minute until
smooth. Stir in ¼ *cup unwhipped*
cream. Freeze 5 minutes.
Meanwhile, slice *2 bananas*; dip in
ReaLemon® brand and drain.
Arrange on bottom of crust. Pour
filling over bananas; cover. Chill at
least 2 hours. In small mixer bowl,
whip remaining ¾ *cup* cream.
Spread on top of pie. Slice
remaining banana; dip in
ReaLemon® brand, drain and
garnish pie. Refrigerate leftovers.

Banana Split Brownie Pie

★ ★ ★ ★

Makes one 9-inch pie

1 (12.9- or 15-ounce) package
   fudge brownie mix
2 medium bananas, sliced,
   dipped in ReaLemon®
   Lemon Juice from
   Concentrate and well
   drained
Borden® or Meadow Gold®
   Vanilla, Chocolate and
   Strawberry Ice Creams
Hot Fudge Sauce (page 399)
Chopped toasted pecans
Borden® or Meadow Gold®
   Whipping Cream,
   whipped
Maraschino cherries,
   optional

Preheat oven to 350°. Prepare
brownie mix as package directs.
Spoon batter into greased 9-inch
round layer cake pan; bake 25
minutes. Cool 10 minutes; remove
from pan. On serving plate, place
brownie; top with bananas, scoops
of ice cream and Hot Fudge Sauce.
Garnish with nuts, whipped cream
and cherries if desired. Serve
immediately. Freeze leftovers.

*Top to bottom: Banana Split Brownie
Pie and Microwave Banana
Caramel Pie*

Peach Mince Cobbler

★ ★ ★ ★

Makes 10 to 12 servings

Pastry for 2-crust pie
1 (27-ounce) jar None Such® Ready-to-Use Mincemeat (Regular *or* Brandy & Rum)
¾ cup chopped walnuts
2 (21-ounce) cans peach pie filling

Place rack in lowest position in oven; preheat oven to 425°. Divide dough in half; roll *each* half 1½ inches larger than 2-quart shallow baking dish. Line dish with half the pastry. Combine mincemeat and nuts; pour into prepared dish. Top with pie filling, then remaining pastry. Cut slits near center; seal and flute. Bake 30 to 35 minutes or until golden. Serve warm.

Apple Cobbler Deluxe

★ ★ ★ ★

Makes 8 to 10 servings

Pastry for 1-crust pie
3 pounds all-purpose apples, cored, pared and sliced (about 8 cups)
2 tablespoons ReaLemon® Lemon Juice from Concentrate
½ cup unsifted flour
½ to ¾ cup sugar
1½ teaspoons ground cinnamon
1 teaspoon ground nutmeg
¼ cup chopped walnuts *or* raisins
1 (16-ounce) jar Bama® Pineapple Preserves

Preheat oven to 375°. In large bowl, sprinkle apples with ReaLemon® brand. Combine flour, sugar, cinnamon and nutmeg; toss with apples and nuts. Add preserves; mix well. Turn into buttered 2-quart baking dish. Roll pastry 1½ inches larger than baking dish; place over apples. Cut slits near center; seal and flute. Bake 1 hour or until golden brown. Serve warm.

Easy Lemon Cream Pie

★ ★ ★ ★

Makes one 9-inch pie

1 (9-inch) baked pastry shell
1 (14-ounce) can Eagle® Brand Sweetened Condensed Milk (NOT evaporated milk)
1 (8-ounce) container Borden® or Meadow Gold® Sour Cream
½ cup ReaLemon® Lemon Juice from Concentrate
Yellow food coloring, optional
Borden® or Meadow Gold® Whipping Cream, whipped *or* whipped topping

Preheat oven to 350°. In medium bowl, beat sweetened condensed milk and sour cream. Stir in ReaLemon® brand and food coloring if desired. Pour into prepared pastry shell; bake 10 minutes. Cool. Chill. Spread with whipped cream. Garnish as desired. Refrigerate leftovers.

Strawberry Cheese Pie
★★★★

Makes one 9-inch pie

- 1 (9-inch) baked pastry shell or graham cracker crumb crust
- 1 (8-ounce) package cream cheese, softened
- 1 (14-ounce) can Eagle® Brand Sweetened Condensed Milk (NOT evaporated milk)
- ⅓ cup ReaLemon® Lemon Juice from Concentrate
- 1 teaspoon vanilla extract
- 1 quart (about 1½ pounds) fresh strawberries, cleaned and hulled
- 1 (16-ounce) package prepared strawberry glaze, chilled

In large mixer bowl, beat cheese until fluffy. Gradually beat in sweetened condensed milk until smooth. Stir in ReaLemon® brand and vanilla. Pour into prepared pastry shell. Chill 3 hours or until set. Top with strawberries and desired amount of glaze. Refrigerate leftovers.

Left to right: Sour Cream Lemon Pie and Light Custard Cheese Pie

Sour Cream Lemon Pie

★ ★ ★ ★

Makes one 9-inch pie

1 (9-inch) graham cracker
  crumb crust or baked
  pastry shell
1¼ cups sugar
⅓ cup cornstarch
2 eggs
½ cup ReaLemon® Lemon
  Juice from Concentrate
1½ cups boiling water
1 tablespoon margarine or
  butter
  Yellow food coloring,
  optional
½ cup Borden® or Meadow
  Gold® Sour Cream, at
  room temperature

In heavy saucepan, combine sugar,
cornstarch and eggs; mix well. Over
medium heat, gradually stir in
ReaLemon® brand then water,
stirring constantly. Cook and stir
until mixture boils and thickens.
Cook 1 minute longer. Remove
from heat. Add margarine, stirring
until melted. Add food coloring if
desired. Fold in sour cream. Pour
into prepared crust. Chill. Garnish
as desired. Refrigerate leftovers.

LIME VARIATION: Substitute
ReaLime® Lime Juice from
Concentrate for ReaLemon® brand
and green food coloring for yellow.

Light Custard Cheese Pie
★★★★

Makes 1 pie

1 (16-ounce) container Borden® Lite-line® or Viva® Lowfat Cottage Cheese
1 tablespoon ReaLemon® Lemon Juice from Concentrate
3 eggs
⅓ cup sugar
⅓ cup Borden® Lite-line® or Viva® Protein Fortified Skim Milk
1 teaspoon vanilla extract
1 (6-ounce) packaged graham cracker crumb pie crust
Assorted cut-up fresh fruit

Preheat oven to 350°. In blender container, combine cottage cheese and ReaLemon® brand; blend until smooth. Add eggs, sugar, milk and vanilla; blend until smooth. Pour into prepared crust. Bake 50 minutes or until set. Cool. Chill. Serve with fresh fruit. Refrigerate leftovers.

Spirited Fruit
★★★★

Makes about 3 cups

¼ cup orange-flavored liqueur *or* orange juice
3 tablespoons ReaLemon® Lemon Juice from Concentrate
2 tablespoons sugar
3 cups assorted fresh fruit

In bowl, combine all ingredients, stirring to dissolve sugar. Cover; refrigerate 4 hours or overnight, stirring occasionally. Serve with custard or cheese pies, cake or ice cream. Refrigerate leftovers.

Microwave Chocolate Mousse Pie
★★★★

Makes one 9-inch pie

1 (9-inch) baked pastry shell
4 (1-ounce) squares unsweetened chocolate
1 (14-ounce) can Eagle® Brand Sweetened Condensed Milk (NOT evaporated milk)
2 teaspoons vanilla extract
2 cups (1 pint) Borden® or Meadow Gold® Whipping Cream, whipped

In 2-quart glass measure with handle, combine chocolate, sweetened condensed milk and vanilla; cook on 100% power (high) 2 to 4 minutes, stirring after each minute until chocolate is melted and mixture is smooth. Cool to room temperature, about 1½ hours. Beat until smooth. Fold in whipped cream. Pour into pastry shell. Chill 4 hours or until set. Garnish as desired. Refrigerate leftovers.

Microwave Chocolate Mousse Pie

BORDEN
CLASSICS

★ ★ ★ ★

ReaLemon Meringue Pie

★★★★

Makes one 9-inch pie

1 (9-inch) baked pastry
    shell
1⅔ cups sugar
6 tablespoons cornstarch
½ cup ReaLemon® Lemon
    Juice from Concentrate
4 eggs, separated
1½ cups boiling water
2 tablespoons margarine
    or butter
¼ teaspoon cream of tartar

Preheat oven to 300°. In heavy saucepan, combine *1⅓ cups* sugar and cornstarch; add ReaLemon® brand. In small bowl, beat egg *yolks*; add to lemon mixture. Gradually add water, stirring constantly. Over medium heat, cook and stir until mixture boils and thickens, about 8 to 10 minutes. Remove from heat. Add margarine; stir until melted. Pour into prepared pastry shell. In small mixer bowl, beat egg *whites* with cream of tartar until soft peaks form; gradually add remaining *⅓ cup* sugar, beating until stiff but not dry. Spread on top of pie, sealing carefully to edge of shell. Bake 20 to 30 minutes or until golden. Cool. Chill before serving. Refrigerate leftovers.

ReaLemon Meringue Pie

Streusel Apple Mince Pie

★ ★ ★ ★

Makes one 9-inch pie

1 (9-inch) unbaked pastry shell

3 medium all-purpose apples, cored, pared and thinly sliced

½ cup plus 3 tablespoons unsifted flour

2 tablespoons margarine or butter, melted

1 (27-ounce) jar None Such® Ready-to-Use Mincemeat (Regular *or* Brandy & Rum)

¼ cup firmly packed light brown sugar

1 teaspoon ground cinnamon

⅓ cup cold margarine or butter

¼ cup chopped nuts

Place rack in lowest position in oven; preheat oven to 425°. In large bowl, toss apples with *3 tablespoons* flour and *melted* margarine; arrange in pastry shell. Top with mincemeat. In medium bowl, combine remaining *½ cup* flour, sugar and cinnamon; cut in cold margarine until crumbly. Add nuts; sprinkle over mincemeat. Bake 10 minutes. *Reduce oven temperature to 375°*; bake 25 minutes longer or until golden. Cool. Garnish as desired.

TIP: 1 (9-ounce) package None Such® Condensed Mincemeat, reconstituted as package directs, can be substituted for None Such® Ready-to-Use Mincemeat.

Left to right: Streusel Apple Mince Pie and Traditional Pumpkin Pie

Traditional Pumpkin Pie
★★★★

Makes one 9-inch pie

- 1 (9-inch) unbaked pastry shell
- 1 (16-ounce) can pumpkin (about 2 cups)
- 1 (14-ounce) can Eagle® Brand Sweetened Condensed Milk (NOT evaporated milk)
- 2 eggs
- 1 teaspoon ground cinnamon
- ½ teaspoon ground ginger
- ½ teaspoon ground nutmeg
- ½ teaspoon salt

Preheat oven to 425°. In large mixer bowl, combine all ingredients except pastry shell; mix well. Pour into pastry shell. Bake 15 minutes. *Reduce oven temperature to 350°*; bake 35 to 40 minutes longer or until knife inserted 1 inch from edge comes out clean. Cool. Garnish as desired. Refrigerate leftovers.

MAPLE PECAN TOPPING VARIATION: In small saucepan, combine ½ cup Borden® or Meadow Gold® Whipping Cream, *unwhipped*, and ½ cup Cary's®, Maple Orchards® or MacDonald's™ Pure Maple Syrup; bring to a boil. Boil rapidly 5 minutes or until thickened; stir occasionally. Add ¼ cup chopped toasted pecans. Spread on warm pumpkin pie. (Makes about ¾ cup)

Classic Banana Cream Pie

Classic Banana Cream Pie
★★★★

Makes one 9-inch pie

- 1 (9-inch) baked pastry shell
- 3 tablespoons cornstarch
- 1⅔ cups water
- 1 (14-ounce) can Eagle® Brand Sweetened Condensed Milk (NOT evaporated milk)
- 3 egg *yolks*, beaten
- 2 tablespoons margarine or butter
- 1 teaspoon vanilla extract
- 3 medium bananas ReaLemon® Lemon Juice from Concentrate Borden® or Meadow Gold® Whipping Cream, whipped

In heavy medium saucepan, dissolve cornstarch in water; stir in sweetened condensed milk and egg *yolks*. Cook and stir until thickened and bubbly. Remove from heat; add margarine and vanilla. Cool slightly. Slice *2 bananas;* dip in ReaLemon® brand and drain. Arrange on bottom of pastry shell. Pour filling over bananas; cover. Chill 4 hours or until set. Spread top with whipped cream. Slice remaining banana; dip in ReaLemon® brand, drain and garnish top of pie. Refrigerate leftovers.

Left to right: Sour Cream Mince Pie and Traditional Mince Pie

Sour Cream Mince Pie

★ ★ ★ ★

Makes one 9-inch pie

1 (9-inch) unbaked pastry
  shell
1 (9-ounce) package None
  Such® Condensed
  Mincemeat, crumbled
1 cup apple juice or water
1 tablespoon flour
1 medium all-purpose apple,
  cored, pared and chopped
2 cups (1 pint) Borden® or
  Meadow Gold® Sour
  Cream
2 eggs
2 tablespoons sugar
1 teaspoon vanilla extract
2 to 3 tablespoons chopped
  nuts

Place rack in lowest position in oven; preheat oven to 425°. In small saucepan, combine mincemeat and apple juice. Bring to a boil; boil briskly 1 minute. In medium bowl, stir flour into apples to coat; stir in mincemeat. Pour into pastry shell. Bake 25 minutes. Meanwhile, in small mixer bowl, combine sour cream, eggs, sugar and vanilla; beat until smooth. Pour evenly over mincemeat mixture. Sprinkle with nuts. *Reduce oven temperature to 325°;* bake 20 minutes longer or until set. Cool. Chill thoroughly. Garnish as desired. Refrigerate leftovers.

Traditional Mince Pie
★★★★

Makes one 9-inch pie

Pastry for 2-crust pie
1 (27-ounce) jar None Such®
Ready-to-Use Mincemeat
(Regular *or* Brandy &
Rum)
1 egg yolk plus 2 tablespoons
water, optional

Place rack in lowest position in
oven; preheat oven to 425°. Turn
mincemeat into pastry-lined 9-inch
pie plate. Cover with top crust; cut
slits near center. Seal and flute.
Brush egg mixture over crust if
desired. Bake 30 minutes or until
golden. Cool slightly.

TO USE NONE SUCH®
CONDENSED MINCEMEAT: In
saucepan, combine 2 (9-ounce)
packages None Such® Condensed
Mincemeat, crumbled, and 3 cups
water; bring to a boil. Cook and stir
1 minute. Cool. Turn into pastry-
lined 9-inch pie plate.

Cherry Mince Pie
★★★★

Makes one 9-inch pie

Pastry for 2-crust pie
1 (9-ounce) package None
Such® Condensed
Mincemeat, reconstituted
as package directs
¾ cup chopped walnuts
1 (21-ounce) can cherry pie
filling

Place rack in lowest position in
oven; preheat oven to 425°.
Combine mincemeat and nuts; turn
into pastry-lined pie plate. Top with
pie filling. Cover with top crust; cut
slits near center. Seal and flute. Bake
25 minutes or until golden.

Cherry Cheese Pie
★★★★

Makes one 9-inch pie

1 (9-inch) baked pastry shell
or graham cracker crumb
crust
1 (8-ounce) package cream
cheese, softened
1 (14-ounce) can Eagle®
Brand Sweetened
Condensed Milk (NOT
evaporated milk)
⅓ cup ReaLemon® Lemon
Juice from Concentrate
1 teaspoon vanilla extract
1 (21-ounce) can cherry pie
filling, chilled

In large mixer bowl, beat cheese
until fluffy. Gradually beat in
sweetened condensed milk until
smooth. Stir in ReaLemon® brand
and vanilla. Pour into prepared
crust. Chill 3 hours or until set. Top
with cherry pie filling before
serving. Refrigerate leftovers.

Cherry Cheese Pie

FAMILY FAVORITES

★ ★ ★ ★

Microwave Vanilla Cream Pie

★★★★

Makes one 9-inch pie

1 (9-inch) baked pastry
   shell or graham
   cracker crust
1 (14-ounce) can Eagle®
   Brand Sweetened
   Condensed Milk (NOT
   evaporated milk)
4 egg *yolks*
½ cup water
1 (4-serving size) package
   vanilla flavor pudding
   mix (*not instant*)
1 (8-ounce) container
   Borden® or Meadow
   Gold® Sour Cream
Whipped cream *or*
   whipped topping

In 2-quart glass measure, beat sweetened condensed milk, egg *yolks*, water and pudding mix well. Cook on 100% power (high) 5 to 8 minutes, stirring every minute until thickened and *smooth*. Cool 15 minutes; stir occasionally. Beat in sour cream. Pour into pastry shell. Chill. Top with whipped cream. Garnish as desired. Refrigerate leftovers.

BANANA CREAM PIE: Prepare filling as above. Slice 2 bananas; dip in ReaLemon® Lemon Juice from Concentrate and drain. Arrange in crust. Top with filling. Chill. Top with whipped cream and banana slices.

BUTTERSCOTCH CREAM PIE: Substitute butterscotch flavor pudding mix for vanilla.

CHOCOLATE CREAM PIE: Substitute chocolate flavor pudding mix for vanilla. Increase water to ¾ cup; add 1 (1-ounce) square unsweetened chocolate when cooking filling.

*Top to bottom: Butterscotch Cream
Pie, Banana Cream Pie and
Chocolate Cream Pie*

Left to right: Maple Custard Pie and Deep-Dish Apple Cranberry Tarts

Deep-Dish Apple Cranberry Tarts

★ ★ ★ ★

Makes 6 tarts

1½ **pounds all-purpose apples, cored, pared and sliced (about 4 cups)**

1 **cup fresh cranberries, rinsed and drained**

2 **tablespoons flour**

½ **cup Cary's®, Maple Orchards® or MacDonald's™ Pure Maple Syrup**

3 **tablespoons firmly packed light brown sugar**

2 **tablespoons margarine or butter, melted**

1 **teaspoon ground cinnamon**

½ **(15-ounce) package refrigerated pie crusts (1 crust)**

Additional Cary's®, Maple Orchards® or MacDonald's™ Pure Maple Syrup

¼ **cup chopped walnuts**

Preheat oven to 375°. In medium bowl, toss apples and cranberries with flour. Add pure maple syrup, brown sugar, margarine and cinnamon; mix well. Spoon equal portions into 6 (6-ounce) custard cups. From pie crust, cut 6 (3½-inch) circles; cut slit in each. Place circles on fruit. Brush with additional pure maple syrup and top with walnuts. Place on baking sheet; bake 40 minutes or until apples are tender. Serve warm.

Maple Custard Pie

★ ★ ★ ★

Makes one 9-inch pie

1 (9-inch) unbaked pastry
    shell, pricked
3 eggs
2 cups Borden® or Meadow
    Gold® Milk
½ cup Cary's®, Maple Orchards®
    or MacDonald's™ Pure
    Maple Syrup

Preheat oven to 400°. Bake pastry
shell 5 minutes. Meanwhile, in
medium bowl, beat eggs; add
remaining ingredients. Pour into
prepared pastry shell; *reduce oven
temperature to 350°*. Bake 45
minutes or until knife inserted near
edge comes out clean. Serve warm
or chilled. Garnish as desired.
Refrigerate leftovers.

Peanut Candy Bar Pie

★ ★ ★ ★

Makes one 9-inch pie

1 (9-inch) baked pastry shell
1 (8-ounce) package cream
    cheese, softened
1 (14-ounce) can Eagle®
    Brand Sweetened
    Condensed Milk (NOT
    evaporated milk)
¾ cup creamy peanut butter
1 teaspoon vanilla extract
2 (2-ounce) chocolate-coated
    peanut candy bars,
    chopped into small pieces
1 cup (½ pint) Borden® or
    Meadow Gold® Whipping
    Cream, whipped
½ to ⅔ cup Hot Fudge Sauce
    or chocolate fudge ice
    cream topping, warmed

Peanut Candy Bar Pie

In large mixer bowl, beat cheese
until fluffy. Gradually beat in
sweetened condensed milk then
peanut butter and vanilla until
smooth. Stir in candy pieces. Fold in
whipped cream. Pour into prepared
pastry shell. Freeze 4 hours or until
firm. Remove from freezer 10
minutes before serving. Serve with
Hot Fudge Sauce. Garnish with
additional candy pieces if desired.
Freeze leftovers.

Hot Fudge Sauce: In heavy
saucepan, over medium heat, melt
1 cup (6 ounces) semi-sweet
chocolate chips and 2 tablespoons
margarine or butter with 1 (14-
ounce) can Eagle® Brand
Sweetened Condensed Milk and 2
tablespoons water. Cook and stir
constantly until thickened, about 5
minutes. Add 1 teaspoon vanilla
extract. Serve warm. Refrigerate
leftovers. (Makes about 2 cups)

Frozen Lemon Satin Pie

★ ★ ★ ★

Makes one 9-inch pie

1 (9-inch) graham cracker crumb crust or baked pastry shell
1 (8-ounce) package cream cheese, softened
1 (14-ounce) can Eagle® Brand Sweetened Condensed Milk (NOT evaporated milk)
½ cup cold water
¼ cup ReaLemon® Lemon Juice from Concentrate
1 (4-serving size) package *instant* lemon flavor pudding mix
   Yellow food coloring, optional
1 cup (½ pint) Borden® or Meadow Gold® Whipping Cream, whipped

In large mixer bowl, beat cheese until fluffy. Gradually beat in sweetened condensed milk until smooth. Add water, ReaLemon® brand, pudding mix and food coloring if desired; mix well. Chill 15 minutes. Fold in whipped cream. Pour into prepared crust. Freeze 6 hours or until firm. Serve with Golden Lemon Sauce. Freeze leftover pie.

Golden Lemon Sauce: In heavy saucepan, combine ⅓ cup sugar, 1 tablespoon cornstarch and dash salt. Add ½ cup water, ¼ cup ReaLemon® brand and 1 egg *yolk*; mix well. Over medium heat, cook and stir until thickened and bubbly. Remove from heat; add 1 tablespoon margarine or butter and yellow food coloring if desired. Stir until well blended. Cool slightly. Serve warm. (Makes about 1 cup)

Cookie Crust Lemon Pie

★ ★ ★ ★

Makes one 9-inch pie

1 (20-ounce) package refrigerated sugar cookie dough
1⅓ cups sugar
⅓ cup cornstarch
2 eggs
½ cup ReaLemon® Lemon Juice from Concentrate
1½ cups boiling water
2 tablespoons margarine or butter
   Yellow food coloring, optional
   Additional sugar

Preheat oven to 350°. On floured surface, press *half* the dough into 6-inch circle. With floured side down, press firmly on bottom and up side to rim of 9-inch pie plate to form crust. In heavy saucepan, combine sugar, cornstarch and eggs; mix well. Over medium heat, gradually stir in ReaLemon® brand then water, stirring constantly. Cook and stir until thickened. Cook 1 minute longer. Remove from heat. Add margarine; stir until melted. Add food coloring if desired. Pour into prepared crust. Slice remaining dough into 16 (¼-inch) rounds; arrange on top of filling. Bake 15 minutes or until golden. Sprinkle with sugar. Cool. Chill. Refrigerate leftovers.

LIME VARIATION: Substitute ReaLime® Lime Juice from Concentrate for ReaLemon® brand and green food coloring for yellow.

Top to bottom: Frozen Lemon Satin Pie and Cookie Crust Lemon Pie

Glazed Apple Custard Pie

★★★★

Makes one 9-inch pie

1 (9-inch) unbaked pastry shell, pricked
1½ cups Borden® or Meadow Gold® Sour Cream
1 (14-ounce) can Eagle® Brand Sweetened Condensed Milk (NOT evaporated milk)
¼ cup frozen apple juice concentrate, thawed
1 egg
1½ teaspoons vanilla extract
¼ teaspoon ground cinnamon
3 medium all-purpose apples, cored, pared and thinly sliced
2 tablespoons margarine or butter
Apple Cinnamon Glaze

Preheat oven to 375°. Bake pastry shell 15 minutes. Meanwhile, in small mixer bowl, beat sour cream, sweetened condensed milk, juice concentrate, egg, vanilla and cinnamon until smooth. Pour into pastry shell; bake 30 minutes or until set. Cool. In large skillet, cook apples in margarine until tender-crisp. Arrange on top of pie; drizzle with Apple Cinnamon Glaze. Serve warm or chilled. Refrigerate leftovers.

Apple Cinnamon Glaze: In small saucepan, combine ¼ cup thawed frozen apple juice concentrate, 1 teaspoon cornstarch and ¼ teaspoon ground cinnamon; mix well. Over low heat, cook and stir until thickened. (Makes about ¼ cup)

Lemon Cheesecake Pie

★★★★

Makes one 9-inch pie

1 (9-inch) graham cracker crumb crust
1 (8-ounce) package cream cheese, softened
1 (14-ounce) can Eagle® Brand Sweetened Condensed Milk (NOT evaporated milk)
2 eggs
2 tablespoons ReaLemon® Lemon Juice from Concentrate
1 teaspoon grated lemon rind, optional
2 cups assorted cut-up fresh fruit, chilled
Lemon Sauce

Preheat oven to 350°. In small mixer bowl, beat cheese until fluffy; gradually beat in sweetened condensed milk. Add eggs and ReaLemon® brand; mix well. Stir in rind if desired. Pour into prepared crust. Bake 20 minutes or until set. Cool. Chill thoroughly. Serve with fruit and Lemon Sauce. Refrigerate leftovers.

Lemon Sauce: In small saucepan, combine ⅓ cup sugar, 2 teaspoons cornstarch and dash salt. Add ½ cup water, ¼ cup ReaLemon® brand and 1 egg *yolk*; mix well. Over medium heat, cook and stir until thickened. Remove from heat; stir in 1 tablespoon margarine or butter and yellow food coloring if desired. Cool. Chill. (Makes about 1 cup)

Chocolate Walnut Pie
★★★★

Makes one 9-inch pie

1 (9-inch) unbaked pastry
   shell
6 tablespoons margarine or
   butter
⅓ cup unsweetened cocoa
1 (14-ounce) can Eagle®
   Brand Sweetened
   Condensed Milk (NOT
   evaporated milk)
½ cup water
2 eggs, beaten
½ teaspoon vanilla extract
½ teaspoon maple flavoring
1 cup coarsely chopped
   walnuts

Preheat oven to 350°. In medium
saucepan, over low heat, melt
margarine. Add cocoa; stir until
smooth. Stir in sweetened
condensed milk, water and eggs;
beat well. Remove from heat; stir in
vanilla, flavoring and walnuts. Pour
into pastry shell. Bake 40 to 45
minutes or until center is set. Cool
slightly. Serve warm or chilled.
Garnish as desired. Refrigerate
leftovers.

PIE MAKING HINTS

Pastry Crust
★ ★ ★ ★

Makes one 8- or 9-inch crust

1 cup unsifted flour
½ teaspoon salt
⅓ cup shortening
3 to 4 tablespoons cold water

In medium bowl, combine flour and salt; cut in shortening until crumbly. Sprinkle with water, 1 tablespoon at a time, mixing until dough is just moist enough to hold together. Form into ball. On floured surface, press dough down into a flat circle with smooth edges. Roll out into a circle ⅛-inch thick and about 1½ inches larger than inverted pie plate. Ease dough into pie plate. Trim ½ inch beyond pie plate edge. Fold under; flute edge as desired.

To Bake Without Filling
★ ★ ★ ★

Preheat oven to 450°. Prick bottom and side of pastry shell with fork. Line pastry with aluminum foil; fill with dry beans. Bake 5 minutes; remove beans and foil. Bake 5 to 7 minutes longer or until golden.

To Bake With Filling
★ ★ ★ ★

Preheat oven as directed in recipe. Do not prick pastry shell. Fill and bake as directed.

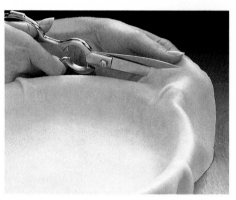

Use kitchen shears or sharp knife to trim dough ½ inch beyond pie plate edge. Fold under extra dough to form rim.

Flute edge as desired.

To keep an unfilled pastry crust from puffing or shrinking during baking, line with aluminum foil and fill with dry beans.

Lemon Pastry

★ ★ ★ ★

Makes one 9-inch pastry crust

1 cup unsifted flour
½ teaspoon salt
⅓ cup shortening
1 egg, beaten
1 tablespoon ReaLemon® Lemon Juice from Concentrate

Preheat oven to 400°. In medium bowl, combine flour and salt; cut in shortening until crumbly. In small bowl, beat egg and ReaLemon® brand. Sprinkle over flour mixture; stir until dough forms a ball. On floured surface, roll out to a circle ⅛-inch thick and about 1½ inches larger than inverted pie plate. Ease dough into pie plate. Trim ½ inch beyond pie plate edge. Fold under; flute edge as desired. Prick with fork. Bake 12 to 15 minutes or until golden.

Crumb Crust

★ ★ ★ ★

Makes one 8- or 9-inch crust

1½ cups graham cracker or chocolate wafer crumbs
¼ cup sugar
6 tablespoons margarine or butter, melted

Combine ingredients; mix well. Press firmly on bottom and up side to rim of 8- or 9-inch pie plate. Chill thoroughly or bake in preheated 375° oven 6 to 8 minutes or until edges are brown. Cool before filling.

Pastry Egg Wash

★ ★ ★ ★

For a more golden crust on a 2-crust pie, beat 1 egg *yolk* with 2 tablespoons water; brush evenly over pastry before baking.

Toasting Coconut and Nuts

★ ★ ★ ★

CONVENTIONAL OVEN: Spread coconut or nuts in shallow pan. Toast in preheated 350° oven 7 to 15 minutes or until golden, stirring frequently.

MICROWAVE OVEN:

Coconut: Spread ½ cup coconut in glass pie plate. Cook on 70% power (medium-high) 5 to 10 minutes or until lightly browned, stirring after each minute.

Nuts: Spread 1 cup nuts in glass pie plate. Cook on 100% power (high) 5 to 8 minutes or until lightly browned, stirring after each minute.

NOTE: In microwave oven, nuts heat quickly and brown evenly. Remove from oven as soon as they begin to brown (browning will continue as they stand). Pie plate and nuts will be very hot after toasting; handle carefully.

JELL-O®
BRAND
Easy Entertaining

Clockwise from top left: Melon Bubbles (page 423), Eggnog Cheesecake (page 430), JELL-O Jigglers (page 459) and Pastry Chef Tarts (page 429)

Introduction

Everyone loves to serve magnificent desserts when they entertain. Most of us, however, think we have neither the time nor the talent to make them. JELL-O *Easy Entertaining* offers the perfect solution to both of these problems.

Contained in this incredible recipe collection are desserts for any occasion. Not only are these irresistible desserts guaranteed to impress your family and friends alike, but they all offer the added bonus of being super-quick and easy to make.

As an added guarantee of success, we have included a special "Tricks of the Trade" chapter complete with no-fail tips that promise to make each and every luscious dessert as beautiful as it is delicious!

Tricks of the Trade

Our professionals share their secrets with you—simple additions guaranteed to add pizzazz to any recipe. These foolproof tips, many with step-by-step photos, ensure perfect results every time and the quick, clever garnish ideas are sure to impress family and friends alike.

Gelatin

Making JELL-O Brand Gelatin is easy—you've probably been doing it since you were little. Just follow the package directions and the results are terrific!

The basic directions as written below are also on the package:

- Add 1 cup boiling water to 1 package (4-serving size) gelatin (2 cups water for 8-serving size). Stir until dissolved, about 2 minutes. Add 1 cup cold water (2 cups for 8-serving size). Chill until set.

- JELL-O Brand Sugar Free Gelatin is prepared in the same way. It can be used in any recipe that calls for JELL-O Brand Gelatin.

Some tips for success

- To make a mixture that is clear and uniformly set, be sure the gelatin is <u>completely</u> dissolved in boiling water or other boiling liquid before adding the cold liquid.

- To double a recipe, just double the amounts of gelatin, liquid and other ingredients used except salt, vinegar and lemon juice. For these, use just 1½ times the amount given in the recipe.

- To store prepared gelatin overnight or longer, cover it to prevent drying. Always store gelatin cakes or pies in the refrigerator.

How to speed up chilling time

- Choose the *right container*—a metal bowl or mold rather than glass, plastic or china. Metal chills more quickly and the gelatin will be firm in less time than in glass or plastic bowls. Also, individual servings in small molds or serving dishes will chill more quickly than large servings.

(continued)

• Speed set (ice cube method): Dissolve gelatin completely in ¾ cup boiling liquid (1½ cups for 8-serving size). Combine ½ cup water and enough ice cubes to make 1¼ cups (1 cup cold water and enough ice cubes to make 2½ cups for 8-serving size). Add to gelatin, stirring until slightly thickened. Remove any unmelted ice. Pour into dessert dishes or serving bowl. Chill. Mixture will be soft-set and ready to eat in about 30 minutes, firm in 1 to 1½ hours. However, <u>do not</u> use this method if you are going to mold the gelatin.

Gelatin Chilling Time Chart

In all recipes, for best results, the gelatin needs to be chilled to the proper consistency. Use this chart as a guideline to determine the desired consistency and the approximate chilling time.

When recipe says:	It means gelatin should...	It will take about:		Use it for...
		Regular set	Speed set*	
"Chill until syrupy"	be consistency of thick syrup	1 hour	3 minutes	glaze for pies, fruits
"Chill until slightly thickened"	be consistency of unbeaten egg whites	1¼ hours	5 to 6 minutes	adding creamy ingredients such as whipped topping, or when mixture will be beaten
"Chill until thickened"	be thick enough so that spoon drawn through it leaves a definite impression	1½ hours	7 to 8 minutes	adding solid ingredients such as fruits or vegetables
"Chill until set but not firm"	stick to the finger when touched and should mound or move to the side when bowl or mold is tilted	2 hours	30 minutes	layering gelatin mixtures
"Chill until firm"	not stick to finger when touched and not mound or move when mold is tilted	Individual molds: at least 3 hours 2- to 6-cup mold: at least 4 hours 8- to 12-cup mold: at least 5 hours or overnight		unmolding and serving

*Speed set (ice cube method) not recommended for molding.

- Ice bath method: Dissolve gelatin according to package directions. Place bowl of gelatin mixture in larger bowl of ice and water; stir occasionally as mixture chills to ensure even thickening.

- Blender method: Place 4-serving size package of gelatin and ¾ cup boiling liquid in blender. (Note: The volume of the 8-serving size package is too large for most blenders.) Cover and blend at low speed until gelatin is completely dissolved, about 30 seconds. Combine ½ cup water and enough ice cubes to make 1¼ cups; add to gelatin. Stir until partially melted. Blend at high speed 30 seconds. Pour into dessert dishes or bowl. Chill until set, at least 30 minutes. Mixture is self-layering and sets with a frothy layer on top, clear layer on bottom.

The Secret to Molding Gelatin

The Mold
- Use metal molds, traditional decorative molds and other metal forms, as well. You can use square or round cake pans, fluted or plain tube pans, loaf pans, metal mixing bowls (the nested sets give you a variety of sizes), or metal fruit or juice cans (to unmold, dip can in warm water, then puncture bottom of can and unmold).

- To determine the *volume of the mold,* measure first with water. Most recipes give an indication of the size of the mold needed. For clear gelatin, you need a 2-cup mold for a 4-serving size package of gelatin, and a 4-cup mold for 8-serving size.

- If mold holds less than the amount called for, pour the extra gelatin mixture into a separate dish and serve at another time. Do not use a mold that is too large, since it would be difficult to unmold. Either increase the recipe or use a smaller mold.

- For easier unmolding, spray mold with non-stick cooking spray before filling mold.

The Preparation
- Use less water in preparing gelatin if it is to be molded. For 4-serving size package, use ¾ cup cold water; for 8-serving size, use 1½ cups cold water. (This adjustment has already been made in recipes in this book that are to be molded.) This makes the mold less fragile and makes unmolding much simpler.

- To arrange fruits or vegetables in molds, chill gelatin until thick, then pour gelatin into mold to about ¼-inch depth. Arrange fruits or vegetables in decorative pattern in gelatin. Chill until set but not firm, then pour remaining thickened gelatin over pattern in mold.

The Unmolding
- First, allow gelatin to set until firm, several hours or overnight. Also, chill serving plate or individual plates on which mold will be served.

- Make certain that gelatin is completely firm. It should not feel sticky on top and should not mound or move to the side if mold is tilted.

- Moisten tips of fingers and gently pull gelatin from edge of mold. Or, use a small metal spatula or pointed knife dipped in warm water to loosen top edge.

(continued)

- Dip mold in warm, not hot, water, just to the rim, for about 10 seconds. Lift from water, hold upright and shake to loosen gelatin. Or, gently pull gelatin from edge of mold.

- Moisten chilled serving plate with cold water; this allows gelatin to be moved after unmolding. Place moistened plate over mold and invert. Shake slightly, then lift off mold carefully. If gelatin doesn't release easily, dip the mold in warm water again for a few seconds. If necessary, move gelatin to center of serving plate.

Unmolding Gelatin

1. Before unmolding, pull gelatin from edge of mold with moist fingers. Or, run small metal spatula or pointed knife dipped in warm water around edge of gelatin.

2. Dip mold in warm water, just to rim, for 10 seconds.

3. Lift from water and gently pull gelatin from edge of mold with moist fingers.

4. Place moistened serving plate on top of mold.

5. Invert mold and plate and shake to loosen gelatin.

6. Gently remove mold and center gelatin on plate.

Pudding Pointers

The recipes in this book use both **JELL-O Pudding and Pie Filling**, which requires cooking, and **JELL-O Instant Pudding and Pie Filling**, which is not cooked. <u>These products are not interchangeable in recipes.</u> Be sure to use the product called for in the recipe.

The basic directions as written below are also on the package:

For JELL-O Pudding and Pie Filling:
- Stir contents of 1 package (4-serving size) pudding mix into 2 cups milk (3 cups for 6-serving size) in medium saucepan. Cook and stir over medium heat until mixture comes to full boil. Pudding thickens as it cools. Serve warm or cold.

- Microwave directions: Stir pudding mix with milk in 1½-quart (2-quart for 6-serving size) microwavable bowl. Microwave on HIGH 6 minutes (8 minutes for 6-serving size), stirring every 2 minutes, until mixture comes to boil. Stir well. Chill. Note: Ovens vary; cooking time is approximate. Microwave method not recommended for ovens below 500 watts.

- For pie, cool cooked pudding 5 minutes, stirring twice. Pour into cooled, baked 8-inch pie shell (9-inch highly fluted or 10-inch for 6-serving size). Chill 3 hours.

- JELL-O Lemon Flavor Pie Filling has different directions that call for eggs, sugar and water rather than milk; follow the package directions to make a delicious lemon meringue pie.

For JELL-O Instant Pudding and Pie Filling:
- Pour 2 cups cold milk (3 cups for 6-serving size) into bowl. Add pudding mix. Beat with wire whisk or at lowest speed of electric mixer until well blended, 1 to 2 minutes. Pour immediately into dishes. Pudding will be soft-set, ready to eat in 5 minutes.

- For pies, beat only 1 minute; mixture will be thin. Pour immediately into cooled, baked pie shell (8-inch for 4-serving size, 9-inch for 6-serving size). Chill at least 1 hour. For chocolate, chocolate fudge, milk chocolate or butterscotch flavors, 4-serving size, reduce milk to 1¾ cups; for chocolate and chocolate fudge flavors, 6-serving size, reduce milk to 2⅔ cups.

- Shaker method: Pour cold milk into leakproof 1-quart container (1½-quart container for 6-serving size). Add pudding mix. Cover tightly. Shake vigorously at least 45 seconds. Pour immediately into dessert dishes or serving bowl.

- Fork-Stir method: Place mix in 1-quart bowl. While stirring with fork, gradually add milk. Stir until blended and smooth, about 2 minutes.

- Blender method: Pour cold milk into electric blender. Add pudding mix; cover. Blend at high speed 15 seconds. Pour immediately into dessert dishes or pie shell.

JELL-O Sugar Free Pudding and Pie Filling and Sugar Free Instant Pudding and Pie Filling can be substituted for their respective cooked and instant pudding mixes.

Citrus Zest Strips

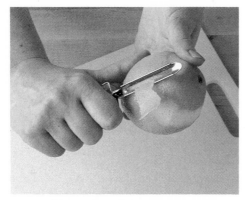

1. Use vegetable peeler to shave off topmost layer from orange peel in wide strips.

2. With sharp knife, cut peel into narrow strips. Use to flavor desserts or as a garnish.

Tinted Coconut

Dilute a few drops of food coloring with ½ teaspoon milk or water; add 1 to 1⅓ cups coconut. Toss with fork until evenly tinted.

Toasted Coconut

Spread coconut in shallow pan. Toast at 350°, stirring frequently, 7 to 12 minutes or until lightly browned. Or toast in microwave oven on HIGH, 5 minutes for 1⅓ cups, stirring several times.

Citrus Fans

1. With sharp knife, cut orange into thin slices.

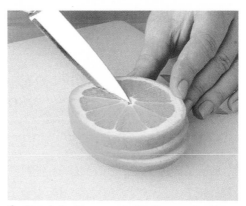

2. Stack 3 slices; cut slit through slices to center.

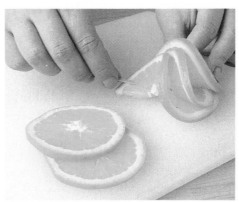

3. Twist slices from slits in opposite directions; twist 3 slices together to give fan effect.

Fruit Fans

1. With sharp knife, cut drained canned pear halves into thin slices (about 5 or 6), cutting up to, but not through, stem ends. (Use same technique for strawberries.)

2. Hold stem end in place and gently fan out slices from stem before placing on plate for fruit desserts or using as garnish.

Frosted Fruit

Use fresh cranberries or green or red seedless grapes. Dip fruit into 1 lightly beaten egg white. (Note: Use only clean eggs with no cracks in shells.) Hold to permit excess egg white to drain off; roll in sugar in flat plate to coat well. Place on tray covered with waxed paper. Let stand until dry.

Whipped Topping Piping

Insert decorating tip in pastry bag; fill with thawed COOL WHIP Whipped Topping. Fold down top of pastry bag. Holding bag firmly with one hand and squeezing topping down into tip, guide tip around surface to be decorated. Double back topping at intervals for decorative wave effect.

Whipped Topping Dollops

1. Swirl spoon, held upright, through thawed COOL WHIP Whipped Topping, creating rippled surface on the topping.

2. Dip spoon into rippled topping to scoop up heaping spoonful of topping, maintaining rippled surface.

3. Gently touch spoon onto surface of dessert and release topping gradually onto surface, pulling spoon up into a crowning tip.

Sauce Swirls

1. Spoon Vanilla Sauce (see page 426 for recipe) onto individual dessert plates. Drop small amounts of sauce (chocolate, raspberry or strawberry) or melted chocolate from spoon at intervals over Vanilla Sauce near rim of plate.

2. Draw wooden pick through sauce, swirling through Vanilla Sauce to create design.

Toasted Nuts

Spread nuts in shallow baking pan. Toast at 400°, stirring frequently, 8 to 10 minutes or until golden brown.

Gumdrop Ribbon

1. Line up gumdrops in a row on surface or sheet of waxed paper sprinkled with sugar. Flatten into long strips with rolling pin, turning frequently to coat with sugar.

2. Cut flattened gumdrops with sharp knife into 1-inch strips.

3. To make bow, fold over four strips to form loops of the bow; place on dessert. Then place a small loop in center to cover center of bow. Cut "V"s at one end of remaining two strips, if desired; place under loops to resemble ends of ribbon.

Gumdrop Flowers

1. Flatten gumdrops with rolling pin on surface or sheet of waxed paper sprinkled with sugar. Roll until very thin (about ¹⁄₁₆ inch thick), turning frequently to coat with sugar.

2. Hold flattened gumdrop at center; overlap edges slightly to give petal effect, pressing piece together at base to resemble flower. For open blossom, bend gumdrop petals outward from center. Insert small piece of gumdrop in centers with wooden pick, if desired. Use wooden pick to attach flowers to cake if necessary.

Quick and Easy

Black Forest Parfaits

1 package (8 ounces)
 PHILADELPHIA BRAND
 Cream Cheese, softened
2 cups cold milk
1 package (4-serving size)
 JELL-O Instant Pudding
 and Pie Filling, Chocolate
 Flavor
1 can (21 ounces) cherry pie
 filling
1 tablespoon cherry liqueur
½ cup chocolate wafer crumbs

BEAT cream cheese with ½ cup of
the milk at low speed of electric
mixer until smooth. Add pudding
mix and remaining milk. Beat until
smooth, 1 to 2 minutes.

MIX together cherry pie filling and
liqueur. Reserve a few cherries for
garnish, if desired. Spoon ½ of the
pudding mixture evenly into
individual dessert dishes; sprinkle
with wafer crumbs. Cover with pie
filling; top with remaining
pudding mixture. Chill until ready
to serve. Garnish with reserved
cherries and additional wafer
crumbs, if desired.

MAKES 4 to 6 servings

Prep time: 15 minutes

Berry Cream Sauce

2 packages (10 ounces each)
 BIRDS EYE Quick Thaw Red
 Raspberries or
 Strawberries, thawed
1½ cups cold half and half or
 milk
1 package (4-serving size)
 JELL-O Instant Pudding
 and Pie Filling, French
 Vanilla or Vanilla Flavor

PLACE raspberries in food
processor or blender; cover.
Process until smooth; strain to
remove seeds. Pour half and half
into medium bowl. Add pudding
mix. Beat with wire whisk until
well blended, 1 to 2 minutes. Stir
in raspberry puree. Let stand 10
minutes or until slightly thickened.
Serve over cake or fruit.

MAKES 3½ cups

Note: Store leftover sauces in
covered containers in refrigerator.

Prep time: 5 minutes

Black Forest Parfaits

Trifle Cups

1 package (4-serving size)
    JELL-O Brand Gelatin,
    Raspberry Flavor
¾ cup boiling water
1 package (10 ounces) BIRDS
    EYE Quick Thaw Red
    Raspberries, thawed
    Ice cubes
12 shortbread or sugar cookies
1½ cups cold half and half or
    milk
1 package (4-serving size)
    JELL-O Instant Pudding
    and Pie Filling, French
    Vanilla or Vanilla Flavor
½ cup thawed COOL WHIP
    Whipped Topping

DISSOLVE gelatin in boiling water.
Drain raspberries, reserving syrup.
Combine syrup and ice cubes to
make 1 cup. Add to gelatin, stirring
until ice is melted. Place bowl in
larger bowl of ice and water. Let
stand, stirring occasionally, until
gelatin is slightly thickened, about
5 minutes. Reserve 6 raspberries
for garnish, if desired. Stir
remaining raspberries into gelatin.

CRUMBLE cookies into individual
dessert dishes. Spoon gelatin
mixture over cookies; chill until
set but not firm.

POUR half and half into small
bowl. Add pudding mix. Beat with
wire whisk until well blended,
about 1 to 2 minutes. Let stand 5
minutes or until slightly thickened.
Fold in whipped topping. Spoon
over gelatin mixture. Chill until
set, about 1 hour. Garnish with
reserved raspberries and additional
whipped topping, if desired.
MAKES 6 servings

Prep time: 20 minutes
Chill time: 1 hour

Pinwheel Cake and Cream

*A quick and easy dessert to make
with any fruit.*

1 package (4-serving size)
    JELL-O Instant Pudding
    and Pie Filling, French
    Vanilla or Vanilla Flavor
2 cups cold milk
1 cup thawed COOL WHIP
    Whipped Topping
1 teaspoon grated orange
    rind
1 small peach or nectarine,
    cut into bite-size pieces
1 pound cake loaf (about
    12 ounces), cut into slices
2 cups summer fruit*

PREPARE pudding mix with milk
as directed on package. Let stand 5
minutes or until slightly thickened.
Fold in whipped topping, orange
rind and peach.

ARRANGE pound cake slices on
serving plate. Spoon pudding
mixture evenly over center of cake
slices. Arrange fruit in pudding
mixture. Chill until ready to serve.
MAKES 10 servings

*We suggest any variety of berries,
seedless grapes or sliced peaches,
nectarines or plums.

Prep time: 15 minutes

Pinwheel Cake and Cream

Orange Cream Timbales

Your guests will love the surprise inside these desserts.

  1 package (4-serving size)
      JELL-O Brand Gelatin,
      Orange Flavor
  1 cup boiling water
  ½ cup cold water
      Ice cubes
  1¾ cups (4 ounces) COOL WHIP
      Whipped Topping, thawed
  1 can (11 ounces) mandarin
      orange sections, well
      drained
      Mint leaves (optional)

DISSOLVE gelatin in boiling water. Combine cold water and ice cubes to make 1 cup. Add to gelatin, stirring until ice is melted. If necessary, place bowl in larger bowl of ice and water; let stand, stirring occasionally, until slightly thickened, about 5 minutes.

FOLD 1⅓ cups of the whipped topping into gelatin mixture. Pour ½ of the gelatin mixture evenly into 6 (6-ounce) custard cups, filling each cup about halfway. Place dollop of remaining whipped topping in center of each dessert; press orange section into each dollop. Fill cups with remaining gelatin mixture. Chill until firm, about 3 hours.

PLACE remaining orange sections in food processor or blender; cover. Process until smooth. Unmold gelatin cups onto individual dessert plates. Spoon orange puree around desserts. Garnish with mint leaves, if desired. (Or omit orange puree. Garnish desserts with whole orange sections and mint.)
MAKES 4 servings

Prep time: 20 minutes
Chill time: 3 hours

Melon Bubbles

  1 package (4-serving size)
      JELL-O Brand Gelatin, any
      flavor
  ¾ cup boiling water
  ½ cup cold water
      Ice cubes
  1 cup melon balls (cantaloupe,
      honeydew or watermelon)
      Mint leaves (optional)

DISSOLVE gelatin in boiling water. Combine cold water and ice cubes to make 1¼ cups. Add to gelatin, stirring until slightly thickened. Remove any unmelted ice. Measure 1⅓ cups gelatin into small bowl; add melon. Pour into individual dessert glasses or serving bowl.

WHIP remaining gelatin at high speed of electric mixer until fluffy, thick and about doubled in volume. Spoon over gelatin in glasses. Chill until set, about 2 hours. Garnish with additional melon balls and mint leaves, if desired.
MAKES 6 to 8 (½-cup) servings

Prep time: 10 minutes
Chill time: 2 hours

Orange Cream Timbales

Ice Cream Shop Pie

Cool, fun and delicious!

1½ cups cold half and half or
    milk
  1 package (4-serving size)
    JELL-O Instant Pudding
    and Pie Filling, any flavor
3½ cups (8 ounces) COOL WHIP
    Whipped Topping, thawed
    Ice Cream Shop Ingredients*
  1 packaged chocolate,
    graham cracker or vanilla
    crumb crust

POUR half and half into large bowl. Add pudding mix. Beat with wire whisk until well blended, 1 to 2 minutes. Let stand 5 minutes or until slightly thickened.

FOLD whipped topping and Ice Cream Shop Ingredients into pudding mixture. Spoon into crust.

FREEZE pie until firm, about 6 hours or overnight. Remove from freezer. Let stand at room temperature about 10 minutes before serving to soften. Store any leftover pie in freezer.

MAKES 8 servings

Rocky Road Pie: Use any chocolate flavor pudding mix and chocolate crumb crust. Fold in ½ cup *each* BAKER'S Semi-Sweet Real Chocolate Chips, KRAFT Miniature Marshmallows and chopped nuts with whipped topping. Serve with chocolate sauce, if desired.

Toffee Bar Crunch Pie: Use French vanilla or vanilla flavor pudding mix and graham cracker crumb crust, spreading ⅓ cup butterscotch sauce onto bottom of crust before filling. Fold in 1 cup chopped chocolate-covered English toffee bars (about 6 bars) with whipped topping. Garnish with additional chopped toffee bars, if desired.

Strawberry Banana Split Pie: Use French vanilla or vanilla flavor pudding mix, reducing half and half to ¾ cup and adding ¾ cup pureed BIRDS EYE Quick Thaw Strawberries with the half and half. Use vanilla crumb crust and line bottom with banana slices. Garnish with whipped topping, maraschino cherries and chopped nuts. Serve with remaining strawberries, pureed, if desired.

Chocolate Cookie Pie: Use French vanilla or vanilla flavor pudding mix and chocolate crumb crust. Fold in 1 cup chopped chocolate sandwich cookies with whipped topping.

Nutcracker Pie: Use butter pecan flavor pudding mix and graham cracker crumb crust. Fold in 1 cup chopped mixed nuts with whipped topping.

Peppermint Stick Pie: Use French vanilla or vanilla flavor pudding mix and chocolate crumb crust. Fold in ½ cup crushed hard peppermint candies, ½ cup BAKER'S Semi-Sweet Real Chocolate Chips and 2 teaspoons peppermint extract with whipped topping.

Prep time: 15 minutes
Freezing time: 6 hours

Top to bottom: Rocky Road Pie; Toffee Bar Crunch Pie; Strawberry Banana Split Pie

Fruit in Cream

Vanilla Sauce (see Pear Fans,
  this page, for recipe)
Assorted fruit*
Quick Chocolate Sauce
  (recipe follows)
Mint leaves (optional)

SPOON Vanilla Sauce onto each
serving plate to cover bottom.
Arrange fruit in sauce. Swirl Quick
Chocolate Sauce through Vanilla
Sauce to form design (see page 416
for directions). Garnish with mint
leaves, if desired.

*We suggest any variety of berries,
mandarin orange sections, melon
balls, halved seedless grapes, sliced
peaches, kiwifruit or plums.

Quick Chocolate Sauce

¾ cup light corn syrup
1 package (4-serving size)
  JELL-O Instant Pudding
  and Pie Filling, Chocolate
  or Chocolate Fudge Flavor
¾ cup evaporated milk or half
  and half

POUR corn syrup into small bowl.
Blend in pudding mix. Gradually
add evaporated milk, stirring
constantly. Let stand 10 minutes or
until slightly thickened.
  MAKES about 2 cups

Prep time: 20 minutes

Note: Store leftover sauces in
covered container in refrigerator.

Pear Fans

*Your guests will think you are an
artist when they see these sauces.*

Canned pear halves, drained
Vanilla Sauce (recipe
  follows)
Berry Cream Sauce (see
  page 418 for recipe)
Cinnamon stick, cut into
  ¾-inch pieces (optional)
Mint leaves (optional)

SLICE pears lengthwise, cutting
almost through stem ends. Place on
individual serving plates; spread to
form fans (see page 415 for
directions). Spoon Vanilla Sauce
around pears. Swirl Berry Cream
Sauce through Vanilla Sauce to
form design (see page 416 for
directions). Place cinnamon stick
and mint leaf at stem end of each
pear, if desired.

Vanilla Sauce

3½ cups cold half and half or
  milk
1 package (4-serving size)
  JELL-O Instant Pudding
  and Pie Filling, French
  Vanilla or Vanilla Flavor

POUR half and half into medium
bowl. Add pudding mix. Beat with
wire whisk until well blended, 1 to
2 minutes. Let stand 10 minutes or
until slightly thickened.
  MAKES 3½ cups

Prep time: 20 minutes

*Top: Pear Fans; bottom:
Fruit in Cream*

Pastry Chef Tarts

1 package (10 ounces) pie
   crust mix
1 egg, beaten
1 to 2 tablespoons cold water
1½ cups cold half and half or
   milk
1 package (4-serving size)
   JELL-O Instant Pudding
   and Pie Filling, French
   Vanilla or Vanilla Flavor
   Assorted berries or fruit*
   Mint leaves (optional)

PREHEAT oven to 425°. Combine pie crust mix with egg. Add just enough water to form dough. Form 2 to 3 tablespoons dough into a round. Press each round onto bottom and sides of each 3- to 4-inch tart pan. (Use tart pans with removable bottoms, if possible.) Pierce pastry several times with fork. Place on baking sheet. Bake for 10 minutes or until golden. Cool slightly. Remove tart shells from pans; cool completely on racks.

POUR half and half into small bowl. Add pudding mix. Beat with wire whisk until well blended, 1 to 2 minutes. Spoon into tart shells. Chill until ready to serve.

ARRANGE fruit on pudding. Garnish with mint leaves, if desired.   *MAKES 10 servings*

*We suggest any variety of berries, mandarin orange sections, melon balls, halved seedless grapes, sliced peaches, kiwifruit or plums.

Note: Individual graham cracker crumb tart shells may be substituted for baked tart shells.

Prep time: 20 minutes
Baking time: 10 minutes

Tropical Breeze

1 package (4-serving size)
   JELL-O Brand Gelatin, any
   flavor
1½ cups boiling tropical blend
   juice
1 tablespoon grated lemon,
   orange or lime rind
½ cup cold water
   Ice cubes
¾ cup light corn syrup
2 egg whites, lightly beaten

DISSOLVE gelatin in boiling juice; stir in rind. Combine cold water and ice cubes to make 1 cup. Add to gelatin, stirring until ice is melted. Stir in corn syrup and egg whites. Place bowl in larger bowl of ice and water. Let stand, stirring occasionally, until gelatin is slightly thickened, about 5 minutes.

BEAT gelatin mixture at high speed of electric mixer until thick and frothy. Pour into 9×5-inch loaf pan. Freeze until firm, about 6 hours or overnight.

SCOOP frozen mixture into individual dessert glasses.
   MAKES 12 servings

NOTE: USE ONLY CLEAN EGGS WITH NO CRACKS IN SHELL.

Prep time: 15 minutes
Freezing time: 6 hours

Pastry Chef Tarts

Holidays and More

Eggnog Cheesecake

You won't want to cut this dessert because it's so pretty, but please do. It tastes as good as it looks.

- 2 packages (5½ ounces each) chocolate-laced pirouette cookies
- ⅓ cup graham cracker crumbs
- 3 tablespoons PARKAY Margarine, melted
- 2 packages (8 ounces each) PHILADELPHIA BRAND Cream Cheese, softened
- 2 cups cold prepared eggnog
- 2 cups cold milk
- 2 packages (4-serving size each) JELL-O Instant Pudding and Pie Filling, French Vanilla or Vanilla Flavor
- 1 tablespoon rum
- ⅛ teaspoon ground nutmeg
  COOL WHIP Whipped Topping, thawed (optional)
  Ribbon (optional)

RESERVE 1 cookie for garnish, if desired. Cut 1-inch piece off 1 end of each of the remaining cookies. Crush 1-inch pieces into crumbs; set aside remaining cookies for sides of cake. Combine cookie crumbs, graham cracker crumbs and margarine until well mixed. Press crumb mixture firmly onto bottom of 9-inch springform pan.

BEAT cream cheese at low speed of electric mixer until smooth. Gradually add 1 cup of the eggnog, blending until mixture is very smooth. Add remaining eggnog, milk, pudding mix, rum and nutmeg. Beat until well blended, about 1 minute. Pour cream cheese mixture carefully into pan. Chill until firm, about 3 hours. Run hot metal spatula or knife around edges of pan before removing sides of pan.

PRESS remaining cookies, cut sides down, into sides of cake. Garnish with whipped topping and reserved cookie, if desired. Tie ribbon around cake, if desired.

MAKES 12 servings

Prep time: 45 minutes
Chill time: 3 hours

Top to bottom: Eggnog Cheesecake;
Holiday Fruitcake (page 432);
Marzipan Fruits (page 432);
Raspberry Gift Box (page 433)

Holiday Fruitcake

A light cake with just a little bit of fruit. The Marzipan Fruits on top are easy to make and turn this dessert into a show stopper.

    1 cup chopped candied fruit
    ⅔ cup pitted dates, chopped
    ½ cup chopped walnuts
    ¼ cup brandy or orange juice
    1 package (6-serving size)
        JELL-O Instant Pudding
        and Pie Filling, Vanilla
        Flavor
    1 package (2-layer size)
        yellow cake mix
    4 eggs
    1 cup (½ pint) sour cream
    ⅓ cup vegetable oil
    1 tablespoon grated orange
        rind
    ⅔ cup cold milk
        Marzipan Fruits (recipe
        follows) (optional)

MIX together candied fruit, dates, walnuts and brandy.

RESERVE ⅓ cup pudding mix; set aside. Combine cake mix, remaining pudding mix, eggs, sour cream, oil and orange rind in large bowl. Beat at low speed of electric mixer just to moisten, scraping sides of bowl often. Beat at medium speed 4 minutes. Stir in fruit mixture.

POUR batter into well-greased and floured 10-inch fluted tube pan. Bake at 350° for 45 minutes or until cake tester inserted in center comes out clean. Cool in pan 15 minutes. Remove from pan; finish cooling on wire rack.

BEAT reserved pudding mix and milk in small bowl until smooth. Spoon over top of cake to glaze. Garnish with Marzipan Fruits, if desired.   *MAKES 12 servings*

Prep time: 30 minutes
Baking time: 45 minutes

Marzipan Fruits

    1¾ cups BAKER'S ANGEL FLAKE
        Coconut, finely chopped
    1 package (4-serving size)
        JELL-O Brand Gelatin,
        any flavor
    1 cup ground blanched
        almonds
    ⅔ cup sweetened condensed
        milk
    1½ teaspoons sugar
    1 teaspoon almond extract
        Food coloring (optional)
        Whole cloves (optional)
        Citron or angelica (optional)

MIX together coconut, gelatin, almonds, milk, sugar and extract. Shape by hand into small fruits, or use small candy molds. If desired, use food coloring to paint details on fruit; add whole cloves and citron for stems and blossom ends. Chill until dry. Store in covered container at room temperature up to 1 week.
    MAKES 2 to 3 dozen confections

Prep time: 30 minutes

Raspberry Gift Box

This dessert is impressive as shown, but if you are pressed for time, omit the gumdrop ribbon and garnish with fresh raspberries.

> 2 packages (4-serving size each) or 1 package (8-serving size) JELL-O Brand Gelatin, Raspberry Flavor
> 1½ cups boiling water
> ¾ cup cran-raspberry juice
> Ice cubes
> 3½ cups (8 ounces) COOL WHIP Whipped Topping, thawed
> Raspberry Sauce (recipe follows)
> Gumdrop Ribbon (see page 417 for directions) (optional)
> Frosted Cranberries (see page 415 for directions) (optional)

DISSOLVE gelatin in boiling water. Combine cran-raspberry juice and ice cubes to make 1¾ cups. Add to gelatin, stirring until ice is melted. Chill until slightly thickened. Fold in whipped topping. Pour into 9×5-inch loaf pan. Chill until firm, about 4 hours.

PREPARE Raspberry Sauce, Gumdrop Ribbon and Frosted Cranberries, if desired.

UNMOLD gelatin mixture onto serving plate. Cut Gumdrop Ribbon into 2 (10×1-inch) strips and 1 (5×1-inch) strip. Place strips on raspberry loaf, piecing strips together as necessary, to resemble ribbon. Cut 7 (3×1-inch) strips; form into bow. Place on gumdrop ribbon. Decorate with Frosted Cranberries. Serve with Raspberry Sauce.   *MAKES 8 servings*

Raspberry Sauce

> 2 packages (10 ounces each) BIRDS EYE Quick Thaw Red Raspberries, thawed
> 2 teaspoons cornstarch

PLACE raspberries in food processor or blender; cover. Process until smooth; strain to remove seeds. Combine cornstarch with small amount of the raspberries in medium saucepan; add remaining raspberries. Bring to boil over medium heat, stirring constantly; boil 1 minute. Chill.
     MAKES 2 cups

Prep time: 30 minutes
Chill time: 4 hours

Christmas Popcorn Teddy Bear

"Teddy" is sure to become a Christmas classic, since he is as tasty as he is cute. You don't have to save him just for Christmas. Use this recipe to make all kinds of animals any time of year.

18 cups popped popcorn
1 cup light corn syrup
½ cup sugar
1 package (4-serving size) JELL-O Brand Gelatin, Strawberry or Lime Flavor
Jelly beans or gumdrops (optional)
Ribbon (optional)

PLACE popcorn in large greased bowl. Combine corn syrup and sugar in medium saucepan. Bring to full rolling boil, stirring constantly; boil 1 minute. Remove from heat. Stir in gelatin until dissolved. Pour over popcorn; toss to coat well. Cool 5 minutes.

FORM about ⅔ of the popcorn mixture into 2 balls, one larger than the other, forming bear's body and head. Shape remaining popcorn into arms, legs and ears; attach to body and head. Use jelly beans or gumdrops for eyes and nose. Attach ribbon bow tie, if desired.

MAKES 1 large teddy bear

Popcorn Balls: Prepare popcorn mixture as directed; shape into 2-inch balls. Makes about 2 dozen popcorn balls.

Note: For ease in handling, grease hands slightly before shaping popcorn mixture into desired shapes.

Prep time: 20 minutes

Ginger Bears

1½ cups all-purpose flour
1½ teaspoons ground ginger
1 teaspoon ground cinnamon
½ teaspoon baking soda
½ cup (1 stick) PARKAY Margarine
½ cup firmly packed brown sugar
1 package (4-serving size) JELL-O Pudding and Pie Filling, Butterscotch Flavor
1 egg
Confectioners Sugar Glaze (recipe follows) or 1 tube prepared decorating icing
Ribbon (optional)

MIX together flour, spices and baking soda. Beat margarine at low speed of electric mixer until light and fluffy; beat in sugar, pudding mix and egg. Gradually add flour mixture, beating until smooth after each addition. Chill dough until firm enough to handle.

ROLL out dough to ⅛-inch thickness on floured surface; cut with 3-inch floured teddy bear cookie cutter. Place on greased baking sheets. Bake at 350° for 10 minutes or until lightly browned. Remove; cool on rack. Decorate cooled cookies with Confectioners Sugar Glaze or icing. Attach ribbon bow ties, if desired.

MAKES about 2½ dozen cookies

Confectioners Sugar Glaze

2½ cups confectioners sugar
3 tablespoons (about) hot milk or water

PLACE sugar in small bowl. Gradually add milk, blending well.

MAKES 1⅓ cups

Prep time: 30 minutes
Baking time: 30 minutes

Top: Christmas Popcorn Teddy Bear; bottom: Ginger Bears

Easter Bonnet Cake

It's almost too pretty to eat.

- 1 package (2-layer size)
    yellow cake mix
- 2 packages (4-serving size
    each) JELL-O Instant
    Pudding and Pie Filling,
    Lemon Flavor
- 4 eggs
- 1 cup water
- ¼ cup vegetable oil
- 1½ cups cold milk
- 3½ cups (8 ounces) COOL WHIP
    Whipped Topping, thawed
- 2⅔ cups (7 ounces) BAKER'S
    ANGEL FLAKE Coconut
    Cloth ribbon (optional)
    Gumdrop Flowers (see page
    417 for directions)
    (optional)

COMBINE cake mix, 1 package of the pudding mix, eggs, water and oil in large bowl. Beat at low speed of electric mixer just to moisten, scraping sides of bowl often. Beat at medium speed 4 minutes. Pour 3¼ cups of the batter into greased and floured 1½-quart metal or ovenproof glass bowl; pour remaining batter into greased and floured 12-inch pizza pan. Bake at 350° for 15 minutes for the pan and 50 minutes for the bowl or until cake tester inserted in centers comes out clean.

COOL cakes 10 minutes. Remove from pan and bowl; finish cooling on racks. If necessary, cut thin slice from flat end of bowl-shaped cake so that it will sit flat; split horizontally into 3 layers.

POUR milk into small bowl. Add remaining package of pudding mix. Beat with wire whisk until well blended, 1 to 2 minutes.

PLACE 12-inch cake layer on large serving plate or tray. Spread layer with 1½ cups of the whipped topping. Center bottom layer of bowl-shaped cake on frosted layer; spread with ⅔ of the pudding. Add second layer; spread with remaining pudding. Add top layer, forming the crown.

SPREAD remaining whipped topping over crown. Sprinkle coconut over cake. Tie ribbon around cake crown to form hat band and bow and garnish with Gumdrop Flowers, if desired. Chill until ready to serve.

MAKES 16 servings

Prep time: 45 minutes
Baking time: 50 minutes

Gelatin Easter Baskets

Why use wicker baskets when you can make these baskets and eat them, too?

- 1 package (4-serving size)
    JELL-O Brand Gelatin,
    any flavor
- 1 cup boiling water
- ½ cup cold water
- ½ cup BAKER'S ANGEL FLAKE
    Coconut
    Food coloring
    Jelly beans
    Red string licorice

DISSOLVE gelatin in boiling water. Add cold water. Pour into individual ring molds or 6-ounce custard cups. Chill until firm, about 2 hours.

TINT coconut as desired with food coloring (see page 414 for directions).

(continued)

UNMOLD gelatin onto individual dessert plates. Sprinkle coconut into center of each mold for "grass." Place jelly beans on top of coconut. Cut licorice for basket handles; insert in molds.

MAKES 4 servings

Prep time: 15 minutes
Chill time: 2 hours

*Top: Easter Bonnet Cake (page 436);
bottom: Gelatin Easter Baskets
(page 436)*

Pumpkin Flan

1 package (4½ ounces) JELL-O
   AMERICANA Custard Mix*
2½ cups milk
2 teaspoons grated orange
   rind
¼ teaspoon ground cinnamon
1 egg yolk
1 cup canned pumpkin
   Citrus Fan (see page 414 for
      directions) (optional)
   Mint leaves (optional)

COMBINE custard mix, milk,
orange rind and cinnamon in
medium saucepan; mix in egg yolk.
Cook, stirring constantly, over
medium-low heat until mixture
comes to full boil. Remove from
heat. Add pumpkin, stirring until
well mixed. Pour into 1½-quart
souffle dish or bowl. Chill until
firm, about 3 hours.

DIP flan in hot water; unmold onto
serving plate. Garnish with Citrus
Fan and mint leaves, if desired.
                    MAKES 8 servings

*1 package (4-serving size) JELL-O
Pudding and Pie Filling, Vanilla
Flavor, may be substituted for the
custard mix.

Prep time: 15 minutes
Chill time: 3 hours

> *New variations on an old
> theme. They're wonderful!*

Thanksgiving Cranberry Pie

1 package (15 ounces)
   refrigerated pie crust
   (2 crusts)
1 package (4-serving size)
   JELL-O Brand Gelatin,
   Orange Flavor or any red
   flavor
¾ cup boiling water
½ cup orange juice
1 can (8 ounces) jellied or
   whole berry cranberry
   sauce
1 teaspoon grated orange rind
1 cup cold half and half or
   milk
1 package (4-serving size)
   JELL-O Instant Pudding
   and Pie Filling, French
   Vanilla or Vanilla Flavor
1 cup thawed COOL WHIP
   Whipped Topping
   Frosted Cranberries (see
      page 415 for directions)
      (optional)

PREPARE and bake 1 sheet of the
pie crust in 9-inch pie plate as
directed on package; cool. Cut out
leaf shapes from remaining sheet of
pie crust with small cookie cutter.
Place on ungreased baking sheet;
bake at 450° for 8 minutes or until
golden. Cool.

DISSOLVE gelatin in boiling water.
Add orange juice. Place bowl in
larger bowl of ice and water. Let
stand, stirring occasionally, until
gelatin is slightly thickened, about
5 minutes. Stir in cranberry sauce
and orange rind. Spoon into pie
crust. Chill just until set, about
30 minutes.

(continued)

Top: Pumpkin Flan (page 438); bottom: Thanksgiving Cranberry Pie (page 438)

POUR half and half into medium bowl. Add pie filling mix. Beat with wire whisk until well blended, 1 to 2 minutes. Let stand 2 minutes or until slightly thickened. Fold in whipped topping. Gently spread over gelatin mixture. Place pastry leaves around rim of pie. Chill until firm, about 2 hours. Garnish with additional whipped topping and Frosted Cranberries, if desired.

MAKES 8 servings

Prep time: 30 minutes
Baking time: 20 minutes
Chill time: 2½ hours

Festive Celebrations

Lemon Cheese Tart

2 packages (11 ounces each)
   JELL-O No-Bake
   Cheesecake mix
¼ cup sugar
⅔ cup PARKAY Margarine,
   melted
2 packages (4-serving size
   each) or 1 package
   (8-serving size) JELL-O
   Brand Gelatin, Lemon
   Flavor
2 cups boiling water
1 cup cold water
3 cups cold milk
1½ teaspoons grated lemon rind
   (optional)
1 cup (about) seedless red or
   green grapes, halved
   Mint leaves

MIX cheesecake crust crumbs with sugar in 9-inch springform pan. Stir in margarine. Press crumb mixture firmly onto bottom of pan.

DISSOLVE gelatin in boiling water. Add cold water. Chill until slightly thickened.

MIX milk with cheesecake filling mix and lemon rind at low speed of electric mixer until blended. Beat at medium speed 3 minutes. Pour over crust. Arrange grape halves on top of cheesecake to resemble large grape cluster. Place mint leaves at stem end of cluster. Carefully spoon thickened gelatin over grape cluster and filling. Chill until set, about 3 hours. Run hot metal spatula or knife around edge of pan before removing sides of pan.
MAKES 12 servings

Note: This recipe may be prepared 1 day ahead.

Prep time: 30 minutes
Chill time: 3 hours

Clockwise from top left: Lemon Cheese Tart; Sparkling Punch Bowl (page 442); Almond Heart Napoleons (page 442)

Sparkling Punch Bowl

Prepare this dessert 1 day ahead.

8 packages (4-serving size each) or 4 packages (8-serving size each) JELL-O Brand Gelatin, any flavor
8 cups boiling water
1 bottle (1 liter) ginger ale
Ice cubes
5 cups cut-up fruit*
1 can (20 ounces) pineapple chunks in juice, drained
Mint leaves (optional)

DISSOLVE gelatin in boiling water. Combine ginger ale and ice cubes to make 8 cups. Add to gelatin, stirring until slightly thickened. Remove any unmelted ice. Measure 4 cups of the gelatin; set aside. Fold cut-up fruit and pineapple chunks into remaining gelatin. Pour into large punch bowl. Chill until set but not firm.

WHIP reserved gelatin at high speed of electric mixer until fluffy, thick and about doubled in volume. Spoon over gelatin in punch bowl. Chill until firm, about 2 hours. Garnish with additional fruit and mint leaves, if desired.

MAKES 32 servings

*We suggest sliced bananas, strawberries or grapes.

Note: If large punch bowl is not available, use smaller bowl and pour extra gelatin mixture into punch cups.

Prep time: 20 minutes
Chill time: 2 hours

Almond Heart Napoleons

1 package (17¼ ounces) frozen puff pastry sheets
1¼ cups cold half and half or milk
2 tablespoons almond liqueur*
1 package (4-serving size) JELL-O Instant Pudding and Pie Filling, French Vanilla or Vanilla Flavor
½ cup confectioners sugar
2 teaspoons (about) hot water
1 square BAKER'S Semi-Sweet Chocolate, melted

THAW puff pastry as directed on package. Preheat oven to 350°. Unfold pastry. Using 2-inch heart-shaped cookie cutter, cut each sheet into 12 hearts. Bake on ungreased baking sheets for 20 minutes or until golden. Remove from baking sheets. Cool on racks. When pastry is completely cooled, split each heart horizontally in half.

POUR half and half and liqueur into small bowl. Add pudding mix. Beat with wire whisk until well blended, 1 to 2 minutes. Chill 10 minutes.

SPREAD about 1 tablespoon of the pudding mixture onto bottom half of each pastry; top with remaining pastry half.

(continued)

STIR together confectioners sugar and hot water in small bowl to make thin glaze. Spread over hearts. (If glaze becomes too thick, add more hot water until glaze is of desired consistency.) Before glaze dries, drizzle chocolate on top to form thin lines. Draw wooden pick through chocolate to make design. Chill until ready to serve.

MAKES 2 dozen pastries

*½ teaspoon almond extract may be substituted for 2 tablespoons almond liqueur.

Note: Pastry may be cut and baked 1 day ahead. Assemble recipe no more than 6 hours before serving.

Prep time: 30 minutes
Baking time: 20 minutes

Pineapple Bombe

      2 cans (20 ounces each)
          pineapple slices, drained
      8 maraschino cherries,
          stemmed and halved
   2½ cups cold milk
      2 packages (4-serving size
          each) JELL-O Instant
          Pudding and Pie Filling,
          French Vanilla or Vanilla
          Flavor
   3½ cups (8 ounces) COOL WHIP
          Whipped Topping, thawed
      1 pound cake loaf (about
          12 ounces), cut into
          14 slices

LINE 2-quart bowl with plastic wrap. Arrange about 16 pineapple slices on bottom and sides of lined bowl, pushing slices as closely together as possible. Place cherry half, cut side up, in center of each pineapple slice.

POUR milk into large bowl. Add pudding mix. Beat with wire whisk until well blended, 1 to 2 minutes. Let stand 5 minutes. Fold in ½ of the whipped topping.

SPREAD about ⅓ of the pudding mixture over pineapple in bowl. Place about 6 cake slices over pudding layer; press down gently. Arrange 5 pineapple slices over cake slices. Layer with ⅓ of the pudding mixture, 4 cake slices and remaining pineapple. Cover with remaining pudding; top with remaining cake slices. Press down gently. Cover with plastic wrap. Chill at least 1 hour.

INVERT dessert onto serving platter. Carefully remove plastic wrap. Garnish with remaining whipped topping.

MAKES 16 servings

Prep time: 30 minutes
Chill time: 1 hour

Lemon Berry Terrine

1 pound cake loaf (about
   12 ounces)
1 package (8 ounces)
   PHILADELPHIA BRAND
   Cream Cheese, softened
2 cups cold milk
1 package (4-serving size)
   JELL-O Instant Pudding
   and Pie Filling, Lemon
   Flavor
1 teaspoon grated lemon rind
3½ cups (8 ounces) COOL WHIP
   Whipped Topping, thawed
1 pint strawberries, stems
   removed

LINE bottom and sides of 8×4-inch loaf pan with waxed paper.

CUT rounded top off pound cake; reserve for snacking or other use. Trim crusts from pound cake. Cut cake horizontally into 5 slices. Line bottom and long sides of loaf pan with 3 cake slices. Cut another cake slice in half; place on short sides of pan.

BEAT cream cheese at medium speed of electric mixer until smooth. Gradually beat in 1 cup of the milk. Add pudding mix, remaining 1 cup milk and lemon rind. Beat at low speed until blended, 1 to 2 minutes. Fold in 1½ cups of the whipped topping.

SPOON ½ of the filling into loaf pan. Reserve several strawberries for garnish. Arrange remaining strawberries in filling, pressing down slightly. Top with remaining filling. Place remaining cake slice on top of filling. Chill until firm, about 3 hours.

UNMOLD dessert onto serving plate; remove waxed paper. Garnish with remaining whipped topping and strawberries.
MAKES 16 servings

Prep time: 30 minutes
Chill time: 3 hours

Apricot Pear Tart

1⅓ cups shortbread cookie or
   graham cracker crumbs
2 tablespoons sugar
¼ cup PARKAY Margarine,
   melted
1 package (4-serving size)
   JELL-O Brand Gelatin,
   Apricot Flavor
1 cup boiling water
⅔ cup cold water
1¾ cups (4 ounces) COOL WHIP
   Whipped Topping, thawed
½ teaspoon ground ginger
1 can (16 ounces) pear halves,
   drained
   Mint leaves
   Cinnamon stick, cut into
   ¾-inch pieces

MIX together cookie crumbs, sugar and margarine in small bowl. Press crumb mixture onto bottom of 9-inch springform pan.

DISSOLVE gelatin in boiling water. Add cold water. Measure ¾ cup gelatin; set aside. Chill remaining gelatin until slightly thickened. Fold in whipped topping and ginger. Spoon over crust.

CHILL measured gelatin until slightly thickened. Slice pears lengthwise, cutting almost through stem ends; arrange on whipped topping mixture in pan, fanning each pear slightly (see page 415 for

(continued)

directions). Place mint leaf and cinnamon stick at stem end of each pear. Carefully spoon thickened gelatin over pears and filling. Chill until firm, about 3 hours. Run hot metal spatula or knife around edge of pan before removing sides of pan.

MAKES 12 servings

Prep time: 30 minutes
Chill time: 3 hours

Clockwise from top: Apricot Pear Tart (page 444); JELL-O Creamy Jigglers (page 459); Lemon Berry Terrine (page 444)

Mitt Cut-Up Cake

1 package (2-layer size) yellow
    cake mix
1 cup cold milk
1 package (4-serving size)
    JELL-O Instant Pudding
    and Pie Filling, Chocolate
    or Chocolate Fudge Flavor
3½ cups (8 ounces) COOL WHIP
    Whipped Topping, thawed
    Chocolate sprinkles
    String licorice
    JELL-O Jigglers (see page 459
    for recipe) (optional)

PREPARE cake mix as directed on package. Pour 2 cups of the batter into greased and floured 1-quart ovenproof bowl; pour remaining batter into greased and floured 9-inch round cake pan. Bake at 325° for 50 minutes or until cake tester inserted in centers comes out clean. Cool 15 minutes. Remove from pan and bowl; finish cooling on racks. Cut cake as shown in Diagram 1.

POUR milk into medium bowl. Add pudding mix. Beat with wire whisk until well blended, 1 to 2 minutes. Fold in 2½ cups of the whipped topping.

SPREAD pudding mixture over sides and top of 9-inch layer. Use remaining whipped topping to cover bowl-shaped cake; place over 9-inch layer. Decorate with chocolate sprinkles and licorice to resemble mitt and ball (Diagram 2). Chill cake until ready to serve. Arrange star-shaped Jigglers around cake, if desired.

MAKES 12 servings

Prep time: 30 minutes
Baking time: 50 minutes

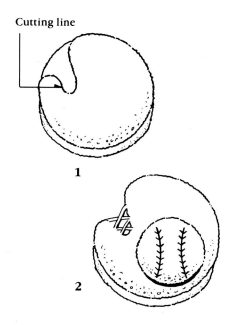

Cutting line

1

2

Snack Mix

4 cups popped popcorn
2 cups thin pretzel sticks
2 cups crisp corn cereal
    squares
1 cup peanuts
½ cup raisins
6 tablespoons PARKAY
    Margarine, melted
1 package (4-serving size)
    JELL-O Brand Gelatin, any
    flavor

PLACE popcorn, pretzels, cereal, peanuts and raisins in large bowl. Add margarine; toss to coat well. Sprinkle with gelatin; toss until evenly coated.

MAKES 10 cups

Prep time: 10 minutes

Clockwise from top left: Winner's Circle Layered Dessert (page 448); Snack Mix; Mitt Cut-Up Cake; JELL-O Jigglers (page 459)

Winner's Circle Layered Dessert

4½ cups cold milk
  3 packages (4-serving size each) JELL-O Instant Pudding and Pie Filling, French Vanilla or Vanilla Flavor
1¾ cups (4 ounces) COOL WHIP Whipped Topping, thawed
  4 packages (4-serving size each) or 2 packages (8-serving size each) JELL-O Brand Gelatin, Strawberry Flavor
  3 cups boiling water
  2 cups cold water
    Ice cubes
  2 cups blueberries
  2 cups sliced strawberries

POUR milk into large bowl. Add pudding mix. Beat with wire whisk until well blended, 1 to 2 minutes. Let stand 5 minutes. Fold in 1 cup of the whipped topping; chill.

DISSOLVE ½ of the gelatin in 1½ cups of the boiling water. Combine 1 cup of the cold water and ice cubes to make 1½ cups. Add to dissolved gelatin, stirring until slightly thickened. Remove any unmelted ice. Stir in ½ of the blueberries and strawberries. Spoon into 4-quart bowl. Chill 15 minutes or until thickened. Meanwhile, prepare remaining gelatin as directed above. Stir in remaining fruit.

TOP gelatin mixture in serving bowl with ½ of the pudding mixture, then remaining gelatin mixture. Chill 15 minutes or until thickened. Top with remaining pudding mixture. Chill until firm, about 3 hours. Garnish with remaining whipped topping and additional fruit, if desired.
MAKES 32 servings

Prep time: 30 minutes
Chill time: 4 hours

Chocolate Berry Torte

"Berry" beautiful and delicious.

  1 package (2-layer size) chocolate cake mix
  1 package (4-serving size) JELL-O Instant Pudding and Pie Filling, Chocolate or Chocolate Fudge Flavor
  4 eggs
  1 cup water
  ¼ cup vegetable oil
  3 cups cold milk
  2 tablespoons chocolate or coffee liqueur (optional)
  2 packages (4-serving size each) JELL-O Instant Pudding and Pie Filling, French Vanilla or Vanilla Flavor
1¾ cups (4 ounces) COOL WHIP Whipped Topping, thawed
  2 pints strawberries

(continued)

COMBINE cake mix, chocolate pudding mix, eggs, water and oil in large bowl. Blend at low speed of electric mixer just to moisten, scraping sides of bowl often. Beat at medium speed 4 minutes. Pour into 2 greased and floured 9-inch round cake pans. Bake at 350° for 35 to 40 minutes or until cake tester inserted in centers comes out clean. Cool in pans 15 minutes. Remove from pans; finish cooling on racks.

POUR milk and liqueur into large bowl. Add vanilla pudding mix. Beat with wire whisk until well blended, 1 to 2 minutes. Let stand 5 minutes. Fold in whipped topping. Chill 15 minutes.

CUT each cake layer in half horizontally. Reserve a few strawberries for garnish; slice remaining strawberries. Place 1 cake layer on serving plate; top with ¼ of the pudding mixture and ⅓ of the sliced strawberries. Repeat layers, using remaining cake, pudding mixture and sliced strawberries, ending with pudding mixture. Chill at least 1 hour. Garnish with reserved strawberries.

MAKES 12 servings

Prep time: 30 minutes
Baking time: 35 minutes
Chill time: 1 hour

Butterfly Cupcakes

1 cup cold milk
1 package (4-serving size) JELL-O Instant Pudding and Pie Filling, any flavor
3½ cups (8 ounces) COOL WHIP Whipped Topping, thawed
24 cupcakes
    Sprinkles
    Pastel confetti candies
    Black string licorice, cut into 2-inch strips

POUR milk into medium bowl. Add pudding mix. Beat with wire whisk until well blended, 1 to 2 minutes. Fold in whipped topping. Reserve 1 teaspoon pudding mixture.

CUT tops off cupcakes. Cut each top in half; set aside. Spoon 2 heaping tablespoons pudding mixture onto each cupcake; top with sprinkles. For each cupcake, insert 2 top halves of cupcake, cut sides together, in pudding mixture, raising outside ends slightly to resemble butterfly wings. Lightly dip confetti candies into reserved pudding mixture; arrange on cupcake wings. Insert string licorice in pudding mixture to resemble antennae. Chill until ready to serve.

MAKES 2 dozen cupcakes

Prep time: 25 minutes

Fun for Children

Gelatin Tilt

1 package (4-serving size)
   JELL-O Brand Gelatin, any
   flavor
COOL WHIP Whipped
   Topping, thawed
   (optional)
JELL-O Jigglers (see page 459
   for recipe) (optional)

PREPARE gelatin as directed on
package. Measure ⅔ cup gelatin
into small bowl; chill until slightly
thickened. Pour remaining gelatin
into parfait or any stemmed glasses,
filling each glass about ½ full. Tilt
glasses in refrigerator by catching
bases of glasses between bars of
refrigerator rack and leaning tops
of glasses against wall. Chill until
set but not firm.

WHIP reserved gelatin at high
speed of electric mixer until fluffy
and thick. Spoon lightly over set
gelatin in glasses. Chill upright
until set, about 2 hours. Garnish
with whipped topping and JELL-O
Jigglers, if desired.

MAKES 4 servings

Prep time: 20 minutes
Chill time: 2 hours

Microwave Popcorn Balls

¼ cup (½ stick) PARKAY
   Margarine
1 bag (10½ ounces) KRAFT
   Miniature Marshmallows
1 package (4-serving size)
   JELL-O Brand Gelatin, any
   flavor
12 cups popped popcorn
1 cup peanuts (optional)

COMBINE margarine and
marshmallows in large
microwavable bowl. Microwave on
HIGH 1½ to 2 minutes or until
marshmallows are puffed. Add
gelatin; stir until well blended.
Pour marshmallow mixture over
combined popcorn and peanuts.
Stir to coat well. Shape into balls or
other shapes with greased hands.
*MAKES about 2 dozen
popcorn balls*

Prep time: 10 minutes

*Clockwise from top left: Gelatin Tilt;
JELL-O Jigglers (page 459); Pitcher's
Mounds (page 452); Microwave
Popcorn Balls; "Out of the Park"
Pudding-Wiches (page 452)*

Fruity Dip

Kids love to dip food. They will have lots of fun dipping cookies, fruit or even fingers into this delicious treat.

1 package (8 ounces)
    PHILADELPHIA BRAND
    Cream Cheese, softened
1 package (4-serving size)
    JELL-O Brand Gelatin, any
    flavor
¼ cup milk
    Assorted fruit and cookies*

STIR cream cheese in small bowl until smooth. Gradually stir in gelatin and milk until well blended. Chill until ready to serve. Let stand at room temperature to soften slightly, if necessary. Garnish with fruit, if desired. Serve with fruit and cookies.

MAKES 1½ cups

*We suggest sliced apples or pears, grapes or strawberries.

Prep time: 5 minutes

Pitcher's Mounds

1 package (4-serving size)
    JELL-O Instant Pudding
    and Pie Filling, Chocolate
    Flavor
2 cups cold milk
3½ cups (8 ounces) COOL WHIP
    Whipped Topping, thawed
1 package (16 ounces)
    chocolate sandwich
    cookies, crushed
8 to 10 (8-ounce) paper or
    plastic cups

PREPARE pudding mix with milk as directed on package. Let stand 5 minutes. Fold in whipped topping and ½ of the crushed cookies.

PLACE about 1 tablespoon crushed cookies in each cup. Fill cups

about ¾ full with pudding mixture. Top with remaining crushed cookies. Chill until set, about 1 hour. Place toy sports figure in center of each "mound," if desired.

MAKES 8 to 10 servings

Prep time: 15 minutes
Chill time: 1 hour

"Out of the Park" Pudding-Wiches

½ cup peanut butter
1½ cups cold milk
1 package (4-serving size)
    JELL-O Instant Pudding
    and Pie Filling, any flavor
    Assorted cookies
    Sprinkles (optional)

STIR peanut butter in small bowl until smooth. Gradually stir in milk. Add pudding mix. Beat with wire whisk or at low speed of electric mixer until well blended, 1 to 2 minutes.

SPREAD pudding mixture about ½ inch thick on cookie. Top with second cookie, pressing cookies together lightly and smoothing edges of pudding mixture with spatula. Coat edges with sprinkles, if desired. Repeat making sandwiches with remaining cookies and filling. Freeze until firm, about 3 hours.

MAKES about 2 dozen
pudding-wiches

Note: Pudding-wiches can be wrapped and stored in freezer up to 2 weeks.

Prep time: 15 minutes
Freezing time: 3 hours

Fruity Dip

Merry-Go-Round Cake

This makes an ordinary cake into a carousel of fun.

- **1 package (6-serving size) JELL-O Instant Pudding and Pie Filling, Vanilla Flavor**
- **1 package (2-layer size) yellow cake mix**
- **4 eggs**
- **1 cup water**
- **¼ cup vegetable oil**
- **⅓ cup BAKER'S Semi-Sweet Real Chocolate Chips, melted**
- **⅔ cup cold milk Sprinkles (optional) Paper carousel roof (directions follow)**
- **3 plastic straws**
- **6 animal crackers**

RESERVE ⅓ cup pudding mix. Combine cake mix, remaining pudding mix, eggs, water and oil in large bowl. Beat at low speed of electric mixer just to moisten, scraping sides of bowl often. Beat at medium speed 4 minutes. Pour ½ of the batter into greased and floured 10-inch fluted tube pan. Mix chocolate into remaining batter. Spoon over batter in pan; cut through with spatula in zigzag pattern to marbleize. Bake at 350° for 50 minutes or until cake tester inserted in center comes out clean. Cool in pan 15 minutes. Remove from pan; finish cooling on rack.

BEAT reserved pudding mix and milk in small bowl until smooth. Spoon over top of cake to glaze. Garnish with sprinkles, if desired.

CUT 10- to 12-inch circle from colored paper; scallop edges, if desired. Make 1 slit to center (Diagram 1). Overlap cut edges to form carousel roof; secure with tape (Diagram 2). Cut straws in half; arrange on cake with animal crackers. Top with roof.

MAKES 12 servings

Prep time: 30 minutes
Baking time: 50 minutes

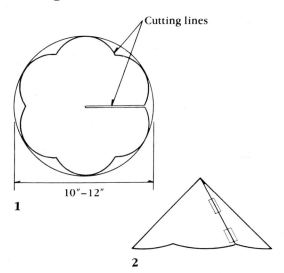

Carousel Gelatin Cups

- **1 package (4-serving size) JELL-O Brand Gelatin, any red flavor**
- **Teddy bear cookies or animal crackers**
- **COOL WHIP Whipped Topping, thawed**

PREPARE gelatin as directed on package. Pour into individual serving dishes. Chill until firm, about 2 hours. Arrange cookies around inside rim of each dish. Garnish with whipped topping.

MAKES 4 servings

Prep time: 10 minutes
Chill time: 2 hours

Merry-Go-Round Cake

Gelatin Sundaes

1 package (4-serving size)
    JELL-O Brand Gelatin,
    any flavor
¾ cup boiling water
½ cup cold water
    Ice cubes
1 pint ice cream, any flavor
1 cup thawed COOL WHIP
    Whipped Topping
¼ cup chopped nuts

DISSOLVE gelatin in boiling water. Combine cold water and ice cubes to make 1¼ cups. Add to gelatin, stirring until slightly thickened. Remove any unmelted ice.

SPOON ice cream and gelatin alternately into tall sundae dishes, ending with gelatin and filling to within ½ inch of top of dish. Top with whipped topping and nuts.
    MAKES 4 servings

Prep time: 15 minutes

Sailboats

1 package (4-serving size)
    JELL-O Brand Gelatin, any
    flavor
1 can (8 ounces) peach slices,
    drained
½ cup banana slices
    Paper and wooden picks for
    sails

PREPARE gelatin as directed on package. Chill until slightly thickened. Reserve 8 peach slices for garnish. Stir remaining peach and banana slices into gelatin. Pour into 4 individual dessert dishes. Chill until firm, about 2 hours.

TOP gelatin with reserved peach slices. Cut 4 small triangles from paper to make sails (decorate sails with crayons, if desired). Insert wooden picks through sails; place in gelatin.   *MAKES 4 servings*

Prep time: 20 minutes
Chill time: 2 hours

Funny Faces

These desserts, as much fun for kids to make as they are to eat, make a great activity for a party or just a rainy day.

1 package (4-serving size)
    JELL-O Instant Pudding
    and Pie Filling, any flavor
2 cups cold milk
    BAKER'S ANGEL FLAKE
    Coconut*
    Popped popcorn
    Assorted candies and nuts
    Sprinkles

DECORATE individual dessert dishes with paper cutouts, if desired.

PREPARE pudding mix with milk as directed on package. Let stand 5 minutes. Spoon pudding into decorated dessert dishes. Make faces on pudding with coconut, popcorn, candies, nuts and sprinkles. Chill until ready to serve.   *MAKES 4 servings*

*Coconut may be tinted, if desired (see page 414 for directions).

Prep time: 20 minutes

Funny Faces

> *JELL-O Jiggler gelatin snacks in all colors and shapes! Following is a fun assortment of JELL-O Jiggler recipes guaranteed to put a smile on any child's face.*

JELL-O Creamy Jigglers
Gelatin Snacks

2½ cups boiling water or boiling
   fruit juice
 4 packages (4-serving size
   each) or 2 packages
   (8-serving size each)
   JELL-O Brand Gelatin,
   any flavor
 1 cup cold milk
 1 package (4-serving size)
   JELL-O Instant Pudding
   and Pie Filling, Vanilla
   Flavor

ADD boiling water to gelatin. Dissolve completely; cool to room temperature.

POUR milk into small bowl. Add pudding mix. Beat with wire whisk until well blended, 1 to 2 minutes. Quickly pour into gelatin. Stir with wire whisk until well blended. Pour into 13×9-inch pan. Chill until firm, about 3 hours.

DIP pan into warm water about 15 seconds for easy removal of JELL-O Jigglers. Use cookie cutters to cut decorative shapes (umbrellas for showers, etc.). Remove from pan. Cut remaining gelatin into cubes.
    *MAKES about 3 dozen
    JELL-O Jigglers*

Prep time: 15 minutes
Chill time: 3 hours

JELL-O Jigglers
Gelatin Snacks

2½ cups boiling water or boiling
   fruit juice
 4 packages (4-serving size
   each) or 2 packages
   (8-serving size each)
   JELL-O Brand Gelatin,
   any flavor

ADD boiling water to gelatin. Dissolve completely. Pour into 13×9-inch pan. Chill until firm, about 3 hours.

DIP pan in warm water about 15 seconds for easy removal of JELL-O Jigglers. Use cookie cutters to cut decorative shapes in gelatin (hearts for Valentine's Day, pumpkins for Halloween, stars for sports parties, etc.). Remove from pan. Cut remaining gelatin into cubes.
    *MAKES about 3 dozen
    JELL-O Jigglers*

Notes: For thicker JELL-O Jigglers, use 8- or 9-inch square pan.

To use ice cube trays or JELL-O Jiggler molds, pour dissolved gelatin into 2 or 3 ice cube trays. Chill until firm, about 2 hours. To remove, dip trays in warm water about 15 seconds. Moisten tips of fingers; gently pull from edges and remove from trays.

Prep time: 10 minutes
Chill time: 3 hours

JELL-O Jigglers

JELL-O Jiggler Surprises
Gelatin Snacks

2½ cups boiling water or boiling
    fruit juice
  4 packages (4-serving size
    each) or 2 packages
    (8-serving size each)
    JELL-O Brand Gelatin,
    any flavor
    Banana slices
    Strawberry slices
    Canned pineapple slices, cut
    into bite-size pieces

ADD boiling water to gelatin.
Dissolve completely. Pour into
13×9-inch pan. Arrange fruit in
gelatin so that when cut into
decorative shapes, each will
contain 1 piece of fruit. Chill until
firm, about 3 hours.

DIP pan in warm water about 15
seconds for easy removal of JELL-O
Jigglers. Use cookie cutters to cut
gelatin into decorative shapes.
Remove from pan. Cut remaining
gelatin into cubes.
MAKES about 3 dozen
JELL-O Jigglers

Prep time: 10 minutes
Chill time: 3 hours

JELL-O Tropical Jigglers
Gelatin Snacks

2½ cups boiling water or boiling
    fruit juice
  4 packages (4-serving size
    each) or 2 packages
    (8-serving size each)
    JELL-O Brand Gelatin,
    Strawberry-Banana or
    Orange Flavor
  1 can (8 ounces) crushed
    pineapple in juice,
    undrained

ADD boiling water to gelatin.
Dissolve completely. Stir in
pineapple. Pour into 13×9-inch
pan. Chill until firm, about 3
hours.

DIP pan in warm water about 15
seconds for easy removal of JELL-O
Jigglers. Use cookie cutters to cut
decorative shapes in gelatin.
Remove from pan. Cut remaining
gelatin into cubes.
MAKES about 3 dozen
JELL-O Jigglers

JELL-O Vegetable Jigglers: Use
lemon, lime or orange flavor
gelatin. Omit pineapple. Stir in
½ cup each shredded carrot, finely
chopped celery and finely chopped
cucumber and 3 tablespoons
vinegar.

Prep time: 10 minutes
Chill time: 3 hours

*JELL-O Jigglers (page 459); JELL-O
Jiggler Surprises; JELL-O Tropical
Jigglers; JELL-O Creamy Jigglers (page
459); JELL-O Vegetable Jigglers*

Celebrates BAKING

Clockwise from top right: Orange No-Bake Cheesecake (page 470), Double Nut Chocolate Chip Cookies (page 476), Carrot Cake (page 467) and Chocolate Cherry Cake (page 501)

Twin Angel Food Party Pies

12 to 16 servings

1 package Duncan Hines® Angel Food
    Cake Mix

FILLING

2 packages (4-serving size) chocolate
    instant pudding and pie filling mix
3 cups milk
½ teaspoon almond extract

1 container (16 ounces) frozen non-dairy
    whipped topping, thawed and
    divided
1 can (21 ounces) cherry pie filling

1. Preheat oven to 375°F.

2. Prepare, bake and cool cake following package directions.

3. Cut cake in half horizontally with serrated knife. Place on serving plates with cut sides up. Cut around cake 1½-inches from outer edge, down ¾-inch and through to center. Gently pull out cut cake to leave a 1½-inch wide rim. Fill center hole with removed cake. Repeat for second half.

4. **For filling**, combine both packages of pudding mix in large bowl. Prepare following package directions, using 3 cups milk and ½ teaspoon almond extract. Fold in 2 cups whipped topping.

5. Fill each cake with half the pudding mixture. Spoon half the cherry pie filling around outer edge of each cake. Garnish each cake with dollops of whipped topping. Refrigerate until ready to serve. To serve, cut filled cake as you would a pie.

■ *Tip: Try different flavor combinations of instant pudding and pie filling such as vanilla instant pudding and pie filling mix and blueberry pie filling.*

Twin Angel Food Party Pie

Carrot Cake

CAKE

1 package Duncan Hines® Moist Deluxe
  Yellow Cake Mix
2 cups grated fresh carrots
1 can (8 ounces) crushed pineapple,
  undrained
½ cup water

3 eggs
½ cup Crisco® Oil or Crisco®
  Puritan® Oil
½ cup finely chopped pecans
2 teaspoons cinnamon

FROSTING

2 packages (3 ounces each) cream
  cheese, softened
⅓ cup butter or margarine, softened

1½ teaspoons vanilla extract
3½ cups confectioners sugar
1 teaspoon milk

1. Preheat oven to 350°F. Grease and flour 13×9×2-inch pan.

2. **For cake**, combine cake mix, carrots, pineapple, water, eggs, oil, pecans and cinnamon in large bowl. Beat at low speed with electric mixer until moistened. Beat at medium speed for 2 minutes. Pour batter into pan. Bake at 350°F for 35 to 40 minutes or until toothpick inserted in center comes out clean. Cool in pan.

3. **For frosting**, combine cream cheese, butter and vanilla extract in large bowl. Beat at medium speed with electric mixer until smooth. Gradually add confectioners sugar and milk, mixing well. Spread on cooled cake. Refrigerate until ready to serve.

■ *Tip: Score cake into serving pieces and garnish with pineapple tidbits and pecan halves.*

Cherry Angel Delight

1 package Duncan Hines® Angel Food
  Cake Mix
2 envelopes whipped topping mix
1 package (8 ounces) cream cheese,
  softened and cut in small pieces

1⅓ cups confectioners sugar
1 can (21 ounces) cherry pie filling

1. Preheat oven to 375°F.

2. Prepare, bake and cool cake following package directions.

3. Prepare topping mix following package directions. Add cream cheese. Beat until smooth. Add confectioners sugar. Mix until blended.

4. Trim crust from cake. Cut into bite-size pieces. Place half the cake pieces in a 13×9×2-inch pan. Cover with half the cheese mixture. Repeat with remaining cake. Cover with remaining cheese mixture. Refrigerate several hours or overnight.

5. Spread pie filling over top of dessert. Refrigerate until ready to serve.

■ *Tip: If you're trying to cut down on calories, use reduced-calorie cream cheese and pie filling.*

Carrot Cake

Fudge Marble Pound Cakes

36 slices

1 package Duncan Hines® Moist Deluxe
   Fudge Marble Cake Mix
1 package (4-serving size) vanilla instant
   pudding and pie filling mix

4 eggs
1 cup water
⅓ cup Crisco® Oil or Crisco®
   Puritan® Oil

1. Preheat oven to 350°F. Grease and flour two 9×5×3-inch loaf pans.

2. Set aside cocoa packet. Combine cake mix, pudding mix, eggs, water and oil in large bowl. Beat at medium speed with electric mixer for 2 minutes. Measure 1 cup batter. Place in small bowl. Stir in cocoa packet.

3. Spoon half the yellow batter in each loaf pan. Spoon half the chocolate batter on top of yellow batter in each pan. Run knife through batters to marble. Bake at 350°F for 45 to 50 minutes or until toothpick inserted in center comes out clean. Cool in pans 5 minutes. Carefully loosen cakes from pans. Invert onto cooling rack. Cool completely. Cut loaves in ½-inch slices.

■ *Tip: To make fudge marble ice cream sandwiches, cut ½ gallon brick of fudge marble ice cream into ½-inch slices. Put ice cream slices between slices of pound cake.*

Lemon Cooler

12 servings

1 package Duncan Hines® Moist Deluxe
   Lemon Supreme Cake Mix
½ cup butter or margarine, melted
1 package (8-serving size) lemon gelatin
1 package (4-serving size) lemon gelatin
3 cups boiling water

⅓ cup lemon juice
2 teaspoons grated lemon peel
1 quart vanilla ice cream
   Whipped cream and additional grated
   lemon peel, for garnish

1. Preheat oven to 350°F. Grease and flour 13×9×2-inch pan.

2. Combine cake mix and melted butter in large bowl. Beat on low speed with electric mixer until crumbs form. Spread in pan. Bake at 350°F for 20 minutes. Cool completely.

3. Combine both gelatin packages and boiling water in large bowl. Stir until gelatin is dissolved. Add lemon juice and peel. Stir. Spoon ice cream into hot gelatin mixture. Stir until ice cream melts. Refrigerate until mixture starts to thicken. Pour over cooled crust. Refrigerate until firm.

4. Cut into 3×3-inch squares. Serve topped with whipped cream sprinkled with grated lemon peel, if desired.

■ *Tip: You can use other fruit flavored gelatins in place of lemon.*

Fudge Marble Pound Cake

Orange No-Bake Cheesecake

12 to 16 servings

CRUST

1 package Duncan Hines® Moist Deluxe
    Pineapple Supreme Cake Mix

½ cup butter or margarine, melted

FILLING

1 package (4-serving size) orange gelatin
1 cup boiling water
2 teaspoons grated orange peel
2 packages (8 ounces each) cream
    cheese, softened

1 cup whipping cream
½ cup dairy sour cream
1 can (11 ounces) Mandarin orange
    segments, drained

1. Preheat oven to 350°F.

2. **For crust**, combine cake mix and melted butter in large bowl. Mix at low speed with electric mixer until crumbs form. Pour into 9-inch springform pan. Lightly press crumbs 1 inch up sides. Smooth remaining crumbs out in bottom of pan. Bake at 350°F for 20 minutes. Cool.

3. **For filling**, dissolve gelatin in boiling water in small bowl. Add orange peel. Refrigerate until mixture begins to thicken.

4. Beat cream cheese until smooth in large bowl. Gradually beat in gelatin.

5. Beat whipping cream until stiff in small bowl. Fold into orange cream cheese mixture. Pour into cooled crust. Refrigerate until firm, about 3 hours.

6. Drop teaspoonfuls of sour cream around edge of cheesecake. Garnish with drained orange segments.

■ *Tip: You can use other fruit flavored gelatin in place of orange. Garnish with appropriate fruit.*

Coconut Crunch Cakes

16 servings

1 package Duncan Hines® Moist Deluxe
    Butter Recipe Golden Cake Mix
1 cup flaked coconut, divided

6 tablespoons butter or margarine,
    melted
¾ cup firmly packed brown sugar

1. Preheat oven to 375°F. Line two 9-inch round cake pans with aluminum foil.

2. To toast coconut, sprinkle ½ cup coconut in bottom of each pan. Bake at 375°F for about 5 minutes. Stir frequently so coconut toasts evenly.

3. Combine melted butter and sugar in medium bowl. Stir until well mixed. Spoon evenly over coconut.

4. Prepare cake following package directions. Pour batter over sugar-coconut mixture. Bake at 350°F for 30 to 35 minutes or until toothpick inserted in center comes out clean. Invert onto serving plate. Remove foil. Serve warm or at room temperature.

■ *Tip: For most recipes, unless specified, you can use either light or dark brown sugar.*

Orange No-Bake Cheesecake

Heavenly Chocolate Cream Pies

CRUST

1 package Duncan Hines® Moist Deluxe Swiss Chocolate Cake Mix

¾ cup butter or margarine

1st LAYER

1 package (8 ounces) cream cheese

1 cup confectioners sugar

1 cup frozen non-dairy whipped topping, thawed

2nd LAYER

2 packages (4-serving size each) chocolate instant pudding and pie filling mix

3 cups milk

3rd LAYER

2 cups frozen non-dairy whipped topping, thawed and divided

1. Preheat oven to 350°F. Grease two 9-inch pie pans.

2. **For crust**, combine cake mix and butter in large bowl. Cut butter in using pastry blender or 2 knives. Put half the crumbs in each pan. Press up sides and on bottom of each pan. Bake at 350°F for 15 minutes. Cool.

3. **For 1st layer**, combine cream cheese and confectioners sugar in small bowl. Beat at medium speed with electric mixer until smooth. Stir in 1 cup whipped topping. Spread half the mixture evenly over each crust. Refrigerate.

4. **For 2nd layer**, prepare pudding mix following package directions using 3 cups milk. Spoon half the pudding over cream cheese mixture in each pan. Refrigerate.

5. **For 3rd layer**, spread 1 cup whipped topping on each pie. Refrigerate until ready to serve.

Note: One container (8 ounces) frozen non-dairy whipped topping will be enough for recipe.

■ *Tip: For **Heavenly Lemon Cream Pies** use Duncan Hines® Moist Deluxe Lemon Supreme Cake Mix in place of Moist Deluxe Swiss Chocolate Cake Mix and lemon instant pudding and pie filling mix in place of chocolate pudding and pie filling mix.*

Heavenly Chocolate Cream Pie

Orange Coconut Fudge Cake

1 can (6 ounces) Citrus Hill® Orange
    Juice Concentrate, thawed

CAKE

1 package Duncan Hines® Moist Deluxe
    Butter Recipe Fudge Cake Mix

¾ cup Citrus Hill® Orange Juice (see step
    #2 below)

3 eggs

½ cup butter or margarine, softened

2 tablespoons orange liqueur, optional

FROSTING

1 cup evaporated milk

¾ cup sugar

3 egg yolks

¼ cup butter or margarine

2 tablespoons Citrus Hill® Frozen
    Orange Juice concentrate, thawed
    (see step #2 below)

1 teaspoon vanilla extract

2 cups chopped pecans

1 cup flaked coconut

1. Preheat oven to 375°F. Grease and flour two 9-inch round cake pans.

2. Measure 2 tablespoons orange juice concentrate. Set aside for frosting. Reconstitute remaining concentrate using ⅓ cup less water than package directions.

3. **For cake**, combine cake mix, orange juice, eggs, butter and liqueur in large bowl. Mix, bake and cool cake following package directions.

4. **For frosting**, combine evaporated milk, sugar, egg yolks and butter in medium saucepan. Cook on medium heat, stirring constantly, until mixture comes to boil and thickens. Remove from heat. Stir in reserved orange juice concentrate and vanilla extract. Add pecans and coconut. Cool. Place one cake layer on serving plate. Spread with thin layer of frosting. Top with second cake layer. Frost top and sides with remaining frosting. Refrigerate until ready to serve.

■ *Tip: Garnish cake with orange slices or twists.*

Orange Coconut Fudge Cake

Double Nut Chocolate Chip Cookies

3 to 3½ dozen cookies

1 package Duncan Hines® Moist Deluxe
   Yellow Cake Mix
½ cup butter or margarine, melted
1 egg

1 cup semi-sweet chocolate chips
½ cup finely chopped pecans
1 cup sliced almonds, divided

1. Preheat oven to 375°F. Grease baking sheet.

2. Combine cake mix, melted butter and egg in large bowl. Beat at low speed with electric mixer until just blended. Stir in chocolate chips, pecans and ¼ cup sliced almonds. Shape rounded tablespoonfuls dough into balls. Place remaining ¾ cup sliced almonds in shallow bowl. Press top of cookie in almonds. Place on baking sheet, 1 inch apart.

3. Bake at 375°F for 9 to 11 minutes or until lightly browned. Cool 2 minutes on baking sheet. Remove to cooling rack.

■ *Tip: To prevent cookies from spreading too much, allow baking sheet to cool completely before baking each batch of cookies.*

Chocolate Toffee Bars

48 bars

1 package Duncan Hines® Moist Deluxe
   Yellow Cake Mix
¾ cup Butter Flavor Crisco®
1 egg

2 tablespoons milk
¾ cup semi-sweet chocolate chips
¾ cup almond brickle chips

1. Preheat oven to 350°F. Grease 13×9×2-inch pan.

2. Combine cake mix, Butter Flavor Crisco, egg and milk in large bowl. Beat at low speed with electric mixer until blended. Press into pan.

3. Bake at 350°F for 22 to 25 minutes or until lightly browned. Remove from oven. Sprinkle with chocolate chips. Return to oven for 3 more minutes. Spread melted chips evenly. Sprinkle brickle chips over chocolate. Cool. Cut into 1½×1-inch bars.

■ *Tip: You can use finely chopped nuts in place of brickle chips.*

Double Nut Chocolate Chip Cookies

Strawberries and Cream Cheesecake Tarts

24 mini cheesecakes

CRUST

1 package Duncan Hines® Moist Deluxe Strawberry Supreme Cake Mix

¼ cup butter or margarine, melted

FILLING

2 packages (8 ounces each) cream cheese, softened

3 eggs

¾ cup sugar

1 teaspoon vanilla extract

TOPPING

1½ cups dairy sour cream

¼ cup sugar

12 fresh strawberries

1. Preheat oven to 350°F. Place 2½-inch foil liners in 24 muffin cups.

2. **For crust**, combine cake mix and melted butter in large bowl. Beat at low speed with electric mixer for 1 minute. Divide mixture evenly in muffin cups. Level but do not press.

3. **For filling**, combine cream cheese, eggs, ¾ cup sugar and vanilla extract in medium bowl. Beat at medium speed with electric mixer until smooth. Spoon evenly into muffin cups.

4. Bake at 350°F for 20 minutes or until mixture is set.

5. **For topping**, combine sour cream and ¼ cup sugar in small bowl. Spoon evenly over cheesecakes. Return to oven for 5 minutes. Cool.

6. Garnish each cheesecake with strawberry half. Refrigerate until ready to serve.

■ *Tip: If you use dark colored muffin pans, reduce the oven temperature to 325°F to prevent over-baking the tarts.*

Lemon Cookies

3 dozen cookies

1 package Duncan Hines® Moist Deluxe
    Lemon Supreme Cake Mix
2 eggs
⅓ cup Crisco® Oil or Crisco®
    Puritan® Oil

1 tablespoon lemon juice
¾ cup chopped nuts or flaked coconut
    Confectioners sugar

1. Preheat oven to 375°F. Grease baking sheets.

2. Combine cake mix, eggs, oil and lemon juice in large bowl. Beat at low speed with electric mixer until well blended. Add nuts. Shape into 1-inch balls. Place on baking sheet, 1 inch apart. Bake at 375°F for 6 or 7 minutes or until lightly browned. Cool 1 minute on baking sheet. Remove to cooling rack. Dust with confectioners sugar.

■ *Tip: You can frost cookies with 1 cup confectioners sugar mixed with 1 tablespoon lemon juice in place of dusting cookies with confectioners sugar.*

Raspberry Meringue Bars

36 bars

BASE

1 package Duncan Hines® Moist Deluxe
    Yellow Cake Mix

½ cup butter or margarine, melted
2 egg yolks

TOPPING

2 egg whites
½ cup sugar
1 cup chopped walnuts

1 cup raspberry preserves
½ cup flaked coconut

1. Preheat oven to 350°F.

2. **For base**, combine cake mix, melted butter and egg yolks in large bowl. Beat at low speed with electric mixer for 1 minute. Spread in ungreased 13×9×2-inch pan.

3. Bake at 350°F for 15 minutes or until lightly browned.

4. **For topping**, beat egg whites in medium bowl at high speed with electric mixer until foamy and double in volume. Beat in sugar. Continue beating until meringue forms firm peaks. Fold in walnuts.

5. Spread raspberry preserves over crust. Sprinkle with coconut. Spread meringue over top.

6. Bake at 350°F for 25 minutes. Cool in pan. Cut into bars.

■ *Tip: You can use other flavor preserves in place of raspberry.*

Lemon Cookies

Quick and Easy Nutty Cheese Bars

24 bars

BASE

1 package Duncan Hines® Moist Deluxe Butter Recipe Golden Cake Mix

¾ cup chopped pecans or walnuts
¾ cup butter or margarine, melted

TOPPING

2 packages (8 ounces each) cream cheese, softened

1 cup firmly packed brown sugar
¾ cup chopped pecans or walnuts

1. Preheat oven to 350°F. Grease and flour 13×9×2-inch pan.

2. **For base**, combine cake mix, ¾ cup pecans and melted butter in large bowl. Stir until well blended. Press mixture into bottom of pan.

3. **For topping**, combine cream cheese and brown sugar in medium bowl. Stir with spoon until well mixed. Spread evenly over base. Sprinkle with ¾ cup pecans.

4. Bake at 350°F for 25 to 30 minutes or until edges are browned and cheese topping is set. Cool completely. Cut into bars. Refrigerate leftovers.

■ *Tip: For successful baking, using the correct measuring cup is important. A lipped measuring cup is for measuring liquids and a flush rimmed cup is for measuring dry ingredients.*

Fudge Marble Bars

32 bars

1 package Duncan Hines® Moist Deluxe Fudge Marble Cake Mix
¼ cup plus 1 tablespoon water, divided
2 eggs

¼ cup butter or margarine, softened
1 cup semi-sweet chocolate chips
½ cup chopped pecans

1. Preheat oven to 350°F. Grease 13×9×2-inch pan.

2. Set aside cocoa packet. Combine cake mix, ¼ cup water, eggs and butter in large bowl. Beat at low speed with electric mixer until just blended.

3. Measure ½ cup batter into small bowl. Add cocoa packet, chocolate chips and remaining 1 tablespoon water. Stir until blended.

4. Add pecans to yellow batter. Spread in pan. Spoon chocolate batter on top. Run knife through batters to marble.

5. Bake at 350°F for 22 to 27 minutes or until toothpick inserted in center comes out clean. Cool. Cut into bars.

■ *Tip: For **Fudge Marble Mint Bars**, use mint chocolate chips in place of semi-sweet chocolate chips.*

Chocolate Peanut Butter Cookies

3½ dozen cookies

1 package Duncan Hines® Moist Deluxe
  Devil's Food Cake Mix
¾ cup Jif® Extra Crunchy Peanut Butter

2 eggs
2 tablespoons milk
1 cup candy-coated peanut butter pieces

1. Preheat oven to 350°F. Grease baking sheets.

2. Combine cake mix, peanut butter, eggs and milk in large bowl. Beat at low speed with electric mixer until blended. Stir in peanut butter pieces.

3. Drop by slightly rounded tablespoonfuls onto baking sheet. Bake at 350°F for 7 to 9 minutes or until lightly browned. Cool 2 minutes on baking sheet. Remove to cooling rack.

■ *Tip: You can use 1 cup peanut butter flavored chips in place of peanut butter pieces.*

Swiss Chocolate Crispies

4 dozen cookies

1 package Duncan Hines® Moist Deluxe
  Swiss Chocolate Cake Mix
½ cup Butter Flavor Crisco®
½ cup butter or margarine, softened

2 eggs
2 tablespoons water
3 cups crisp rice cereal, divided

1. Combine cake mix, Butter Flavor Crisco, butter, eggs and water in large bowl. Beat at low speed with electric mixer for 2 minutes. Fold in 1 cup cereal. Refrigerate 1 hour.

2. Crush remaining 2 cups cereal into coarse crumbs.

3. Preheat oven to 350°F. Grease baking sheets.

4. Shape dough into 1-inch balls. Roll in crushed cereal. Place on baking sheets about 1 inch apart.

5. Bake at 350°F for 11 to 13 minutes or until lightly browned. Cool 1 minute on baking sheets. Remove to cooling rack.

■ *Tip: For evenly baked cookies, place baking sheet in center of oven, not touching sides.*

Chocolate Peanut Butter Cookies

Jelly Roll Diploma

8 to 10 servings

1 package Duncan Hines® Angel Food
   Cake Mix
1 cup water
¾ cup Crisco® Oil or Crisco®
   Puritan® Oil
¼ cup all-purpose flour

3 eggs
½ teaspoon vanilla extract
2 tablespoons grated lemon peel
   Confectioners sugar
⅔ cup any red jam or preserves
   Ribbon for bow

1. Preheat oven to 350°F. Line a 15½×10½×1-inch jelly-roll pan with waxed paper and grease the waxed paper. Place 2½-inch paper or foil liners in 24 muffin cups.*

2. Combine water and egg white packet (blue) in large bowl. Beat at low speed with electric mixer for 1 minute. Beat at high speed until very stiff peaks form. Combine flour packet (red), oil, flour, eggs, vanilla extract and lemon peel in medium bowl. Beat at low speed until blended. Beat at medium speed for 3 minutes. Fold beaten egg whites into yellow batter. Pour enough batter into jelly-roll pan to fill to within one-fourth inch of top. Spread evenly.

3. Bake at 350°F about 30 minutes, or until toothpick inserted in center comes out clean. Immediately invert cake onto dish towel covered with confectioners sugar. Peel off paper and trim edges of cake. Roll up with towel jelly-roll fashion. Cool. Unroll cake and spread with jam. Reroll. Sprinkle top with confectioners sugar. Tie a ribbon around diploma.

*For cupcakes, while jelly roll cake is baking, spoon remaining batter into muffin cups, filling each about two-thirds full. Bake at 350°F for 15 to 20 minutes. Cool. Frost as desired. Makes 24 cupcakes.

■ *Tip: For Graduation prediction cupcakes write predictions such as "Your job interview will be a winner" on small piece of white paper. Roll up. Tuck paper in small cut in bottom of each cake. Frost as desired.*

Jelly Roll Diploma

Harvey Wallbanger's Cake

12 to 16 servings

1 package Duncan Hines® Moist Deluxe
    Orange Supreme Cake Mix
3 eggs
¾ cup Citrus Hill® Orange Juice

⅓ cup Crisco® Oil or Crisco®
    Puritan® Oil
⅓ cup Galliano®
¼ cup vodka
    Confectioners sugar

1. Preheat oven to 350°F. Grease and flour 10-inch Bundt® pan.

2. Combine cake mix, eggs, orange juice, oil, Galliano and vodka in large bowl. Beat at medium speed with electric mixer for 4 minutes. Pour into pan. Bake at 350°F for 45 to 50 minutes, or until toothpick inserted in center comes out clean. Cool in pan 25 minutes. Invert onto serving plate. Cool completely. Dust with confectioners sugar.

■ *Tip: For a non-alcoholic cake, use ½ cup plus 1 tablespoon water in place of Galliano and vodka.*

Baked Alaska

10 to 12 servings

½ gallon ice cream, softened

1 package Duncan Hines® Moist Deluxe
    White Cake Mix

MERINGUE

4 egg whites, at room temperature
½ teaspoon cream of tartar

¾ cup sugar
½ teaspoon vanilla extract

1. Line 2-quart round bowl with plastic wrap. Press softened ice cream into bowl. Freeze until firm.

2. Preheat oven to 350°F. Grease and flour two 8-inch round cake pans.

3. Prepare, bake and cool cake following package directions. Place one layer on heatproof platter. (Freeze other layer in airtight plastic bag for a quick dessert at a later time.)

4. **For meringue**, beat egg whites in medium bowl at high speed with electric mixer until foamy. Add cream of tartar. Gradually beat in sugar. Add vanilla extract. Beat 5 minutes or until thick and glossy.

5. To assemble, unmold ice cream on top of cake layer. Remove plastic wrap. Spread meringue over ice cream and cake. Cover completely. Return to freezer for 15 minutes.

6. Reheat oven to 450°F. Bake Alaska 4 or 5 minutes or until lightly browned. Serve immediately.

■ *Tip: Baked Alaska can be assembled earlier in the day and frozen. Bake meringue at serving time; or bake ahead and freeze until ready to serve.*

Easter Basket Cupcakes

24 cupcakes

1 package Duncan Hines® Moist Deluxe
   Yellow Cake Mix
3 tablespoons plus 1½ teaspoons water
6 drops green food coloring
1½ cups shredded coconut

1 container (16 ounces) Duncan Hines®
   Vanilla Layer Cake Frosting
½ pound assorted colors jelly beans
24 assorted colors pipe cleaners

1. Preheat oven to 350°F. Place 2½-inch paper liners in 24 muffin cups.

2. Prepare, bake and cool cupcakes following package directions.

3. Combine water and green food coloring in large container with tight fitting lid. Add coconut. Shake until coconut is evenly tinted green.

4. Frost cupcakes with vanilla frosting. Sprinkle coconut over frosting. Press 3 jelly beans into coconut on each cupcake. Bend pipe cleaners to form handles. Push into cupcakes.

■ *Tip: You can make fruit baskets by placing fruit slices on top of frosting in place of coconut and jelly beans.*

Fruit Parfaits

6 servings

1 package Duncan Hines® Moist Deluxe
   Yellow Cake Mix
2 cups fresh peaches, peeled and diced
1 cup miniature marshmallows
¼ cup flaked coconut

1½ cups whipping cream
2 tablespoons confectioners sugar
½ teaspoon almond extract
6 peach slices

1. Preheat oven to 350°F. Grease and flour two 9-inch round cake pans.

2. Prepare, bake and cool cake following package directions.

3. Cut one cake layer into 1-inch cubes. Place in large bowl. (Freeze other cake in large airtight plastic bag to use later.) Add diced peaches, marshmallows and coconut to cake. Toss to mix.

4. Combine whipping cream, confectioners sugar and almond extract in large bowl. Beat at high speed with electric mixer until stiff. Set aside enough whipped cream for garnish. Fold remaining whipped cream into cake mixture. Spoon into 6 parfait dishes. Top each with reserved whipped cream and peach slice. Refrigerate until ready to serve.

■ *Tip: For a quick dessert, defrost frozen cake and cut cake in half vertically. Frost one half. Stack other half on top. Frost uncut sides and top for half a cake, which will serve 6 to 8.*

Easter Basket Cupcakes

Rainbow Sorbet Torte

10 to 12 servings

4 pints assorted flavors sorbet
1 package Duncan Hines® Moist Deluxe
    White Cake Mix

Assorted fruit, for garnish

1. Line bottom of 8-inch round cake pan with aluminum foil. Soften one pint of sorbet. Spread evenly in pan. Return to freezer until firm. Run knife around edge of pan to loosen sorbet. Remove from pan. Wrap in foil and return to freezer. Repeat for other flavors.

2. Preheat oven to 350°F. Grease and flour two 8-inch round cake pans.

3. Prepare, bake and cool cake following package directions for No Cholesterol recipe.

4. To assemble torte, cut both cake layers in half horizontally. Place one cake layer on serving plate. Top with one layer sorbet. Peel off foil. Repeat for all cake and sorbet layers. Wrap aluminum foil around plate and cake. Return to freezer until ready to serve. To serve, garnish top with fruit.

■ *Tip: This is a good make-ahead dessert. Whole torte can be served or you may use only a few slices at a time.*

Spicy Oatmeal Raisin Cookies

4 dozen cookies

1 package Duncan Hines® Moist Deluxe
    Spice Cake Mix
4 egg whites
1 cup quick-cooking oats (not instant or
    old-fashioned)

½ cup Crisco® Oil or Crisco®
    Puritan® Oil
½ cup raisins

1. Preheat oven to 350°F. Grease baking sheets.

2. Combine cake mix, egg whites, oats and oil in large bowl. Beat at low speed with electric mixer until blended. Stir in raisins. Drop by rounded teaspoons onto baking sheets.

3. Bake at 350°F for 7 to 9 minutes or until lightly browned. Cool 1 minute on baking sheets. Remove to cooling rack.

■ *Tip: You may use other Duncan Hines® cake mix flavors in place of Spice Cake Mix.*

Rainbow Sorbet Torte

Strawberry Basket

1 package Duncan Hines® Moist Deluxe
    White Cake Mix

GLAZE

3 cups medium-size strawberries, divided   1 tablespoon cornstarch
⅓ cup water   Red food coloring
¼ cup sugar

FROSTING

1 container (16 ounces) Duncan Hines®   1 tablespoon plus 2 teaspoons cocoa
    Vanilla Layer Cake Frosting

1. Preheat oven to 350°F. Grease and flour two 8-inch square pans.

2. Prepare, bake and cool cake following package directions for No Cholesterol recipe.

3. **For glaze**, wash berries. Remove stems and leaves. Simmer ½ cup berries with water for 2 minutes in small saucepan. Push mixture through sieve into small bowl. Return to saucepan. Combine sugar and cornstarch in small cup. Add to berry juice. Cook until glaze is thickened and clear. Stir in 3 drops food coloring. Set aside.

4. **For frosting**, mix vanilla frosting and cocoa until smooth in small bowl.

5. To assemble, place one layer on serving plate. Frost with ⅓ cup cocoa frosting. Top with second layer. Cut into top of cake 1 inch in from all four edges; cut down 1 inch deep. Lift out cut section with pancake turner. (One inch rim will be left on top layer.) Frost outside and top rim of cake with cocoa frosting. Spoon 2 tablespoons glaze in cut out area. Spread evenly. Fill with remaining strawberries, pointed ends up. Brush berries with remaining glaze. Make basket pattern in frosting using four-tine fork.

■ *Tip: For a delicious snack, spread leftover frosting between graham crackers.*

Mexican Chocolate Cake

1 package Duncan Hines® Moist Deluxe   1 container (16 ounces) Duncan Hines®
    Dark Dutch Fudge Cake Mix   Dark Dutch Fudge Layer Cake
1 teaspoon cinnamon   Frosting

1. Preheat oven to 350°F. Grease and flour two 9-inch round cake pans.

2. Prepare, bake and cool cake following package directions for No Cholesterol recipe.

3. Stir cinnamon into dark dutch fudge frosting; frost tops and sides of cake.

■ *Tip: Always use a cooling rack to cool cake layers. If you place warm cake layers on a plate to cool, the cake will become soggy and stick to the plate.*

Strawberry Basket

Raspberry Swirl Cake

12 to 16 servings

1 package Duncan Hines® Moist Deluxe
French Vanilla Cake Mix

RASPBERRY SAUCE

1 package (12 ounces) frozen
raspberries, thawed
2 tablespoons seedless raspberry jam
1 tablespoon cornstarch

1 tablespoon water
1 container (16 ounces) Duncan Hines®
Cream Cheese Layer Cake Frosting

1. Preheat oven to 350°F. Grease and flour two 9-inch round cake pans.

2. Prepare, bake and cool cake following package directions for No Cholesterol recipe.

3. **For raspberry sauce**, place sieve over small saucepan. Push raspberries through sieve with spoon. Discard seeds. Add jam. Dissolve cornstarch in water in small cup. Add to saucepan. Cook on medium heat, stirring constantly, until sauce comes to boil and thickens. Cool.

4. To assemble, place one cake layer (bottom-side up) on plate. Spread with raspberry sauce, reserving enough to drizzle on top. Place second layer on top. Frost sides and top of cake with cream cheese frosting. Drizzle with remaining sauce. Run knife through frosting and sauce to swirl.

■ *Tip: You may use strawberries and strawberry jam in place of the raspberries and raspberry jam.*

Refrigerated Peach Sheet Cake

12 servings

1 package Duncan Hines® Moist Deluxe
White Cake Mix
1 package (4-serving size) peach flavored
gelatin

1 cup boiling water
1 container (8 ounces) frozen non-dairy
whipped topping, thawed
1 medium peach, sliced

1. Preheat oven to 350°F. Grease and flour 13×9×2-inch pan.

2. Prepare and bake cake following package directions for No Cholesterol recipe. Cool 5 minutes.

3. Dissolve gelatin in boiling water in small bowl. Cool until slightly thickened.

4. Poke holes in top of cake with toothpick or long-tined fork. Gradually pour gelatin mixture over cake. Refrigerate for 2 hours.

5. To serve, frost cake with whipped topping. Garnish with peach slices. Cut into 3-inch squares.

■ *Tip: You can use other flavors of gelatin and fresh fruit, such as apricot, raspberry or strawberry.*

Raspberry Swirl Cake

Piña Colada Cake

16 servings

1 package Duncan Hines® Moist Deluxe
   Pineapple Supreme Cake Mix

FILLING

2 cups milk
1 package (8 ounces) cream cheese,
   softened
1 package (4-serving size) vanilla instant
   pudding and pie filling mix

¾ teaspoon rum flavoring or extract
1 can (8½ ounces) crushed pineapple,
   well drained

TOPPING

2 cups frozen non-dairy whipped
   topping, thawed
½ cup flaked coconut, for garnish

½ cup pineapple tidbits, for garnish
½ cup maraschino cherries, for garnish

1. Preheat oven to 350°F. Grease and flour 10-inch tube pan.

2. Prepare, bake and cool cake following package directions for original recipe.

3. Cut cooled cake into three equal layers (see Tip).

4. **For filling**, combine milk, cream cheese, pudding mix and flavoring in small bowl. Beat at medium speed with electric mixer for 2 minutes.

5. To assemble, place one cake layer on serving plate. Spread with half the pudding mixture. Top with half the crushed pineapple. Repeat with second cake layer and remaining filling. Place third cake layer on top.

6. **For topping**, spread whipped topping on sides and top of cake. Refrigerate until ready to serve. Garnish with coconut, pineapple tidbits and cherries, if desired.

■ *Tip: To cut cake evenly, measure cake with ruler. Divide into 3 equal layers. Mark with toothpicks. Cut through layers using toothpicks as guide.*

Piña Colada Cake

Chocolate Cherry Cake

12 to 16 servings

1 package Duncan Hines® Moist Deluxe
    Dark Dutch Fudge Cake Mix
1 package (8 ounces) cream cheese,
    softened
½ cup butter or margarine, softened

½ teaspoon almond extract
1 pound confectioners sugar (3½ to
    4 cups)
1 cup frozen dark sweet cherries,
    thawed, chopped, and well drained

1. Preheat oven to 350°F. Grease and flour two 9-inch round cake pans.

2. Prepare, bake and cool cake following package directions.

3. Place cream cheese, butter and almond extract in large bowl. Beat at medium speed of electric mixer until smooth. Gradually add sugar, mixing well after each addition. Measure ¾ cup of cream cheese mixture. Place in small bowl. Stir in cherries.

4. Place one cake layer on serving plate. Spread with cherry mixture. Place other layer on top. Frost sides and top with plain cream cheese frosting. Garnish top with cherries, if desired. Refrigerate until ready to serve.

■ *Tip: You can use either fresh or canned dark sweet cherries in place of frozen.*

Banana Mousse Spice Cake

12 to 16 servings

1 package Duncan Hines® Moist Deluxe
    Spice Cake Mix
1 cup milk
⅔ cup sugar
1 envelope unflavored gelatin

2 eggs, beaten
2 medium-size ripe bananas
1 tablespoon lemon juice
1 cup whipping cream
    Additional bananas, for garnish

1. Preheat oven to 350°F. Grease and flour 13×9×2-inch pan.

2. Prepare, bake and cool cake following package directions.

3. Combine milk, sugar and gelatin in medium saucepan. Cook on medium heat until mixture comes to boil. Remove from heat. Slowly stir half of hot mixture into beaten eggs. Return mixture slowly to pan while stirring. Cook on low heat 1 minute, stirring constantly. Refrigerate until thickened.

4. Mash bananas in small bowl. Stir in lemon juice. Stir into gelatin mixture. Beat whipping cream until stiff in large bowl; fold into gelatin mixture. Spread over top of cooled cake. Refrigerate until ready to serve. Garnish with additional banana slices, if desired (see Tip).

■ *Tip: To prevent fresh fruit from turning brown, slice bananas, peaches, apples, nectarines and pears into a little lemon or orange juice.*

Chocolate Cherry Cake

Strawberry Celebration Cake

1 package Duncan Hines® Moist Deluxe
   Strawberry Supreme Cake Mix
1 cup strawberry jam, divided

1 container (16 ounces) Duncan Hines®
   Cream Cheese Layer Cake Frosting
Fresh strawberries, for garnish

1. Preheat oven to 350°F. Grease and flour 10-inch tube pan.

2. Prepare, bake and cool cake following package directions. Refrigerate cake several hours for easier cutting.

3. Cut cake horizontally into three layers (see Tip). Heat strawberry jam in small saucepan. Place one cake layer on serving plate. Spread with ½ cup jam. Place second layer on top. Spread with remaining jam. Top with third layer.

4. Frost with cream cheese frosting. Garnish with sliced strawberries, if desired. Refrigerate until ready to serve.

■ *Tip: To cut evenly, measure cake with ruler. Divide into three equal layers. Mark with toothpicks. Cut through layers using toothpicks as guide.*

Fresh Fruit 'n Cream Bundt Cake

16 servings

1 package Duncan Hines® Moist Deluxe
   French Vanilla Cake Mix
1 package (4-serving size) lemon instant
   pudding and pie filling mix
5 eggs, divided
¾ cup water

¼ cup Butter Flavor Crisco®
1 cup sugar
⅓ cup Citrus Hill® Orange Juice
1½ tablespoons lemon juice
1 cup whipping cream
Mixed fresh fruit

1. Preheat oven to 350°F. Grease and flour 10-inch tube pan or Bundt® pan.

2. Combine cake mix, pudding mix, 4 eggs, water and Butter Flavor Crisco in large bowl. Beat at low speed with electric mixer until just blended. Beat at medium speed 2 minutes. Bake at 350°F for 45 to 55 minutes or until toothpick inserted in center comes out clean. Cool following package directions.

3. Beat remaining 1 egg with fork in heavy 1-quart saucepan until blended. Stir in sugar, orange juice and lemon juice. Cook on medium heat, stirring constantly, 10 minutes or until mixture just comes to boil. Remove from heat. Refrigerate until chilled, about 30 minutes.

4. Beat whipping cream until stiff in large bowl. Just before serving fold whipped cream into sauce. To serve, spoon sauce over cake slices. Garnish with fresh fruit.

■ *Tip: You can usually find a good variety of mixed fresh fruit at a salad bar.*

Strawberry Celebration Cake

Banana Cream Cake

12 to 16 servings

1 package Duncan Hines® Moist Deluxe
  Banana Supreme Cake Mix
1 package (4-serving size) vanilla
  pudding and pie filling mix
  (not instant)

1½ cups milk
1 cup whipping cream
1 cup miniature marshmallows
3 medium-size ripe bananas, sliced

1. Preheat oven to 350°F. Grease and flour two 9-inch round cake pans.

2. Prepare, bake and cool cake following package directions.

3. Cook pudding following package directions using 1½ cups milk. Place waxed paper on surface of pudding. Refrigerate until cool, about 30 minutes.

4. Beat whipping cream until stiff in large bowl. Fold into cooled pudding. Fold in marshmallows and bananas.

5. Cut each cake layer in half horizontally (see Tip). Place one cut cake layer on serving plate. Spoon on one-fourth banana mixture. Spread to edges. Repeat for remaining layers saving enough for top of cake. Refrigerate until ready to serve.

■ *Tip: To cut each cake evenly, measure cake with ruler. Divide into 2 equal layers. Mark with toothpicks. Cut through layers using toothpicks as guide.*

Fruit Tarts

4 dozen tarts

1 package Duncan Hines® Moist Deluxe
  French Vanilla Cake Mix
¾ cup Butter Flavor Crisco®
2 tablespoons milk
1 egg

1 package (8 ounces) cream cheese,
  softened
Assorted fresh fruit (such as bananas,
  green grapes, kiwi, pineapple tidbits,
  strawberries or peaches)

1. Combine cake mix, Butter Flavor Crisco, milk and egg in large bowl. Beat at low speed with electric mixer until ingredients are blended. Refrigerate dough 1 hour.

2. Preheat oven to 375°F. Grease baking sheets.

3. Shape dough into 1-inch balls. Bake at 375°F for 10 to 12 minutes or until lightly browned. Cool on baking sheets 1 minute. Remove to cooling rack.

4. Spread each tart with cream cheese. Cut fruit into bite-size pieces. Arrange on top of cream cheese. Serve immediately.

■ *Tip: Undecorated tarts will keep frozen in airtight container for up to 6 weeks.*

Banana Cream Cake

Fruit and Yogurt Topped Cake

12 servings

1 package Duncan Hines® Moist Deluxe
White Cake Mix
2 containers (8 ounces each) low-fat fruit
yogurt, any flavor

Fresh fruit (same fruit as yogurt)

1. Preheat oven to 350°F. Grease and flour 13×9×2-inch pan.

2. Prepare, bake and cool cake following package directions.

3. To serve, cut cake into 3-inch squares. Place on serving plates. Spoon yogurt over each serving. Top with fresh fruit.

■ *Tip: When baking cakes, it's best not to open the oven door while the cake is baking. The sudden rush of cooler air can cause the cake to fall.*

Dump Cake

12 to 16 servings

1 can (20 ounces) crushed pineapple,
undrained
1 can (21 ounces) cherry pie filling
1 package Duncan Hines® Moist Deluxe
Yellow Cake Mix

1 cup chopped pecans or walnuts
½ cup butter or margarine, cut into thin
slices

1. Preheat oven to 350°F. Grease 13×9×2-inch pan.

2. Dump undrained pineapple into pan. Spread evenly. Dump in pie filling. Spread evenly. Sprinkle cake mix evenly over cherry layer. Sprinkle pecans over cake mix. Dot with butter. Bake at 350°F for 50 minutes or until top is lightly browned. Serve warm or at room temperature.

■ *Tip: You can use Duncan Hines® Moist Deluxe Pineapple Supreme Cake Mix in place of Yellow Cake Mix.*

Fruit and Yogurt Topped Cake

Cherry Filled Chocolate Cake

12 to 16 servings

1 package Duncan Hines® Moist Deluxe
   Devil's Food Cake Mix
2 envelopes whipped topping mix
1 package (4-serving size) chocolate
   instant pudding and pie filling mix

1¼ cups milk
¼ teaspoon almond extract
1 can (21 ounces) light cherry pie filling,
   divided

1. Preheat oven to 350°F. Grease and flour two 9-inch round cake pans.

2. Prepare, bake and cool cake following package directions.

3. Combine topping mix, pudding mix, milk and almond extract in medium bowl. Beat at medium speed with electric mixer until stiff, about 3 minutes.

4. To assemble, place one cake layer on serving plate. Make a 1-inch wide by ½-inch high ring of chocolate mixture around top edge of cake.

5. Reserve ¾ cup of cherry filling. Spoon remaining filling in center of cake. Spread to edge of chocolate ring. Place second cake layer on top. Spoon reserved cherries in center; spread into a circle.

6. Frost sides of cake and over top edge to ring of cherries with remaining chocolate mixture. Refrigerate at least 1 hour before serving. Store leftovers in refrigerator.

■ *Tip: You can use other fruit pie filling or other flavors pudding mix in place of the cherry pie filling and chocolate pudding.*

Peach Chantilly

12 servings

1 package Duncan Hines® Moist Deluxe
   White Cake Mix
2 containers (8 ounces each) peach
   yogurt

1 cup frozen non-dairy whipped topping,
   thawed
2 peaches
   Nutmeg

1. Preheat oven to 350°F. Grease and flour 13×9×2-inch pan.

2. Prepare, bake and cool cake following package directions.

3. Place yogurt in small bowl. Fold in whipped topping. Finely dice 1 peach; fold into topping. Cut second peach into 12 thin slices.

4. To serve, cut cake into 3-inch squares. Place on serving plates. Spoon topping on each serving; top with peach slice. Sprinkle with nutmeg.

■ *Tip: You can use other yogurt flavors and fresh fruit in place of peach yogurt and peaches.*

Pineapple Cream Supreme

16 servings

1 package Duncan Hines® Moist Deluxe
   Pineapple Supreme Cake Mix
1 package (8 ounces) cream cheese,
   softened
2 tablespoons milk

1 package (4-serving size) vanilla instant
   pudding and pie filling mix
1 can (8 ounces) crushed pineapple,
   undrained
1½ cups fresh blueberries, optional

1. Preheat oven to 350°F. Grease and flour 13×9×2-inch pan.

2. Prepare, bake and cool cake following package directions.

3. Beat cream cheese in small bowl at medium speed with electric mixer until smooth. Add milk; beat until creamy. Add pudding mix; beat until mixed. Add pineapple; beat 1 minute. Fold in blueberries by hand. Spread over top of cooled cake. Refrigerate until ready to serve.

■ *Tip: To keep the cake's fresh flavor, tent aluminum foil over top of pan and seal edges tightly.*

Fruit Cocktail Cake

12 servings

1 package Duncan Hines® Moist Deluxe
   Yellow Cake Mix
1 package (4-serving size) lemon instant
   pudding and pie filling mix
4 eggs
1 can (16 ounces) fruit cocktail,
   undrained

1 cup flaked coconut
¼ cup Crisco® Oil or Crisco®
   Puritan® Oil
¼ cup quartered maraschino cherries
½ cup chopped walnuts

1. Preheat oven to 350°F. Grease and flour 13×9×2-inch pan.

2. Combine cake mix, pudding mix, eggs, fruit cocktail, coconut, oil and cherries in large bowl. Beat at medium speed with electric mixer for 4 minutes. Pour into pan. Sprinkle top with walnuts. Bake at 350°F for 45 to 50 minutes or until toothpick inserted in center comes out clean. Cool in pan. Cut into 3-inch squares.

■ *Tip: You can use Duncan Hines® Moist Deluxe Pineapple Supreme or Moist Deluxe Banana Supreme Cake mix in place of Yellow Cake Mix.*

Carousel Cake

12 to 16 servings

1 package Duncan Hines® Moist Deluxe
   Cake Mix (any flavor)
1 container (16 ounces) Duncan Hines®
   Vanilla or Cream Cheese Layer Cake
   Frosting

Assorted garnishes such as chopped
   nuts, toasted coconut, mini chocolate
   chips, peanut butter chips, jelly
   beans, slivered almonds, chocolate
   decors or colored decors

1. Preheat oven to 350°F. Grease and flour two 9-inch round cake pans.

2. Prepare, bake and cool cake following package directions.

3. Frost cake with vanilla frosting. Score top of cake into 8 equal wedges. Top each wedge with a different garnish of your choice.

■ *Tip: Change decorations for seasonal or party themes.*

Black Eyed Susan Cake

12 to 16 servings

1 package Duncan Hines® Moist Deluxe
   Fudge Marble Cake Mix
1 container (16 ounces) Duncan Hines®
   Chocolate Layer Cake Frosting

1 container (16 ounces) Duncan Hines®
   Lemon Layer Cake Frosting

1. Preheat oven to 350°F. Grease and flour two 9-inch round cake pans.

2. Prepare, bake and cool cake following package directions.

3. Place one cake layer on serving plate. Frost with chocolate frosting to within ¼ inch of edge. Place second layer on top. Frost top with chocolate frosting to within 1½ inches of edge.

4. Frost sides and top edge with lemon frosting. Use knife to pull out and swirl frosting on top to decorate.

■ *Tip: For a delicious snack, spread leftover frosting between vanilla wafers.*

Carousel Cake

Clown Cupcakes

12 clown cupcakes

1 package Duncan Hines® Moist Deluxe
  Yellow Cake Mix
12 scoops vanilla ice cream
1 package (12 count) sugar ice cream
  cones

1 container (7 ounces) refrigerated
  aerosol whipped cream
Assorted colored decors
Assorted candies for eyes, nose and
  mouth

1. Preheat oven to 350°F. Place 2½-inch paper liners in 24 muffin cups.

2. Prepare, bake and cool cupcakes following package directions.

3. To assemble each clown, remove paper from cupcake. Place top-side down on serving plate. Top with a scoop of ice cream. Place cone on ice cream for hat. Spray whipped cream around bottom of cupcake for collar. Spray three small dots up front of cone. Sprinkle whipped cream with assorted colored decors. Use candies to make clown's face.

Note: This recipe makes 24 cupcakes: 12 to make into "clowns" and 12 to freeze for later use. Cupcakes will keep frozen in airtight container for up to 6 weeks.

■ *Tip: For easier preparation, make the ice cream balls ahead of time. Scoop out balls of ice cream, place on baking sheet or in bowl and return to freezer to firm.*

Polka-Dot Cookies

4 dozen cookies

1 package Duncan Hines® Moist Deluxe
  Yellow Cake Mix
¾ cup Butter Flavor Crisco®

2 eggs, separated
1 tablespoon milk
Assorted colored decors

1. Preheat oven to 375°F. Grease baking sheets.

2. Combine cake mix, Butter Flavor Crisco, egg yolks and milk in large bowl. Shape into 1-inch balls.

3. Beat egg whites slightly in small bowl. Dip balls into egg whites. Roll in assorted colored decors. Bake at 375°F for 8 to 10 minutes or until lightly browned. Cool on baking sheet 1 minute. Remove to cooling rack.

■ *Tip: You can frost cookies with any flavor Duncan Hines® frosting instead of rolling cookies in assorted colored decors.*

Clown Cupcakes

Ice Cream Cookie Sandwich

2 pints chocolate chip ice cream, softened
1 package Duncan Hines® Moist Deluxe Dark Dutch Fudge Cake Mix

½ cup butter or margarine, softened

1. Line bottom of one 9-inch round cake pan with aluminum foil. Spread ice cream in pan. Return to freezer until firm. Run knife around edge of pan to loosen ice cream. Remove from pan. Wrap in foil and return to freezer.

2. Preheat oven to 350°F. Line bottom of two 9-inch round cake pans with aluminum foil. Place cake mix in large bowl. Add butter. Mix until crumbs form. Place half the cake mix in each pan. Press lightly. Bake at 350°F for 15 minutes or until browned around edges; do not overbake. Cool 10 minutes. Remove from pans. Remove foil from cookie layers. Cool completely.

3. To assemble, place one cookie layer on serving plate. Top with ice cream. Peel off foil. Place second cookie layer on top. Wrap in foil and freeze 2 hours. To keep longer, store in airtight container.

■ *Tip: You can use lemon sherbet and Duncan Hines® Moist Deluxe Lemon Supreme Cake Mix in place of chocolate chip ice cream and Moist Deluxe Dark Dutch Fudge Cake Mix.*

Dessert Pizza Pies

24 servings

1 package Duncan Hines® Moist Deluxe Yellow Cake Mix
1 egg
½ cup butter or margarine
2 packages (8 ounces each) cream cheese, softened

½ cup confectioners sugar
1½ cups strawberry jam
½ cup candy coated chocolate pieces
1 ounce white chocolate, shaved

1. Preheat oven to 350°F. Grease 10-inch circle on 2 baking sheets.

2. For crust, combine cake mix, egg and butter in large bowl. Beat at low speed with electric mixer until blended. Place half the mixture in center of each greased circle. Press evenly to edge of circle. Bake at 350°F for 15 minutes or until lightly browned. Cool on baking sheets.

3. For topping, combine cream cheese and confectioners sugar in small bowl. Beat at low speed with electric mixer until smooth. Spread over cooled circles. Spread ¾ cup strawberry jam on top of cream cheese layer. Decorate each with ¼ cup chocolate pieces. Sprinkle with shaved white chocolate. Cut each circle into 12 servings.

■ *Tip: You can use any candy pieces in place of chocolate pieces.*

Ice Cream Cookie Sandwich

Banana Split Refrigerator Cake

12 servings

1 package Duncan Hines® Moist Deluxe
　Banana Supreme Cake Mix
1 envelope whipped topping mix
1 package (4-serving size) vanilla instant
　pudding and pie filling mix
1½ cups milk
1 teaspoon vanilla extract
6 maraschino cherries, drained and
　halved

1 medium-size ripe banana, sliced
½ cup thinly sliced fresh pineapple pieces
¼ cup coarsely chopped pecans or
　walnuts
½ cup hot fudge ice cream topping,
　warmed

1. Preheat oven to 350°F. Grease and flour 13×9×2-inch pan.

2. Prepare, bake and cool cake following package directions.

3. Combine topping mix, pudding mix, milk and vanilla extract in large bowl. Beat at medium speed with electric mixer until stiff. Spread over cooled cake. Place maraschino cherry halves, banana slices, pineapple pieces and chopped pecans randomly on topping. Drizzle with fudge topping. Refrigerate until ready to serve. Cut into 3-inch squares.

■ *Tip: To prevent banana slices from darkening, slice into small amount diluted lemon juice. Drain thoroughly before placing on cake.*

Butterfly Cake

12 to 16 servings

1 package Duncan Hines® Moist Deluxe
　Yellow or Lemon Supreme Cake Mix
2 containers (16 ounces) Duncan Hines®
　Vanilla or Cream Cheese Layer Cake
　Frosting, divided

Red food coloring
Red licorice laces
Pastel candy wafers

1. Preheat oven to 350°F. Grease and flour two 9-inch round cake pans.

2. Prepare, bake and cool cake following package directions.

3. Fill and frost with vanilla frosting as for 2 layer cake. Refrigerate cake 1 hour for easier handling. Place remaining frosting in small bowl. Add a few drops red food coloring to tint frosting pink.

4. To assemble, cut cake in half. Place on serving plate with round sides touching and with cut sides out. Outline with pink frosting using decorator's tube (see Note). Arrange 2 licorice laces for feelers. Decorate with candy wafers for spots.

Note: If decorator's tube is not available, place tinted frosting in small airtight plastic bag. Seal top and cut off a tiny bottom corner to use as tip.

■ *Tip: Leftover cake will keep frozen in airtight container for up to 6 weeks.*

Banana Split Refrigerator Cake

Rainbow Cupcakes

CAKE

1 package Duncan Hines® Moist Deluxe Fudge Marble Cake Mix

Red and green food coloring

FROSTING

1 pound confectioners sugar (3½ to 4 cups)
½ cup Butter Flavor Crisco®
⅓ cup milk

1 teaspoon vanilla extract
2 tablespoons cocoa
Red and green food coloring
Assorted colored decors

1. Preheat oven to 350°F. Place 2½-inch paper liners in 24 muffin cups.

2. **For cake**, set aside cocoa packet. Prepare cake mix following package directions. Divide batter into thirds and place in 3 different bowls. Stir cocoa packet into one. Add 5 drops red food coloring to another. Add 5 drops green food coloring to the third. Stir each just until blended.

3. Layer 1 tablespoon of each color batter into each muffin cup. Bake at 350°F for 20 to 25 minutes. Cool completely.

4. **For frosting**, combine sugar, Butter Flavor Crisco, milk and vanilla extract in medium bowl. Beat at low speed with electric mixer until blended. Scrape bowl. Beat at high speed for 2 minutes.

5. Divide frosting into thirds and place in 3 different bowls. Add cocoa to one. Add a few drops red food coloring to another. Add a few drops green food coloring to the third. Stir each until well blended. Frost cupcakes with a small amount of each color frosting. Sprinkle with assorted colored decors.

■ *Tip: An easy way to fill muffin cups is to place the batter in a 2- or 4-cup glass measure. Pour desired amount of batter into each muffin cup. Use a spatula to stop the flow of batter.*

Rainbow Cupcakes

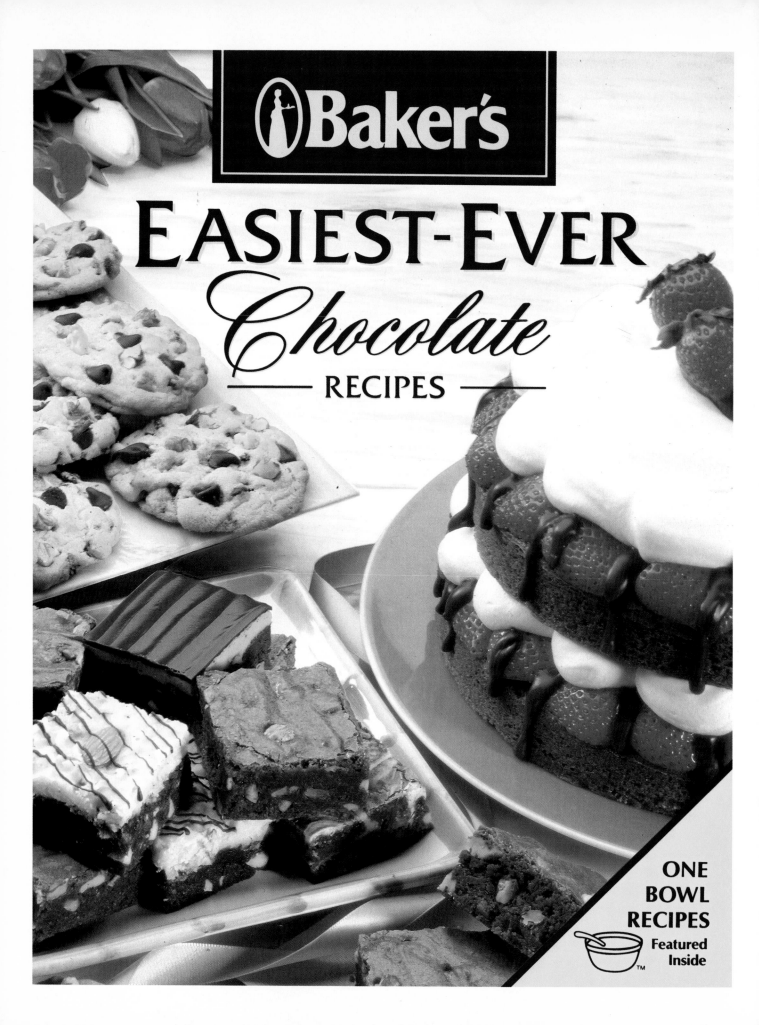

Baker's

EASIEST-EVER
Chocolate
— RECIPES —

ONE BOWL RECIPES
Featured Inside

Clockwise from top left: BAKER'S Chocolate Chip Cookies (page 541), Chocolate Strawberry Shortcake (page 558), ONE BOWL Brownies (page 531), Almond Macaroon Brownies (page 536), German Sweet Chocolate Cream Cheese Brownies (page 534) and Peanut-Layered Brownies (page 536)

INTRODUCTION

''I didn't know it could be so easy!'' This has been the popular response to BAKER'S new ONE BOWL recipes. Discover how to prepare delicious *homemade* brownies, cookies and more in about the same amount of time it would normally take to prepare a mix.

BAKER'S EASIEST-EVER CHOCOLATE RECIPES features over 50 of these no-fuss ONE BOWL recipes, each one bursting with the velvety richness of BAKER'S chocolate. And since everything is assembled in a single bowl, cleanup couldn't be easier!

Since no BAKER'S recipe collection would be complete without the tried-and-true classics, we have also included a selection of BAKER'S all-time irresistible favorites—indulgent Wellesley Fudge Cake, sinfully-rich Chocolate Pecan Pie and our most popular German Sweet Chocolate Cake are only a few. Many have been updated to include shortcuts and baking tips to make these classics easier to prepare than ever before!

Whether an experienced baker or just a beginner, BAKER'S EASIEST-EVER CHOCOLATE RECIPES promises virtually foolproof results every time. Taste them for yourself!

What Makes ONE BOWL Recipes So Easy

The BAKER'S ONE BOWL method includes ways to cook and bake that save you time, effort and messy cleanups, yet assures delicious results!

 Look for this ONE BOWL Symbol throughout the book. It provides a quick way to identify which recipes require the use of a single bowl. Here are some of the ONE BOWL techniques that make cooking and baking with BAKER'S virtually foolproof and almost as easy as using a mix.

- **No more burning chocolate.** The BAKER'S method of microwaving chocolate squares with other ingredients from the recipe gives you a **no-watch, no-burn** way to melt chocolate.

- **No sifting flour.** Our recipes call for all-purpose flour—no fancy cake flour. And there's **no sifting at all.** (Just spoon flour lightly into a measuring cup and level off.)

- **No extra bowls.** Most of the recipes in this book have been designed to use a single bowl. We've kept the number of utensils and bowls to a minimum.

- **No complicated recipes to follow.** Our recipes have been developed with your busy schedule in mind. We wrote our recipes in clear, step-by-step language so you can follow them **quickly and easily.**

- **Microwave shortcuts.** Whenever possible, we show you how to use your microwave oven for shortcuts that save you time in preparing the recipe.

- **Time planners.** Every recipe has Preparation Time, Baking Time, Chill Time or Freezing Time listed, so you know exactly which recipe to pick for the amount of time you have to spend. Our preparation times start from the point when all ingredients have been assembled. It is a good practice to assemble all the ingredients you need before you begin.

- **No exotic ingredients.** Our recipes call for only those ingredients you can find at your local supermarket.

- **No unusual pans.** The pans called for in our recipes are ones our research tells us most people have in their kitchens. When there is a choice of pans, we tell you.

TIPS AND TECHNIQUES

Cooking and Baking Tips

It is important to follow the recipe exactly and measure ingredients carefully.
- use a glass "liquid" measuring cup to measure liquids and a set of "dry" measuring cups to measure dry ingredients
- always use **measuring** spoons

When a recipe tells you to beat, you may use an electric mixer or beat by hand vigorously with a wooden spoon.

Coconut and Baking Powder. When a recipe calls for coconut or baking powder, we recommend using BAKER'S ANGEL FLAKE Coconut and CALUMET Baking Powder.

Margarine or butter. We list the product first that will give the best results in the recipe. In a few recipes, we list butter first, because the flavor is desirable in the recipe; however, margarine will give a satisfactory result.

Use regular stick margarine or butter in all BAKER'S recipes. Soft, light or diet margarine may not produce the desired result.

Whipped topping. When a recipe calls for COOL WHIP Whipped Topping or whipped cream, be sure to refrigerate the finished recipe until serving time. Any leftovers should also be refrigerated.

Microwave ovens. Microwave ovens vary in wattage, and therefore cooking times can vary. These recipes were developed in 600 to 700 wattage ovens. Since microwaves vary in wattage, cooking times can vary. To make it easy for you, we say "or until margarine is melted" or "until mixture boils," so you can be assured that the recipe will turn out right.

HIGH ALTITUDE DIRECTIONS. Some recipes in this book have been adjusted for high altitude preparation. Call our toll-free number 9 a.m. to 4 p.m. (EST) weekdays (Continental U.S.) for information: **1-800-431-1001**

Chocolate Tips

When melting chocolate, remember:

1. We highly recommend using the microwave method for melting chocolate whenever possible. Chocolate scorches easily on top of the stove; use **very low** heat and a heavy saucepan.

2. Semi-sweet chocolate and GERMAN'S Sweet Chocolate will hold their shape and may not look melted until they are stirred. However, unsweetened chocolate will become somewhat liquid while melting.

3. When melting chocolate alone, use a completely dry container and stirring utensil. Even a tiny drop of moisture will cause the chocolate to stiffen. If this happens, add 1 teaspoon solid vegetable shortening (not butter or margarine) for each square of chocolate. Stir until smooth.

Storing Chocolate

Store chocolate in a cool, dry place, below 75°F., if possible. At higher temperatures, the cocoa butter melts and rises to the surface. When this happens, the chocolate develops a pale, gray color called "bloom." This condition does not affect the flavor or quality of the chocolate in any way. The original color will return when the chocolate is melted.

Chocolate Substitutions

Most recipes are so carefully developed and tested that you can be assured of successful results only if you follow the recipe exactly. Generally, it is best not to substitute a sweet or semi-sweet chocolate for an unsweetened chocolate and vice versa.

Melting Unsweetened and Semi-Sweet Chocolate—Microwave

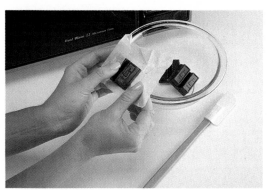

1. To melt BAKER'S Unsweetened or Semi-Sweet Chocolate, place unwrapped chocolate in microwavable dish.

2. For 1 square chocolate, microwave on HIGH 1 to 2 minutes or until almost melted, stirring after each minute. Remove from microwave. **Stir until completely melted.** Add 10 seconds for each additional square of chocolate.

Melting GERMAN'S Sweet Chocolate—Microwave

To melt BAKER'S GERMAN'S Sweet Chocolate, place unwrapped (4 ounce) bar chocolate, broken in half, in microwavable dish. Microwave on HIGH 1½ to 2 minutes or until almost melted, stirring after each minute. Remove from microwave. **Stir until completely melted.**

Melting Chocolate—Saucepan Preparation

Place chocolate, unwrapped, in heavy saucepan over **very low** heat, stirring constantly, until chocolate is just melted.

Melting Chocolate and Margarine—Saucepan Preparation

Heat chocolate and margarine* in heavy saucepan over **very low** heat, **stirring constantly,** until chocolate is just melted.

Melting Chocolate and Water—Saucepan Preparation

Heat chocolate and water* in heavy saucepan over **very low** heat, **stirring constantly,** until chocolate is melted and mixture is smooth.

How to Melt Caramels—Saucepan Preparation

Heat caramels and milk or cream* in heavy saucepan over very low heat, **stirring constantly.**

*Use amounts called for in recipe.

Try these finishing touches to make your recipes extra-special. Garnishes may be stored in a freezer in an airtight container for up to 6 months.

Grating Chocolate

Grate only 1 square of BAKER'S Semi-Sweet Chocolate or ½ package of BAKER'S GERMAN'S Sweet Chocolate at a time over large holes of hand grater. Sprinkle grated chocolate over cakes, pies and desserts.

Shaving Chocolate

Pull vegetable peeler across surface of 1 square of BAKER'S Semi-Sweet Chocolate or 3-square strip of BAKER'S GERMAN'S Sweet Chocolate. Sprinkle shaved chocolate on cakes, desserts or pies.

Chocolate Curls

1. Melt 4 squares BAKER'S Semi-Sweet Chocolate or 1 package (4 ounces) BAKER'S GERMAN'S Sweet Chocolate. Spread with spatula into very thin layer on cookie sheet. Refrigerate until firm, but still pliable, about 10 minutes.

2. To make curls, slip tip of straight-side metal spatula under chocolate. Push spatula firmly along cookie sheet, under chocolate, so chocolate curls as it is pushed. (If chocolate is too firm to curl, let stand a few minutes at room temperature; refrigerate again if it becomes too soft.) Carefully pick up each chocolate curl by inserting wooden pick in center. Lift onto waxed paper-lined cookie sheet. Refrigerate until firm, about 15 minutes. Arrange on desserts. (Lift with wooden pick to prevent breakage or melting.) Refrigerate until ready to use.

Chocolate Drizzle

1. Place 1 square BAKER'S Semi-Sweet Chocolate in a zipper-style plastic sandwich bag. Close bag tightly. Microwave on HIGH about 1 minute or until chocolate is melted. Fold down top of bag tightly and snip a tiny piece off 1 corner (about ⅛ inch).

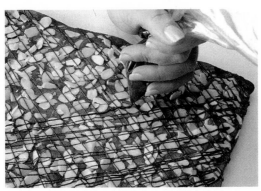

2. Holding top of bag tightly, drizzle chocolate through opening over brownies, cookies, cakes or desserts.

Chocolate Doodles

1. Melt chocolate, following directions for Chocolate Drizzle. Drizzle chocolate into free-form designs onto waxed paper-lined cookie sheet. (Or draw design on paper, cover with waxed paper and drizzle chocolate over design.) Refrigerate until firm, about 30 minutes.

2. Use as garnish for cakes and other desserts.

Chocolate Cups

1. Melt 1 package (8 ounces) BAKER'S Semi-Sweet Chocolate. Spread chocolate over the inside of 10 aluminum foil baking cups or double-layered paper baking cups, using a spoon or brush to completely coat all surfaces with a layer of chocolate. Set cups in muffin pans. Refrigerate until firm, about 1 hour. (Small bon bon cups may also be used.)

2. Holding cup in one hand, carefully peel off paper or aluminum foil. Refrigerate until ready to use.

Chocolate Leaves

1. Melt 4 squares BAKER'S Semi-Sweet Chocolate or 1 package (4 ounces) BAKER'S GERMAN'S Sweet Chocolate. Using a narrow spatula or brush, spread chocolate over undersides of washed and dried non-toxic leaves (such as lemon, rose or grape ivy) to form a smooth, thick coating. Avoid spreading chocolate to very edge of leaf to prevent chocolate from running onto top side of leaf. Place leaves on waxed paper-lined tray. Refrigerate until chocolate is firm, about 15 minutes.

2. Carefully peel away leaves from chocolate. Refrigerate chocolate leaves until ready to use.

Chocolate Cutouts

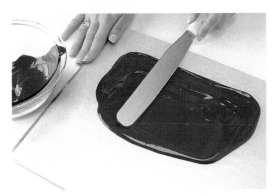

1. Melt 4 squares BAKER'S Semi-Sweet Chocolate or 1 package (4 ounces)BAKER'S GERMAN'S Sweet Chocolate. Pour onto waxed paper-lined cookie sheet; spread to ⅛-inch thickness with spatula. Refrigerate until firm, about 15 minutes.

2. Cut out shapes with cookie cutters.

3. Immediately lift shapes carefully from waxed paper with spatula or knife. Refrigerate until ready to use.

Dipping Fruit and Nuts

Melt BAKER'S Semi-Sweet Chocolate or BAKER'S GERMAN'S Sweet Chocolate. Dip fruit or nuts into melted chocolate, covering at least half; let excess chocolate drip off. Arrange on waxed paper-lined tray. Let stand or refrigerate until chocolate is firm. **Do not freeze.**

Chopping Chocolate
Using a large knife, cut chocolate on cutting board into chunks.

Toasting Nuts
Spread nuts in a shallow pan. Toast at 400°F., stirring frequently, 8 to 10 minutes or until golden brown.

Toasting Coconut
Spread coconut in a shallow pan. Toast at 350°F., stirring frequently, 7 to 12 minutes or until lightly browned. Or, toast in microwave oven on HIGH, 5 minutes for 1⅓ cups coconut, stirring several times.

BROWNIES

ONE BOWL
Brownies

ONE BOWL RECIPE

4 squares BAKER'S Unsweetened
    Chocolate
¾ cup (1½ sticks) margarine or
    butter
2 cups sugar
3 eggs
1 teaspoon vanilla
1 cup all-purpose flour
1 cup chopped nuts (optional)

HEAT oven to 350°F.

MICROWAVE chocolate and margarine in large microwavable bowl on HIGH 2 minutes or until margarine is melted. **Stir until chocolate is completely melted.**

STIR sugar into melted chocolate mixture. Mix in eggs and vanilla until well blended. Stir in flour and nuts. Spread in greased 13×9-inch pan.

BAKE for 30 to 35 minutes or until toothpick inserted into center comes out with fudgy crumbs. **Do not overbake.** Cool in pan; cut into squares.

Makes about 24 brownies

Prep time: 10 minutes
Baking time: 30 to 35 minutes

Tips
• For cakelike brownies, stir in ½ cup milk with eggs and vanilla. Increase flour to 1½ cups.
• When using a glass baking dish, reduce oven temperature to 325°F.

Peanut Butter Swirl Brownies

Creamy peanut butter and rich chocolate make a super flavor combination.

PREPARE ONE BOWL Brownie batter (page 531) as directed, reserving 1 tablespoon of the margarine and 2 tablespoons of the sugar. Add reserved ingredients to ⅔ cup peanut butter; mix well.

PLACE spoonfuls of peanut butter mixture over brownie batter. Swirl with knife to marbleize. Bake at 350°F for 30 to 35 minutes or until toothpick inserted into center comes out with fudgy crumbs. Cool in pan; cut into squares.

Makes about 24 brownies

Prep time: 15 minutes
Baking time: 30 to 35 minutes

Tip
• For more peanut butter flavor, use 1 cup peanut butter.

Rocky Road Brownies

Kids will love these quick and easy brownies!

PREPARE ONE BOWL Brownies (page 531) as directed. Bake at 350°F for 30 minutes.

SPRINKLE 2 cups KRAFT Miniature Marshmallows, 1 cup BAKER'S Semi-Sweet Real Chocolate Chips and 1 cup chopped nuts over brownies immediately. Continue baking 3 to 5 minutes or until topping begins to melt together. Cool in pan; cut into squares.

Makes about 24 brownies

Prep time: 15 minutes
Baking time: 35 minutes

German Sweet Chocolate Brownies

> 1 package (4 ounces) BAKER'S GERMAN'S Sweet Chocolate
> ¼ cup (½ stick) margarine or butter
> ¾ cup sugar
> 2 eggs
> 1 teaspoon vanilla
> ½ cup all-purpose flour
> ½ cup chopped nuts

HEAT oven to 350°F.

MICROWAVE chocolate and margarine in large microwavable bowl on HIGH 2 minutes or until margarine is melted. **Stir until chocolate is completely melted.**

STIR sugar into melted chocolate mixture. Mix in eggs and vanilla until well blended. Stir in flour and nuts. Spread in greased 8-inch square pan.

BAKE for 25 minutes or until toothpick inserted into center comes out with fudgy crumbs. **Do not overbake.** Cool in pan; cut into squares.

Makes about 16 brownies

Prep time: 10 minutes
Baking time: 25 minutes

Coconut-Pecan Brownies

PREPARE German Sweet Chocolate Brownie batter as directed. Pour into pan.

MIX 1⅓ cups BAKER'S ANGEL FLAKE Coconut, ½ cup chopped pecans and ¼ cup firmly packed brown sugar in same bowl. Add ¼ cup milk; toss to coat well. Spoon over brownie batter. Bake at 350°F for 40 minutes. Cool in pan; cut into squares.

Top to bottom: Peanut Butter Swirl Brownies (page 532); Rocky Road Brownies (page 532)

German Sweet Chocolate Cream Cheese Brownies

BROWNIE LAYER:
  1 package (4 ounces) BAKER'S
    GERMAN'S Sweet Chocolate
¼ cup (½ stick) margarine or butter
¾ cup sugar
  2 eggs
  1 teaspoon vanilla
½ cup all-purpose flour
½ cup chopped nuts

CREAM CHEESE LAYER:
  4 ounces PHILADELPHIA BRAND
    Cream Cheese, softened
¼ cup sugar
  1 egg
  1 tablespoon all-purpose flour

HEAT oven to 350°F.

MICROWAVE chocolate and margarine in large microwavable bowl on HIGH 2 minutes or until margarine is melted. **Stir until chocolate is completely melted.**

STIR ¾ cup sugar into melted chocolate mixture. Mix in 2 eggs and vanilla until well blended. Stir in ½ cup flour and nuts. Spread in greased 8-inch square pan.

MIX cream cheese, ¼ cup sugar, 1 egg and 1 tablespoon flour in same bowl until smooth. Place spoonfuls over brownie batter. Swirl with knife to marbleize.

BAKE for 35 minutes or until toothpick inserted into center comes out with fudgy crumbs. **Do not overbake.** Cool in pan; cut into squares.

Makes about 16 brownies

Prep time: 20 minutes
Baking time: 35 minutes

Chocolate Brownie Pie

  1 package (4 ounces) BAKER'S
    GERMAN'S Sweet Chocolate
¼ cup (½ stick) margarine or butter
¾ cup sugar
  2 eggs
  1 teaspoon vanilla
½ cup all-purpose flour
½ cup chopped nuts
    Ice cream, any flavor
    Regal Chocolate Sauce (page 574)
    Strawberries (optional)

HEAT oven to 350°F.

MICROWAVE chocolate and margarine in large microwavable bowl on HIGH 2 minutes or until margarine is melted. **Stir until chocolate is completely melted.**

STIR sugar into melted chocolate mixture. Mix in eggs and vanilla until well blended. Stir in flour and nuts. Spread in greased and floured 9-inch pie plate.

BAKE for 25 minutes or until toothpick inserted into center comes out with fudgy crumbs. **Do not overbake.** Cool in pie plate.

SERVE with ice cream and Regal Chocolate Sauce. Garnish with strawberries, if desired.

Makes 8 servings

Prep time: 20 minutes
Baking time: 25 minutes

*Top to bottom: German Sweet Chocolate Cream Cheese Brownies (page 534);
Coconut-Pecan Brownies (page 532); Chocolate Brownie Pie (page 534)*

Peanut-Layered Brownies

BROWNIE LAYER:
  4 squares BAKER'S Unsweetened
    Chocolate
  ¾ cup (1½ sticks) margarine or
    butter
  2 cups granulated sugar
  3 eggs
  1 teaspoon vanilla
  1 cup all-purpose flour
  1 cup chopped peanuts

PEANUT BUTTER LAYER:
  1 cup peanut butter
  ½ cup powdered sugar
  1 teaspoon vanilla

GLAZE:
  4 squares BAKER'S Semi-Sweet
    Chocolate
  ¼ cup (½ stick) margarine or butter

HEAT oven to 350°F.

MICROWAVE unsweetened chocolate and ¾ cup margarine in large microwavable bowl on HIGH 2 minutes or until margarine is melted. **Stir until chocolate is completely melted.**

STIR granulated sugar into melted chocolate mixture. Mix in eggs and 1 teaspoon vanilla until well blended. Stir in flour and peanuts. Spread in greased 13×9-inch pan.

BAKE for 30 to 35 minutes or until toothpick inserted into center comes out with fudgy crumbs. **Do not overbake.** Cool in pan.

MIX peanut butter, powdered sugar and 1 teaspoon vanilla in separate bowl until well blended and smooth. Spread over brownies.

MICROWAVE semi-sweet chocolate and ¼ cup margarine in small microwavable bowl on HIGH 2 minutes or until margarine is melted. **Stir until chocolate is completely melted.** Spread over peanut butter layer. Cool until set. Cut into squares.

Makes about 24 brownies

Prep time: 20 minutes
Baking time: 30 to 35 minutes

Almond Macaroon Brownies

ONE BOWL RECIPE

BROWNIE LAYER:
  6 squares BAKER'S Semi-Sweet
    Chocolate
  ½ cup (1 stick) margarine or butter
  ⅔ cup sugar
  2 eggs
  1 teaspoon vanilla
  1 cup all-purpose flour
  ⅔ cup toasted chopped almonds

CREAM CHEESE TOPPING:
  4 ounces PHILADELPHIA BRAND
    Cream Cheese, softened
  ⅓ cup sugar
  1 egg
  1 tablespoon all-purpose flour
  1 cup BAKER'S ANGEL FLAKE
    Coconut
    Whole almonds (optional)
  1 square BAKER'S Semi-Sweet
    Chocolate, melted (page 525)
    (optional)

HEAT oven to 350°F.

MICROWAVE 6 squares chocolate and margarine in large microwavable bowl on HIGH 2 minutes or until margarine is melted. **Stir until chocolate is completely melted.**

STIR ⅔ cup sugar into melted chocolate mixture. Mix in 2 eggs and vanilla until well blended. Stir in 1 cup flour and ⅓ cup of the chopped almonds. Spread in greased 8-inch square pan.

MIX cream cheese, ⅓ cup sugar, 1 egg and 1 tablespoon flour in same bowl until smooth. Stir in the remaining ⅓ cup chopped almonds and the coconut. Spread over brownie batter. Garnish with whole almonds, if desired.

BAKE for 35 minutes or until toothpick inserted into center comes out with fudgy crumbs. **Do not overbake.** Cool in pan. Drizzle with 1 square melted chocolate, if desired.

Makes about 16 brownies

Prep time: 20 minutes
Baking time: 35 minutes

Top to bottom: Peanut-Layered Brownies (page 536); Almond Macaroon Brownies (page 536); Walnut Crunch Brownies (page 538)

Walnut Crunch Brownies

ONE BOWL RECIPE

BROWNIE LAYER:
 4 squares BAKER'S Unsweetened
  Chocolate
 ¾ cup (1½ sticks) margarine or
  butter
 2 cups granulated sugar
 4 eggs
 1 teaspoon vanilla
 1 cup all-purpose flour

WALNUT TOPPING:
 ¼ cup (½ stick) margarine or butter
 ¾ cup firmly packed brown sugar
 2 eggs
 2 tablespoons all-purpose flour
 1 teaspoon vanilla
 4 cups chopped walnuts

HEAT oven to 350°F.

MICROWAVE chocolate and ¾ cup margarine in large microwavable bowl on HIGH 2 minutes or until margarine is melted. **Stir until chocolate is completely melted.**

STIR granulated sugar into melted chocolate mixture. Mix in 4 eggs and 1 teaspoon vanilla until well blended. Stir in 1 cup flour. Spread in greased 13×9-inch pan.

MICROWAVE ¼ cup margarine and brown sugar in same bowl on HIGH 1 minute or until margarine is melted. Stir in 2 eggs, 2 tablespoons flour and 1 teaspoon vanilla until completely mixed. Stir in walnuts. Spread mixture evenly over brownie batter.

BAKE for 45 minutes or until toothpick inserted into center comes out with fudgy crumbs. **Do not overbake.** Cool in pan; cut into squares.

     Makes about 24 brownies

Prep time: 20 minutes
Baking time: 45 minutes

Saucepan preparation for topping: Melt margarine in 1½-quart saucepan over low heat. Stir in ¾ cup brown sugar; cook 1 minute. Continue as above.

Caramel-Layered Brownies

ONE BOWL RECIPE

 4 squares BAKER'S Unsweetened
  Chocolate
 ¾ cup (1½ sticks) margarine or
  butter
 2 cups sugar
 3 eggs
 1 teaspoon vanilla
 1 cup all-purpose flour
 1 cup BAKER'S Semi-Sweet Real
  Chocolate Chips
1½ cups chopped nuts
 1 package (14 ounces) KRAFT
  Caramels
⅓ cup evaporated milk

HEAT oven to 350°F.

MICROWAVE chocolate and margarine in large microwavable bowl on HIGH 2 minutes or until margarine is melted. **Stir until chocolate is completely melted.**

STIR sugar into melted chocolate mixture. Mix in eggs and vanilla until well blended. Stir in flour. Remove 1 cup of batter; set aside. Spread remaining batter in greased 13×9-inch pan. Sprinkle with chips and 1 cup of the nuts.

MICROWAVE caramels and milk in same bowl on HIGH 4 minutes, stirring after 2 minutes. Stir until caramels are completely melted and smooth. Spoon over chips and nuts, spreading to edges of pan. Gently spread reserved batter over caramel mixture. Sprinkle with the remaining ½ cup nuts.

BAKE for 40 minutes or until toothpick inserted into center comes out with fudgy crumbs. **Do not overbake.** Cool in pan; cut into squares.

     Makes about 24 brownies

Prep time: 20 minutes
Baking time: 40 minutes

Caramel-Layered Brownie (page 538)

COOKIES AND BARS

BAKER'S Chocolate Chip Cookies

ONE BOWL RECIPE

1 cup (2 sticks) margarine or butter, softened
¾ cup firmly packed brown sugar
¾ cup granulated sugar
1 teaspoon vanilla
2 eggs
2¼ cups all-purpose flour
1 teaspoon baking soda
¼ teaspoon salt
1 package (12 ounces) BAKER'S Semi-Sweet Real Chocolate Chips
1 cup chopped nuts (optional)

HEAT oven to 375°F.

BEAT margarine, sugars, vanilla and eggs until light and fluffy. Mix in flour, baking soda and salt. Stir in chips and nuts. Drop by rounded teaspoonfuls, 2 inches apart, onto ungreased cookie sheets.

BAKE for 8 to 10 minutes or until golden brown. Remove from cookie sheets to cool on wire racks.

Makes about 6 dozen cookies

Prep time: 15 minutes
Baking time: 8 to 10 minutes

Chocolate Sugar Cookies

3 squares BAKER'S Unsweetened
   Chocolate
1 cup (2 sticks) margarine or butter
1 cup sugar
1 egg
1 teaspoon vanilla
2 cups all-purpose flour
1 teaspoon baking soda
¼ teaspoon salt
   Additional sugar

MICROWAVE chocolate and margarine in large microwavable bowl on HIGH 2 minutes or until margarine is melted. **Stir until chocolate is completely melted.**

STIR 1 cup sugar into melted chocolate mixture until well blended. Stir in egg and vanilla until completely mixed. Mix in flour, baking soda and salt. Refrigerate 30 minutes.

HEAT oven to 375°F. Shape dough into 1-inch balls; roll in additional sugar. Place on ungreased cookie sheets. (If a flatter, crisper cookie is desired, flatten ball with bottom of drinking glass.)

BAKE for 8 to 10 minutes or until set. Remove from cookie sheets to cool on wire racks.

Makes about 3½ dozen cookies

Prep time: 15 minutes
Chill time: 30 minutes
Baking time: 8 to 10 minutes

Jam-Filled Chocolate Sugar Cookies

PREPARE Chocolate Sugar Cookie dough as directed; roll in finely chopped nuts in place of sugar. Make indentation in each ball; fill center with your favorite jam. Bake as directed.

Chocolate-Caramel Sugar Cookies

PREPARE Chocolate Sugar Cookie dough as directed. Roll in finely chopped nuts in place of sugar. Make indentation in each ball; bake as directed. Microwave 1 package (14 ounces) KRAFT Caramels with 2 tablespoons milk in microwavable bowl on HIGH 3 minutes or until melted, stirring after 2 minutes. Fill centers of cookies with caramel mixture. Drizzle with melted BAKER'S Semi-Sweet Chocolate (page 527).

Quick Chocolate Macaroons

1 square BAKER'S Unsweetened
   Chocolate
1⅓ cups BAKER'S ANGEL FLAKE
   Coconut
⅓ cup sweetened condensed milk
½ teaspoon vanilla

HEAT oven to 350°F.

MELT chocolate in large microwavable bowl on HIGH 1 to 2 minutes or until almost melted, stirring after each minute. **Stir until chocolate is completely melted.** Stir in coconut, condensed milk and vanilla. Drop from teaspoonfuls, 1 inch apart, onto well-greased cookie sheets.

BAKE for 10 to 12 minutes or until set. Immediately remove from cookie sheets to cool on wire racks.

Makes about 2 dozen cookies

Prep time: 10 minutes
Baking time: 10 to 12 minutes

Top to bottom: Chocolate Sugar Cookies (page 542); Jam-Filled Chocolate Sugar Cookies (page 542); Chocolate-Caramel Sugar Cookies (page 542)

Banana Split Bars

⅓ cup margarine or butter, softened
1 cup sugar
1 egg
1 banana, mashed
½ teaspoon vanilla
1¼ cups all-purpose flour
1 teaspoon CALUMET Baking Powder
¼ teaspoon salt
⅓ cup chopped nuts
2 cups KRAFT Miniature Marshmallows
1 cup BAKER'S Semi-Sweet Real Chocolate Chips
⅓ cup maraschino cherries, drained and quartered

HEAT oven to 350°F.

BEAT margarine and sugar until light and fluffy. Add egg, banana and vanilla; mix well. Mix in flour, baking powder and salt. Stir in nuts. Pour into greased 13×9-inch pan.

BAKE for 20 minutes. Remove from oven. Sprinkle with marshmallows, chips and cherries. Bake 10 to 15 minutes longer or until toothpick inserted in center comes out clean. Cool in pan; cut into bars.

Makes about 24 bars

Prep time: 20 minutes
Baking time: 30 to 35 minutes

Chocolate Peanut Butter Bars

2 cups peanut butter
1 cup sugar
2 eggs
1 package (8 ounces) BAKER'S Semi-Sweet Chocolate
1 cup chopped peanuts

HEAT oven to 350°F.

BEAT peanut butter, sugar and eggs in large bowl until light and fluffy. Reserve 1 cup peanut butter mixture; set aside.

MELT 4 squares of the chocolate (page 525). Add to peanut butter mixture in bowl; mix well. Press into ungreased 13×9-inch pan. Top with reserved peanut butter mixture.

BAKE for 30 minutes or until edges are lightly browned. Melt the remaining 4 squares chocolate; spread evenly over entire surface. Sprinkle with peanuts. Cool in pan until chocolate is set. Cut into bars.

Makes about 24 bars

Prep time: 15 minutes
Baking time: 30 minutes

Layered Chocolate Cheese Bars

¼ cup (½ stick) margarine or butter
1½ cups graham cracker crumbs
¾ cup sugar
1 package (4 ounces) BAKER'S GERMAN'S Sweet Chocolate
1 package (8 ounces) PHILADELPHIA BRAND Cream Cheese, softened
1 egg
1 cup BAKER'S ANGEL FLAKE Coconut
1 cup chopped nuts

HEAT oven to 350°F.

MELT margarine in oven in 13×9-inch pan. Add graham cracker crumbs and ¼ cup of the sugar; mix well. Press into pan. Bake for 10 minutes.

MELT chocolate (page 525). Stir in the remaining ½ cup sugar, the cream cheese and egg. Spread over crust. Sprinkle with coconut and nuts; press lightly.

BAKE for 30 minutes. Cool; cut into bars.

Makes about 24 bars

Prep time: 20 minutes
Baking time: 40 minutes

Top plate (clockwise from top): Layered Chocolate Cheese Bars (page 544);
Banana Split Bars (page 544); Chocolate Peanut Butter Bars (page 544)

545

Double Chocolate Chunk Cookies

4 squares BAKER'S Semi-Sweet
    Chocolate
½ cup (1 stick) margarine or butter,
    slightly softened
½ cup granulated sugar
¼ cup firmly packed brown sugar
1 egg
1 teaspoon vanilla
1 cup all-purpose flour
½ teaspoon CALUMET Baking
    Powder
¼ teaspoon salt
¾ cup chopped walnuts (optional)
4 squares BAKER'S Semi-Sweet
    Chocolate

MELT 1 square chocolate (page 525); set aside. Cut 3 squares chocolate into large (½-inch) chunks; set aside.

BEAT margarine, sugars, egg and vanilla until light and fluffy. Stir in 1 square melted chocolate. Mix in flour, baking powder and salt. Stir in chocolate chunks and walnuts. Refrigerate 30 minutes.

HEAT oven to 375°F. Drop dough by heaping tablespoonfuls, about 2 inches apart, onto greased cookie sheets. Bake for 8 minutes or until lightly browned. Cool 5 minutes on cookie sheets. Remove and finish cooling on wire racks.

MELT 4 squares chocolate (page 525). Dip ½ of each cookie into melted chocolate. Let stand on waxed paper until chocolate is firm.

Makes about 2 dozen cookies

Prep time: 30 minutes
Chill time: 30 minutes
Baking time: 8 minutes

Double Chocolate Chunk Mocha Cookies

PREPARE Double Chocolate Chunk Cookies as directed, adding 2 tablespoons instant coffee to the margarine mixture before beating.

Chocolate Fantasies

A chocoholic's dream cookie.

4 squares BAKER'S Semi-Sweet
    Chocolate
4 squares BAKER'S Unsweetened
    Chocolate
½ cup (1 stick) margarine or butter
2 eggs
1 cup sugar
¼ cup all-purpose flour
1 cup BAKER'S Semi-Sweet Real
    Chocolate Chips
1 cup finely chopped pecans

MICROWAVE chocolate squares and margarine in large microwavable bowl on HIGH 3 minutes, stirring after 2 minutes. **Stir until chocolate is completely melted.**

BEAT eggs in large bowl until thick and light in color. Gradually beat in sugar. Stir in melted chocolate mixture. Mix in flour. Stir in chips and pecans. Refrigerate 30 minutes.

HEAT oven to 350°F. Shape dough into 1½-inch balls. Place 2 inches apart on ungreased cookie sheets.

BAKE on middle rack of oven for 12 to 15 minutes or until set. Cool 5 minutes on cookie sheets. Remove and finish cooling on wire racks.

Makes about 2½ dozen cookies

Prep time: 15 minutes
Chill time: 30 minutes
Baking time: 12 to 15 minutes

Double Chocolate Chunk Cookies (page 546) 547

Chocolate Lace Cornucopias

ONE BOWL
RECIPE

These beautiful rolled cookies will make an impressive ending to any meal.

½ cup firmly packed brown sugar
½ cup corn syrup
¼ cup (½ stick) margarine or butter
4 squares BAKER'S Semi-Sweet
    Chocolate
1 cup all-purpose flour
1 cup finely chopped nuts
    Whipped cream or COOL WHIP
    Whipped Topping, thawed

HEAT oven to 350°F.

MICROWAVE sugar, corn syrup and margarine in large microwavable bowl on HIGH 2 minutes or until boiling. Stir in chocolate until completely melted. Gradually stir in flour and nuts until well blended.

DROP by level tablespoonfuls, 4 inches apart, onto foil-covered cookie sheets.

BAKE for 10 minutes. Lift foil and cookies onto wire rack. Cool on wire rack 3 to 4 minutes or until cookies can be easily peeled off foil. Remove foil; finish cooling cookies on wire rack that has been covered with paper towels.

PLACE several cookies, lacy side down, on foil-lined cookie sheet. Heat at 350° for 2 to 3 minutes or until slightly softened. Remove from foil, one at a time, and roll lacy side out to form cones. Cool completely. Just before serving, fill with whipped cream.

Makes about 30 cornucopias

Prep time: 20 minutes
Baking time: 12 to 13 minutes

Saucepan preparation: Mix sugar, corn syrup and margarine in 2-quart saucepan. Bring to boil over medium heat, stirring constantly. Remove from heat; stir in chocolate until melted. Continue as above.

Chocolate Date Bars

4 squares BAKER'S Semi-Sweet
    Chocolate
2 cups chopped dates
¾ cup water
⅓ cup corn syrup
¾ cup (1½ sticks) margarine or
    butter, slightly softened
1 cup firmly packed brown sugar
1¾ cups all-purpose flour
½ teaspoon baking soda
¼ teaspoon salt
1½ cups quick oats

MICROWAVE chocolate, dates, water and corn syrup in large microwavable bowl on HIGH 3 minutes; stir. Microwave 2 minutes longer or until thickened. Cool.

HEAT oven to 400°F. Beat margarine and sugar in separate bowl. Mix in flour, baking soda and salt. Stir in oats. Press ½ the mixture evenly into greased 13×9-inch pan. Spread with chocolate mixture; top with the remaining oat mixture.

BAKE for 25 minutes or until topping is golden brown. Cool in pan; cut into bars.

Makes about 35 bars

Prep time: 30 minutes
Baking time: 25 minutes

Saucepan preparation: Mix chocolate, dates, water and corn syrup in 1-quart saucepan; stir over low heat until thickened. Continue as above.

Chocolate Lace Cornucopias (page 548)

CAKES AND BREADS

ONE BOWL
Chocolate Cake

ONE BOWL RECIPE

6 squares BAKER'S Semi-Sweet
    Chocolate
¾ cup (1½ sticks) margarine or
    butter
1½ cups sugar
  3 eggs
  2 teaspoons vanilla
2½ cups all-purpose flour
  1 teaspoon baking soda
  ¼ teaspoon salt
1½ cups water

HEAT oven to 350°F.

MICROWAVE chocolate and margarine in large microwavable bowl on HIGH 2 minutes or until margarine is melted. **Stir until chocolate is completely melted.**

STIR sugar into melted chocolate mixture until well blended. Beat in eggs, one at a time, with electric mixer until completely mixed. Add vanilla. Add ½ cup of the flour, the baking soda and salt; mix well. Beat in the remaining 2 cups flour alternately with water until smooth. Pour into 2 greased and floured 9-inch layer pans.

BAKE for 35 minutes or until toothpick inserted into center comes out clean. Cool in pans 10 minutes. Remove from pans to cool on wire racks. Fill and frost as desired.

Makes 12 servings

Prep time: 15 minutes
Baking time: 35 minutes

Black Forest Cake (as shown): Mix 1 can (21 ounces) cherry pie filling, drained, and ¼ cup cherry liqueur (or ½ teaspoon almond extract). Spoon evenly over 1 cake layer. Spread 1½ cups thawed COOL WHIP Whipped Topping over cherries; top with second cake layer. Frost top and sides with additional 2 cups whipped topping. Garnish as desired. Refrigerate.

Semi-Sweet Chocolate Glaze

ONE BOWL RECIPE

3 squares BAKER'S Semi-Sweet
   Chocolate
3 tablespoons water
1 tablespoon margarine or butter
1 cup powdered sugar
½ teaspoon vanilla

MICROWAVE chocolate, water and margarine in large microwavable bowl on HIGH 1 to 2 minutes or until chocolate is almost melted, stirring once. **Stir until chocolate is completely melted.**

STIR in sugar and vanilla until smooth. For thinner glaze, add ½ to 1 teaspoon additional water.

Makes about ¾ cup

Prep time: 10 minutes

Chocolate Chunk Banana Bread

ONE BOWL RECIPE

2 eggs, lightly beaten
1 cup mashed ripe bananas (about
   3 medium bananas)
⅓ cup vegetable oil
¼ cup milk
2 cups all-purpose flour
1 cup sugar
2 teaspoons CALUMET Baking
   Powder
¼ teaspoon salt
1 package (4 ounces) BAKER'S
   GERMAN'S Sweet Chocolate,
   coarsely chopped
½ cup chopped nuts

HEAT oven to 350°F.

STIR eggs, bananas, oil and milk until well blended. Add flour, sugar, baking powder and salt; stir until just moistened. Stir in chocolate and nuts. Pour into greased 9×5-inch loaf pan.

BAKE for 55 minutes or until toothpick inserted into center comes out clean. Cool in pan 10 minutes. Remove from pan to cool on wire rack.

Makes 1 loaf

Prep time: 20 minutes
Baking time: 55 minutes

Tip
• For easier slicing, wrap bread and store overnight.

Chocolate Chunk Sour Cream Muffins

1½ cups all-purpose flour
½ cup sugar
1½ teaspoons CALUMET Baking
   Powder
½ teaspoon cinnamon
¼ teaspoon salt
2 eggs, lightly beaten
½ cup milk
½ cup sour cream or plain yogurt
¼ cup (½ stick) margarine, melted
1 teaspoon vanilla
1 package (4 ounces) BAKER'S
   GERMAN'S Sweet Chocolate,
   chopped

HEAT oven to 375°F.

MIX flour, sugar, baking powder, cinnamon and salt; set aside. Stir eggs, milk, sour cream, margarine and vanilla in large bowl until well blended. Add flour mixture; stir until just moistened. Stir in chocolate.

FILL 12 paper- or foil-lined muffin cups ⅔ full with batter.

BAKE for 30 minutes or until toothpick inserted into center comes out clean. Remove from pan to cool on wire rack.

Makes 12 muffins

Prep time: 15 minutes
Baking time: 30 minutes

Top left to bottom right: Chocolate Chunk Sour Cream Muffins (page 552);
Chocolate Chunk Banana Bread (page 552)

Easy Chocolate Cheesecake

This recipe gives you the richness of chocolate and the indulgence of cheesecake in one fabulous dessert.

CRUST:
1¾ cups chocolate cookie or graham
   cracker crumbs
2 tablespoons sugar
⅓ cup margarine or butter, melted

FILLING:
2 packages (4 ounces each) BAKER'S
   GERMAN'S Sweet Chocolate
2 eggs
⅔ cup corn syrup
⅓ cup heavy cream
1½ teaspoons vanilla
2 packages (8 ounces each)
   PHILADELPHIA BRAND Cream
   Cheese, cubed and softened

HEAT oven to 325°F.

COMBINE cookie crumbs, sugar and margarine in 9-inch pie plate or 9-inch springform pan until well mixed. Press into pie plate or onto bottom and 1¼ inches up sides of springform pan.

MICROWAVE 1½ packages of the chocolate in microwavable bowl on HIGh 1½ to 2 minutes or until almost helted, stirring after 1 minute. **Stir until completely melted.**

BLEND eggs, corn syrup, cream and vanilla ∞ electric blender until smooth. With blender running, gradually add cream cheese, blending until smooth. Blend in melted chocolate. Pour into crust.

BAKE for 50 to 55 minutes or until firm. Cool on wire rack. Cover; refrigerate. Just before serving, melt the remaining ½ package chocolate and drizzle over top (page 527).

Makes 8 servings

Prep time: 25 minutes
Baking time: 50 to 55 minutes

2 eggs
6 squares BAKER'S Semi-Sweet
   Chocolate, melted (page 525)
   COOL WHIP Whipped Topping,
   thawed (optional)
   Chocolate Doodles (page 527)
   (optional)

HEAT oven to 350°F.

COMBINE crumbs and margarine in 9-inch springform pan until well mixed. Press onto bottom and 1¼ inches up sides of pan. Bake for 10 minutes.

MICROWAVE caramels and milk in large microwavable bowl on HIGH 1½ minutes. Stir; microwave 1 minute longer. Stir until caramels are completely melted and smooth. Pour into crust. Top with pecans.

BEAT cream cheese, sugar and vanilla until well blended. Add eggs; beat wellMix in chocolate; pour over pecans.

BAKE for 40 minutes or until firm. Cool on wire rack. Cover; refrigerate. Garnish with whipped topping and Chocolate Doodles, if desired.

Makes 12 servings

Prep time: 30 minutes
Baking time: 40 minutes

Easy Chocolate Cheesecake (page 554)

1 cup buttermilk or sour milk*
2 teaspoons vanilla
1 cup finely chopped nuts
   Powdered sugar (optional)
   Chopped nuts (optional)

HEAT oven to 350°F.

MIX flour, baking soda and salt; set aside. Beat margarine and sugar in large bowl until light and fluffy. Add eggs, one at a time, beating well after each addition. Stir in chocolate.

ADD flour mixture alternately with buttermilk, beating after each addition until smooth. Mix in vanilla and 1 cup nuts. Pour into 5 greased and floured 5×3-inch loaf pans.

BAKE about 50 minutes or until toothpick inserted into centers comes out clean. Cool in pans 10 minutes. Remove from pans to cool on wire racks. Sprinkle with powdered sugar; garnish with chopped nuts, if desired.

Makes 5 loaves

Prep time: 30 minutes
Baking time: 50 minutes

*To make sour milk, add 1 tablespoon vinegar to 1 cup milk; let stand 5 minutes.

Tip
• Loaves may also be baked in 2 (9×5-inch) loaf pans. Bake 1 hour.

¼ teaspoon salt
1 cup (½ pint) sour cream or plain
   yogurt
1 teaspoon baking soda
½ cup (1 stick) margarine or butter,
   softened
1 cup sugar
2 eggs
½ teaspoon vanilla

HEAT oven to 350°F.

MIX chocolate, nuts, ¼ cup sugar and cinnamon; set aside. Mix flour, baking powder and salt; set aside. Combine sour cream and baking soda; set aside.

BEAT margarine and 1 cup sugar in large bowl until light and fluffy. Add eggs, one at a time, beating well after each addition. Add vanilla. Add flour mixture alternately with sour cream mixture, beginning and ending with flour mixture. Spoon ½ the batter into greased 9-inch square pan. Top with ½ the chocolate-nut mixture, spreading carefully with spatula. Repeat layers.

BAKE for 30 to 35 minutes or until cake begins to pull away from sides of pan. Cool in pan; cut into squares.

Makes 9 servings

Prep time: 30 minutes
Baking time: 30 to 35 minutes

*Top to bottom: Chocolate Nut Loaf (page 556); Chocolate Chunk
Coffee Cake (page 556)*

Chocolate Strawberry Shortcake

2 pints strawberries, hulled and cut in half
2 tablespoons sugar
1 teaspoon vanilla
2 (9-inch) layers ONE BOWL Chocolate Cake (page 551)
Semi-Sweet Chocolate Glaze (page 552)
3½ cups (8 ounces) COOL WHIP Whipped Topping, thawed
Chocolate-dipped strawberries (page 529) (optional)

MIX strawberries, sugar and vanilla. Spoon ½ of the strawberries on 1 cake layer. Drizzle with ½ the chocolate glaze; top with ½ the whipped topping. Repeat layers. Garnish with chocolate-dipped strawberries, if desired. Refrigerate.

Makes 12 servings

Prep time: 15 minutes

Wellesley Fudge Cake

This rich, chocolate cake frosted with Easy Fudge Frosting will enhance any special occasion.

4 squares BAKER'S Unsweetened Chocolate
1¾ cups sugar
½ cup water
1⅔ cups all-purpose flour
1 teaspoon baking soda
¼ teaspoon salt
½ cup (1 stick) margarine or butter, softened
3 eggs
¾ cup milk
1 teaspoon vanilla

HEAT oven to 350°F.

MICROWAVE chocolate, ½ cup of the sugar and the water in large microwavable bowl on HIGH 1 to 2 minutes or until chocolate is almost melted, stirring once. **Stir until chocolate is completely melted.** Cool to lukewarm.

MIX flour, baking soda and salt; set aside. Beat margarine and the remaining 1¼ cups sugar in large bowl until light and fluffy. Add eggs, one at a time, beating well after each addition. Add flour mixture alternately with milk, beating after each addition until smooth. Stir in chocolate mixture and vanilla. Pour into 2 greased and floured 9-inch layer pans.

BAKE for 30 to 35 minutes or until cake springs back when lightly pressed. Cool in pans 10 minutes. Remove from pans to cool on wire racks. Frost as desired.

Makes 12 servings

Prep time: 30 minutes
Baking time: 30 to 35 minutes

Easy Fudge Frosting

4 squares BAKER'S Unsweetened Chocolate
2 tablespoons margarine or butter
4 cups powdered sugar
½ cup milk
1 teaspoon vanilla

MICROWAVE chocolate and margarine in large microwavable bowl on HIGH 1 minute or until margarine is melted. **Stir until chocolate is completely melted.**

STIR in sugar, milk and vanilla until smooth. Let stand, if necessary, until of spreading consistency, stirring occasionally. Spread quickly. (Add 2 to 3 teaspoons additional milk if frosting becomes too thick.)

Makes about 2½ cups or enough to frost tops and sides of 2 (8- to 9-inch) layer cakes

Prep time: 10 minutes

Chocolate Strawberry Shortcake (page 558)

559

German Sweet Chocolate Cake

This has been our most-requested recipe for years.

---

1 package (4 ounces) BAKER'S GERMAN'S Sweet Chocolate
½ cup water
2 cups all-purpose flour
1 teaspoon baking soda
¼ teaspoon salt
1 cup (2 sticks) margarine or butter, softened
2 cups sugar
4 egg yolks
1 teaspoon vanilla
1 cup buttermilk
4 egg whites
Classic Coconut-Pecan Filling and Frosting (recipe follows)

HEAT oven to 350°F. Line bottoms of three 9-inch layer pans with waxed paper.

MICROWAVE chocolate and water in large microwavable bowl on HIGH 1½ to 2 minutes or until chocolate is almost melted. **Stir until chocolate is completely melted.**

MIX flour, baking soda and salt; set aside. Beat margarine and sugar until light and fluffy. Add egg yolks, one at a time, beating well after each addition. Stir in melted chocolate and vanilla. Add flour mixture alternately with buttermilk, beating after each addition until smooth.

BEAT egg whites until they form stiff peaks. Gently stir into batter. Pour batter into prepared pans.

BAKE for 30 minutes or until cake springs back when lightly touched.

REMOVE from oven; immediately run spatula between cake and sides of pans. Cool in pans 15 minutes. Remove from pans; peel off waxed paper. Cool on wire racks.

SPREAD Classic Coconut-Pecan Filling and Frosting between layers and over top of cake.

Makes 12 servings

Prep time: 35 to 40 minutes
Baking time: 30 minutes

Tip
• This delicate cake will have a flat, slightly sugary top crust that tends to crack. This is normal and the frosting will cover it up.

Classic Coconut-Pecan Filling and Frosting

ONE BOWL RECIPE

1½ cups (12 ounce can) evaporated milk
1½ cups sugar
4 egg yolks, lightly beaten
¾ cup (1½ sticks) margarine or butter
1½ teaspoons vanilla
2 cups BAKER'S ANGEL FLAKE Coconut
1½ cups chopped pecans

COMBINE milk, sugar, egg yolks, margarine and vanilla in saucepan. Cook over medium heat until mixture thickens and is golden brown, about 12 minutes, stirring constantly. Remove from heat.

STIR in coconut and pecans. Beat until cool and of spreading consistency.

Makes about 4¼ cups or enough to fill and frost top of 1 (3-layer) cake, frost tops of 2 (13×9-inch) cakes or frost 24 cupcakes

Prep time: 20 minutes

Top to bottom: German Sweet Chocolate Cake (page 560) with Classic Coconut-Pecan Filling and Frosting (page 560); Wellesley Fudge Cake (page 558) with Easy Fudge Frosting (page 558)

561

German Sweet Chocolate Pie

ONE BOWL RECIPE

1 package (4 ounces) BAKER'S
 GERMAN'S Sweet Chocolate
⅓ cup milk
1 package (3 ounces)
 PHILADELPHIA BRAND Cream
 Cheese, softened
2 tablespoons sugar (optional)
3½ cups (8 ounces) COOL WHIP
 Whipped Topping, thawed
9-inch prepared crumb crust
Chocolate Shavings or Curls
 (page 526) (optional)

MICROWAVE chocolate and 2 tablespoons of the milk in large microwavable bowl on HIGH 1½ to 2 minutes or until chocolate is almost melted, stirring halfway through heating time. **Stir until chocolate is completely melted.**

BEAT in cream cheese, sugar and the remaining milk until well blended. Refrigerate to cool, about 10 minutes.

STIR in whipped topping gently until smooth. Spoon into crust. Freeze until firm, about 4 hours. Garnish with Chocolate Shavings or Curls, if desired.

Makes 8 servings

Prep time: 20 minutes
Freezing time: 4 hours

Saucepan preparation: Heat chocolate and 2 tablespoons of the milk in saucepan over very low heat until chocolate is melted, stirring constantly. Remove from heat. Continue as above.

Chocolate Pecan Pie

This is a delicious variation on a traditional Southern favorite.

---

    1 package (4 ounces) BAKER'S
        GERMAN'S Sweet Chocolate
    2 tablespoons margarine or butter
    1 cup corn syrup
    ⅓ cup sugar
    3 eggs
    1 teaspoon vanilla
    1½ cups pecan halves
    1 unbaked 9-inch pie shell
        COOL WHIP Whipped Topping,
        thawed (optional)

HEAT oven to 350°F.

MICROWAVE chocolate and margarine in large microwavable bowl on HIGH 2 minutes or until margarine is melted. **Stir until chocolate is completely melted.**

STIR in corn syrup, sugar, eggs and vanilla until well blended. Stir in pecans, reserving 8 halves for garnish, if desired. Pour filling into pie shell.

BAKE for 55 minutes or until knife inserted 1 inch from center comes out clean. Cool on wire rack. Garnish with whipped topping and chocolate-dipped pecan halves (page 529), if desired.

Makes 8 servings

Prep time: 20 minutes
Baking time: 55 minutes

Chocolate Peanut Butter Pie

You'll hear cheers from the peanut gallery when you make this tasty pie.

    ¾ cup (1½ sticks) margarine or
        butter
    ¾ cup peanut butter
    ½ cup firmly packed brown sugar
    5¼ cups (12 ounces) COOL WHIP
        Whipped Topping, thawed
        Chocolate Nut Crust (page 568)
        Peanuts (optional)
    2 squares BAKER'S Semi-Sweet
        Chocolate, melted (page 525)
        (optional)

BEAT margarine, peanut butter and sugar until well blended. Reserve ¼ cup of the whipped topping for garnish. Gently stir in the remaining 5 cups whipped topping until mixture is smooth and creamy. Spoon into Chocolate Nut Crust.

REFRIGERATE until firm, about 4 hours. Garnish with reserved whipped topping. Sprinkle on peanuts and drizzle with melted chocolate, if desired.

Makes 10 to 12 servings

Prep time: 20 minutes
Chill time: 4 hours

Decorative Pie Crust Tips
• Make a prepared pie shell look homemade. Before baking, reflute the edge to make a higher, prettier crust.
• Use an extra unbaked pie shell as decoration on pies. Cut out small shapes (leaves, hearts, diamonds, etc.), moisten and place on moistened pastry rim, overlapping edges slightly. Press into place.

Chocolate Pecan Pie (page 564)

Sweetheart Pie

1 package (8 ounces) BAKER'S Semi-
   Sweet Chocolate
⅔ cup corn syrup
1 cup (½ pint) heavy cream
3 eggs
1 unbaked 9-inch pie shell
2 tablespoons sugar
½ teaspoon vanilla
1 pint strawberries, cleaned, hulled
   and sliced
   Chocolate Cutouts (page 529)
   (optional)

HEAT oven to 350°F.

MELT 6 squares of the chocolate (page
525). Stir in corn syrup and ½ cup of the
cream. Add eggs, one at a time, beating
well after each addition. Pour into pie shell.

BAKE for 45 minutes or until knife inserted
1 inch from center comes out clean. Cool
on wire rack. (Center of pie will sink after
cooling.)

WHIP the remaining ½ cup cream, the
sugar and vanilla until soft peaks form;
spoon into center of cooled pie. Top with
strawberries. Melt the remaining 2 squares
chocolate and drizzle over strawberries
(page 527). Garnish with Chocolate
Cutouts, if desired.

Makes 8 servings

Prep time: 30 minutes
Baking time: 45 minutes

Mocha-
Almond Pie

2 squares BAKER'S Unsweetened
   Chocolate
2 squares BAKER'S Semi-Sweet
   Chocolate
½ cup (1 stick) margarine or butter
1 tablespoon instant coffee
1 cup sugar
¼ cup corn syrup
3 eggs
2 tablespoons sour cream or plain
   yogurt
1 teaspoon vanilla
1 unbaked 9-inch pie shell
½ cup sliced almonds

HEAT oven to 350°F.

MICROWAVE chocolates, margarine and
instant coffee in large microwavable bowl
on HIGH 2 minutes or until margarine is
melted. **Stir until chocolate is
completely melted.**

STIR in sugar and corn syrup. Beat in eggs,
sour cream and vanilla. Pour into pie shell;
sprinkle with almonds.

BAKE for 45 minutes or until knife inserted
1 inch from center comes out clean. Cool
on wire rack.

Makes 8 to 10 servings

Prep time: 15 minutes
Baking time: 45 minutes

Saucepan preparation: Heat chocolate,
margarine and instant coffee in 2-quart
saucepan over very low heat until just
melted, stirring constantly. Remove from
heat. Continue as above.

Cream and Custard Pies
• To avoid spoilage, refrigerate pies
with cream or custard fillings as soon
as they have cooled. Refrigerate
leftovers immediately.

Top to bottom: Chocolate Sweetheart Pie (page 566); Mocha-Almond Pie (page 566); Chocolate Peanut Butter Pie (page 564)

Chocolate Raspberry Tart

An easy and impressive dessert that your family and friends will love.

---

1 package (4-serving size) JELL-O Pudding and Pie Filling, Vanilla Flavor
1¾ cups half and half or milk
1 Chocolate Crumb Crust (recipe follows), baked in 9-inch tart pan and cooled
1 pint raspberries, cleaned
2 squares BAKER'S Semi-Sweet Chocolate, melted (page 525)

MICROWAVE pie filling mix and half and half in large microwavable bowl on HIGH 3 minutes; stir well. Microwave 3 minutes longer; stir again. Microwave 1 minute or until mixture comes to a boil. Cover surface with plastic wrap. Refrigerate at least 4 hours.

SPOON filling into Chocolate Crumb Crust just before serving. Arrange raspberries on top of filling. Drizzle with melted chocolate (page 527).

Makes 8 to 10 servings

Prep time: 30 minutes
Chill time: 4 hours

Saucepan preparation: Combine pie filling mix and half and half in 2-quart saucepan. Cook over medium heat until mixture comes to a full boil, stirring constantly. Continue as above.

Chocolate Crumb Crust

---

3 squares BAKER'S Semi-Sweet Chocolate
3 tablespoons margarine or butter
1 cup graham cracker crumbs

HEAT oven to 375°F.

MICROWAVE chocolate and margarine in microwavable bowl on HIGH 2 minutes or until margarine is melted. **Stir until chocolate is completely melted.**

STIR in crumbs. Press mixture onto bottom and up sides of tart pan or pie plate. Freeze 10 minutes. Bake for 8 minutes. Cool on wire rack.

Makes 1 (9-inch) crust

Prep time: 5 minutes
Freezing time: 10 minutes
Baking time: 8 minutes

Chocolate Nut Crust

---

6 squares BAKER'S Semi-Sweet Chocolate
1 tablespoon margarine or butter
1½ cups toasted finely chopped nuts

Line 9-inch pie plate with foil.

MICROWAVE chocolate and margarine in large microwavable bowl on HIGH 2 minutes or until margarine is melted. **Stir until chocolate is completely melted.**

STIR in nuts. Press mixture onto bottom and up sides of prepared pie plate. Refrigerate until firm, about 1 hour. Remove crust from pie plate; peel off foil. Return crust to pie plate or place on serving plate. Refrigerate.

Makes 1 (9-inch) crust

Prep time: 15 minutes
Chill time: 1 hour

Crumb Crust Pies
• To serve crumb crust pies, dip pie plate just to rim in hot water for 30 seconds. Cut; serve.

Chocolate Raspberry Tart (page 568) with Chocolate Crumb Crust (page 568)

569

Desserts and Sauces

Chocolate Plunge

ONE BOWL RECIPE

⅔ cup corn syrup
½ cup heavy cream
1 package (8 ounces) BAKER'S Semi-Sweet Chocolate *or* 2 packages (4 ounces each) BAKER'S GERMAN'S Sweet Chocolate
Assorted fresh fruit (strawberries, sliced kiwifruit, pineapple, apples or bananas) or cake cubes

MICROWAVE corn syrup and cream in large microwavable bowl on HIGH 1½ minutes or until mixture boils. Add chocolate; stir until melted. Serve warm as a dip with fresh fruit or cake cubes.

Makes 1½ cups

Prep time: 10 minutes

Saucepan preparation: Heat corn syrup and cream in 2-quart saucepan until boiling, stirring constantly. Remove from heat. Continue as above.

Chocolate Truffle Loaf

2 cups heavy cream
3 egg yolks, lightly beaten
2 packages (8 ounces each) BAKER'S Semi-Sweet Chocolate
½ cup corn syrup
½ cup (1 stick) margarine or butter
¼ cup powdered sugar
1 teaspoon vanilla
Raspberry Sauce (recipe follows)

LINE 8½ × 4½ × 2½-inch loaf pan with plastic wrap.

MIX ½ cup of the cream with egg yolks. Heat chocolate, corn syrup and margarine in heavy 2-quart saucepan over medium heat until chocolate is melted, stirring constantly. Add egg mixture; cook 3 minutes or until thickened, stirring constantly. Cool to room temperature.

BEAT the remaining 1½ cups cream, the sugar and vanilla until stiff peaks form. Gently stir in chocolate mixture until no streaks remain. Pour into prepared pan. Refrigerate overnight or freeze 3 hours. Invert onto serving plate. Remove pan and peel off plastic wrap. Serve with Raspberry Sauce.

Makes 12 servings

Prep time: 30 minutes
Freezing time: 3 hours

Raspberry Sauce

1 package (10 ounces) frozen raspberries in light syrup, thawed
⅓ cup corn syrup
¼ cup orange liqueur (optional)

RESERVE a few raspberries for garnish, if desired. Puree the remaining raspberries; strain to remove seeds. Stir in corn syrup and liqueur.

Makes about 1¼ cups

Prep time: 10 minutes

Party Baskets

A delicious chocolate cup you can fill with fruit, ice cream or anything you want.

1 package (8 ounces) BAKER'S Semi-Sweet Chocolate, melted (page 525)
Ice cream, any flavor, or fresh fruit
Regal Chocolate Sauce (page 574)
Chopped nuts, sprinkles, candies, additional fruit, whipped cream (optional)

COAT inside of paper- or foil-lined muffin cups with melted chocolate (page 528). Place in muffin pans. Refrigerate 30 minutes or until chocolate hardens. Peel off paper or foil.

PLACE scoop of ice cream or fresh fruit in each cup. Top with Regal Chocolate Sauce. Garnish with nuts, sprinkles, candies, additional fruit or whipped cream, if desired.

Makes 10 servings

Prep time: 20 minutes
Chill time: 30 minutes

Clockwise from top left: Chocolate Truffle Loaf (page 572) with Raspberry Sauce (page 572); Party Baskets (page 572) with Regal Chocolate Sauce (page 574)

573

Chocolate Almond Pear Torte

An elegant dessert for any party.

CRUST:
⅔ cup all-purpose flour
2 tablespoons sugar
⅓ cup margarine or butter
½ cup toasted finely chopped almonds

TOPPING:
4 squares BAKER'S Semi-Sweet Chocolate
½ cup (1 stick) margarine or butter
½ cup sugar
⅓ cup heavy cream
2 eggs, lightly beaten
½ teaspoon vanilla
1 can (16 ounces) pear halves, drained and thinly sliced
½ cup toasted coarsely chopped almonds

HEAT oven to 375°F.

MIX flour and 2 tablespoons sugar; cut in ⅓ cup margarine until mixture resembles coarse crumbs. Stir in finely chopped almonds. Press firmly onto bottom of 9-inch springform pan or onto bottom and sides of 9-inch pie plate. Bake for 10 minutes.

MICROWAVE chocolate and ½ cup margarine in large microwavable bowl on HIGH 2 minutes or until margarine is melted. **Stir until chocolate is completely melted.**

STIR in ½ cup sugar and cream, mixing well. Stir in eggs and vanilla. Pour over crust.

ARRANGE pear slices over filling. Sprinkle with coarsely chopped almonds. Bake for 35 to 40 minutes or until toothpick inserted into center comes out almost clean. (Center may be slightly soft.) Cool on wire rack. Refrigerate.

Makes 8 servings

Prep time: 30 minutes
Baking time: 45 to 50 minutes

Regal Chocolate Sauce

This chocolate sauce will make any dessert regal.

2 squares BAKER'S Unsweetened Chocolate
⅓ cup water
½ cup sugar
3 tablespoons margarine or butter
¼ teaspoon vanilla

MICROWAVE chocolate and water in microwavable bowl on HIGH 1½ minutes. **Stir until chocolate is completely melted.**

STIR in sugar. Microwave 1 minute. Stir. Microwave 2 minutes longer; stir in margarine and vanilla.

Makes about 1 cup

Prep time: 10 minutes

Saucepan preparation: Heat chocolate and water in saucepan over low heat, stirring constantly, until chocolate is melted and mixture is smooth. Add sugar; bring to a boil. Boil for 2 to 3 minutes or until slightly thickened, stirring constantly. Remove from heat; stir in margarine and vanilla.

Variations
Orange-Chocolate Sauce: Prepare Regal Chocolate Sauce as directed, substituting 1 tablespoon orange liqueur for the vanilla.

Almond-Chocolate Sauce: Prepare Regal Chocolate Sauce as directed, substituting 1 tablespoon almond liqueur for the vanilla.

Mocha Sauce: Prepare Regal Chocolate Sauce as directed, adding 1 to 2 tablespoons instant coffee with sugar.

Cinnamon-Chocolate Sauce: Prepare Regal Chocolate Sauce as directed, adding ½ teaspoon cinnamon with sugar.

Chocolate Almond Pear Torte (page 574)

CANDIES AND TREATS

ONE BOWL
Chocolate Fudge

1 package (8 ounces) BAKER'S Semi-Sweet Chocolate
⅔ cup sweetened condensed milk
1 teaspoon vanilla
⅛ teaspoon salt
½ cup chopped nuts (optional)

MICROWAVE chocolate and milk in 1½-quart microwavable bowl on HIGH 1 minute; stir well. Microwave 1 minute longer. **Stir until chocolate is completely melted and smooth.**

STIR in vanilla, salt and nuts. Spread into greased 8×4- or 9×5-inch loaf pan. Refrigerate until firm; cut into squares.

Makes about 2 dozen candies

Prep time: 10 minutes
Chill time: 30 minutes

Tip
• Recipe may be doubled; spread into greased 8-inch square pan.

Saucepan preparation: Heat chocolate and milk in 2-quart saucepan over very low heat, stirring constantly, until chocolate is melted and mixture is smooth. Remove from heat. Continue as above.

Clockwise from top right: Rocky Road Fudge (page 578); Peanut Butter Fudge (page 578); ONE BOWL Chocolate Fudge

Peanut Butter Fudge

PREPARE ONE BOWL Chocolate Fudge (page 577) and spread into pan as directed. Immediately drop ¼ cup peanut butter by rounded spoonfuls on top of fudge. Swirl peanut butter through fudge with knife to marbleize. Refrigerate and cut into squares.

Makes about 2 dozen candies

Prep time: 10 minutes
Chill time: 30 minutes

Rocky Road Fudge

PREPARE ONE BOWL Chocolate Fudge (page 577) as directed, adding 1 cup KRAFT Miniature Marshmallows to fudge with the vanilla, salt and nuts. Refrigerate and cut into squares.

Makes about 2 dozen candies

Prep time: 10 minutes
Chill time: 30 minutes

Fantasy Fudge

- ¾ cup (1½ sticks) margarine or butter
- 3 cups sugar
- ⅔ cup evaporated milk
- 1 package (8 ounces) BAKER'S Semi-Sweet Chocolate, broken into pieces
- 1 jar (7 ounces) KRAFT Marshmallow Creme
- 1 teaspoon vanilla
- 1 cup chopped nuts

MICROWAVE margarine in 4-quart microwavable bowl on HIGH 1 minute or until melted. Add sugar and milk; mix well.

MICROWAVE on HIGH 3 minutes; stir. Microwave 2 minutes longer or until mixture begins to boil; mix well. Microwave 3 minutes; stir. Microwave 2½ minutes longer. Let stand 2 minutes.

STIR in chocolate until melted. Add marshmallow creme and vanilla; mix well. Stir in nuts. Pour into greased 13×9-inch pan. Cool at room temperature; cut into squares.

Makes about 4 dozen candies

Prep time: 20 minutes

Saucepan preparation: Mix margarine, sugar and milk in heavy 3-quart saucepan. Bring to full boil, stirring constantly. Boil 5 minutes over medium heat, stirring constantly to prevent sticking. Remove from heat. Continue as above.

Chocolate Marshmallow Haystacks

- 1 package (3 ounces) PHILADELPHIA BRAND Cream Cheese, softened
- 2 tablespoons milk
- 2 cups powdered sugar
- 2 squares BAKER'S Unsweetened Chocolate, melted (page 525), cooled slightly
- ¼ teaspoon vanilla
- 3 cups KRAFT Miniature Marshmallows
- BAKER'S ANGEL FLAKE Coconut

BEAT cream cheese and milk until well blended. Gradually add sugar. Mix in chocolate and vanilla. Stir in marshmallows.

DROP by rounded teaspoonfuls into coconut; roll until well coated. Place on waxed paper-lined tray. Refrigerate until firm, about 1 hour.

Makes about 4 dozen candies

Prep time: 15 minutes
Chill time: 1 hour

Top to bottom: Chocolate Marshmallow Haystacks (page 578); Fantasy Fudge (page 578); Chocolate Caramel Drops (page 580)

579

Chocolate Caramel Drops

24 KRAFT Caramels (about 7 ounces)
2 tablespoons heavy cream
1 cup (about) pecan halves
4 squares BAKER'S Semi-Sweet
    Chocolate, melted (page 525)

MICROWAVE caramels and cream in large microwavable bowl on HIGH 1½ minutes; stir. Microwave 1½ minutes longer; stir until caramels are completely melted. Cool.

PLACE pecan halves on lightly greased cookie sheets in clusters of 3. Spoon caramel mixture over nuts, leaving ends showing. Let stand until set, about 30 minutes. Spread melted chocolate over caramel mixture. Let stand until chocolate is set.

Makes about 2 dozen candies

Prep time: 20 minutes
Standing time: 30 minutes

Saucepan preparation: Heat caramels and cream in heavy 2-quart saucepan over very low heat until caramels are melted, stirring constantly. Continue as above.

Chocolate-Coated Almond Toffee

1 cup (2 sticks) butter or margarine
1 cup sugar
3 tablespoons water
1 tablespoon corn syrup
½ cup toasted chopped almonds
6 squares BAKER'S Semi-Sweet
    Chocolate, melted (page 525)
⅓ cup toasted finely chopped
    almonds

COOK butter, sugar, water and corn syrup in heavy 2-quart saucepan over medium heat until mixture boils, stirring constantly. Boil gently, stirring frequently, 10 to 12 minutes or until golden brown and very thick. (Or until ½ teaspoon of mixture will form a hard, brittle thread when dropped in 1 cup cold water.)

REMOVE from heat. Stir in ½ cup almonds. Spread evenly into well-buttered 15½×10½×1-inch baking pan. Let stand until almost cool to the touch.

SPREAD melted chocolate over toffee; sprinkle with ⅓ cup almonds. Let stand until chocolate is firm. Break into pieces.

Makes about 1½ pounds candy

Prep time: 30 minutes

Easy Chocolate Truffles

1 package (8 ounces)
    PHILADELPHIA BRAND Cream
    Cheese, softened
3 cups powdered sugar
1½ packages (12 ounces) BAKER'S
    Semi-Sweet Chocolate, melted
    (page 525)
1½ teaspoons vanilla
    Ground nuts, unsweetened cocoa
    or BAKER'S ANGEL FLAKE
    Coconut, toasted

BEAT cream cheese until smooth. Gradually add sugar, beating until well blended. Add melted chocolate and vanilla; mix well. Refrigerate about 1 hour. Shape into 1-inch balls. Roll in nuts, cocoa or coconut. Store in refrigerator.

Makes about 5 dozen candies

Prep time: 15 minutes
Chill time: 1 hour

Variation
• To flavor truffles with liqueurs, omit vanilla. Divide truffle mixture into thirds. Add 1 tablespoon liqueur (almond, coffee or orange) to each third mixture; mix well.

Top to bottom: Easy Chocolate Truffles (page 580); Chocolate-Coated Almond Toffee (page 580)

ACKNOWLEDGMENTS

The publishers would like to thank the companies and organizations listed below for the use of their recipes in this publication.

Almond Board of California
American Lamb Council
Armour Swift-Eckrich
Best Foods, a Division of CPC International Inc.
Blue Diamond Growers
Borden Kitchens, Borden, Inc.
California Poultry Industry Federation
California Tree Fruit Agreement
Canned Food Information Council
Checkerboard Kitchens, Ralston Purina Company
Chef Paul Prudhomme's Magic Seasoning
    Blends™
Clear Springs Trout Company
Contadina Foods, Inc., Nestlé Food Company
Delmarva Poultry Industry, Inc.
Del Monte Foods
Diamond Walnut Growers, Inc.
Dole Food Company, Inc.
Florida Department of Citrus
The Fresh Garlic Association
Heinz U.S.A.
Hershey Chocolate U.S.A.
The HVR Company
Kellogg Company
Kikkoman International Inc.
The Kingsford Products Company
Kraft General Foods, Inc.
Lawry's® Foods, Inc.
Libby's, Nestlé Food Company
Thomas J. Lipton Co.
McIlhenney Company
Nabisco Foods Group
National Broiler Council
National Fisheries Institute
National Live Stock and Meat Board
National Pork Producers Council
Nestlé Specialty Products Company
Ocean Spray Cranberries, Inc.
Oklahoma Peanut Commission
Pace Foods, Inc.
Perdue Farms
The Procter & Gamble Company, Inc.
The Quaker Oats Company
Reckitt & Colman Inc.
Roman Meal Company
StarKist Seafood Company
Uncle Ben's Rice
USA Rice Council
Western New York Apple Growers Association
Wisconsin Milk Marketing Board

PHOTO CREDITS

The publishers would like to thank the companies and organizations lised below for the use of their photographs in this publication.

Almond Board of California
American Lamb Council
Armour Swift-Eckrich
Best Foods, a Division of CPC International Inc.
Borden Kitchens, Borden, Inc.
Canned Food Information Council
Checkerboard Kitchens, Ralston Purina Company
Chef Paul Prudhomme's Magic Seasoning
    Blends™
Clear Springs Trout Company
Contadina Foods, Inc., Nestlé Food Company
Del Monte Foods
Dole Food Company, Inc.
The HVR Company
The Kingsford Products Company
Kraft General Foods, Inc.
Lawry's® Foods, Inc.
Libby's, Nestlé Food Company
Thomas J. Lipton Co.
Nabisco Foods Group
National Broiler Council
National Live Stock and Meat Board
National Pork Producers Council
The Procter & Gamble Company, Inc.
Reckitt & Colman Inc.
StarKist Seafood Company
Uncle Ben's Rice
USA Rice Council

INDEX

A

All-American Cheeseburgers, 190
Almonds
  Almond Brown Rice Stuffing, 168
  Almond Chicken, 268
  Almond Chicken Paprika, 56
  Almond-Chocolate Sauce, 574
  Almond Heart Napoleons, 442
  Almond Macaroon Brownies, 536
  Almond Pastry Crust, 378
  Apple Almond Mince Pie, 379
  California Nut Pie, 376
  Cheddar Almond Muffins, 326
  Chicken Almond Stir-Fry, 35
  Chicken Ragout with Chilies,
    Tortillas and Goat Cheese, 26
  Chocolate Almond Pear Torte, 574
  Chocolate-Coated Almond Toffee,
    580
  Double Nut Chocolate Chip
    Cookies, 476
  Honey Almond Grilling Glaze, 232
  Marzipan Fruits, 432
  Mexican-Style Almond Chicken
    Salad, 23
  Mince Almond Pie, 382
  Mocha-Almond Pie, 566
  Orange-Almond Scallops, 291
  Parmesan Almond Muffins, 326
  Pork Ball Stir-Fry, 99
  Two Tone Muffins, 347
Antipasto Rice, 174
Appetizers & Snacks
  Bandito Buffalo Wings, 14
  Bits o' Teriyaki Chicken, 19
  Cheddar-Rice Patties, 136
  Chicken Pâté, 139
  Chilled Shrimp in Chinese Mustard
    Sauce, 253
  Chinatown Stuffed Mushrooms, 249
  Cucumber Canapés, 132
  Curried Chicken Puffs, 16
  Deluxe Fajita Nachos, 10
  Easy Wonton Chips, 248
  Egg Rolls, 253
  Fruity Dip, 452
  Garlicky Gilroy Chicken Wings, 19
  Glazed Ginger Chicken, 17
  JELL-O Creamy Jigglers Gelatin
    Snacks, 459
  JELL-O Jigglers Gelatin Snacks, 459

Appetizers & Snacks, *continued*
  JELL-O Jiggler Surprises Gelatin
    Snacks, 460
  JELL-O Tropical Jigglers Gelatin
    Snacks, 460
  JELL-O Vegetable Jigglers, 460
  Mexican Appetizer Cheesecake, 17
  Mexican Rice Cakes, 138
  Oriental Chicken Wings, 249
  Oriental Salsa, 252
  Peach-Mint Salsa, 12
  Rice Cake De-Light, 136
  Savory Shrimp Cheese Cups, 359
  Shrimp Toast, 254
  Snack Mix, 446
  Spicy Chicken Bundles, 250
  Spring Rolls, 250
Apples
  Almond Brown Rice Stuffing, 168
  Apple Almond Mince Pie, 379
  Apple Cobbler Deluxe, 386
  Apple-Cranberry Muffins, 319
  Apple Date Nut Muffins, 349
  Apple Grape Punch, 239
  Apple Spice Muffins, 339
  Apple-Walnut Muffins, 343
  Cheesy Bacon 'n Apple Muffins, 310
  Curried Scallops in Rice Ring, 161
  Deep-Dish Apple Cranberry Tarts, 398
  French Toast Strata Pie, 369
  Glazed Apple Custard Pie, 402
  Harvest Rice, 172
  Lemony Apple Oat Muffins, 309
  Sausage Skillet Dinner, 82
  Streusel Apple Mince Pie, 392
  Stuffed Chicken with Apple Glaze,
    59
  Taffy Apple Muffins, 332
Apricot and Walnut Brown Rice
  Stuffing, 173
Apricot Pear Tart, 444
Apricot Walnut Mince Pie, 375
Arroz Blanco, 170
Artichokes
  Antipasto Rice, 174
  California Salmon Pie, 358
  Garlic Shrimp with Noodles, 110
  Grilled Chicken Salad, 144
  Mediterranean Phyllo Pie, 365
  Paella Salad, 26
Asparagus
  Buddha's Delight, 298
  Gourmet Chicken Bake, 60
  Mandarin Beef, 68
  Shanghai Chicken with Asparagus
    and Ham, 272
Autumn Seafood Bake, 104

B

K

Kabobs
    Barbecued Sausage Kabobs, 206
    Beef Kabobs Italiano, 188
    Buffalo Turkey Kabobs, 214
    Charcoal Beef Kabobs, 186
    Chicken Kabobs in Pita Bread, 14
    Chicken Kabobs with Peanut Sauce, 216
    Chicken Vegetable Kabobs, 219
    Curried Beef and Fruit Kabobs, 207
    Garlic Skewered Shrimp, 286
    Grilled Turkey with Vegetable Pizzazz, 208
    Herb Marinated Chicken Kabobs, 62
    Lamb Shaslek, 201
    Oriental Chicken Kabobs, 275
    Oriental Steak Kabobs, 192
    Seafood Kabobs, 220
    Seafood-Vegetable Kabobs, 226
    Shrimp and Steak Kabobs, 223
Kamaaina Spareribs, 206
Kansas City Burgers, 190
Kung Po Chicken, 281

L

Lakeside Lobster Tails, 223
Lamb
    Butterflied Leg of Lamb with Orange Sauce, 197
    Grilled Lamb Fajitas, 196
    Lamb Shaslek, 201
    Raspberry-Glazed Lamb Ribs, 202
    Spicy Lamb Burgers, 194
Layered Chocolate Cheese Bars, 544
Leek Cream, 224
Lemon
    Cookie Crust Lemon Pie, 400
    Easy Lemon Cream Pie, 386
    Frozen Lemon Angel Pie, 374
    Frozen Lemon Satin Pie, 400
    Golden Lemon Sauce, 400
    Heavenly Lemon Cream Pies, 473
    Lemonade, 234
    Lemon Berry Terrine, 444
    Lemon Cheesecake Pie, 402
    Lemon Cheese Tart, 440
    Lemon Cloud Pie, 382
    Lemon Cookies, 481
    Lemon Cooler, 468
    Lemon Fish Roll-Ups, 105

Lemon, *continued*
    Lemon Glaze, 309
    Lemon Honey Chicken, 38
    Lemon Pastry, 405
    Lemony Apple Oat Muffins, 309
    Lemony Light Cooler, 238
    Low Calorie Lemonade, 234
    Minted Lemonade, 234
    Pink Lemonade, 234
    ReaLemon Meringue Pie, 390
    Slushy Lemonade, 234
    Sour Cream Lemon Pie, 388
    Sour Cream Lemon Streusel Muffins, 336
    Sparkling Lemonade, 234
    Velvety Lemon Lime Pie, 378
Lemon Cheesecake Pie, 402
Light Custard Cheese Pie, 389
Lime
    Halibut with Cilantro and Lime, 290
    Honey-Lime Glazed Chicken, 274
    Margarita Parfait Pie, 372
    Velvety Lemon Lime Pie, 378
Lite Quencher, 239
Louisiana Tomato-Rice Gumbo, 107
Low Calorie Lemonade, 234

M

Ma Po Tofu, 301
Magic Grilled Fish, 222
Maiden Mary, The, 234
Mai Tai Slush, 236
Mandarin Beef, 68
Mandarin Chicken Salad, 24
Mandarin Muffins, 323
Manhattan Burgers, 190
Maple Custard Pie, 399
Maple Pecan Topping, 393
Margarita Parfait Pie, 372
Marinated Cucumbers, 300
Marinated Vegetable Salad, 144
marinating tips, 183
Marzipan Fruits, 432
Meat Patties with Chinese Gravy, 264
Meatza Pizza Pie, 366
Mediterranean Phyllo Pie, 365
Melon Bubbles, 423
Merry-Go-Round Cake, 455
Mexican Appetizer Cheesecake, 17
Mexican Beef Stir-Fry, 77
Mexican Chicken Kiev, 41
Mexican Chocolate Cake, 495
Mexican Rice Cakes, 138

V

METRIC CONVERSION CHART

VOLUME MEASUREMENT (dry)

⅛ teaspoon = .5 mL
¼ teaspoon = 1 mL
½ teaspoon = 2 mL
¾ teaspoon = 4 mL
1 teaspoon = 5 mL
1 tablespoon = 15 mL
2 tablespoons = 25 mL
¼ cup = 50 mL
⅓ cup = 75 mL
⅔ cup = 150 mL
¾ cup = 175 mL
1 cup = 250 mL
2 cups = 1 pint = 500 mL
3 cups = 750 mL
4 cups = 1 quart = 1 L

VOLUME MEASUREMENT (fluid)

1 fluid ounce (2 tablespoons) = 30 mL
4 fluid ounces (½ cup) = 125 mL
8 fluid ounces (1 cup) = 250 mL
12 fluid ounces (1½ cups) = 375 mL
16 fluid ounces (2 cups) = 500 mL

WEIGHT (MASS)

½ ounce = 15 g
1 ounce = 30 g
3 ounces = 85 g
3.75 ounces = 100 g
4 ounces = 115 g
8 ounces = 225 g
12 ounces = 340 g
16 ounces = 1 pound = 450 g

DIMENSION

1/16 inch = 2 mm
⅛ inch = 3 mm
¼ inch = 6 mm
½ inch = 1.5 cm
¾ inch = 2 cm
1 inch = 2.5 cm

OVEN TEMPERATURES

250°F = 120°C
275°F = 140°C
300°F = 150°C
325°F = 160°C
350°F = 180°C
375°F = 190°C
400°F = 200°C
425°F = 220°C
450°F = 230°C

BAKING PAN SIZES

Utensil	Size in Inches/Quarts	Metric Volume	Size in Centimeters
Baking or	8×8×2	2 L	20×20×5
Cake pan	9×9×2	2.5 L	22×22×5
(square or	12×8×2	3 L	30×20×5
rectangular)	13×9×2	3.5 L	33×23×5
Loaf Pan	8×4×3	1.5 L	20×10×7
	9×5×3	2 L	23×13×7
Round Layer	8×1½	1.2 L	20×4
Cake Pan	9×1½	1.5 L	23×4
Pie Plate	8×1¼	750 mL	20×3
	9×1¼	1 L	23×3
Baking Dish	1 quart	1 L	
or Casserole	1½ quart	1.5 L	
	2 quart	2 L